THE EVERYDAY PRACTICE OF PUBLIC ART

The Everyday Practice of Public Art: Art, Space and Social Inclusion is a multidisciplinary anthology of analyses exploring the expansion of contemporary public art issues beyond the built environment.

It follows the highly successful publication *The Practice of Public Art* (eds Cartiere and Willis), and expands the analysis of the field with a broad perspective which includes practicing artists, curators, activists, writers and educators from North America, Europe and Australia, who offer divergent perspectives on the many facets of the public art process.

The collection examines the continual evolution of public art, moving beyond monuments and memorials to examine more fully the development of socially engaged public art practice. Topics include constructing new models for developing and commissioning temporary and performance-based public artworks; understanding the challenges of a socially engaged public art practice vs. social programming and policymaking; the social inclusiveness of public art; the radical developments in public art and social practice pedagogy; and unravelling the relationships between public artists and the communities they serve.

The Everyday Practice of Public Art offers a diverse perspective on the increasingly complex nature of artistic practice in the public realm in the twenty-first century.

Cameron Cartiere is an Associate Professor at Emily Carr University of Art + Design (Vancouver, Canada). She is the author of *RE/Placing Public Art*, co-author of *The Manifesto of Possibilities: Commissioning Public Art in the Urban Environment*, and co-editor of *The Practice of Public Art* (with Shelly Willis).

Martin Zebracki is a Lecturer (Assistant Professor) in Critical Human Geography at the University of Leeds (UK). He has published various academic articles, journal issues and book chapters on public art and social engagement. He is the author of *Public Artopia: Art in Public Space in Question*.

"Finally a publication that attempts to explore the multiple, complex elements that make up contemporary art in the public sphere. *The Everyday Practice of Public Art* traces the changes in contemporary public practice through a broad reaching series of essays: from the growth of social practice in educational institutions, to the problematics of city public art regeneration programs, to an analysis of art as a catalyst for social transformation. This publication asks the question – why public art, what is happening now and what can and should art in the public sphere be doing for us?"

Dee Hibbert-Jones, *Associate Professor of Art, University of California, Santa Cruz*

"This book is a reminder that social practice is also an acknowledgement of different perspectives, new histories, collaboration. The authors of these texts do us a service by bringing new voices and views to the already robust debate."

Suzanne Lacy, *Chair, MFA Public Practice, Otis College of Art and Design*

"A wonderful collection that takes *public* art as a socially engaged practice seriously. Theoretically, practically and politically engaged, this book does much to advance debates on art and the social world."

Loretta Lees, *Professor of Human Geography and Director of Research, University of Leicester*

"This volume deserves to become essential reading for researchers interested in understanding the processes underpinning the production of public art, its inscription and its contribution to social inclusion. Its value lies in the broad definition given to public art, amply reflected in the case studies, and particularly to the structuring of the discussion. The editors are to be applauded for their innovative approach in teasing out socially engaged public art practices, not least in emphasising the pedagogic routes underpinning production, its evolution and through bringing together authors representing a suitably diverse range of disciplinary backgrounds."

Ronan Paddison, *Emeritus Professor of Geography, University of Glasgow*

THE EVERYDAY PRACTICE OF PUBLIC ART

Art, Space and Social Inclusion

*Edited by Cameron Cartiere
and Martin Zebracki*

Routledge
Taylor & Francis Group

LONDON AND NEW YORK

First published 2016
by Routledge
2 Park Square, Milton Park, Abingdon, Oxon OX14 4RN

and by Routledge
711 Third Avenue, New York, NY 10017

Routledge is an imprint of the Taylor & Francis Group, an informa business

British Library Cataloguing-in-Publication Data
A catalogue record for this book is available from the British Library

Library of Congress Cataloging-in-Publication Data
The everyday practice of public art : art, space, and social inclusion / Edited by Cameron Cartiere and Martin Zebracki.
pages cm
Includes bibliographical references and index.
1. Public art--Social aspects. I. Cartiere, Cameron, editor. II. Zebracki, Martin, 1984- editor.
N8825.E94 2015
701'.03--dc23
2015020724

ISBN: 978-1-138-82920-6 (hbk)
ISBN: 978-1-138-82921-3 (pbk)
ISBN: 978-1-315-73788-1 (ebk)

Typeset in Bembo
by Saxon Graphics Ltd, Derby

MIX
Paper from
responsible sources
FSC
www.fsc.org   FSC® C013056

Printed and bound in Great Britain by
TJ International Ltd, Padstow, Cornwall

CONTENTS

List of illustrations   *viii*

Acknowledgements   *x*

List of contributors   *xi*

Introduction   1
Cameron Cartiere and Martin Zebracki

PART I
The social practice of public art   **11**

1   Through the lens of social practice: considerations on a public
    art history in progress   13
    Cameron Cartiere

2   Politicizing publics: a social framework for public artworks   27
    Andrew Hewitt and Mel Jordan

3   Placing murals in Belfast: community, negotiation and change   45
    Lesley Murray

4   The everyday agonistic life after the unveiling: lived
    experiences from a public art World Café   63
    Martin Zebracki

PART II
The education of a public artist   83

5   Creating the global network: developing social and
    community practice in higher education   85
    Dean Merlino and Susan Stewart

6   Throwing stones in the sea: Georg Simmel, social practice
    and the imagined world   103
    Ted Purves

7   Open Engagement: accessible education for socially
    engaged art   120
    Jen Delos Reyes

8   "Context is half the work": developing doctoral research
    through arts practice in culture   141
    Anne Douglas

PART III
The spatial fabric of public art and social practice   159

9   Public art as a function of urbanism   161
    John Bingham-Hall

10 Listening in certain places: public art for the post-regenerate
    age   177
    Elaine Speight

11 Antagonistic spaces: on small, interventionist and socially
    engaged public art   193
    Justin Langlois and Danielle Sabelli

12 Why public art? Urban parks and public art in the twenty-
    first century   208
    Joni Palmer

PART IV
Visual timeline **223**

13 A collective timeline of socially engaged public art practice
    1950–2015   225
    Cameron Cartiere, Sophie Hope, Anthony Schrag, Elisa Yon
    and Martin Zebracki

References   *242*
Index   *254*

ILLUSTRATIONS

1.1	*Consequences of a Gesture* (1993), Daniel J. Martinez.	20
1.2	*Alison Lapper Pregnant* (2005), Marc Quinn.	23
2.1	*Nowhereisland* (2012), Alex Hartley.	35
2.2	*Gramsci Monument* (2013), Thomas Hirschhorn.	38
2.3	*Node* (2011), STEALTH.unlimited (Ana Džokić and Marc Neelen) and architects María Camila Vélez and Yesenia Rodríguez.	41
3.1	Mural in an alleyway.	52
3.2	A 're-imaged' mural.	56
3.3	*Guernica.*	59
4.1	*Expansion* (1967), Toon Slegers.	69
4.2	*Expansion* (1967), Toon Slegers.	70
4.3	Impression of the host–guest role-play workshop pursuing the World Café discussion method.	72
6.1	*Bliz-aard Ball Sale* (1983), David Hammons.	106
6.2	*One Stop Knock-Off Shop* (2014), Anastasia Klose.	110
7.1	Open Engagement visual identity evolution, Jen Delos Reyes.	121
7.2	"Bodies of Knowledge: Sourcing Disability Experience", a lunchtime discussion focused on disability and access at Open Engagement: Life/Work, 2014.	137
8.1	*New Cullen Ceiling* (2004), Robert Orchardson.	146
8.2	"Seminar 1: Working in Public" (2007), Suzanne Lacy, Grant Kester and participants.	150
8.3	*Plein Air: The Ethical Aesthetic Impulse* (2010), Reiko Goto Collins. Peacock Visual Arts, Aberdeen, Scotland.	153
9.1	*Space Syntax.*	166
9.2	Map of Catford town centre.	171

10.1   *Open to the Public* (2013), Wouter Osterholt and Katja van Driel.   187
10.2   *Harris Flights* (2013), *In Certain Places* and Research Design.   188

Timeline illustrations

13.1   Cage and Cunningham (1953), Black Mountain College
        Research Project.   228
13.2   Situationist International (1957), Cosio d'Arroscia, Italy.   229
13.3   *Make a Salad* (2014), Allison Knowles.   230
13.4   "The Town Artist project" (1968–1978), David Harding.   231
13.5   *La Familia Obrera*, (Blue Collar Family) (1968), Oscar Bony.   231
13.6   *The Great Wall of Los Angeles* (1976–ongoing), Judith E. Baca.   232
13.7   *Touch Sanitation Performance* (1979–1980), Mierle Laderman
        Ukeles.   233
13.8   *Floyd Road Mural* (1974), Carol Kenna, Stephen Lobb and Rick
        Walker.   233
13.9   *7000 Eichen, Action, documenta 7* (1982–1987), Joseph Beuys.   234
13.10   *Chambres d'Amis* (1986), Jan Hoet.   235
13.11   *Heidelberg Project* (1986–ongoing), Tyree Guyton.   235
13.12   *Consequences of a Gesture* (1993), Daniel J. Martinez.   236
13.13   *Project Row Houses* (1993-ongoing), Rick Lowe.   236
13.14   *Mecca* (1999–2000), Anna Best.   237
13.15   HORKEŠKART (2000), Škart.   238
13.16   *Become the Bike Bloc Laboratory for Insurrectionary Imagination*
        (2009), Platform.   239
13.17   Het Blauwe Huis (The Blue House) (2005–2009), Jeanne van
        Heeswijk in collaboration with Hervé Paraponaris and Dennis
        Kaspori.   239
13.18   *Conflict Kitchen* (2010), Jon Rubin and Dawn Weleski.   240
13.19   *Digital Natives* (2011), Lorna Brown, Clint Burnham and diverse
        artists.   240

ACKNOWLEDGEMENTS

An anthology, by its very nature, is a group effort and this one was no exception. The collective labour to produce this work spanned several academic and professional disciplines, continents, borders and time zones. We would like to thank all of the authors who contributed their unique perspectives, depth of knowledge and genuine passion for the public art field within the pages of this book. Your enthusiasm and heartfelt support made this project possible.

We would particularly like to thank our copy reviewer, Nicolas Kojey-Strauss, and our indexer, Noeline Bridge, for their most welcome support. Thank you to our editor Natalie Foster and editorial assistant Sheni Kruger.

The design of the timeline benefited from the creative talents of Elisa Yon, and we would like to extend our appreciation to all the artists, organizations and individuals who lent their material to make this visual slice of public art history possible.

We would like to give special thanks to Emily Carr University of Art + Design, Faculty of Culture and Community; to the University of Leeds, School of Geography and to our personal environments for being with us in good spirit.

CONTRIBUTORS

John Bingham-Hall is a researcher at Theatrum Mundi, a network of artists and urbanists based in LSE Cities, London School of Economics, UK, where he develops programming for cross-disciplinary discussion about cultural and public space in the city. He is also a PhD candidate at The Bartlett, University College, London, working on neighbourhood communication ecologies in London and tutor in critical contexts for design at Central St Martins, University of the Arts, London. With an academic background in both music and urban studies plus experience developing temporary use projects and arts programming with Argent LLP and the Architecture Foundation, his on-going interest has been in the production of the public through culture, communication and the use of urban space.

Cameron Cartiere is an Associate Professor at Emily Carr University of Art + Design, Vancouver, Canada. She is a practitioner, writer and researcher specializing in public art, urban renewal and environmental issues. She is the author of *RE/Placing Public Art*, co-editor of *The Practice of Public Art* and co-author of *The Manifesto of Possibilities: Commissioning Public Art in the Urban Environment*. As part of her research on the sustainable effects of public art, Cartiere is collaborating with artists, writers, scientists, and new media researchers to convert neglected greenways and brownfield sites within British Columbia into native pollinator pastures, using public art as the driving force for environmental renewal.

Jen Delos Reyes is a creative labourer, educator, writer and radical community arts organizer. Her practice is about working with institutions and creating and supporting sustainable artist-led culture. Delos Reyes worked at Portland State University from 2008 to 2014 to create the first flexible residency Art and Social Practice MFA in the United States and devised curricula that focused on place, engagement and dialogue. She is the director and founder of Open Engagement, an international annual conference on socially engaged art that has been active since 2007 and also hosted seven other conferences in the USA and Canada.

Anne Douglas is Research Professor of Art in Public Life, Grays School of Art, Robert Gordon University, Aberdeen, Scotland. She co-founded and directs *On the Edge* research (2001–present), a programme of doctoral and postdoctoral research in which the practice of art forms a crucial element of an experimental approach. Douglas has published on a number of research themes, including the artist as leader, improvisation, experimentation and experiential knowledge. Douglas co-authored *The Artistic Turn* (2009) with Kathleen Coessens and Darla Crispin, then research fellows at the Orpheus Institute of Research in Music, Ghent. She was a 2014 Macgeorge Fellow, University of Melbourne.

Andrew Hewitt is Senior Lecturer in Social Art Practice, School of the Arts, University of Northampton. He is an academic and a practising artist. Hewitt's research and practice is based within the field of public art, and is concerned with the conceptions and the politics of publics and art. He works with Dave Beech and Mel Jordan as the Freee art collective who produce slogans, billboards and publications that aim to challenge the commercial and bureaucratic colonization of the public sphere. Their work has been shown at the Liverpool Biennial and the Istanbul Biennial. Hewitt is a founding co-editor of *Art & the Public Sphere Journal* (Intellect).

Sophie Hope is a Lecturer in the Film, Media and Cultural Studies Department at Birkbeck College, University of London. Her practice-based research investigates the relationships between art and society. Projects have included hosting dinners about art and politics in 1984 (www.1984dinners.net); exploring physical relationships to immaterial labour (www.manuallabours.co.uk) and creating a Social Art Map tracing narratives of socially engaged art in London. She has also written and co-devised programmes to explore the ethics and politics of work in the cultural and creative industries and notions of employability within higher education (e.g. www criticalworkplacements.org.uk).

Mel Jordan is Reader in Art and the Public Sphere and Senior Tutor in Sculpture, Royal College of Art. She is an academic and a practising artist. Jordan is particularly concerned with the publishing and dissemination of ideas and the formation of opinion, or what Jürgen Habermas describes as the "public sphere". Jordan is a member of the Freee art collective who produces slogans, billboards and publications. Freee's work has been shown at the Liverpool Biennial and the Istanbul Biennial. Jordan is a principal editor of *Art & the Public Sphere Journal* (Intellect).

Justin Langlois is an Assistant Professor in the Faculty of Culture and Community and Academic Coordinator of the Imagining Our Future initiative at Emily Carr University of Art + Design, Vancouver, Canada . He is the co-founder and research director of Broken City Lab, an artist-led interdisciplinary research collective working to explore the complexities of locality, infrastructures and participation in relation to civic engagement and social change, and director of the artist-run education initiative, The School for Eventual Vacancy. His practice explores collaborative structures, critical pedagogy and custodial frameworks as tools for gathering, learning and making together.

Dean Merlino is Coordinator of Teaching and Learning, Community Cultural Development Graduate Program, Centre for Cultural Partnerships, University of Melbourne, Australia. With a background in music performance and teaching, Dean is interested in how community practices are taught at tertiary level and the global contexts of learning. He is engaged internationally to speak on this topic and has worked with training institutions to develop teaching and research philosophies. He is currently completing his PhD on the sonic elements of cultural transmission titled '… And the trumpet shall sound: the cosmological function of sound and music'.

Lesley Murray is a Senior Lecturer in Social Science at the University of Brighton, UK where her research centres around urban mobilities. Lesley previously worked as a transport researcher for the London Research Centre and the Greater London Authority, before moving to Transport for London. She completed a PhD in 2007, followed by an ESRC-funded postdoctoral fellowship at the University of Brighton. Her research includes collaborations with artists, architects and creative writers. She has recently co-edited the collection *Researching and Representing Mobilities* and has published extensively in the field of mobilities, including on the intersections between mobile and visual methods.

Joni Palmer is a Visiting Associate Professor in Environmental Design at the University of Colorado at Boulder. For over 25 years her professional life has been a blend of practice and academia. She has worked with design and planning firms in Boston, Seattle, Denver, and San Francisco, and has taught in a variety of disciplinary programmes across the USA. As an urban and cultural geographer, she conducts work in the realms of landscape studies, public arts, cultural planning and visual representations.

Ted Purves is an Associate Professor of Social Practice at California College of the Arts and is Chair of the MA in Social Practice and Public Forms. He produces socially based projects in collaboration with Susanne Cockrell under the umbrella name of Fieldfaring (www.fieldfaring.org). Their most recent project, The Red Bank Pawpaw Circle, a large public planting, was completed in Cincinnati 2012. His book, *What We Want is Free: Generosity and Exchange in Recent Art*, was published by SUNY Press in 2005. A significantly expanded and revised edition was released in 2014.

Danielle Sabelli is an artist, researcher and lawyer with a practice focused on exploring and addressing structural inequity and front-line intervention. She is the co-founder of Broken City Lab, an artist-led interdisciplinary research collective working to explore the complexities of locality, infrastructures and participation in relation to civic engagement and social change. She works in poverty law on Unceded Coast Salish Territory in the downtown Eastside of Vancouver, Canada.

Anthony Schrag is a freelance artist. He is currently completing a practice-based PhD at Newcastle University, UK, exploring conflict and participatory practices. He has worked across the UK as well as internationally and is currently based in Scotland. He works in a participatory manner, and central to his practice is a broader discussion about the place of art in the wider social context. He has been the recipient of numerous awards, including those from Creative Scotland and the British Arts Council; the Dewar Arts Award; the 2011 Standpoint Futures public residency award, as well as a Henry Moore Artist Fellowship.

Elaine Speight is a Research Associate in the School of Art, Design and Performance at the University of Central Lancashire, UK, where she curates the In Certain Places project. As a curator, artist and educator, Speight has worked for organizations including Liverpool Biennial, UP Projects and Creative Partnerships, and taught arts management at Birkbeck College, University of London. She has also initiated a number of independent collaborative projects, such as "Pest" (2008–10) – a series of publications and commissions that explored artist-led initiatives in the UK, Europe and Canada.

Susan Stewart is the Founding Dean of the Faculty of Culture and Community at Emily Carr University of Art + Design, Vancouver, Canada. She leads research and pedagogical innovation in social and community engagement. As well as serving as an administrator, arts educator and social practice researcher, Stewart is a trans-disciplinary artist and has produced documentary video, photography, writing and multimedia performance and installations. Recent work is concerned with the relational, ecological and political aspects of the social body and considers notions of social sustainability within the context of environmental and cultural crisis.

Elisa Yon is a public art coordinator with the City of Richmond Public Art Program in British Columbia, Canada. She assists in managing a wide range of public art programmes – from major commissions for civic facilities to community-based artist residencies and temporary site-specific projects. As an artist based in Vancouver, she continues to develop a research-based practice situated at the intersection of public art, social practice and architecture. Her work often aims to reveal a collective consciousness of place and identity through site-responsive interventions and participatory methods of inquiry and production.

Martin Zebracki is a Lecturer (Assistant Professor) in Critical Human Geography in the Citizenship and Belonging Research Group in the School of Geography at the University of Leeds, UK. With an academic background in cultural geography and the history of art, he employs discursive, observational, participatory and multi-media methodologies to examine his intersecting core ethnographic interests in public art, social engagement and inclusiveness, queer citizenship and gender and sexual diversity within everyday in-vivo contexts of Western city spaces. On these topics Zebracki has published various articles, journal issues and book chapters and is actively involved in international academic committees and conferencing. A full list of academic work and activities can be retrieved from www.zebracki.org.

INTRODUCTION

Cameron Cartiere and Martin Zebracki

An anecdotal reintroduction

In 2013–14, the City of Philadelphia Mural Arts Program marked its 30th anniversary. Founded in 1984, the programme utilizes one of the most recognized public art forms, the mural, to "create art with others to transform places, individuals, communities and institutions" (City of Philadelphia Mural Arts Program 2015a). By 2009, the Mural Arts Program had completed 3,000 installations in the city. But in 2013, as the programme staff paused to look back at its history and consider its forward trajectory, they considered a different means of participatory practice to examine the social dimensions of art in the public realm. They turned to the internationally renowned social practice artist team called Lucy + Jorge Orta. As part of their on-going series of ritual meals staged throughout the world, the Ortas collaborated with Mural Arts to stage the 34th event in the series: *70 x 7 The Meal, act XXXIV*. The goal of the project was to gather a diverse collection of people from across the city around a series of interconnected communal tables to eat together while discussing and debating the politics of contemporary food production and the potential role heirloom foods can play to create healthier food systems that are more ecologically responsive.

On 5 October 2013 over 900 people sat down to the collective meal in Thomas Paine Plaza, located in the heart of Philadelphia. At the event, participants were encouraged to discuss issues of food production, genetically modified organisms (GMOs,) heirloom food revival and food advocacy. In addition to the communal meal, there was an additional project that distributed free food kits containing table runners designed by the Ortas, heirloom produce and recipes that allowed 400 citywide participants the opportunity to produce heirloom dishes at their own tables.

What is remarkable about this moment in public art history is not the scope nor scale of this project. Lucy + Jorge Orta have already produced numerous events involving hundreds of participants at a time, and they even aspire to create a meal across London's Millennium Bridge that would engage 8,000 guests. What makes *70 x 7 The Meal, act XXXIV* particularly noteworthy is that the commissioner was Mural Arts. *70 x 7 The Meal, act XXXIV* was not merely the kick-off event for the thirtieth anniversary but the culmination of a series Mural Arts had launched five months previously – *What We Sow*.

> *What We Sow* takes the future of Mural Arts beyond a genre-specific format and expands on the social and civic foundation of the mural tradition by addressing the relationship between local communities, regional ecologies, global economies, and the politics of food production. By working with contemporary artists who are at the forefront of public art, and of community-based co-production, Mural Arts aims to catalyse new networks and new participants from all social backgrounds who have a shared interest in finding spaces for civic engagement based on active dialogue and collective experience.
>
> *(City of Philadelphia Mural Arts Program 2015b)*

For an organization founded on the development of murals, one of the oldest and most traditional of public art formats, to acknowledge the importance of a different kind of social practice through the *What We Sow* series and the commissioning of the Ortas' thirty-fourth meal at such a momentous point in their history, denotes a significant shift in the acknowledgement of community-engaged practices that has become evident across the broader arts field and geographical humanities.

Shifting public art ontologies and practices

Since the National Endowment for the Arts established their first public art programme in 1967, with the purpose of bringing to the public the best "artwork outside of museum walls", public art programmes have proliferated throughout the United States and abroad. Rather quickly, *public art* replaced the previously accepted moniker of *public sculpture,* which was mostly used to describe sculptures and installations sited in public places and funded by public institutions. Now, public art is more commonly used by public art administrators to describe municipal, state and government programmes.

While a definitive, single-sentence definition of public art may never be attainable, there are recognized directions within public art practice that serve to define the field. In the *Practice of Public Art*, Cartiere and Willis (2008, p. 15) addressed this challenge with the development of a working definition of public art:

> *Public art is art outside of museums and galleries and must fit within at least one of the following categories:*[1]
> 1   in a place freely accessible or visible to the public: *in public*
> 2   concerned with, or affecting the community or individuals: *public interest*

3 maintained for or used by the community or individuals: *public place*
4 paid for by the public: *publicly funded*

Therefore, under the vast umbrella of public art one finds permanent works, temporary works, interventions, socially engaged practice, political activism, service art, performance, site-specific works, community-produced projects, monuments, memorials, spatial practice, interdisciplinary activism, contextual practice, social practice art, virtually mediated art practice and, let us not forget, plunk and plop art – this is certainly not an exhaustive list and none of these terms are mutually exclusive. Temporary works can be site-specific and memorials can exist as interventions. The practices of public art weave in and around themselves, existing in layers. Public art can incorporate a single object or an entire street or cityscape. Public art exists in urban centres, suburbia, rural regions, cyberspace and contexts of augmented realities and economic and art spaces of international flows. Public art has crept into every corner of our society and perhaps, in part, that is why it is one of the most controversial and misinterpreted art disciplines and subjects of study today.

Within the small collection of texts that delve into the annals of public art, there is little discussion of permanent works that do not incite controversy. For many, the discourse and history of public art is still frozen at the base of *Tilted Arc*. In 2001, art historian Harriet Senie wrote the definitive examination of Richard Serra's sculpture in *The Tilted Arc Controversy*. Perhaps her most significant contribution to the history of *Tilted Arc* was to examine the works that were sited in New York's Federal Plaza after the ill-fated arc was dismantled. In this way, Senie freed us to move forward, challenging the field to allow *Tilted Arc* to be(come) a significant milestone in the history of public art rather than the final destination of public art history.

Rationale and buildup

Through *The Practice of Public Art*, Cartiere and Willis (2008) accepted Senie's challenge and continued the conversation beyond the Federal Plaza, past the early territories of new genre public art and into the complexities of sited and situated public art practice. With the development of this new companion, *The Everyday Practice of Public Art* continues the journey and provides an expanded territory of socially engaged public art practice. This multidisciplinary anthology examines the continual evolution of the public art field with essays that explore new models for developing and commissioning permanent or temporary and community-centred public artworks, understanding the challenges of public art that address social conditions as well as the social inclusiveness of public art and unravelling the pedagogical relationships between public artists and the communities they serve. In 1995, the book *Mapping the Terrain*, (edited by artist and educator Suzanne Lacy) championed the need for a different form of criticism for public art whose core was socially engaged practice. This mode of public artwork was to become identified as "new genre public art".[2] The writers in *The Everyday Practice of Public Art* expand the critical discussions developed within Lacy's anthology by questioning and dissecting the parameters of socially engaged public art practice using contemporary examples.

The chapters in *The Everyday Practice of Public Art* are divided into three sections that correspond respectively to the anthology's main themes: the social practice of public art, the education of a public artist and the spatial fabric of public art and social practice. We reclaim the rich and extensive histories of socially engaged art by offering a visual timeline of significant works and events that can be expanded by the greater public art community. Within these pages we continue to expect ambiguities and contradictions along art, space and social inclusion and in so doing hope to inspire the public art debate. We aspire to offer solutions to be challenged and gauged across a range of 'glocal' communities and within a multiplicity of practices.

Section one: the social practice of public art

In the first section of this anthology, writers examine the social practice of public art from various perspectives. 'Through the Lens of Social Practice: Considerations on a Public Art History in Progress' examines a very specific and personal historical trajectory of socially engaged practice within the larger context of the public art field. The context for social practice within public art has been quietly evolving, building a critical mass in terms of its tangible real-world outcomes, and consequently its influence on practitioners in the field as well as thinkers and educators. But an examination of the history of social practice requires a different positioning, as all histories are subjective. If social practice is based on lived experience, would the history of such a practice not then be a very personal and highly variable reflection on the past?

This notion of positioning is continued in 'Politicizing Publics: A Social Framework for Public Artworks', where the authors reflect upon the function and methods of contemporary public art by proposing the need to differentiate between conceptions of public space, public realm and the public sphere when considering both the production of artworks and the audiences of an artwork. Although conventionally understood as neutral, public space is increasingly administered with less opportunity for political address and more room for commercial advertising, leisure and consumption. The customary tendency of articulating public art in relation to space and place is undermined by the acknowledgement that neither the artwork nor the space in which it is located are free from meaning and associations. The rise of shared space dedicated to consumption results in an absence of places where people can gather socially (i.e. meaningfully) in the public realm. This chapter asks: can the public artwork demarcate new spaces to congregate, and moreover can artworks 'call' for public assembly? This chapter examines a series of artworks sited in the public realm that enable the production of new social spaces through utilizing a social practice methodology.

'Placing Murals in Belfast: Community, Negotiation and Change' acknowledges that public art is a battleground of myriad complexity in Belfast, and discourses of 'community' are often at its core. Street murals, in particular, are negotiators of cultural divergence, producing mobile city spaces. Community is place-specific and often embraces and celebrates historical connections while resisting (new) spatial connections. In this way it can appear immobile and immobilizing. This chapter is centred round research on street murals in Belfast that explores how mobility is mediated through visual experiences of urban space, with discourses of 'community' emerging as a key theme. It looks at the way in which community materializes through murals and whether parochialism in street art in fact perpetuates city tensions and spatial division. The author grapples with the negotiation of public art in Belfast within the context of community, state measures to control the city's visual streetscapes and a city edging towards 'normality'.

'The Everyday Agonistic Life after the Unveiling: Lived Experiences from a Public Art World Café' discusses the mundane practices within the purview of permanent physical public art along issues of social difference and inclusiveness. The analysis is based on an interactive expert role-play workshop in World Café discussion style (cf. Brown and Isaacs 1995) about the dismantled and relocated abstract sculpture *Expansie* (the Dutch word for expansion), created by a locally well-known sculptor, in the city of Eindhoven. The chapter is concerned with social geographies of meaningful encounters within the everyday lived experiences of public art. The argument particularly engages with social public art practice as an agonistic sphere, one of potential conflict and open, ardent dialogues between ambivalent vistas. In the workshop, participants were expected to critically discuss official (i.e. institutional) aftercare and social engagement with *Expansion*. It encompassed host–guest role-plays in which participants alternated between the roles of three main actors involved in the recent relocation of the artwork: the curator of a Dutch multinational bank, local residents and a municipal cultural policymaker. The dialectic host–guest tenet conjured up queries and contentions about what artists, cultural policymakers, the diverse everyday users of public space and any interested individuals and civil society parties expect from the aftercare for public art over space, time and in terms of ownership and accountability.

Section two: the education of a public artist

In section two, we turn our attention to the education of a public artist. In 'Creating the Global Network: Developing Social and Community Practice in Higher Education' educators from two significant social practice programmes (in Australia and Canada) (look at the historical conditions that characterized early iterations of non-formalized practice before exploring the rise of higher-education degrees which recognize and reward community and social practice in four different national contexts (Canada, the United States, the United Kingdom and Australia). The authors explore why an international dialogue between higher-education programmes is essential to ensure they cater to the needs of a globalized practice, and offer a proposal for what such a dialogue might look like. They also expand on why students (as current and future practitioners and leaders) play the most important role in this network. Ultimately they develop a view that the pedagogic philosophy of community practice in a globalized world, which has been both under-examined and undervalued, is potentially short-changing the student and future practitioner's experience, learning, and ability to creatively and meaningfully contribute to society as they engage within communities and cultures.

'Throwing Stones in the Sea: Georg Simmel, Social Practice and the Imagined World' continues the pedagogical discussion with an in-depth examination of the development and evolution of the Social Practice Workshop at the California College of the Arts (CCA). As a professor of Social Practice, with the specific mandate to begin a Graduate Level curriculum that focused on artistic practice at the intersection between art and the public (and counter-public) spheres, the author unpacks the questions he utilized to develop the graduate programme: how does art interact with the social world? What does it change? How does it work with specific communities, or serve to create them? How are the boundaries of a specific community even determined in a time of escalating globalization? How might the critical language of the arts apply to larger social forms? When does the practice of art bleed so far into other areas of 'participatory culture' that it becomes something else? These questions are the same ones that he still considers, nine years later. While the questions have stayed the same, what has changed in the last nine years of teaching is the body of theories that the faculty uses to provide frameworks for the students. For the students, two years is a very short time to refine one's art practice to focus on the social and public spheres, let alone to understand the complexities of sociology, political philosophy, economics and cultural studies that might be brought to bear when trying to understand even a small, local community with any level of depth. As such, the theoretical framework that CCA works with has become increasingly considered. This chapter outlines some of the changes the programme has made and charts some of the pedagogical frameworks that the programme uses to bring student practice into the world.

'Open Engagement: Accessible Education for Socially-Engaged Art' takes a different approach to examine educational opportunities for artists interested in social practice. Begun as the author's graduate student thesis project and the basis of her master's education, it is now a major foundation for her work as an educator. Open Engagement started as a hybrid project that used a conference on socially engaged art practices as its foundation and incorporated elements including workshops, exhibitions, residencies, pedagogy, curatorial practice and collaboration. Since the first Open Engagement conference in 2007, the event has become a key meeting point for people interested in socially engaged art. From 2010 to 2013, Open Engagement was based at Portland State University and was planned in conjunction with the Art and Social Practice graduate students. Through discussions and planning sessions with students, all aspects of the conference were determined, including the themes of exploration for the year, the selection of keynote presenters, review of submissions, scheduling, partnerships and all aspects of organizing. This chapter examines the conference as a site of education for socially engaged art, and looks to the 2014 relocation of the conference to the Queens Museum as a means of opening the potential of how we learn from one another in the field – museums, funders, artists, students, publics and educators.

'"Context is Half the Work": Developing Doctoral Research Through Arts Practice in Culture' traces the evolution of the Gray's School of Art doctoral programme, *On the Edge*. This programme is developing practice-led research into the changing nature of arts practice in the public sphere. The remote rural culture of north-east Scotland uniquely informs this research in ways that are relational more than hierarchical. Vernacular culture is already rich in creativity and meaning. As such, it is a resource for the artist. The programme seeks to establish public art practice as profoundly research-led as well as epistemic. It orientates the voice and experience of the artist as an important contributor to producing knowledge in this complex field, alongside those of the critic, historian and theorist. The programme supports individuals across arts practice, policy development and curatorial practice, exploring issues with cultural leaders, inhabitants and academics from disciplines including anthropology and philosophy. Each doctoral project establishes unique exploratory threads, deploying metaphor as a way to grasp the particularity of their artistic approach as a contribution to a shared discourse. Co-operation between individuals creates feedback loops into the research process. The chapter explores a number of case studies of completed doctoral research, evaluating the permeability between artistic production and engagement.

Section three: the spatial fabric of public art and social practice

In section three of this anthology, the authors unravel the spatial fabric of public art and social practice. 'Public Art as a Function of Urbanism' summarizes an empirical study whose approach to public art was to start with real objects in space and combine modelling of urban form with a critical understanding of art styles to suggest a rigorous means for testing and investigating locative implications of public art. The author utilizes London's borough of Lewisham as his case study – a diverse stretch of urbanity ranging from an inner-city 'creative hub' to semi-suburban residential and park areas, laying claim to ownership of 52 public artworks including community murals, street furniture and freestanding sculptures. Drawing from methods laid out in space-syntax theories of urban form, empirical measurements of network accessibility, visibility and space usage for each artwork were analysed using geographic information system (GIS) software and observed on the ground. Clear patterns emerged in the responses of artists and commissioning processes to specific spatial attributes such as urban density, segregation or high visibility, leading on to a discussion that synthesizes the ideologies inherent in urban form with patterns of ownership, commissioning and style in public artworks. Particularly highlighted within the chapter are a spatial description of the difference between pre- and post-war planning styles and the associated disappearance of the monument as a form of public art.

'Listening in Certain Places: Public Art for the Post-Regenerate Age' focuses on the commissioning of public art during the 2000s that often became linked to the regeneration of UK towns and cities. Commonly associated with other 'place-making' activities, such as urban design, art became widely regarded as a low-cost way to help create an identity for redevelopment schemes and to engage local people in regeneration processes. Criticized by some as the instrumentalization of public art to advance social agendas and promote gentrification, this approach has also been impeded by the recent economic crisis, which has led to a marked decline in regeneration schemes. Against this backdrop, therefore, the challenge for today's public art commissioners, curators and artists is to develop new approaches to producing and articulating the value of art within the post-regenerate city. This chapter proposes the notion of 'place listening' as one such possible approach. Using *Taking In Certain Places* – a public art programme developed in 2003 in response to the (now abandoned) plan to regenerate the city of Preston – as a case study, the author describes how public art continues to help shape our cities. In contrast to the top-down approach typified by regeneration, however, she suggests that public art practitioners have begun to adopt an approach that engenders intimate, sensorial forms of place knowledge, providing the foundations for informing urban futures in embodied and surprising ways.

'Antagonistic Spaces: On Small, Interventionist, and Socially Engaged Public Art' offers an artist-based perspective to unfold the political capacity of public art not necessarily to make tangible social change but to harness a political imagination towards demonstrating and actualizing different ways to be in the world together. As co-founders of Broken City Lab, the authors explore a number of the collective's projects to argue, as in *The Everyday Agonistic Life after the Unveiling*, that socially engaged public art can act as a productive site for the development of antagonistic spaces of exchange that can cultivate capacities for critical engagement with our cities, their infrastructures and communities. Ranging from momentary pop-up installations to long-term community-embedded programming, Broken City Lab has aimed to engage and problematize the role that artists can and are expected to play in the public sphere. However, if socially engaged public art is expected to have the capacity to act as a catalyst for social transformation, as a site for experimental forms of living and organizing or as an incubator for critical democracy, then one must ask about the implications of the language that so often frames core elements of these projects, such as 'audience engagement', 'participation' and 'public'. Further, the authors examine the challenges of interventionist public art in relation to its legibility, instrumentalization and co-optation that invariably inform the way such work is sanctioned, supported and shared.

'Why Public Art? Urban Parks and Public Art in the Twenty-First Century' explores spatial fabric through the role of art in urban public parks, being a burgeoning phenomenon in neo-liberal urban spaces across the world. In particular reference to The High Line in New York, the author asks: what does public art do for this park and for its publics? The author examines the motivations behind rationales and support for various types of art in urban parks, particularly in environments where parks constitute a curious form and strategy of private–public orchestrated space, creating new 'hybrid park realities'. This chapter is an exploratory project, a means by which the author aims to advance the field by bringing three arenas of practice and thought – urban parks, public art and neo-liberalism – into a trialectic construct. This furthers what is becoming a platform to critically interlink the (alternative) futures of culture, arts and public space along the meaning and rescaling of the site-specificness and social inclusiveness of urban parks.

Section four: visual timeline

The fourth and final section of this anthology is an ambitious collaboration, 'A Collective Timeline of Socially Engaged Public Art Practice, 1950–2015'. In developing the chapter, the authors immediately recognized that they could not hope to present the entire timeline of socially engaged public artworks over the past half millennium, but they could instead present a highly subjective one that acts as a starting point for inquiry. In the spirit of the collaborative underpinnings of 'new genre public art', they wove together selected, intertwined histories chosen by five public art scholars. These individuals operate in various locations and professions within the field, and their selections reflect their varied interests: from the activist to the aesthetic; from the historical to happenings; from the local to the global. While the legacy of socially engaged art stretches back much further, the boundaries for the timeline were set at 1950 and 2015 to allow for a relatively focused chronology of an already complex and expansive topography. The contributors recognize the North American/Northern European focus of their selections. This has been for auto-ethnographical and practical rather than conceptual reasons, and they note that the practices of southern, eastern and 'non-centralized' geographies are brimming with significant examples of this sort of work that the Global North can – and should – value and learn from.

In the same vein, this limited selection does not try to present a holistic definition of the practice but hopes to have incorporated the milestone events that surround, shape and guide this way of working, including changes to political landscapes, policy shifts and social movements. It is hoped that these conversations with the history of this extensive public art practice can offer challenges and helpful guidance that encourage us to reinterpret, rethink and continue to problematize our current and future experiences and narratives.

Through the collection of perspectives brought together in this anthology, we recognize the outstanding role of socially engaged public art in our society. This vital practice is uniquely part of art history and everyday socio-cultural geographies. It contributes to the on-going desire to identify and understand our citizenships and belongings: 'who' are we and to whom and to which spaces do we belong? It contributes to social change, it shocks, it excites, it challenges social conventions, it has meaning, it educates, it inspires, it celebrates and remembers, it draws us together (includes) and pulls us apart (excludes), it envisages new paradigms and crosses disciplines, it is a catalyst for change in the political, economic and cultural sphere, and so on and so forth. The work that falls within the category of social practice art should not be considered disenfranchised. Socially engaged public artwork is a legitimate voice in the canon of contemporary and place-aware art.

Notes

1 We acknowledge that these definitional criteria leave room for other interpretations, as works of public art may be funded by public-private partnership schemes, not necessarily be freely accessible to the publics at large, or mediated in the public digital-virtual sphere only.
2 In her introductory essay to *Mapping the Terrain*, Suzanne Lacy (1995, p. 19) coined the phrase *new genre public art* to describe "visual art that uses both traditional and nontraditional media to communicate and interact with a broad and diversified audience about issues directly relevant to their lives". The key identifier for *new genre* was public art "based on engagement." (ibid.).

PART I
The social practice of public art

THROUGH THE LENS OF SOCIAL PRACTICE

Considerations on a public art history in progress

Cameron Cartiere

The year 1989 will be remembered for numerous events, many of which marked the end of an era: the fall of the Berlin Wall, the break-up of the Soviet Union, the last days of apartheid, the Tiananmen Square massacre that brought an end to pro-democracy demonstrations in Beijing, the final hours of the Reagan era (the end of Thatcherism was not far behind) and the end of the cold war, officially declared over by presidents Bush and Gorbachev.

Against this backdrop of political endgames, 1989 was a significant year for public art in North America. It was the year that Richard Serra's *Tilted Arc* was removed from Federal Plaza in New York City. It was also the year that artist collectives such as Group Material and ACT UP were starting to lead the charge to combat ignorance and prejudice in the midst of the AIDS epidemic, turning the *Silence = Death* pink triangle into a warning symbol that change was not only needed, it was no longer optional.

While politicians were closing the book on many of their failed endeavours, 1989 was also the year that a new chapter was being opened in the art world. In particular, it was a year of planning and preparation for the expansion of a changing category of public art practice: Projects such as *Places with a Past*, *Mapping the Terrain* and *Culture in Action* were in development – complex projects that required the coordination and cooperation of numerous groups of artists, volunteers and community stakeholders. As with the end of any decade, new trends and concerns became more manifest as collectively we looked back on the accomplishments and failures of the field, and planned ahead for the challenges of the next ten years. There was an uneasy energy, particularly in the museum world, as curators and educators grappled with how best to develop exhibitions and programmes for 1992 (which would celebrate the quincentenary of Columbus's arrival in the 'new world') in light of the emerging backlash coming from the multicultural movement.

Soon, this collective planning and exploration would usher in a new approach to public art that would eventually come to be known as social practice.

This chapter examines a very specific and personal historical trajectory of socially engaged practice within the larger context of the public art field. This presents a challenge, as – despite the fact that public art touches the daily lives of millions of people and that millions of dollars are spent commissioning public works around the world, leading to a proliferation and diversity of art created for the public realm – critical recognition of public art remains limited and our engagement is often based on individual influences and encounters that do not fit neatly into an easily quantifiable 'public'.

Public art is a complex, multifaceted discipline, and it is this very diversity and multiplicity that lies at the heart of its struggle not only for critical recognition but also for an understanding and recognition of a shared history. Indeed, with such an analytical challenge overshadowing the field, it is not surprising that those engaged in a less permanent or object-based practice might want to distance themselves from the moniker of public art (though it has been my experience that many social practice artists who are not willing to refer to their work as 'public art' are nonetheless willing to access public art funding). However, I would argue that disavowing oneself from the expansive field of public art also means cutting oneself off from the compelling and engaging history of those who have spent decades working in the public realm. I find this most evident when talking with students and emerging artists who have stumbled into this type of activity.

When taking on the challenge of considering a history of public art for *The Practice of Public Art* (Cartiere and Willis 2008), my concern was with the position of public art in the broader context of art history, grappling with a definition of public art that could embrace the vast spectrum of activity that falls across a field as diverse as ours. That field includes sculpture, performance, activism, social engagement, place-making, monuments and memorials, and a range of other artistic practices that are difficult to categorize but share the common ground of existing in and for the public realm. There was also the challenge of considering the public relationships between temporary and permanent works, particularly during a time when many arts administrators were considering how to revisit the definition of 'permanent' in relation to the accession and de-accession of their public art collections. Should that be five years, ten years, an indefinite period of time? An additional consideration was determining what our ontological position was in terms of defining the public realm within the context of public art practice. Here we recognized the need to expand beyond publicly owned streets and buildings, parks, rights of way and civic spaces to include privately owned spaces that allowed public access (such as shopping malls, banks, housing developments, etc.), airports and other transportation hubs that required a ticket (metros, buses, ferries, etc.) and even private works that were in the public view. Taking an expansive position on this territory allowed for a broader inclusion of the everyday spaces we move through where unexpected encounters with art might occur.

Meanwhile, if the last two decades have not been overly kind to public art in terms of its academic recognition, the field of social practice within public art has been quietly evolving, building a critical mass in terms of its tangible real-world outcomes, and therefore its influence on practitioners in the field as well as on thinkers and educators. But an examination of the history of social practice requires a different positioning. All histories are subjective. It is an old adage that states, "history is written by the victors."[1] If social practice is based on lived experience (Thompson 2012), would the history of such a practice not then be a very personal and highly variable reflection of the past? Even if there were an agreed upon starting point (Alan Kaprow's first use of the term 'happening' in 1957, or the often referenced formation of the Situationists also in 1957), the selected path through the following years would vary greatly depending on the personal experiences, professional interests and political influences of each author.[2]

The fact is, social practice is rooted in the real world – in people, relationships and communities. A more effective way to analyse its true impact is therefore to look at its evolution through personal, professional and political perspectives. By examining the development of social practice through this multifaceted lens, this chapter will develop an overview of how contemporary public practice is now being shaped by it; chart its gradual recognition in academic and educational circles; explore the relationship between social practice and public institutions; and trace some of the significant contributions of social practice to public art history.

Social practice as a lived experience

In the anthology, *Living as Form: Socially Engaged Art From 1991–2011*, Creative Time curator Nato Thompson takes up the challenge of unpacking the multiple layers of a practice that spans the gamut from theatre to architecture, design to dinner parties, political activism to media campaigns. But in doing so, he also points out the limitations of the current language used in the contemporary art world to describe and define the nature of this range of work.

> Socially engaged art may, in fact, be a misnomer. Defying discursive boundaries, its very flexible nature reflects an interest in producing effects and affects in the world rather than focusing on the form itself. In doing so, this work has produced new forms of living that force a reconsideration and perhaps new language altogether.
>
> *(Thompson 2012, p. 32)*

Thompson is certainly not the first writer to raise the inadequacies of a discursive language to address an art form that has quickly evolved beyond the parameters of contemporary critical debate (Phillips 1999, Cartiere 2008, Bishop 2012). Rosalind Krauss took up the cause in her seminal essay, "Sculpture in the expanded field" (1979) as sculpture moved off the plinth and into the landscape with the likes of Richard Long, Mary Miss, and Walter de Maria. In 1989, Suzanne Lacy was developing a collective, critical response to the radical changes in public art as works continued to expand from public sculptural forms to public practices.[3] Lacy was serving as the Dean of Fine Arts at the California College of Arts and Crafts[4] and I had just taken up the role as coordinator of exhibitions and public programmes for the college galleries. It was through this position that I had a front row seat to the discussions and debates that would manifest the terminology for 'new genre public art' as I embarked on an adventure with Lacy and a team of intrepid artists, curators, educators, students, as well as dedicated volunteers attempting to 'map the terrain' of a particular form of public art that had moved off the traditional plinth and into the realm of community life.

Professional interests: engaging the institution – institutional critique redux

The evolution of the phrase, "new genre public art" is most often associated with Lacy's anthology, *Mapping the Terrain: New Genre Public Art* (1995), but for a handful of writers, curators, artists, project managers and volunteers, the phrase evokes memories of hours of talking (facilitated discussion groups, lunchtime breakout sessions, hallway catch-ups, choreographed dinners and animated dialogues at the bar); months of planning, coordinating and managing the countless details of a substantial public programme and retreat (flight bookings, equipment, transportation, meals, press, documentation, etc.); and the years of influence (curatorial, artistic, academic) this singular event has had on the lives of those who participated in the process.

   The resulting collection of texts did not merely evolve out of the project but was always an integral part of the overall structure of the programme. Writers were invited to develop their initial ideas in advance of the event and these ideas served as the platform from which we could all discuss and debate the evolution of the field at that particular moment. My role was to work with the planning team to coordinate the public programme at the San Francisco Museum of Modern Art (1991). The event was designed as a kind of town hall meeting with an impressive roster of performers and speakers[5] such as Suzi Gablik, Walter Hood Jr and Patricia Phillips who poked, prodded and provoked a debate into being around our collective understanding of how public art was changing as a reflection of our current social conditions. I remember the lecture hall at SFMOMA's former location in the San Francisco Legion of Honor being filled to capacity, so much so that we had to set up an overflow room to accommodate the public demand to attend the event (it was here that I learned that in the field of social practice, no job is too big or too small, it just needs to get done). I also remember running the microphone up and down the aisles from speaker to speaker as the evening unfolded and ushering the retreat attendees onto buses as we shuttled off into the night, heading north to Napa Valley for two days of intense discussions that would expand on those initial ideas and eventually result in the writings that completed the anthology.

While much of the *Mapping the Terrain* event was planned, including the topics for the discussion groups and the order of speakers, this was a living event filled with unexpected obstacles, unplanned opportunities and unforeseen outcomes. This was a major shift from my previous curatorial experiences of gallery exhibitions and artist lectures. The countless hours of unseen labour involved in the complex planning and management of *Mapping the Terrain* were similar to those I had encountered in a gallery context; however, the unforeseen and unpredictable effects of the project were radically different. Within a museum or gallery context, an exhibition or programme is often curating *for* a public. But this project was fundamentally different from any work I had been involved with previously. *Mapping the Terrain* was not only opening up the potential of curating *with* a public, it was also exploring the concept of curating *in* public.

Political influences: socialists living in a capitalist world

One of the participants and writers at *Mapping the Terrain* was Mary Jane Jacob and in 1991 when the event took place, she was between two significant curatorial projects that radically influenced not only my curatorial trajectory but also, I would venture, impacted on a generation of young curators and artists around the world. The first exhibition, *Places with a Past: New Site-Specific Art in Charleston* had opened for the Spoleto Festival on 24 May and ran for three months, closing on 4 August 1991. So when Jacob came to San Francisco in November of the same year for *Mapping the Terrain*, her experience in Charleston was still quite fresh. The exhibition featured an impressive selection of artists: Christian Boltanski, Chris Burden, James Coleman, Houston Conwill, Estella Conwill Majozo, Joseph DePace, Kate Ericson and Mel Ziegler, Ian Hamilton Finlay, Gwylene Gallimard, Jean-Marie Mauclet, Antony Gormley, Ann Hamilton, David Hammons, Ronald Jones, Narelle Jubelin, Liz Magor, Elizabeth Newman, Joyce Scott, Cindy Sherman, Lorna Simpson, Alva Rogers and Barbara Steinmen. The works within this exhibition were a radical departure from those that had been developed for previous arts festivals and biennials. The artists involved produced works that were reflective of the specific locations in which each was sited. They not only responded to the topography of specific locations (both natural and artificial physical landscapes) but each grappled with the unique history, political context and/or social condition of the places selected. Many of the works were installations based in unusual locations (a former jail, a disused auto repair shop or a church), but a few ventured far outside the confines of an enclosed environment to sit boldly in front of the public eye. These were not works that occupied the traditional territory of the public plaza or the raised plinth. These were works that were firmly rooted in the neighbourhoods in which they were sited – works that not only spoke to a specific public but also to the social and cultural concerns of that public.[6] This exhibition was not one curated for the usual festival art crowd of collectors, gallery owners or corporate funders. This was curating for a *public*.

In his extremely favourable *New York Times* review of the exhibition, critic Michael Brenson noted:

> The sailing was not always smooth. The exhibition did not appeal to Gian Carlo Menotti, the founder and artistic director of the Spoleto Festival U.S.A., who threatened to resign over it at a board meeting last October. "It was not his idea of art", said Claudia Keenan of the festival's press office. At the same meeting, however, he agreed to go along with what the board wanted. "He has in some ways resigned himself to the show," Ms. Keenan said (1991).

Given the critical success of the exhibition, one would think that Menotti might have reconsidered his initial position on the exhibition. However, as noted in Brenson's 2013 reflection piece on *Places with a Past*,

> Menotti did not want this exhibition. On May 30 (1991) Allan Kozinn reported in the *Times* that "in an extraordinarily fiery statement, delivered to the board on Monday, Mr. Menotti attacked the show again, describing it as 'nothing more than silly, sophomoric stunts, justified by even sillier explanations.' When a member of the board quoted Michael Brenson's favorable review of the exhibition in the *New York Times* on Monday as part of a resolution in support of the curator, Mary Jane Jacob, Mr. Menotti stormed out of the meeting." Two years later, Menotti resigned from the Festival.
> *(Brenson 2013)*

As highlighted earlier, and as Brenson reminds us in a second article, it is important to consider the contextual period in which this work was taking place. In addition to the political turmoil of the day, "the National Endowment for the Arts was thrown into crisis by right-wing indignation over impudent photographs of naked men and children by Robert Mapplethorpe and the incendiary 'Piss Christ' of Andres Serrano" (ibid.). In June 1989, when the Washington Project for the Arts announced its intention to present Mapplethorpe's final exhibition, *The Perfect Moment*, more than a hundred members of Congress criticized the NEA for supporting Mapplethorpe's works. In July 1989, Senator Jesse Helms (a Republican from North Carolina) proposed an amendment to an Interior Department bill that would prohibit the NEA from using funds for the dissemination, promotion or production of obscene or indecent materials or materials denigrating a particular religion. Fortunately the amendment did not pass; however, Congress did return to the issue when it passed a 1990 Appropriations Bill which contained restrictions affecting NEA grant-making procedures. In April 1990, *The Perfect Moment* opened to the public in Cincinnati, Ohio. This moment marked the first criminal trial of an art museum over the content of an exhibition in the USA, as Ohio's Hamilton County grand jury accused the Cincinnati Contemporary Arts Center and its director, Dennis Barrie, of two misdemeanour counts each.[7] For Barrie, the charges carried the threat of a maximum penalty of a year in jail and fines of up to $2,000; for the art centre, the maximum fine could have been $10,000. Fortunately, the director and the art centre were found not guilty, but the 'culture wars' were now in full swing.

It was in the heat of this climate that Jacob launched her second pivotal exhibition, *Culture in Action*, which brought into focus for me, the concept of curating *in public*.

Personal experiences: curating in public

One could argue that art in the public realm enjoys a tremendously broad and abundant audience. For example, the works adorning the walls of the New York subway system (MTA) are seen by millions of riders daily. The MTA reported that in September 2014, single-day ridership numbers exceeded six million travellers on five different days.[8] But how do we know what impact these works might have on the lives of daily commuters or out-of-town visitors? This has been the challenge of public arts administrators for decades. There is anecdotal evidence: letters of support (or opposition), chance comments, online discussions and reactionary debate that indicate that at least some of the general public take notice. However the real challenge has always been trying to track the impact on those who do not feel compelled to write to the editor, sign a petition or start an online forum (often) denouncing the arrival of a new public work. How do we understand that audience of millions of people who pass through the gates on the way down to the subway platforms at Canal Street station heading for the A, C or E line under the watchful eyes of the 180 bronze crows, grackles and blackbirds of Walter Martin and Paloma Muñoz's *A Gathering* (2001)? Do they simply appreciate the humour of such an unexpected sight, perched on the gates and railings at the entrance of the station? Do they find the scene a bit too 'Hitchcockian', a bit too menacing? Do they even notice while they negotiate the electronic commands of the MTA fare machine as they hurry to top up their subway cards while their approaching train rattles up to the platform? Unlike New York's Museum of Modern Art, where visitors are counted at the door and have (presumably) crossed the threshold to engage with art, it is much more difficult to determine the engagement of the audience that passes by the work of Martin and Muñoz. As someone who lived in New York City and was a frequent user of the MTA system, I can attest to the fact that public art on the subway made the crush of daily commuting just a bit less miserable for me. While I never went out of my way to see the work, I always enjoyed passing by those bronze birds if I needed to venture to Canal Street.

It could be said that the audience for social practice public art is often much more immediate than that of a sited permanent work, particularly one deep in the underground caverns of the MTA system. A social practice-based work is often developed with a specific group of people, around a series of concerns or questions and in response to particular social conditions. With such intimate connection to their audience, curators and artists have access to more direct and immediate feedback about the impact of the work on their initial audience. But as the audience broadens through the concentric circles of Lacy's model, it becomes much more difficult to trace, and much more challenging to comprehend, the lasting effects that any type of public art might have imprinted on its audience. The Martin and Muñoz work has stayed with me. I remember those birds fondly; I have shown the work in presentations about public art and transportation; I have cited it as an example that public art made of bronze does not have to be limited to memorial figures frozen in time. And in doing so, I have presented this work to a different audience – an audience that may never see the work in situ but might still experience some visual or intellectual impact.

Continuing with this concept of the ripple effects of a public artwork, I return to *Culture in Action*. I never had direct experience with *Culture in Action*. I wasn't able to tour the streets of Chicago and happen upon Daniel Martinez's parade, *Consequences of a Gesture*, or enjoy *Tele-Vecindario*, the street level video block party on West Erie Street. My engagement with *Culture in Action* was as a member of the circle of encounter described by Lacy's audience model as the "audience of myth and memory" (Lacy 1995, p. 178). And yet, this work had a profound influence on the development of my curatorial thinking, on my transition out of the gallery and into the public realm and on my continued writing and research.

FIGURE 1.1 *Consequences of a Gesture* (1993), Daniel J. Martinez. Trafalgar Square, London.
Credit: John McWilliams for Sculpture Chicago/Mary Jane Jacob.

In her article on the influence of *Mapping the Terrain* 20 years after the event, Stephanie Smith describes Lacy's audience model quite extensively, but also quite distinctly and it merits repeating here.

> This visual model succinctly delineates a wider range than the usual dyad of "artist" and "audience". Based on varied points of connection to a work's production and reception, these circles begin with the person most responsible for the work – the artist – at the centre, and then move out through collaborators and eventually on to "the audience of myth and memory". These categories are fluid: individuals might move through each of the circles, which, Lacy argues, offer complementary sites for critical analysis beyond the traditional moment of aesthetic interaction in which a person encounters a "finished" product (be it a painting, a sculpture or a performance). If we think of *Mapping the Terrain* as an artwork, for instance, we might consider that first circle of origination and responsibility as a rather tight one defined by Lacy's creative vision for this project, based in her particular aesthetic and intellectual approaches and strongly influenced by her feminist organisational methods. Then we might consider how the project was presented for and experienced by those who intersected with early manifestations of *Mapping the Terrain*, either as collaborators and co-creators or as audience members. We might further consider the latter as involving two overlapping groups: those who experienced the public performative elements of "City Sites" and the conference, and those who encountered the book in the mid-1990s soon after it was published. We might look at the media audience—press coverage of the individual parts and early reviews — and also the book's longer arc of resonance (or dissonance) within current conversations.
>
> *(Smith 2011)*

So, 20 odd years after *Mapping the Terrain* and *Culture in Action*, I find myself at an interesting moment and one that we often advocate for when asked to evaluate public art. We advocate for time – time for the work to 'settle in' to the landscape, the community, and the memory; for reactionary emotions towards change to calm; for the ripples of influence and effect to move outward and if possible, to travel back to the work. While I was directly involved in many aspects of the *Mapping the Terrain* event which allowed me to experience the fluidity of audience that Lacy aspired to create and that Smith so eloquently describes above, I wonder why I still refer to *Culture in Action* as the more personally influential. During *Mapping the Terrain*, I was at times directly engaged and at other times peripherally involved in every level of Lacy's audience model, be it as collaborator, immediate audience, media audience, and most certainly now as "audience of myth and memory" (Lacy 1995, p. 178). For those of us who experienced *Mapping the Terrain* in 1991, the process of developing the project and the execution of the actual event has taken on almost mythical proportions and my memory of the experience serves as a form of record, not only in this chapter but also in my recollection of the event during presentations in the classroom, at conferences and in conversation. Yet throughout my career, it has been *Culture in Action* to which I have turned for curatorial guidance and inspiration. It has not been until now that I have realized to what extent my direct involvement in the former event prepared me to fully appreciate and understand the execution of the latter project.

While this may read as quite a belated and somewhat implausible breakthrough, I expose this slightly awkward personal revelation as a way to continue a discussion about the lived experience of public art. Thompson refers to socially engaged art as "living as form" which he describes as:

> Socially engaged art is not an art movement. Rather, these cultural practices indicate a new social order – ways of life that emphasize participation, challenge power, and span disciplines ranging from urban planning and community work to theatre and the visual arts.
>
> *(Thompson 2012, p. 19)*

But if social practice is about engaging in a lived experience, one shared with a community of common interest, is not all public art a form of shared experience, shared with a public that one may simply never meet face-to-face? This brings me back to the idea of our collective public art history and the influences that many public works – some sited and permanent, some community-based and quite temporary – have had on my understanding of the broader field of work in the public realm. Looking back, I can mention several personally influential works: Mel Chin's *Revival Field* (1990), Isamu Noguchi's *California Scenario* (1982), Seyed Alavi's *Where is Fairfield?* (1995), Platform's *Gog & Magog* (2002–7), Rachel Whiteread's *House* (1993), Christo and Jeanne-Claude's *Gates* (1979–2005) and Marc Quinn's *Alison Lapper Pregnant* (2005) just to name a few that easily fit under Thompson's description of socially engaged art. Ultimately, I can think of no singular work that challenges power more directly and more poetically than Quinn's, which situated an 11 foot 6-inch carved white marble sculpture of an eight months' pregnant disabled woman on the Fourth Plinth in London's Trafalgar Square, in sharp contrast to the military figures on the other three plinths.

At the time that *Alison Lapper Pregnant* occupied the Fourth Plinth, I lived in London and would often see the work as I rode by on the bus. If I was walking in the neighbourhood, I would make a point of going by to see the sculpture and spend some time looking up at the marble figure, her lap often filled with Trafalgar Square's famous pigeons. I was always able to rally some latent inner strength looking at this figure of a woman born with altered limbs (Lapper was born with shortened legs and no arms as a result of a chromosomal disorder) caught forever at the brink of a tremendous odyssey: about to set sail on the voyage of motherhood, a challenging journey of its own, with no arms to hold, feed or comfort a child. Yet the pose of the figure was confident and the small flock of pigeons nestled in her lap oddly reassuring. Of the four figures situated on pedestals around the square, she was by

FIGURE 1.2   *Alison Lapper Pregnant* (2005), Marc Quinn. Trafalgar Square, London. *Credit*: Anthony Carr.

far the most heroic. Even Lord Nelson, high atop his column, one arm severed in battle, could not measure up to the lifetime of challenges and achievements that Quinn's sculpture captures with this moment in the life of Alison Lapper.[9] I was not alone in this encounter – I was sharing my experience with hundreds of people standing in the square, whose names I didn't know and whose faces I would never see again. I was also sharing my experience with an expansive media audience, as there were copious newspaper articles about the emotional impact this work had on the public, commentaries questioning our ideas of beauty and ability and the social conditions that limit or support disabled people in contemporary society – many of the social issues and political concerns that Thompson highlights as indicative of socially engaged art.

Finding one's place in a history in progress

"Why are you the best person to do this work?" This is not a question that the studio artist is often asked. If they demonstrate any kind of creative talent, aptitude for materials, and/or conceptual thinking, that is usually enough to carry the banner of 'artist'. Even if one does not possess any of the aforementioned attributes but has the tenacity to claim the title (along with some requisite eccentricities), they will often go unchallenged. However, for the students and artists that I work with in this continually evolving territory of socially engaged public art, it is a question I pose often. Ours is a practice that not only engages people, it is dependent upon their participation to exist. With that engagement comes a level of social responsibility that is not necessarily required of studio practice. Examining our shared history reveals countless artists who have taken on the challenge of working successfully in this mode and a common thread is often the extended period of time they have devoted to developing the community relationships that underpin the work. To that point, I can think of no better artist to close this reflective quasi-historical chapter than one of the most long-standing public-realm practitioners in our field, Mierle Laderman Ukeles.

Ukeles has held the position of artist-in-residence for the New York Sanitation Department since 1977. Within this unpaid position, she has created renowned works such as *Touch Sanitation* (1978–84), a durational performance work involving shaking the hand of every New York City sanitation worker (over 8,500 of them) and expressing gratitude for their labour with the phrase, "Thank you for keeping New York City alive"; *Flow City* (1985–96) a visitor centre at the 59ᵗʰ Street Marine Transfer Station in Manhattan, allowing audiences a view of the transfer process of the garbage flowing out of the city onto barges for transportation to landfill sites; and *Freshkills Park* (1989– continuing), the rehabilitation of what was once the world's largest landfill site into a 2,200 acre park (three times the size of New York's Central Park). Bringing this chapter full circle, it is interesting to note that 1989 was when Ukeles began advocating for such a park – she later became one of the contributors to the Freshkills Park master plan. She has been commissioned to develop a permanent viewing platform for the south section of the park with two related earthworks. The timeline for the completion of this extensive project is long. The park to date has been decades in the making and the completion of all five phases of the restoration is likely to be decades away, yet Ukeles (now in her 70s) continues to work along the same trajectory, with the same commitment to her extended community. The maintenance art that has been her practice for over four decades is a model for contemporary artists engaged in public art and social practice with any community. Her *Manifesto of Maintenance Art 1969*, originally penned as a proposal for the exhibition CARE, speaks more to a way of being within a practice than to the practice itself. Her consideration of maintenance is a fundamental component of her artistic practice, and community engagement is as evident in her work today as it was in 1969: "maintenance … preserve the new; sustain the change; protect progress; defend and prolong the advance; renew the excitement; repeat the flight… keep the home fires burning" (Ukeles 1969 cited in Lippard 1997, p. 221).

With Ukeles' philosophies of maintenance in mind, I recognize that my list of influential public artworks changes constantly. Today, as I read about Cuban officials detaining Tania Bruguera (another noteworthy social practice artist),[10] I am reminded of an additional work, *The Year of the White Bear and Two Undiscovered Amerindians Visit the West* (1992–94) a collaborative performance piece by Coco Fusco and Guillermo Gómez-Peña. While I have only experienced this work as a member of the audience of media and of myth and memory, it has stayed with me and has informed my views on how we comprehend and challenge ideas of "otherness". Each of us involved with art in the public realm will have our own history of influence, but it is crucial that we recognize that we possess a shared history. That as we move forward to take on the challenges of contemporary society, we should not only look to the past for ideas and influences, but we should also look to the side at works just to the left and right of our own particular practice, to gain support and different approaches to a shared goal of engaging our public audiences in ways that are politically critical and socially empowered, and far less passive than the traditional public position of simply being a spectator.

Notes

1 This quote is often attributed to Sir Winston Churchill but is of unknown origin. Versions of this quote include "history is written by the winners", or "conquerors".

2 Such variations are evident in the collectively produced social practice timeline in the last chapter of this anthology.

3 An important precursor to *Mapping the Terrain* was a series of experimental, site-specific lectures called "City Sites: Artists and Urban Strategies" (1989) featuring ten artists, many of whom would return to the Bay Area to participate in *Mapping the Terrain*. Along with Lacy, the City Sites artists included Judy Baca, Helen and Newton Harrison, Lynn Hershman, Marie Johnson-Calloway, Allan Kaprow, Mierle Laderman Ukeles, John Malpede and Adrian Piper

4 Since 2003 the institution has dropped 'craft' from its moniker and is now referred to as the California College of the Arts: https://www.cca.edu/about/history

5 Other speakers included: Juana Alicia, Judy Baca, Sheila Levrant de Bretteville, Mel Chin, Estella Conwill Májozo, Houston Conwill, Jennifer Dowley, Patricia Fuller, Anna Halprin, Ann Hamilton, Jo Hansen, Helen Harrison, Lynn Hershman, Mary Jane Jacob, Chris Johnson, Allan Kaprow, Suzanne Lacy, Hung Liu, Alf Löhr, Yolanda Lopez, Lucy Lippard, Leopoldo Mahler, Jill Manton, David Mendoza, Richard Misrach, Peter Pennekamp, Lynn Sowder, Mierle Laderman Ukeles, Carlos Villa and more. See http://www.suzannelacy.com/mapping-the-terrain/

6 Most notable of these works were Kate Ericson and Mel Ziegler's *Camouflaged History* and *House of the Future* by David Hammons.

7 "In the Spring of 1990, the Contemporary Arts Center (CAC) in Cincinnati, Ohio, held an exhibit of photographs by the late artist Robert Mapplethorpe. The exhibit was controversial from the start because of the openly homosexual nature of much of Mapplethorpe's work and was well covered in the Cincinnati press. There was a great deal of negative public reaction, and rumors spread that the city of Cincinnati would attempt to close down the exhibit under Ohio's obscenity statute, which makes it illegal for any person to 'Promote,... display ... or exhibit ... any obscene material.' The CAC's director, Dennis Barrie, attempted a preemptive strike aimed at heading off an obscenity prosecution. The CAC filed an action for a declaratory judgment, which is a type of civil lawsuit, on March 27, 1990, in Hamilton County (which includes Cincinnati) Municipal Court. CAC asked the court to declare the exhibit not obscene, but on April 6, 1990, the court refused and dismissed the action. The next day, the Hamilton County Grand Jury indicted CAC and Barrie for criminal violations of the Ohio obscenity statute. Of the approximately 175 pictures in the exhibit, seven were particularly controversial and were the focus of the ensuing trial. Two pictures were of naked minors, one male and one female, with a 'lewd exhibition or graphic focus on the

genitals'. The other five were of adult men in unusual sadomasochistic poses" (http://law.jrank.org/pages/3469/Mapplethorpe-Obscenity-Trial-1990.html).

8 See http://www.mta.info/news-subway-new-york-city-transit-ridership-record-breaking/2014/10/22/more-6-million-customers-ride.

9 Alison Lapper graduated in 1993 with a first-class honours degree in fine art from the University of Brighton and in 2014 she was awarded an honorary doctorate by the same university. In 2003 she was awarded a MBE for her service to the arts. See: http://www.theguardian.com/artanddesign/2014/jul/28/artist-alison-lapper-doctorate-university-brighton.

10 See http://www.e-flux.com/announcements/on-the-detention-of-cuban-artist-tania-bruguera-by-coco-fusco.

2

POLITICIZING PUBLICS

A social framework for public artworks

Andrew Hewitt and Mel Jordan

Introduction

As early as 1996, in her essay "What is Public Art?: Time, Place and Meaning", Hilde Hein explores what constitutes public art. Suggesting that "the concept of public art has undergone radical changes", she acknowledges that "todays public artworks may be impermanent and discontinuous, like the installations of Suzanne Lacy" (Hein 1996, p. 2). Thus, like the concept of space, "public art became first an object *in* public space, and then a sculpting of that space as objects too evaporated, leaving only relations behind" (ibid.).

For Doreen Massey space is a social construction that is always under production; space is never fixed but continually being (re)formed. The move from imagining space as a physical entity to the recognition of it as a social and contingent concept (Massey 2005) is not unlike the trajectory that contemporary art takes – contemporary art shifts from unique physical objects to incorporate social and performative means of production. Artists use action and intervention as a way of performing their social critique – participatory art practice, relational aesthetics and new genre public art can be described as an art that engages directly *with* the political imagination as opposed to representing it.

Jurgen Habermas's theory of the Bourgeois Public Sphere (Habermas 1989) [1962] – as well as other scholars' expansions of public sphere theory (Benhabib, Mouffe and Fraser) – have been utilized by both W. J. T. Mitchell (Mitchell 1992) and Rosalyn Deutsche (Deutsche 1996) to analyse the practice of public art.

By employing the term 'public sphere' as opposed to the term 'public space', we are better able to understand the internal contradictions of 'publicness' and ask what actually constitutes a public space. This is in contrast to the way in which the word 'public' is traditionally used in the expressions 'public art' and 'art in public places', which usually refer pragmatically to the siting of an art work in an 'outside' space. And although the rhetoric around this practice uses the terminology of democracy as Rosalyn Deutsche observes, the divisions between desirable and undesirable publics still remain.

> Following a $1.2-million reconstruction of the park, a neighborhood group, Friends of Jackson Park – a group the *Times* consistently mistakes for both "the community" and "the public" –decided to lock the newly installed park gates at night. The City Parks Department, lacking sufficient personnel to close the park, welcomed "public" help in protecting public space, a defense they equated with evicting homeless people from city parks. "The people who hold the keys," announced the *Times,* "are determined to keep a park a park".
>
> *(Deutsche 1996, p. 276)*

Habermas describes the bourgeois public sphere as being made up of private individuals; what makes it public is simply that they publish their opinions ((Habermas 1989) [1962]). These shared opinions remain the views of private individuals, but by being published they become part of the collective attempt to arrive at common values, decisions and potential actions. And as Susen explains,

> The public sphere is nothing but the socialised expression of individuals' reciprocally constituted autonomy: individuals are autonomous not in isolation from but in relation to one another, that is, in relation to a public of autonomous beings.
>
> *(Susen 2011, p. 42)*

The key idea that we take from Jürgen Habermas is not the concept of the public within the public sphere, but the activity of publishing ((Habermas 1989) [1962]). As such, the public is neither an empirical body, nor a spatial concept. The public sphere is a *performative* arrangement; it is the activity of 'going public' or 'making something public' that fills particular places and spaces with public life. And this is why the public can emerge in private, commercial and mobile spaces too, such as the coffee house, the magazine, the parlour, the Working Men's Club, the political party and the pub (Beech, et al. 2007).

The use of a public sphere theory framework to emphasize the social and political interactions within the term 'public' resonates with Massey's theory that space is too often understood as formal, physical and static. Thus we can move away from the original physical description of both 'public' and 'space' within the discourse of public art.

Furthermore, by taking into account that the social turn in art practices is allied with the public realm, the public domain and public space, and is understood to include temporary artworks that engage people in their production, we identify a parallel set of concerns between Massey's explanation of space and Habermas's articulation of the public sphere. Hence we propose that the notion of the 'social' in the term 'social art practice' and the term 'public' in 'public art' should be understood as discursive constructs. The 'social', understood as in the 'social production of being' as opposed to a set of sociable interactions or chance meetings; the 'public' recognized as a contingent body of citizens with a degree of shared purpose or common experience rather than a placid community of abstractly equal individuals (ibid.).

By bringing these two theories together, we can better understand participatory art practice. By distinguishing which artworks rely on a limited understanding of the concepts of 'space' and 'public', and which ones operate with an expanded engagement with 'space' and 'public', we can begin to articulate the different social relations of production within specific artworks. Appreciating this, we argue, enables us to better analyse in what ways artworks are *public*.

In order to do this, we examine three artworks: *Nowhereisland*, by Alex Hartley, *Gramsci Monument* by Thomas Hirschhorn and *Node* by Stealth. Utilizing this framework we develop three instances in which the notion of 'publicness' is employed in contemporary artworks: We describe these as:

- Picturing Publics – a picturing of people as part of the artwork.
- Educating Publics – the function of the artwork is to enable a distribution of knowledge by the artist.
- Benefiting Publics – the artist provides a service or product for a specific community in which the result and consequences enable a practical enhancement of the users' lives.

No space like a public sphere

As Hein points out, art historian Patricia Phillips acknowledges the importance of asking what the meaning of public is within the term 'public art'. She recognizes the changing concept of *public* in a mass media context when she says:

> The millions of television viewers of the lighted apple's descent in New York's Times Square New Year's Eve celebration are as much a part of the public spectacle as are the thousands of witnesses on the street. Only the meaning of the word 'public' has changed, becoming more 'psychologically internalised' as a result of developments in urban and information systems.
>
> *(Hein 1996)*

Habermas's 1989 ([1962]) concept of the bourgeois public sphere is a virtual or imaginary community that does not exist in any specific location. However, a portion of the public sphere comes into being in every conversation in which private individuals assemble to form a public body. Similarly, there is not a singular form of public sphere. For Habermas, contemporary opinion formation can occur through any number of means and can be a combination of processes (for example, in correspondence via letters, printed media, the internet or phone technology, informal meetings in the street, in a public building, in the home, a local shop, park or street), or can be organized as a more formal system of association such as a labour union or a political organization.

Both Habermas and Massey understand social relations as political. Habermas's account of the bourgeois public sphere (ibid.) is a historical description of the development of liberal democracy. Massey insists on the multiplicity of space and warns against turning "space into time". This view advances the way we think about globalization; currently a single historical trajectory is inferred by the dominant terminology of 'developed and developing' countries: This trajectory inevitably suggests a hierarchy along which 'developing' countries will progress to the state of 'developed' countries. Such an arrangement fails to take into account the contingencies of space and time. Consequently, it reverts to a notion of progress through accumulated historical understanding, directed by prevailing nation states (Massey and Warburton 2013).

From public spaces to public assembly

For the purposes of this text we broadly define public space as accessible spaces which are generally open to people – parks, roads and pavements, beaches, as well as spaces that are owned by the state or the people: public libraries, national parks, government buildings – including objects and services that are paid for by taxes such as military bases etc. (Parkinson 2012). There is an important distinction between a public space and a public assembly, as the places in which people gather can be both publicly owned as well as commercially instigated. For example, they include the marketplace, coffee shops, football stadiums, theatres, churches, etc.

There is no question that disputes over public space are still an essential part of politics. Notwithstanding the collective agreement that access to physical space alone is not the formation of a counter-public sphere, we do however need to meet somewhere and in some place – be it physical or virtual – to generate our collective opinions. The act of addressing the question of what constitutes public space – and furthermore to whom it belongs – is central to political transformation. As Doreen Massey notes, "space is the dimension that presents us with the existence of the other; space is the dimension of multiplicity" and therefore "it is space that presents us with the question of the social"(Massey and Warburton 2013).

The right to public assembly is a stipulated human right; Article 20 of The Universal Declaration of Human Rights (UN 2014), states that "everyone has the right to freedom of peaceful assembly and association". The purpose of the congregation is the key to the difference between a public assembly and an audience of an event. A public assembly is comprised of active publics with an opinion to share. The *content* of a public gathering is the reason why people attend, and the subject under discussion is what attracts passers-by to join in. When discussing the impact of the Occupy movement's occupation of St Paul's Cathedral, Massey says:

> While I was there people who had nothing to do with the occupation came
> up to me and asked questions and talked and it seemed to me that what they

managed briefly to create there was a really public space, which means it was a place for the creation of a public, of politically engaged subjects if you like, of people who would talk to each other about the wider world.

(Massey and Warburton 2013)

To be sure, accidental publics like shoppers and passers-by can join an existing public assembly and become part of the public sphere, but a bystander is not converted into a public by the formal act of gathering alone (Jordan 2011).

Under neo-liberalism the interests of capital have dominated public spaces. Spaces traditionally understood as 'public' have been turned into places of economic consumption, not just through commercial advertising but also through state interventions that have led to the physical reshaping of civic spaces, entertainment venues and the high street (ibid.). However as Massey believes, space is a product of our relations with each other, which inevitably includes the matter of power within these interactions. When we become aware of the unequal distribution of power of some groups over others, or power of some places over others, this translates into the political (Massey and Warburton 2013). It is through social exchanges that we transform public spaces into political places. Being a passer-by is negotiable: we all have the capacity to change our status while in the public realm; each one of us has the agency to interfere, act up and protest, and lots of us do (Jordan 2011).

A public assembly is predicated on social principles and is not simply a physical spatial entity. Understanding this concept can affect the way we consider the 'public' within 'public art', and it enables us to recognize the limitations of declaring an artwork 'public' when it is installed in a 'public' (usually outside) space. In addition, state-commissioned and publically funded artworks are also not necessarily public, and an artwork does not necessarily have to be funded by the state for it to be acknowledged as 'public'. In this sense, the definition of an artwork's 'publicness' is defined by the way it operates within the public sphere of opinion formation (politics) as opposed to its technical specifications.

Public art towards participatory art

During the 1990s UK cultural policy encouraged artists to work in the public realm within culture-led regeneration projects. Due to significant increases in the funding of the arts, opportunities for new commissions and project development increased and artists established new approaches to working in the public realm. Groups such as Muf and Public Works developed interdisciplinary methods that provided new models of art practice in urban and rural contexts. Other artists, such as Jeremy Deller, Mark Wallinger and Liam Gillick, combined their work in the commercial gallery sector with projects in the publicly funded sector, either with art galleries or in publicly funded regeneration contexts.

In the last ten years, theories of art and participation have centred on ideas by Bourriaud, Bishop and Kester. Bourriaud's 'Relational Aesthetics' (Bourriaud 2002) has been influential in advocating non-object-based practices. His theory redefines the political as "models of sociability" and "micro-utopias" in the space provided by the art institution. Bishop is critical of Bourriaud's 'Relational Aesthetics', outlining three issues in this theory that she finds problematic: activation, authorship and community. First, she says, there is an emphasis on an active subject being formed via participation in an artwork. Second, co-authorship is presented as non-hierarchical production – the matter of power is overlooked. And third, due to a perceived crisis in community relations, the restoration of a social bond is imagined through participatory art projects. Bishop is critical of arguments made for the virtues of 'Relational Aesthetics', claiming that the participant lacks a distinct role in these exchanges; being neither an author nor a collaborator, the potential for subjects to become an activated public is limited (Bishop 2006, p. 180). The implication here is that Bishop believes that some forms of participation are hegemonic. To support her point, she reminds us of how "participation is used by business as a tool for improving efficiency and workforce morale" (ibid.)

According to Bishop, there are two potential outcomes of participation. One is disruptive and interventionist, the other constructive and ameliorative. Bishop believes that Bourriaud's concept of participation in relational aesthetics is both constructive and ameliorative in its 'convivial' encounter with the other. She claims that while taking coffee or sharing a meal does reconfigure what art can be, his theory diminishes antagonism in favour of acts of sociability. This 'micro-utopian' togetherness is made frictionless as members undertake a communal activity such as eating together. She accuses Bourriaud of putting 'sociability' or 'conviviality' where dissent and critique should be (ibid.).

Bishop has entered into a series of debates with Grant Kester, who advocates the dialogical as a form of art practice. In her critique of social artworks, Bishop sets up a tension by contrasting ideas of aesthetics and ethics. Bishop discusses the ethics of authorship in dialogic art practices. In Kester's theory of dialogic aesthetics, she sees a "trend toward identity politics – respect of the other, recognition of difference, protection of fundamental liberties, inflexible mode of political correctness – [meaning] a rejection of art that might offend or trouble its audience" (Bishop 2004, p. 67). Bishop describes Kester as being against sophisticated art and theory, and suggests that his position undermines art's political potential.

It is worth pointing out here that although Bishop complains about the sociability of 'Relational Aesthetics', she herself reverts to a formal question of art's ontology; for her the value in relational aesthetics is in its ability to question what is acceptable as art. Considered in this way, she reduces the social relations in art to functioning merely to innovate; formal techniques of what art can be are deemed the primary goal for socially engaged art practice. This has repercussions on her overall critique of relational aesthetics as it presupposes a commitment to the concept of nomination as a convincing method for the production of art practice. We would say that this is contrary to the intentions of the first generation of artists making social artworks. Furthermore, Bishop neglects to consider the potential political associations that might be formed from an initial convivial encounter.

Picturing people: *Nowhereisland*

Alex Hartley's project *Nowhereisland* was commissioned as one of the 12 art projects selected for 'Artists Taking the Lead', the 2012 Cultural Olympiad commission for the south-west UK. *Nowhereisland* was devised by Alex Hartley, who while on an expedition to the Arctic discovered an island revealed by receding ice that he declared to be a new nation, an idea that led to the *Nowhereisland* project. "*Nowhereisland* is a floating sculpture, which is comprised of glacial moraine that the artist removed from the Arctic archipelago in the Norwegian region of Svalbard" (Nowhereisland 2014).

In fact, *Nowhereisland* was manufactured by MDM Props, London. The island is a 60-metre-long steel structure, with fibreglass and resin used to form the island's surface; the glacial moraine retrieved from the High Arctic was scattered over the finished structure. The manufacture of the sculpture required the fabricators to wear masks, boiler suits taped at their wrists, as well as ankle protectors and safety boots.[1]

The website claims that *Nowhereisland* was pulled from the High Arctic to the south-west of England, where it undertook a 500-mile trip around the south-west coast (ibid). However, as it was made in London it is not clear what part of the island was pulled from the High Arctic.

The environmental agenda would appear to be a key motivation for the production of *Nowhereisland,* as is evident in claims made in the promotion of the project. Statements about the project make clear a critique of contemporary life, contrasting the quiet, unpopulated Arctic with the social conditions of the busy world, and the impact of the latter upon the former. The website states:

> *Nowhereisland* began in a place far from the noise of the urban centres of the Western world. Far (it would seem) from the passport controls and security checks of our journeys across national boundaries. Far from the riots and protests of our streets. Far from the ringing of our phones, the buzzing of our cash points, the tapping of our keyboards. And yet of course, *Nowhereisland* began in exactly the place in which all the actions made by us and decisions made for us are brought to bear – the Arctic (ibid.).

In an attempt to point to the cause and effect of global warming, the social world is described as crowded and noisy in contrast to the tranquil landscape of the arctic region. The consequence of this is that *Nowhereisland* is therefore demarcated as a flat, objective space, denying the "throwntogetherness" of space that Massey endorses (Massey 2005).[2] "To hold onto the idea of open space is a dubious concept" (ibid, p. 152) and presents a deworlded view of the problems we collectively face. The idea that we can achieve a space without people, nations states and technology can only be an ideological construct; this romanticized notion of being alone and therefore individual is utilized by neo-liberalism to ward off threats of collectivity. It is reasonable to imagine that many people accept and understand the deleterious effect industrialization and global capital are having upon our environment, yet it is unclear how crucial a romantic, solipsistic world of explorers, tall ships and artistic integrity is for inquiring into what constitutes a responsible geography.

Audiences congregated on points along the south-west coastline to catch a glimpse of the island. The island's mobile embassy (a motor vehicle) arrived in ports and towns to represent the visiting nation. As well as a mobile museum, it was also a vehicle that functioned to provide interpretation for the project at points on the coastline. The website describes it as "a place at which citizenship can be conferred, ceremonial duties undertaken and it will carry with it the stories of its origins and will gather new stories as it moves from location to location" (Nowhereisland 2014).

Certainly the project aimed to raise awareness of eco-politics. Looking to galvanize people's imagination, it encouraged them to engage in thinking about what they wanted the island (and, by association, the world) to be like, through a 'vox pop' method of immediate response. The top ten propositions put forward by Nowhereian citizens included "Every child will be read to each night" and "Every Nowhereian has the right to be silent" and "Every Nowhereian has the right to be heard" (ibid.). These demands seem tame, and in fact they are not as radical as the Universal Declaration of Human Rights, which was adopted in 1948 and warns against slavery and servitude, supports the right to be able to eat and keep warm, and promotes the right to belong to a nation.

The project team imagined the island as a tool intended to be outside of current thinking on political matters, as well as a catalyst for urgent action. Simon Anholt (one of the 52 resident thinkers of *Nowhereisland*) says it's about the opportunity to "stop the world, I want to get off" and "it's the first *non-country*, a piece of truly neutral territory where people can get outside the system to think about the system" (Anholt 2011). In this way, the project encourages viewers to turn their back on the particularities of space and time. It is therefore no surprise that the propositions suggested by its new citizens rely on generic and universal ideas of public good.

Nowhereisland's constitution was to be devised by its citizens by eliciting answers to questions about migration, sovereignty and global warming, as well as inviting responses to what life would be like in a place where we could begin again. In this way, the project does have the possibility to become a public sphere as it offers the opportunity to meet and exchange ideas about how people want to live. However, the abstract notion of the concept of *Nowhereisland* means that there is not much at stake, nothing to actually invest in, because this is not a step towards a real exchange of opinion: instead, it catches fanciful ideas for potential change.

Anholt makes it clear that, he sees its value in its independence. "There could be no better vantage-point to take a fresh, clear, cool, hard non-country look at the world and see what we can do to solve these non-country problems" (ibid.).

This disregards the question of art's autonomy from the social sphere as a crucial consideration for a generation of artists occupied with the social function of art.

FIGURE 2.1 *Nowhereisland* (2012), Alex Hartley.
Credit: Max McClure.

While we are not searching for a quantifiable amount of change affected by Hartley's project, more importantly we would expect a challenge to the aesthetic role of the artwork as well as alternatives to art's autonomy. That is not to say artists have to offer up pragmatic solutions, but it is not much to ask that they be aware of the politics of space and notions of the public when they utilize these concepts in the production of their artworks.

Public engagement was seen as a key component of the project. However, it seems engagement here is used loosely as a term that speaks of audiences, onlookers and passers-by. A significant claim for 'engagement' is made by the project team in the evaluation report, (as evidenced by the number of people involved), which actually constitutes audiences as well as project partners. There are photographs of the project that includes people looking out to sea at *Nowhereisland,* as well as audience members pictured with the mobile embassy. These images demonstrate evidence of popular interest in the artwork. As they represent people engaged with the sculpture, this manifests as publicity and is managed through the interpretation of the artwork.

Educating publics: *Gramsci Monument*

In 1999, Thomas Hirschhorn began making monuments to philosophers; to date he has completed monuments to Spinoza (Amsterdam 1999), Deleuze (Avignon 2000), Bataille (Documenta 11 Kassel 2002), Gramsci (New York 2013). Hirschhorn describes these monuments as precarious; they are purposefully temporary in order to be "a monument for a limited time" (Hirschhorn 2014). They differ from conventional sculptural tributes which commemorate the life of an authorized individual, typically of someone who has served in wars and campaigns, contributed to science, technology or industry, or is a member of royalty. And in doing so, Hirschhorn attempts to break the authority of the usual type of statue, by conceiving his monuments as "community commitments" (ibid.).

Hirschhorn's monuments are composed of at least two parts: first, what Hirschhorn calls the "classical-part", which is a representation of the thinker, depicting his head or body, and second the "information part", which comprises all types of material including books, videotapes, statements and biographical documents.[3] It is in this way that the concept of the monument is extended to include not only a depiction of the philosopher but, more significantly, to also embrace his work. His version of a monument marks a decisive shift away from statues that manifest as representations of a person's form. Hirschhorn proposes that we should celebrate the contribution that these philosophers have made by collectively engaging with their work rather than publishing what they looked like, for he does not care for the convention of figurative representation (ibid.). This tactic succeeds in socializing the formerly autonomous monument, and furthermore it (re)activates the work of these thinkers, thus enabling viewers, publics and onlookers to engage in their ideas in the here and now.

For his latest work, the *Gramsci Monument* (commissioned by Dia Art Foundation in 2013), he developed a project, which was sited in a working-class area of New York. From July to September 2013, *Gramsci Monument* was open seven days a week on the grounds of Forest Houses, a New York City Housing Authority development in the Morrisania neighbourhood in the borough of the Bronx (Dia Art Foundation 2013).

The *Gramsci Monument* takes the form of a village hall with functioning rooms and spaces for a library, discussion space, exhibition space, canteen, museum, classroom, along with facilities including a newspaper, workshop, computer room and radio station. The temporary construction was built by residents of Forest Houses; the buildings were constructed using Hirschhorn's trademark materials, – plywood, tape, tarpaulin sheets and rough-sawn timber, adorned with slogans, instructions and information.

A programme of events ran daily between 10am and 7pm, which included political and philosophical lectures, theatre performances, children's workshops and art classes run by Hirschhorn. My mission, says Hirschhorn, "is to establish a new term of monument, provoke encounters, create an event, think Gramsci today" (ibid.).

His monuments rethink the conventional idea of statues, presenting structures that introduce people to new ways of tribute. This is not formal innovation but political engagement. The intention here is to think political for political action. Hirschhorn talks of the monuments in terms of encounters; however his desire for the encounter is one based on the pursuit of active assembly, not happenstance, convivial meetings.

There is no doubt that the *Gramsci Monument* project sits awkwardly in its physical siting; this is Hirschhorn's intention. He spent a considerable amount of time choosing the location, and the people with whom to work. Visiting Forest Houses in the south Bronx puts most art 'insiders' in unfamiliar territory; conversely residents of Forest Houses are comfortable in these environs but almost certainly are not used to thinking about contemporary art (there, and maybe not at all). The insertion of the artwork in this particular place is part of the way Hirschhorn asks political questions about the function of culture and the problems of social division.

The *Gramsci Monument* temporarily alters the material economic and social conditions of the site. The south Bronx residents accept their guest, as Hirschhorn's visit has been negotiated with key community leaders who ratified his temporary tenure of the green space between the apartment buildings. People take from the project what they want (and here there are material choices), they accept the windfall of paid work, the physical changes to their locale, the spectacle of the visual intervention, the rush of strangers who come to visit the neighbourhood. And when the project is completed and is broken down they benefit from a share in Hirschhorn's materials and equipment.

The monuments to philosophers are not permanent but mirror the duration of contemporary art exhibitions, enabling Hirschhorn and his projects to occupy a new spatial and social territory before moving onto the next place and project. The monuments are for commemorating and engaging with the likes of Gramsci; they are not for quiet, isolated contemplation. Instead, they address collective exchange as well as functioning as a type of pedagogic apparatus.

The political education of viewers or visitors to the monument places an emphasis on learning about the significance of the critical thinker in question.

Hirschhorn's educational framework introduces ideas of political thought and subjectivity reminiscent of the adult education of the 'New Left' in post-war UK, which included writers and activists such as Raymond Williams, Ralph Miliband and E.P. Thompson. This approach to educational practice was significant, as it promoted a discussion of a 'history from below', as a way to examine literature, culture in general as well as political theory. According to Tom Steele and Richard Taylor, it "produced a much greater interest in Marxist theory in Britain than ever before and many student dissidents subsequently sought careers in adult education and its more radical offshoot, community education" (Steele and Taylor 2004, p. 586). Certainly the English translation of Antonio Gramsci's *Prison Notebooks* in 1971 was influential: Gramsci emphasized the idea of 'cultural struggle', education having a pivotal role in the transformation of class structure. This was mirrored in the view of Williams, Thompson and Hoggart.

> Gramsci's concept of hegemony referred directly back to the early Marx of *The German Ideology* and claimed that the ruling class ruled more by the consent of the subordinate classes to their ideas and values than by direct coercion – although this, of course, was always the ultimate backup. Constructing the counter-hegemony therefore became the rationale for many adult educators.
>
> *(ibid, p. 587)*

FIGURE 2.2 *Gramsci Monument* (2013), Thomas Hirschhorn.
Credit: Romain Lopez.

Hirschhorn is equally informed by the notion of the 'organic intellectual': an idea that contested the concept of an intellectual class and called for the acknowledgement that all work, including *manual* work, involved the intellect. Thus all types of workers were capable of intellectual development and political understanding. For sure, Hirschhorn's project does not have the structural capacity to effect change on the scale of the introduction of adult education in post-war Britain, but it has at its core a critical intention of understanding how culture needs to operate towards social transformation. Gramsci did not want to further educate people in order for them to fit more effectively into the existing apparatus of education, but rather his project proposed to alter the social structures of education in order to recognize and endorse different forms of knowledge. Thus, managing the (re)education of the public is not the sort of change Gramsci wanted. Gramsci calls for the actual (social, economic and political) apparatus to be restructured, and this is the purpose of Gramsci's formulations of hegemony. For Gramsci the practice of hegemony is precisely what keeps the apparatus intact.

The question is whether a monument to Gramsci extends beyond the pragmatics of educating publics to disrupting the way things are managed. Hirschhorn's *Gramsci Monument* may not be an all-out attack on the ideological state apparatus, but it can be considered as an acknowledgement of the need for political and social change.

Benefiting publics: *Node*

Nodos de Desarrollo Cultural No. 1 (Cultural Development Node No. 1) is a project by the group STEALTH.[4] It is an architectural project that aims to extend and enlarge the activities of the Cultural Development Center of Moravia (CDCM), located in a poor district of Medellín in Colombia.

STEALTH have developed a number of low-cost temporary 'buildings' to house and extend the existing cultural community development programme. Through the use of locally sourced materials – much of it recycled – and the use of local craft skill and labour, they have been able to design and build structures that function as neighbourhood centres. The area of Moravia is where much salvage work and recycling is done, so STEALTH worked to utilize the availability of these types of materials as a component of the final project. STEALTH envisage this example of the *Node* as a prototype, and propose that similar urban situations can adopt the method they have employed. Therefore by utilizing freely available materials as well as local skills and labour to produce architectural arrangements, no two 'Nodes' will look the same. The premise of the *Node* is to formulate the process as a template and acknowledge that the structures will vary from site to site (STEALTH.unlimited 2015).

In August 2010 STEALTH held three workshops in Medellín with El Puente Lab and a number of architects, artists and architecture students. The group recognized that shared space was a key problem in Moravia, an area that has a large population drawn from rural districts to work in manufacturing and construction industries, as well as the informal subsistence economies that emerge in such large new communities. The area has no central planning and hence few services. It is densely populated without building regulations, which has led to narrow streets and no 'public' space. As STEALTH observe, the project's aim was to "tackle the lack of cultural spaces in a marginalised, densely populated neighbourhood, and in addition, work under the condition of a low budget, using recycled materials and strict conditions of use of public space" (ibid.).

The workshop team established the methodology for the Node project and began to identify available materials and workable design solutions, while looking for potential spaces where the structures could be sited. Three buildings were designed that offered functional spaces for community use. In the case of one building made of steel, the doors, windows and chassis of a bus formed its base. This example shows the required innovation in this context but also hints at a vernacular that marks out the project in terms of form and aesthetics. This methodology enabled them to have access to a space in which to conduct their community programme, which includes reading and literacy, health and wellbeing, as well as visual art workshops. The space is also adaptable for other social activities, for example as a community kitchen.

It was El Puente Lab – a small group of urban activists – that invited STEALTH to Moravia to develop a project. El Puente Lab aims to literally form bridges with other cities in the world to create alliances that bring good ideas to their context, a move that has led them to work with urbanists, designers and architects from the Netherlands, Italy and the UK. Their motto is "we have to be self-sustaining", as they accept that due to the political, economic and social challenges facing Colombia they cannot wait for an intervention by the state or by businesses but must first establish community-based development before looking for outside support for their ideas. They use cultural work, including art, video and events as a means to engender awareness and garner support and participation in their initiatives (El Puente Lab 2014).

STEALTH is an architectural practice. As urban designers and architects, they aim to "shape opportunities where various fields of investigation meet and where thinking about possible future(s) of the city is mobilised" (STEALTH.unlimited 2015). In this way, STEALTH place an emphasis on the technical, on infrastructures *for* people, and – in the case of the *Node* project – by providing spaces for social activity where no civic spaces had existed before.

They state that they "consider space both a tool and an agency, and focus on innovative aspects of sometimes hidden, temporary or unplanned urban practices that challenge ways in which to create physical aspects of the city, and of its culture" (ibid.). Culture, for them, is thus a means to stimulate social change. This concept is not unfamiliar, although the political and economic situation in Moravia is very different from the post-industrial conditions in the UK, for example. Under New Labour the UK was subject to forms of culture-led regeneration which included gallery education programmes or community development, and were employed to produce change in 'hard to reach' communities. However, STEALTH are interested in bottom-up practices to effect change, and use their skills and experience to promote alternative ideas to urban planning and civic organization. STEALTH encourage the "shared authoring of urban space and culture" (ibid.) and perceive their interventions as a mix of urban research, visual arts, spatial intervention and cultural activism, employing the potential within the organization of urban space for social transformation.

The concrete benefits to the users of this art project are obvious. It provides spaces for education and social interaction, and although the structures are temporary, they are provisional architecture and therefore distinct from Hirschhorn's temporary cardboard and wood constructions. We acknowledge that the question of whether this project constitutes art is fundamental to a conventional comparison of the *Node* with *Nowhereisland* or the *Gramsci Monument*. However, we would like to suspend the urge to address this ontological question and rather focus again on our inquiry, which is concerned with asking in what way is this work *public*.

Through the *Node* project, STEALTH bring a civil society model of social organization to Moravia, and they acknowledge the limitation of their project when they recognize that these temporary structures do not replace the need for permanent buildings. They say:

> the context of Moravia – a neighborhood that is undergoing major changes that will continue in the coming years – and the requirement to install with

salvaged materials from the city have forced us to adopt a flexible design approach instead of waiting for the location to a new building.

(STEALTH.unlimited 2015)

The manifestation of STEALTH's work into actual structural assistance can be considered as a charitable act. This type of intervention is pragmatic and directly affects the quality of people's day-to-day lives. Charity is not only the complex mixture of ethics and politics, but can also be comprehended through space and time. In fact, it must be understood as contingent, and each act must be assessed in the context of the situation in which it is carried out.

Evaluating the notion of charity as a generic concept is unhelpful and suggests a static view of ethics and politics. However, what is at stake is the function of aid as a hegemonic influence. If the results of charitable acts stop people from transforming their lives into something more economically sustainable, then charity plays a repressing role for dominant political ideologies. Charity can be considered 'public', if through the stabilization of resources it enables the politicization of subjects. Yet if it suppresses people's action and deters them from working towards a better future, then its role is one of controlling marginalized publics and of benefiting powerful publics. The growth of charity within neo-liberalism demonstrates the preference for individual acts over infrastructural change.

FIGURE 2.3   *Node* (2011), STEALTH.unlimited (Ana Džokić and Marc Neelen) and architects María Camila Vélez and Yesenia Rodríguez.
Credit: Andrés Galeano.

Conclusion

This chapter specifically addresses the issues of *publicness* within public artworks and attempts to further understand what we mean by it. By bringing together Doreen Massey's concept of space and Jürgen Habermas's theory of the public sphere, we develop a critical framework that enables us to recognize the importance of the political when considering the term *public*. At the same time, by acknowledging its wide range of use – from defining a type of space to characterizing a mass of bodies – we call for artists to understand the complexity of the *public*.

Art criticism is limited in how it understands *publics* and relational artworks, because of its long-standing preoccupation with the object. As art historian Claire Bishop (Bishop 2012) points out, participatory art is a relatively underdeveloped area of critical analysis, since the curator who commissioned the project typically writes and publishes most of the project documentation. Bishop acknowledges that this is logistical because of the nature of these projects, which are usually site-specific and temporal, but, even so, this is a disadvantage when attempting a critical analysis of the artworks produced. In her essay "Responsible Criticism: Evaluating Public Art", Senie (2003) suggests a series of questions that should be asked of public artworks, but the function of these enquiries are to aid art criticism and to evaluate the social function of the specific public artwork.

What we are suggesting here is that by further describing the ways in which publics are utilized and enabled within and for artworks (both as the content and material of certain works as well as the way that artworks address particular publics), we enable a more accurate understanding of art and politics. However we need to recognize this proposed arrangement of art and the social as having a far wider significance than simply enabling a new definition of terms. This understanding needs to enable a new articulation of art and politics. In this chapter we have sought to discuss the way in which artworks utilize notions of publics, and to this end we have proposed three ways of considering art and the concept of publics: Picturing Publics, Educating Publics and Benefiting Publics.

We argue that the picturing of publics sees the managing of opinion formation. This is problematic from a public spherian point of view as this results in a manipulative publicity that advocates art as a public good. Habermas believes that the misuse of publicity undermines the political public sphere. He says, "Even arguments are translated into symbols to which again one can not respond by arguing but only by identifying with them" (Habermas 1989 [1962], p. 206).

Nowhereisland is neither a public sphere nor a contingent space. Its social intervention becomes one with which to nominate spaces of environmental concern as apart from the people that live on the planet. In this way, the project manages people as part of its technical format, as well as utilizing the public body as a publicity tool with which to promote and justify its existence. Yet the work is separated from the social as well as the political, through its physical and social distance from its onlookers, which approximates to a desire for autonomy. As Massey makes clear, "instituting democratic public spaces necessitates operating with a concept of spatiality which keeps always under scrutiny the play of the social relations which construct them" (Massey 2005, p. 153). *Nowhereisland* is a folly to publicness as it operates as both a symbol of the public and the political.

Educating the public is clearly a time-invested activity, and Hirschhorn is dedicated to proposing an alternative way for others to engage with conceptual and philosophical ideas about how to live and be. The *Gramsci Monument* is the fourth in the series of monuments dedicated to philosophers (the previous three are for Bataille, Spinoza and Deleuze). If post-structuralist interpretations of Spinoza and Gramsci focus upon discourse and language, practice and action are viewed through intertextuality and an aestheticised idea of life. What Hirschhorn does to these thinkers in the monument projects is to position them within the social and material world, publishing them and arranging them to be engaged with and communicated through.

The *Gramsci Monument* is distinct from Hirschhorn's other monuments in that the content of Gramsci's work was aimed at the politicization of the public through the notion of the organic intellectual: You could say that this relates to the methods that Hirschhorn employs within the Monument artworks: i.e. the desire to introduce the residents of Morrisania to Gramsci's ideas and writings. Hirschhorn's *Gramsci Monument* may not be as 'Gramscian' as Hirschhorn would have it, but there is no getting away from the fact that his acts of engaging with publics have a political purpose.

Node by STEALTH utilizes a social definition of both space and public, as does the pedagogic model of the *Gramsci Monument. Node* develops new conceptions of artistic action. In this case we see the 'artist benefactor', the artist as the provider of a service or product for a specific community, in which the result and consequences enable a practical enhancement to the lives of that community. This social function of *Node* is clearly a radical and purposeful intervention into the lives of others. The artwork's relationship to charity, and therefore its place within neo-liberalism, needs more exploration than we have space here to expound.

As early as 1989, Patricia Phillips called for a more precise examination of the notion of public within the field of public art when she said: "The errors of much public art have been its lack of specificity, its tendency to look at society – at the public – too broadly and simply" (Philips 1989b, p. 335).

It's about time we responded to this demand, and for us there can be no public other than a political public. Massey's theory of space and Habermas's account of the public sphere allow us to move away from a universal and convivial interpretation of the public towards a *political* public. Applying their theories to an exploration of the function of the public within public artworks enables us to understand how art not only can picture, educate and benefit its publics but also, more crucially, how art can begin to politicize its publics.

Notes

1   One of Mel Jordan's students worked on the production of the *Nowhereisland* object.

2 The authors note that Doreen Massey is named as a resident thinker of *Nowhereisland* and contributes an existing text published on the website http://nowhereisland.org/resident-thinkers/49/

3 The Royal College of Art, Visual Cultures Lecture: Thomas Hirschhorn, 11 March 2014, introduced by Mel Jordan.

4 STEALTH are Ana Džokić and Marc Neelen, based in both Belgrade and Rotterdam. They established STEALTH in 2000.

3

PLACING MURALS IN BELFAST

Community, negotiation and change

Lesley Murray

Introduction

The association between public art and 'community' is highly contested. Nevertheless, street murals, which are considered to be the art form that precipitated community participation in public art (Cockcroft and Barnet-Sanchez 1993), have been an integral part of the practices of everyday life and the broader spatial politics of the city of Belfast. In this highly segregated city, spatial divisions, in the form of around one hundred material barriers that range up to 13.5 metres in height (Belfast Interface project 2011), the so-called 'peace walls', provide ample resource for Belfast's mural painters. In their contemporary form, murals have tended to depict struggles for social justice: from the early twentieth century in the murals of the Chicano Movement in the USA (Cockcroft and Barnet-Sanchez 1993) to the *Santa's Ghetto* project in the West Bank instigated by the street artist Banksy to highlight the Palestinian struggle (Parry 2010). In Belfast, mural painting has its roots in the representations of working-class identities at a time when the city was a shipyard of global importance in the early twentieth century. They have now to some extent been appropriated by the city authorities in a bid to promote a vibrant regenerated Belfast (for example by the Northern Ireland Tourist Board). These 'sanitized' murals are often set in contrast to those that are rooted in 'community' and speak of political struggle, and which are considered parochial and inward facing and an instrument of continued community segregation. There is a coherent body of literature on the latter (particularly Rolston 1987, 2004, 2012) that details the historic and political legacy of street art in the city.

Like the mural painting on the separation walls of the West Bank in Palestine, mural painting in Belfast intersects with the cultural and political landscape and the divisions within it – here, the cultural divisions between nationalism and unionism. Hence the first murals in the city appeared in east Belfast, on the gable walls of the shipyard workers' terraced housing, in the first decade of the twentieth century. These murals represented the predominantly unionist workforce of the shipyard and the close relationship between the state and unionist popular cultures (Rolston 1987). Mural painting in the principally nationalist west Belfast emerged much later during the 'hunger strikes'[1] of the 1980s. Nowadays, murals depicting local and more global concerns can be found throughout the city, including in more middle-class areas such as the university quarter. Nevertheless, this street art remains coupled with nationalist and unionist interests and while nationalist murals tend to have a wider remit than the nationalist cause, unionist murals continue to depict sectarian positions and are often paramilitary in content. It is for this reason that murals in unionist areas have become the main focus of state funds designated for changing Belfast's muralscape. These come in the form of the state Re-Imaging Communities Programme, a project set up in 2006 following a series of local and regional government failed attempts to remove the city's more antagonistic murals. Managed by the Arts Council of Northern Ireland with an original budget of £3.3m over the first three years (Hill and White 2011, Rolston 2012), these funds are distributed to groups who can demonstrate adherence to the programme's aims. The scheme, however, is much maligned, operating a process of 'aesthetic evangelism'that conflicts with mural practices that promote "self-assertion and self-empowerment" (Rolston 2012, p. 457). Rolston argues that the 're-imaged' murals "say little about the community today, and even less about aspirations for the future" (ibid., p. 460)

Murals as public art both intersect with and form part of the practice of urban space (Deutsche 1996, Miles 1997, Massey and Rose 2003, Whybrow 2011) and this chapter uses the concepts of community, negotiation and change to articulate this interrelationship. Of course, each of these terms is highly contested, and unravelling their complexity brings into question not only the notion of urban art as public but also of urban public space itself and the ways in which it is negotiated by various social groupings within it. For as Massey and Rose (2003) contest, looking at public art and its social and spatial contexts allows us to reflect on the conceptualization of public space itself. A mobilization of place (Massey 1994) allows a detachment of place from the restrictions of the local, and in doing so politicizes it. Through focusing on the contested practices of mural painting in Belfast, this chapter suggests a similar mobilization of the concept of community through public art and the ways in which it becomes over-determined (Sennett 2006) through external intervention. It does this through considering the ways in which murals are negotiated in local contexts and the potential for change that this negotiation produces. Drawing from ethnographic fieldwork in Belfast, the chapter considers the practices around street murals, using particularly illustrative examples.

Re-placing community through art

Much of the arts-based literature on public art is concerned with the ways in which art engages with or intervenes in community space (Miles 1997, Whybrow 2011), whereas the focus in geography is centred on the production of space and the ways in which community has become co-positioned with space as static and uncontested and set against a "geographical fragmentation of our times" which, Massey (1994, p. 146) argues, leads to segregation. Here, community is necessarily static and inward looking, resisting movements within and between. Likewise Young (1990, p. 302) positions community as a spatial grouping that denies difference, particularly difference "in the form of temporal and spatial distancing", which is associated with something wider than local in privileging "face to faceness" as something "authentic" and non-conflictual. Instead Young (ibid., p. 303) argues for a "politics of difference" with "social relations without domination" in which it is possible for people to co-habit space with other people who are strangers but who are not bound by the exclusionary practices of 'community'. This relies on openness and enables the potential for social transformation, as opposed to a romanticization of localness, which leads to a privileging of good local democracy over external controls that is overly simplistic. Place and community are co-produced, since a bounded conceptualization of place leads to a bounded notion of 'community', where community requires a commonality not only of spatial but – in their interrelatedness – of temporal identification, a shared history. Approached from a relatively superficial standpoint it could be said that the nostalgia associated with community murals in Belfast supports this conceptualization, as sectarian imagery projects a memorialized vision of the past (McDowell 2008). Murals are an integral part of the cultural landscape of Belfast and they produce urban experience as mediators of memory, not only in their static imagery but also in the practices around them such as unveilings, parading, marking and re-marking. However, this is premised on an understanding of community as necessarily closed, and abstracted from the generative practices of street art.

An uncritical analysis of the spatialities of Belfast might reveal the characteristics of space that Massey contests. These conceptualizations rely on 'inherited traditions' and are premised on exclusion and stasis, particularly in relation to an increasingly globalized and mobile world. They rely on "the formation of a social geography of us and them; of insiders and outsiders; of those who belong and those who do not" (Massey and Rose 2003, p. 3). The spatial landscape of Belfast is constructed as one that is marked out through extremism and exclusions. Belfast space is highly territorialized, visually segregated through flags, painted kerbstones and murals (Nagle 2009; Shirlow 2003). The potential for transformations of this seemingly closed public space is therefore questionable. However, this supposes a flat, static and immobile visual landscape, whereas it is more likely that in some aspects, some spaces will be more open than others – places where 'diverse social identities' are revealed and enter into dialogue.

In their exploration of public art in Milton Keynes, Massey and Rose (2003) consider public art as a conduit for the mobilization of space, a means to open up space to the political through assessing the varying degrees of negotiation that different forms of public art evoke. In this enlarging of space to encompass areas wider than local geographies, place is disengaged from the local and becomes relational (Massey 1994, 2005). For Massey and Rose (2003) public art is not flat and inert imagery, but its materiality is bound up with the social and cultural practices that surround it; it is therefore necessarily negotiated in public space and, in doing so, creates space. The greater the level of negotiation required, the more 'public' a space becomes. Massey and Rose suggest that the process of creating space through public art is uneven, as this production of space through art "interpellate[s] some 'differences' more than others" (Massey and Rose 2003, p. 9). Public art is therefore part of the negotiation of place, and in its multiplicity of forms it can be a way of making conflict visible so that dialogue becomes possible. However, it is always place-specific and audienced.

The impact of public art therefore relies on an on-going relationship between the artwork and its audience. Belfast's murals become public art through their content and its audiencing, through the practicing of the artwork. However, they are also subject to the processes of 'colonization' of public space through art by dominant powers (Deutsche 1996), whether through the "act of identifying, claiming and accessing a suitable space", which often need the approval of local paramilitary groups (McCormick and Jarman 2005, p. 55) or state funding schemes such as the Re-Imaging Communities Programme. The process of intervention in public space by authoritative organizations is dependent on a fixed notion of space, since it simplifies space so that it may be more easily controlled. This is exemplified in the physical delineations of the 'defensive' architecture that is justified on the basis of community safety and security but also more directly through the re-imaging project. Despite claiming that this project seeks to 'empower' communities, in the removal of images that are considered to be unacceptable in relation to good community relations, space becomes increasingly privatized, closing off public space. An understanding of the role of public art in cities such as Belfast is therefore dependent on distinguishing between material delineations of space, the visual landscapes created by these material divisions, and public art that is contesting such divisions through mobilizing visions to a multiplicity of scales. The alternative 'myth of place' is a version of place that is oversimplified and denies the perpetual fluidity and mobility of places and spaces, maintains hierarchies of power and denies social transformation.

This 'over-determination' of urban space (Sennett 2006) creates segregation and community stasis. In cities like Belfast, this over-determination has become manifest in the material delineation of the urban space in the 'peace walls' and other physical barriers. However, rather than the more traditional 'public spaces' of cities, which have become semi-privatized, Sennet argues that it is at the "territorial edges" of cities where interaction creates diversity and thus creates the urban public. Sennet argues that territorial edges or borders create the new 'public', and are both spatial and sociological (Simmel 1903/2002), where "walls functioned much like cell membranes, both porous and resistant" (Sennett 2006, p. 3). There are interfaces in cities, the 'peace walls' in Belfast and the 'separation barrier' in Jerusalem, where there is the potential, though not always realized, for social interaction. The following explores the porosity of community in both connecting outwards to less local interests and in instigating internal dialogues that are informed by elements of everyday life that may be situated outside the community borders. It is the negotiation of complexity and diversity that makes space and art public.

Researching murals

The methods used in this research draw upon an interpretative methodology that is based on theories of visual culture (Evans and Hall 1999) and critical visual methodologies (Rose 2007). Rose identifies three sites of visualization that are necessarily explored in critical methodologies: the production of images, the image itself and the audiencing of the image. In examining each of these sites there is recognition of the "practical collaboration" (Barthes 1999, p. 63) between the image producer and those who interpret and reinterpret it. It is this collaborative process that produces particular practices around the murals. The ethnographic study of the murals and the data collection, therefore, focused on these three sites of visualization and involved image-makers, images and their 'audiences' in the research. First, interviews were carried out with three muralists in Belfast, two of whom had been creating murals since the early 1980s.[2] Although this was a static group interview with all three muralists, it took place in their studio, where much of their work is imagined and produced.

Second, mobile interviews were undertaken with 'mural tour' guides as we visited the mural sites. These are organized tours, available to the public, although I contacted the organizers in advance with details of my research, asking for the agreement of the tour guides. I also made an audio-visual recording of the tour and took photographs of each of the murals we encountered. This allowed me to engage with the third site of visualization, the audiencing of the murals, providing insights into the ways in which the murals are audienced both by the tour guides themselves and by those who take the tour, which includes both visitors to Belfast and residents who would like to know a little more about its mural history. As we travelled from mural to mural, I carried out a narrative interview, asking about the life experiences of each of the tour guides as well as their experience of the murals. The video allowed me to locate the interview dialogue in place. This method of interviewing and observing, and of understanding the importance of context in interviews draws from my experience of using mobile methods (Murray 2009, 2010; Buscher et al., 2010; Fincham et al. 2010). My visit to Belfast also produced the opportunity to interview a community worker involved in the mural Re-imaging Communities Programme. It emerged, during the interviews, that a number of the interviewees were ex-political prisoners. Although it was not possible to conclude about the impact of this fact on the research, I was mindful that the responses would be more likely to be well informed and highly politicized, an issue similarly encountered by Wiedenhoft Murphy (2010) in her ethnographic study of mural tours in Belfast and by Hercbergs (2012) in her ethnography of tours of Jerusalem led by Palestinian guides.

Representing and producing community – mural in an alleyway

Murals, from their early beginnings in Belfast have represented 'community', where representation is understood as a dynamic process of co-production of community and place (see Murray and Upstone 2014). Hence murals associated with the loyalist cause in the 1690 Battle of the Boyne, and in particular the victor Prince William of Orange, not only depicted the historic scene but also were practised through community associations with the cause. In a simplistic reading of dominant local cultures in the city this sectarian mural represented one of two dominant cultures. However, this masks the diversity of the city's population with, in particular, a recent rise in ethnic diversity through the significant growth of immigration since the enlargement of the European Union in 2004 (Bell et al. 2004). However, there is evidence that, in specific parts of the city, territorial allegiances associated with Loyalism or Nationalism have led to conflict with immigrant groups (Svašek 2008). Dialogue between communities is impeded by imagined and material divides. In some parts of the city it is dangerous to walk on particular sides of the road as this indicates particular cultural affiliation, and in others people make unnecessarily circuitous journeys for health, education and leisure in order to avoid more local services that are associated with the 'other' community (Shirlow 2003; Shirlow and Murtagh 2006). In this sense, community is a vehicle of exclusion, both social and spatial.

Murals are used in certain areas to mark out territory, "to establish and affirm the territorial delineation of working class areas" (McCormick and Jarman 2005, p. 59). Nagle (2009) suggests that such visual displays of territorialization embed exclusionary community practices, and that policies introduced in the name of community cohesion are being directed towards one community or another, rather than fostering cross-community dialogue. He suggests that policy programmes implemented under the umbrella term of 'shared space' reaffirm segregation by denying these alternative stories and supporting traditional community affiliation, and that murals and other visual displays play a key role in this process:

> The sheer volume of ethno-national representations of space which festoon part of the city, delineated through sites of remembrance like murals and commemorative parades, are sources of group affiliation and identity reaffirmation that try to prohibit the emergence of alternative encapsulations.
>
> *(Nagle 2009, p. 330)*

Many of the murals adorning the streets of Belfast evidence this claim. The visual narratives of murals tend to be community focused and offer little potential for cross-community dialogue, propagating communities of sameness rather than communities of difference. Their negotiation is closed to large sections of the population. However, although murals that appear sectarian hinder cross-community dialogue, they nevertheless form part of a dialogue between community and state, and this is particularly pertinent when the authorities impose their version of an acceptable visual landscape. As Paddy, one of the muralists maintained:

> Murals came about in our community through censorship, the amount and level of censorship. People like that were being brutalized and tortured in the prisons and no-one was telling the story, there was no communication, and the first murals went up to highlight that...These images were going back to people all over the world who were thinking: "Hold on – if they were so hated, how come there are big pictures of them in their communities?" That's where the murals came out of, and basically what they were being used for was a blackboard of our discontent … that became the images on the walls.
>
> *(Paddy, muralist)*

Paddy was particularly uncomfortable with the notion that murals are part of a territorialization of space that was exclusionary, as they were a necessary part of the voicing of community concerns in the context of practices of misinformation, especially during periods of intense conflict.

One of the aspects of community that many of the murals seek to portray is based on a particular cultural identity, and in areas that are considered nationalist, links to Celtic culture. Celtic myths form the subject of many of the murals in parts of the city. The mural in Figure 3.1 is an example of this. Situated in an alleyway in a housing estate to the north of the city, the mural depicts an elaborate scene from Celtic mythology. The central figure, Cúchulainn, a Celtic warrior from the Ulster Cycles mythical stories, dominates the mural, a representation of the strength of the community in challenging those who threaten Irish identity. This mural was painted by Gerard Kelly, better known as Mo Chara (meaning 'my friend' in Gaelic), who aims to 're-imagine' and reappropriate space in the process of reidentifying with a sense of Irish cultural identity (Hartnett 2011). The positioning of the mural is at first perplexing, as it is tucked away, not visible to passers-by on the main road. However, this mural, unlike many of the others that are more prominently placed, has been directed towards a particular audience in its placing. It is on a wall opposite a youth club, which had been an Irish language club but has become a youth club with wider concerns, including global sustainability. A small mosaic near the club's door carries a message about curbing environmental destruction. It is clear that Kelly is less interested in mass viewings of this mural and more concerned with directing the gaze of young people using the club towards a vision of their Irish heritage. The tour guide who showed me the mural knew the area, and Kelly himself, well and seemed proud of the contribution the mural makes to the local community.

> This is a masterpiece. This was done by an ex-political prisoner, a Republican, and his pen name is Mo Chara – his name is Gerard Kelly. Mo Chara is actually an ex-political prisoner. He actually travels the world teaching

FIGURE 3.1   Mural in an alleyway.
Credit: Lesley Murray.

young people how to construct murals … He had the scaffolding up… it took him months…I actually called it his Sistine chapel… it took him months. If you'd just look at the detail… the detail there is amazing.

(Seamus, tour guide)

The dialogue created by the mural sits in tension with the more global discourse of the smaller environmental murals in the alleyway, but this creates a dynamism in the space, and an openness. The walls of the alleyway speak to each other, challenging different imaginings, past and present. The dialogue invites and engages different groups within a heterogeneous community, with differing attitudes and visions for the future. The murals are not 'artefacts' sustaining a closed community but are actively practised and negotiated. This practice, which as McCormick and Jarman (2005, p. 51) point out, precludes their presentation as "banal and anonymous expressions of the paramilitary culture", is based both in their political context and their lifecycle: the stories that they tell and those they collude with in writing. This is particularly evident in a mural situated close to the alleyway in Ballymurphy. As Seamus explained:

This is a mural from the Ballymurphy massacre. It was actually constructed from the children and the grandchildren of the ones who were killed during the massacre. Now and again what they do is they come up and write wee personal messages – "Granny I passed my exam" and things like that, so it's a living mural, and then you'd have the core demands of the campaign, and then just this mural here reflecting the … .

(Seamus, tour guide)

This mural appears to exude community – identifying a social group with past tradition, remembering a past that local people do not want to forget, and connecting intergenerationally around a common bond of cultural experience. These active dialogues are evident not only in the practices of the murals in situ but also in their making. The mural painters claim that they could not practice without the support of the community.

People normally ask how do you get on in the communities, but we've never had a problem with that. You see people storing our stuff. Looking after it. I mean, when you go down and start painting, the first thing is the locals come out. "Do you want a cup of tea? Blah blah blah". We even had the same in Liverpool.

(Paddy, muralist)

To equate public art with a homogenous and closed notion of community in Belfast therefore, is an oversimplification. The complexities are illustrated further in the relationships among residents, planners and policymakers in the city.

Negotiating visual space – re-imaging violence

The practices of public space in Belfast involve the negotiation of state policies on the city's visual landscape. The Re-imaging Communities Programme of the Arts Council of Northern Ireland, which was introduced in 2006, is a particularly significant attempt to reorder certain spaces. Resources are made available through this scheme to replace "divisive imagery with imagery that reflects communities in a more positive manner" (Independent Research Solutions 2009, p. viii cited Hill and White 2012, p. 75). These funds are distributed to groups who can demonstrate adherence to the programme's aims through a process of what Rolston (2012) terms "aesthetic evangelism", a process that he argues conflicts with mural practices that promote "self-assertion and self-empowerment" (ibid., p. 457). It is not only the aims of this project that are of interest here but also the choice of title for the programme. In 'Re-imaging communities' the agenda is foremost a sectarian one, as 'communities' here refers not to the streets or walls where the murals are located but the distinct 'communities' to which they are attached.

There is much debate on the motives for attempting to control Belfast's muralscape in the ways that the programme seeks. Hill and White (2011, p. 81) argue that the aim of the state project is to regain territorial control in "seeking to assert the authority of government agencies over the visual environment". As mural painting on walls representing state control may be considered a form of appropriation, this may be a *re*-assertion of authority, in line with Handelman's (2011, p. 72) claim that Jerusalem's separation walls are "utterly without adornment" and "practice absolute division, domination, and sovereignty". Resistance to 'Re-imaging', therefore, is a contestation of state-controlled sectarianism, carried out by members of communities, and this calls into question the ways in which communities become constructed as homogenous and impenetrable. As Shirlow (2003, p. 77) argues, there is no common outlook and set of values within communities and although "in some cases socially dominant groups can claim ownership of a community's fears, phobias and traumas in a desire to triumph [over]particular political discourses", communities are diverse and their characteristics and practices complex. Donal, the community worker, articulated the emotions associated with some of the more militaristic murals:

> When I seen them go up … it was frightening towards me, cause I remember going back to the conflict, this was very similar and this is part of what radicalized me … And actually seeing young people, with schoolbags on their backs and stopping and looking up at them … And people in this community are so frightened to say anything about them and when they do they get their windows broke, or they get a petrol bomb through their front door, or they're physically threatened when they go into the pub at night … Murals really do have this fear factor in the communities, especially new paramilitary murals, you know. If they're old, they accept that and you can get people's mind set talking about getting rid of those murals, because they're not being cared for, they're falling apart.

In relation to the replacement of the murals he went on to say:

> People in the community will then accept the removal of these … There's still a minority of people that want to put up something that's even more paramilitary. But they're in the minority. It's about empowering those residents who want to live in peace and harmony and trust, Indigenous people living together. … there's murals around that as well, advocating for a multi-cultural society, getting people from ethnic backgrounds to get involved in the murals. We hope to be doing one from an Indian background … a paramilitary mural being removed and an ethnic mural in its place, and the kids are going to design that themselves. It's going to be painting-by-numbers with the artists designing it, and the kids are going to be putting the paint on the walls as well. To me, that's going to be really empowering.
>
> *(Donal, community worker)*

Here Donal's 'community' viewpoint is on recognizing diversity and entering into a dialogue about this. He considers the 're-imaging' project as offering the potential to do so. Similarly, one of the mural tour guides makes an optimistic reading of the attempts to re-image Belfast's streetscape: "Here's a mural here. There is an effort to tidy up…these murals were all militaristic but there's a sort of an attitude that people want to change them, and they're becoming more positive" (Finn, tour guide).

However, there is a tension here between efforts to engage the communities and the imposition of a particular visionscape. This is evident in the muralists' unanimous opposition to the programme, as Paddy explains:

> When it first kicked off, it was so ridiculous, besides the fact it was so insulting to people from our communities. You know, we don't need to be re-imaged. Let us build our own idea of ourselves. Don't impose it with this carrot and stick idea of offering money, £3.5m. 'Cause the murals were changing anyhow, 'cause they only reflect what's in the community. Communities are moving ahead. Now I think the Unionists are a bit slower than the Nationalist community, but I think that's also good. To see their cause, you can gauge how far the community has moved by the public art that surrounds them.
>
> *(Paddy, muralist)*

The mural in Figure 3.2 is an example of a 're-imaged' piece of street art. The original mural is shown in a plaque, which has been placed beside the new mural. It is an image depicting two paramilitary, armed figures on each side of the emblem of the Ulster Defence Association (UDA), a loyalist paramilitary group active during the 'troubles' in Northern Ireland (1968–98). The mural specifically represents the Scottish Branch of the UDA. The UDA motto, "Quis Separabit", meaning "who will separate us?" is visible on the emblem, along with the red hand of Ulster and a crown, showing the allegiance of the UDA to both Ulster and the union of the UK. Although the UDA declared a ceasefire in 1994, it did not begin 'demobilization' until 2007, and did not fully decommission its weapons until 2010. The UDA was considered to be a sectarian group that created community tensions, and therefore murals such as the one replaced in Figure 3.2 are deemed to be examples of 'divisive imagery'. These murals were commonly made to order by paramilitary groups, becoming the "calling card of the loyalist paramilitary groups", particularly after the ceasefire period (Rolston 2004, p. 40). Indeed as Rolston (2012) points out, loyalist murals became more belligerent after the end of the 'troubles', and this "spoke volumes regarding loyalist ambivalence about the peace process" (ibid., p. 450). Again, the placing of this mural is important here, as it is in an estate where some prominent loyalist paramilitaries lived, and which they controlled. It is speaking to the loyalist community and the factions within it, rather than beyond.

The mural was replaced through the 'Re-imaging Communities Programme', with an image of children finding gold coins painted by street artist Tim McCarthy. The plaque reads:

FIGURE 3.2 A 're-imaged' mural.
Credit: Lesley Murray.

The Gold Rush mural replaces a paramilitary image of two silhouetted gunmen representing the Scottish Brigade. This new image by artist Tim McCarthy represents an event in July 1969 in Christopher Street when children digging in the rubbish of the then demolished 'Scotch Flats' discovered a hoard of gold sovereigns. Word spread quickly and thus began 'the gold rush'. The project was funded by the Re-imaging Communities programme of the Arts Council of Northern Ireland and delivered by Belfast City Council with the support of the Lower Shankill Community Association. The project would not have been possible without the support and participation of the local community.

One of the mural tour guides gives his account of the content of the image in his own words:

This one here, with the 1969 gold rush. Just behind us here was all small flats and maisonettes. They knocked them down, and in the rubble young children found gold sovereigns, and it was like me telling you, telling someone else. By the end of the day it was told there was gold in the ground, and they were all out with picks and shovels, digging like champions. There was nothing there at all.

(Fred, tour guide)

There are some indications here that the 'Gold Rush' story has been embellished in the process of replacing the mural. Although Tim McCarthy is a street artist with a wealth of experience in community projects, he is not one of the band of mural painters that have been practising mural painting since the early 1980s and this sets artists like Tim McCarthy outside the muralist 'community'. In fact, Paddy suggests that 'Re-imaging' artists are considered to be taking advantage of a situation they previously chose to ignore:

> And when all of this was going on, they ['artists'] were focused on what was happening anywhere else but here. They could have helped our communities. They could have made this life that we've had to endure so much shorter if they had of dealt with the issues.
>
> *(Paddy, muralist)*

At the same time, the muralists claim to be representative of the communities that the Arts Council are similarly claiming to support. The muralists I spoke to refuse to take part in the programme:

> We haven't done any work and won't … They're not real murals. They're on laminated aluminium. … I think the re-imaging will happen from the community. The murals always reflect the community theme: their dreams and aspirations. And I think that re-imaging will start – true re-imaging will happen once the community has moved on. I don't think you can force a thing like stuff like that. … They should be spending that money on things that would benefit the community as a whole, rather than aesthetics.
>
> *(Tom, muralist)*

This is also a very different understanding of 'community' from that of Donal, the community worker, who argues that the group is too frightened to voice their opinions on the murals. What is emerging, therefore, is a not only a diverse but a fluid notion of 'community', whose characteristics depend on different relationships with those who are part of the 'community' and with the state that is attempting to intervene in local affairs. These notions of community are shaped through public art, as the notion of community changes according to its relationship with artwork. It is clear that public art is negotiated between communities and the state. The question remains, however, concerning the extent to which these negotiations shape wider notions of community and create openness.

Affecting change through connection – *Guernica*

Public art creates dialogue but does not necessarily lead to a mobilization of communities if the discussion centres on relatively local concerns. However, mural painting is rarely parochial. Mural projects such as Judith Baca's *Great Wall of Los Angeles* (Cockcroft and Barnet-Sanchez 1993) and Banksy's *Santa's Ghetto* are internationally celebrated. The aim of the latter was to enhance the visibility of the 'separation wall' between Israel and Palestine, with a number of international street artists as well as local artists involved. Although the intervention brought mixed reactions, with some Palestinians objecting to "beautifying the wall", most "welcomed the show of solidarity from the outside world" (Parry 2010, p. 10). Similarly the 'international peace wall' in Belfast reaches out beyond the local community by making connections to campaigns outside Northern Ireland. As the tour guides explain:

> This is the start of the international wall. This would be the loyalist end of it. There's a lot of Palestinian murals. Murals of international content, of universal subjects such as "no racism". The tourism correspondent of the *Guardian* newspaper, about six or seven years ago, called it the number one tourist attraction in what he called the British Isles. It was open 24 hours a day, it was free and it was safe.
>
> *(Seamus, tour guide)*

> This wall here is called international wall or justice wall, and what they'll do here is they'll draw on similarities here and what's going on in the rest of the world.
>
> *(Fred, tour guide)*

The tour guides spoke with some pride about the broad range of issues depicted in these murals. One of these (Figure 3.3) is a copy of Picasso's *Guernica*, the original painting of which is on show at the Museo Reina Sofía in Madrid. Just as the muralists of the 20th century mural renaissance, such as Diego Rivera, were influenced by European modernism (Cockcroft and Barnet-Sanchez 1993), so too are the muralists of Belfast. The three muralists I interviewed painted the mural of Picasso's *Guernica*. For them, this mural represents a coming together of artists from different communities.

> So that's how we got together, and one of the most important things we've done is probably the *Guernica* thing ... That was the first time we worked together publicly... in 2006 or 2007. Just in the advent of the power sharing agreement ... 'Cause of what it represents, sort of the futility of war and the horror of war. We had reached a level of stability, and peace was looking like it was going to hold and things were moving forward. We thought that because of what we do, and because we're so visible in our own communities and represent working-class issues that engage with people on the street. We thought that we should work together...again reflecting what was happening in the bigger politics in and around that time ... to help promote peace.
>
> *(Paddy, muralist)*

FIGURE 3.3 *Guernica.*
Credit: Lesley Murray.

Interestingly, although the muralists tried to acquire funding for the project, they struggled to find financial backing. Eventually a friend of theirs who was starting a small business, as well as a local newspaper, agreed to fund the mural painting. This lack of initial interest contrasts starkly with the reaction to the completed work, which surprised the muralists as did the range of people who volunteered to help out with the painting.

> There was actually Protestants from East Belfast came over. It generated a big buzz around it, like. There was Spanish people, Japanese people, Latin Americans wanting to help out. So it started off us, and ended up about 30 [laughs].
>
> *(Tom, muralist)*

As well as groups of people willing to help out, the mural also eventually attracted attention from the Arts Council of Northern Ireland's Re-imaging Communities Programme.

> The people from Re-imaging came down and they actually tried to claim some responsibility … the culture minister … had heard about what we were doing and the project we were going to be doing in Liverpool[3] and the *Guernica* thing was global. It was in American newspapers and the *Guardian* and everything.
>
> *(Paddy, muralist)*

Guernica has come to represent cross-community dialogue, a conversation that recognizes the importance of acknowledging the past but at the same time making connections beyond the local in a way that opens it up to places beyond in a negotiation of social difference. As Paddy explains:

> So it's looking back on all that in both communities and saying yes, we have the right to celebrate the people who we believe contributed. And most of those people didn't have a chance to understand, cause most were indoctrinated by the past, and it's taken us a while to find that space, to try and find what unites us, how we can resolve all these problems as we made on the statement on *Guernica*, without resorting to armed resistance or violence.
>
> *(Paddy, muralist)*

For Paddy, the murals create direct dialogue between different people, those that audience the murals on the street and those who hear about them.

> I think we're ahead of these people on re-imaging. We're not taking away… One of the things I meant to say about the murals, the murals are not just a visual medium, they're an aural medium. We put these wee hooks on the wall. It's the ones behind us who are discussing them, who pass by later on and discuss and have a conversation and explain.
>
> *(Paddy, muralist)*

A key aspect of the role of murals in producing open communities is their mobility. Those of the international peace wall change regularly. Murals have a "lifespan and a biography" and, as such, the "value of the image will change" (McCormick and Jarman 2005, p. 51). For McCormick and Jarman, the end of the mural is as important as its situatedness. The mural of *The Gold Rush* in Figure 3.2 maintains poignancy not because of the image on the wall now but because of the image it replaced. The mobility of murals is evident not least in their storytelling, which is not only in their material presence but in their disappearing also: a blanked-out wall, once adorned with a paramilitary mural, is now part of an open narrative (ibid., 2005). The loss of mural sites on gable walls, as a result of changes in public-housing design to create 'defensible space', is another story. The changing muralscape represents changing space. For example, the Shankill area, in which the mural in Figure 3.2 is situated, was controlled by specific paramilitary groups and the changing muralscape signalled changes in control. Similarly, there have been various successful campaigns to remove paramilitary murals, involving local newspapers and business organizations, and this represents changing attitudes to these groups, which would at different times have been powerful enough to resist this (McCormick and Jarman 2005, Hill and White 2011). Murals can be powerful in their mobility and practices; murals on the international wall have been influential in a number of social justice campaigns (McCormick and Jarman 2005). These pieces of public art are mobilizing through practice. As McDowell (2008, p. 337) suggests, material cultures have the "ability to influence and mobilise those who read them". This movement of murals creates the more fluid and open notion of community necessary for social transformation. As McCormick and Jarman (2005, p. 52) argue, there is a "need on both sides for permanence in the certainty of the past, which has been replaced by a more fluid and transitory social memory". Hence, murals and community are co-produced, as Tom and Paddy demonstrate:

> Its all about involvement and inclusion and making people feel comfortable … it happens to us all the time. We'll be painting and you hear conversations going on in the background and maybe three or four tourists talking to a local person who happened to pass by. So the person in the community, they love it 'cause they're able to tell their story …That's how the pictures come about, through the community engaging with us.
>
> *(Tom, muralist)*

> It's not totally unconscious, but you are always bearing it in mind. You see, if we didn't do that, the murals would be desecrated. They have to belong to the community. It has to be issues…in lots of cases they don't have to agree with them, but you have to make sure that that mural, the finished product, when you go away, there's something there that relates to that community and the proof is in the pudding – terrible clichés, that's totally the wrong cliché.
>
> *(Danny, muralist)*

For the muralists then, the term 'community' is open. Community for them is self-determining, not in an exclusionary way, but indeed a way that is necessarily reaching out and beyond.

Conclusion

This chapter has illustrated the generative cultural practices of street murals in Belfast, in illuminating the dangers of normative conceptualizations of space and community as fixed and closed. Focusing on three particular mural sites has revealed the myriad faces of community in its interaction with muralists, in acceptance of the art of mural painting and in the creation of new stories as murals are interpreted and practised. The chapter suggests a rethinking of community through the practices of street art, as murals such as the depiction of an Irish myth in an alleyway in Ballymurphy illustrate the ways in which discussions are taking place within communities, and between communities and those outside them. Although there is evidence that some practices are entrenched in the sectarianism that depends on fixed communities, there still appears to be an openness in engaging in dialogue with the state authorities, who are attempting to impose their vision of a peaceful city that has left behind the problems of the past. Like the murals of the

Chicano and Palestinian struggles, murals on the 'international peace wall' represent the connections between local communities and issues in all parts of the world. In this way public art such as mural painting reveals community through making visible the social differences that, as Lefebvre (1996) argues, make the city.

Notes

1 Irish republican prisoners began a hunger strike in 1981 in protest at the withdrawal of Special Category Status. Ten prisoners, including Bobby Sands who during the strike was elected to the UK Parliament, died during the protest.
2 The research project gained ethical approval from the University of Brighton Faculty of Health and Social Science Ethics and Governance Committee. This included a full appraisal of the potential ethical issues that may arise, in particular in using visual methods. Names have been changed to protect the privacy of research participants. Where identification is nevertheless possible due to association with particular murals, participants gave specific agreement in relation to this.
3 In 2007 the muralists were invited to Liverpool by the Liverpool Mural Project to paint a mural of the Beatles as part of a cross-community project.

4

THE EVERYDAY AGONISTIC LIFE AFTER THE UNVEILING

Lived experiences from a public art World Café

Martin Zebracki

Rationale

When we talk about public art, we should talk about social engagement that is as fundamentally complex as the multifacetedness of society. In public space, as we usually know it, there is neither a well-delineated stage, a well-defined audience nor a 'fourth wall'. Rather, what we encounter is 'unstaged' social difference of the everyday. In this chapter I argue that Chantal Mouffe's socio-political notion of *agonism* (Mouffe 2008, 2013) is precisely a productive epistemological framework in which to situate the dynamic social everydayness of public art.

From my academic standpoint as human geographer, this chapter reflects an intermediate stage of my intellectual journey through the everyday practice of permanent physical public art, as seen through the lens of poststructuralist socio-cultural and political theory. In particular, I reconcile social engagement with existing permanent works of public art – and the attendant articulations of social difference and degrees of social inclusiveness – around the Mouffian notion of agonism. Agonism, while acknowledging its ontological complexity, basically reveals the heart of cosmopolitan democraticism that intrinsically offers room for potential conflict and open, ardent dialogues between ambivalent vistas (ibid.). Social engagement with art in public spaces can occur in a completely passive and indifferent fashion, and, although very compelling in and of itself, I am not tapping this particular social behaviour towards public art here. Rather, ensuing from the affective turn in the geographical humanities (Clough 2007, Thrift 2008), I am particularly concerned with social geographies of meaningful encounter (McCormack 2008) with the everyday lived experiences of public art, *after* its unveiling.

We may consider Richard Serra's *Tilted Arc* a textbook example where (radical) meaningful encounter with permanent public art is concerned. Placed in New York's Federal Plaza in 1981 and destroyed through public will in 1989, this example shows, as conveyed by Deutsche (1998) and Senie (1998), how aesthetic opposition to this 3.5-metre-high and 27-metre-long curved steel wall was consonant with social resistance to the urban form and, more generally, to its perceived (mis)uses. *Tilted Arc* was basically a sheer confrontation between perceived aesthetic and utilitarian uses of urban public space as much as it was a conversation piece about the (mis)representations of various social identities (Kelly 1996). In a sense, *Tilted Arc* was a multiscalar radical act. As indicated by Crimp (1986, cited in Deutsche 1992), *Tilted Arc* architecturally turned the plaza into spatial incoherency which, at a symbolic meta-level, may be read as a sweeping attempt to confront everyday life with – and potentially subvert – hegemonic powers of state and societal structure.

Currently, the official (i.e. institutional) aftercare for permanent public art is still under pressure: along aesthetic interest on the one hand and, on the other, utilitarian demands, mainly in the spheres of financial policy and community development. Acknowledging the conceptual merit of agonism in understanding confrontation in public art practice, I empirically situated this notion within a public art research context I am familiar with. Also, I acted on the recent affective turn as well as ethnographic calls to engage further with everyday experience and participatory methods. I embarked on the everyday reality of permanent (although occasionally considered 'superfluous') public artworks after their unveiling in the context of the homonymous Dutch public art expert symposium *After the Unveiling* at Van Abbe Museum in the Dutch city of Eindhoven on 15 September, 2014. At the invitation of Eindhoven's alderman for culture, Mary-Ann Schreurs, and after preliminary inquiry into the dynamics of cultural policy and public art practice in Eindhoven and the Netherlands more broadly, I provided a conceptual talk as well as a participatory role-play workshop about the official aftercare for public art and dimensions of social engagement.

The afterlife of Honoré De Balzac

The trigger for the symposium in Eindhoven was the project *Radio Balzac*, called into existence by the established Dutch artist Arnoud Holleman. This project entailed a profound artistic-environmental dialogue of Holleman with Rodin's sculpture *Honoré De Balzac* (1898) which was situated in the front garden of the Van Abbe Museum from 1965 until 2014. Holleman, who argued that most permanent outdoor artworks are a sign of collective oblivion, set himself the task to "kiss the art awake" so as to actively recollect it – "as if you become aware of the clothes that you are already wearing" (Arnoud Holleman, 15/09/14, talk)[1] As a temporary solution, Holleman placed the artwork on a rotating platform in the inner court of the museum in early 2014. His mission, termed "Balzacification", was to employ this artwork to identify contemporary issues about the practical care for public art at times dictated by crisis, retreating governments and increasing care assignments of local authorities. He argued that through being swayed by these *everyday* issues, it is easy to forget and not come to terms with *structural* 'social traumas'. In historical reference, the *Tilted Arc* case successfully and succeeded to achieve the latter. Holleman contended that moving *Honoré De Balzac* should mark a new beginning in a new place, rather than being restored in its original place. According to him, the accrued "new touch" has given a sequel to collective remembrance and has redeployed its previous archival value (ibid.).

Inspired by Derrida and Dufourmantelle (2000), I consider public art within a framework of hospitality to which I relate my conception of agonism in this chapter. The *Radio Balzac* project, which has peculiarly turned *Honoré De Balzac* inside out within a reformed sense of publicness, was a striking test case to critically ponder on *host* and *guest* roles in social engagement with public art after its unveiling. In my conceptual talk in the early afternoon slot of the expert symposium, I framed this matter within the context of confrontation, agonism and meaningful encounter, essential elements that, in my view, were lacking in the morning debates at the symposium.

Buildup

I first elaborate on the conceptual baggage that I conveyed in a nutshell to the attendants of the symposium. Thereafter, I present my experimental public art World Café discussion method. Based on this method, I convened a 90-minute workshop involving 'relative-empathetic' yet agonistic role-plays in the symposium's afternoon slot. In this workshop, participants were expected to critically discuss official aftercare and social engagement with regard to another salient test case in the city of Eindhoven: *Expansion* [translated from the Dutch: *Expansie*], an abstract public artwork created by the locally well-known sculptor Toon Slegers that was dismantled and relocated. Whereas we may argue that the *Tilted Arc* case demonstrated an ephemeral social outburst – an 'in-your-face' confrontation with hegemonic power – *Expansion* can be seen as a sample of public-art-of-the-everyday that needs to be "kissed awake" in Holleman's rhetoric (which in itself may be viewed as a radical act of a different, intimate calibre). After the methodological discussion, I empirically analyse the host–guest plays, in this case involving the positionalities of three main actors involved in the recent relocation of *Expansion*: a curator of a Dutch multinational bank, residents and a municipal cultural policymaker. Based on my workshop-based study and engagement with agonism, I conclusively conduct a meta-reflection on everyday social engagements with the 'afterlife' of public artworks. There, I also provide pointers as to how this subject can be conceptually and methodologically progressed by follow-up public art studies.

Public art's geographies of meaningful encounter

I consider confrontation, seen on a scale of agonism, as the essence of meaningful encounter within the socially produced spaces of public art (à la Lefebvre 1991). Audience encounters with public art can be orchestrated or stimulated by its enabling actors – including artists and cultural policymakers – or they can be accidental, conscious or subliminal, positive or negative, reactionary or revolutionary, and so on and so forth. Public art encounters produce lived experiences thereof and, depending on their level of criticality, inhabit the *inviting* potential to intently sense everyday life. As such, within a framework of hospitality (Derrida and Dufourmantelle 2000), I regard public art as a hosting platform for a wide range of modalities of agonistic engagement in the interrelated spheres of the political, economic, social, cultural-symbolic and, more recently, the virtual. In these spheres, public art can incite commonplace but also unfamiliar aspects of citizenship and belonging.

The intriguing part of this hospitality mechanism is how, at some point, the host status of public art is dialectically exchanged with the guest status of the publics, including residents, visitors and passers-by. On the basis of their (collaborative) public art encounters, the publics can potentially attain the pedagogical capital to 'host' tools to (re-)define locally mundane as well as cosmopolitan citizenships, belongings and ethics (Derrida 2001, Rancière 2009). These (re)definitions create layers of meaning that, to come full circle, can be fed back to the work-of-art-as-guest so that in its turn it can act as host to follow-up encounters. Following Latour (2007), such dialectical process between host and guest, and between materiality and body/corporeality, entails an iterative and co-existing, more-than-human process through the agonistic window of public art.

Social groundedness

Based on this dialectic host–guest tenet, it is tricky, or even inexpedient, to generalize nomothetically about social engagement with public art, in view of the socially grounded nature of the praxis of public art. In line with a Lefebvrian take on the production of social space (Lefebvre 1991), there are no – nor should there be – absolute predictive and extrapolating models of the social making and embodying of public art. Accordingly, there are no social pre-calculations to make regarding how involved actors perceive and respond to works of art within individual and community settings (Lossau and Stevens 2015). Public art research should, in an idiosyncratic fashion, be grounded from within these social practices that are spatio-temporally unique – one after the other.[2] Such research, therefore, would produce socially situated insights by involving itself in what public art 'does' rather than what it 'is' a priori. An essentialist realm of thought is something to avoid, but by my estimation it is a frequent reality that plagues public art practice. I captured and subsequently deconstructed such essentialism – at times prevalent among the policy and creative enablers of public art – by my notions of 'public artopia' (Zebracki et al. 2010) and 'the bird's-eye doctrine' (Zebracki 2014). These indicate injecting essentialist thoughts and top-down implementations into the everyday practice of public art, respectively.[3] Notwithstanding, as an elaboration of the host–guest tenet, I now provide pointers to frame situated encounters – and as such the agonisms – as part and parcel of what public art 'does'. These pointers conceptually ground the role-plays I conducted with participants in my workshop, while concurrently departing from the idea that these role-plays in their turn acted as test cases of the everyday agonistic realities of public art practice.

In this chapter's focus on permanent works of outdoor art, it is important to acknowledge that their settled state, and hence spatial fixity, can potentially be seen, or fetishised, as frustrating inflexibility within public art discourse (Senie and Webster 1998). Such frustration, as witnessed in the *Tilted Arc* case, often transforms at the critical juncture when new configurations for the work are proposed or enabled. Social engagement with public art is then concerned with asking to what extent the public artwork should, for example, be reinstated or renewed, replaced, dismantled, destroyed, or relocated to a new location (or depot). Apart from the practical and logistic provisos, the parameters of the artwork's future are subjective and emotionally framed among those who engage with – or rather negotiate – its future. The public artwork's settled state becomes interrupted in this social and emotional interplay, and the notion of agonism thus comes into play. A change to the public artwork's status quo recollects the artwork, or "kisses it awake", as Holleman stated. This in itself can be a revealing but also disturbing agonistic process, generating emotions that range from the fostering to the loathing. The confrontations and struggles immanent in such agonistic practice are not there to be overcome per se, but these social disputes in and of themselves can be conducive to positive social meaning-making and change (Büchler and Harding 1997, Mouffe 2007). As such, the public artwork could open up and intimate interaction among those who engage with it, allowing them to contemplate, imagine, contend for and potentially reshape the socio-spatial entourage of the artwork, as well as its locale.

Fluid parameters

Through the perspectives of a wide variety of involved actors – both enablers and publics whom I altogether consider "art engagers" (Zebracki 2015) – the agonistic process in public art's official aftercare can critically put in mind the origin of the artwork: why and how exactly did the work come into being and arrive at this place? Another concern relates to its 'site-specificity' (Kwon 2004): to what extent does the work join in with in-situ social and spatial identities? In the case of classical statuary, one might wonder if it is just a "dope on a pedestal", in the words of the Dutch popular philosopher Prins (2002), or a work that lets people intensively contemplate the social world. Which visions about the future of the public artwork go round? But which ones precisely prevail and are hence imposed through the design table? And what are the power systematics of the underlying agonistic processes? In public art's both pre- and post-unveiling era, the socially politicized divisions of roles between policymakers, the public sector more broadly, the (art) market and the (counter-)publics are not univocal (Deutsche 1996). Their fluctuating, relative and multiscalar dispositions and inherent power constellations and multifaceted agonisms require constant redefinition to understand the parameters of social engagement with the artwork.

Therefore, conceptualizing social engagement with public art requires a spatio-temporally differentiated, *fluid* approach that takes into account individuation and community dynamics from the local societal level through regional and global developments and (anti-)normativities in the domains of politics, the (art) market and social order. Thus, in the spirit of Bauman's (2012) liquid modernity, analysing the aftercare for art in public *space*, needs a grasp of the public *time* that interfaces with the collective past, as well as the actuated present and projected future trajectories. These are all discerned according to the diverse standpoints of the art engagers. Such analytical dynamism would chart, following Žižek's notion (2011) of parallax, *transforming subjectivities* of these art engagers in order to come to grips (inter- and self-critically) with public art's potency of aftercare. This may evoke social change (as modest or radical as this might be in regard to established normativities) and a further intensification of the everyday living environment. As such, deducing from Bluedorn (2002), public art's public time does not follow a neatly coherent and consistent pattern. So, here one can wonder about which spatio-temporal path public art actors take, want to take, or are able to take through agreement and conflict, and how they live through – and envisage social engagement with – public art in the political, economic, social and cultural-symbolic spheres.

I want to emphasize that I frame the fluidity of everyday social engagement with public art in a more-than-human assemblage (Latour 2007). Here, there should be acknowledged that the properties of the public artwork (e.g. its shape, colour, size, position, level of permanency, etc.) and its meanings and 'codes' ascribed by its enablers offer possibilities and simultaneously place limits on the capacities and forms of social engagement with the artwork (Massey and Rose 2003). In this process, we can detect a compelling everyday field of tension between senses of *public ownership* of the artwork mainly on the part of the (counter-)publics, and *public accountability* (Zebracki 2014a, 2014b) mainly on the part of public art's enablers, which was considered in the role-play workshop.

The public art World Café method on *Expansion*

Based on the previous conceptual baggage, I organized a host–guest role-play workshop about social engagement inherent in the official aftercare for public art. My workshop pursued the World Café discussion method (Brown and Isaacs 1995)[4] and I amended it to take into account the specificities of the test case on *Expansion*. Before I elaborate on this method I shall briefly discuss the provenance and evolution of this public artwork. I do this primarily on the basis of first-hand information provided by the curator of the local bank (Respondent #5) and an art and cultural policy adviser of the municipality of Eindhoven (Respondent #4), who were both involved in *Expansion*'s relocation in 'real' life. They provided a brief introduction to this relocation from their own professional standpoints in the symposium's morning slot.

Expansion: a passe-partout

Expansion is an abstract sculpture by Toon Slegers that was placed on a public traffic-rich site in front of a Dutch multinational bank in the centre of Eindhoven in 1967 (Figure 4.1). This artwork can be considered a direct reference to the then spirit of urban expansion. Due to the demolition of the bank headquarters, which is being rebuilt at the moment of writing, *Expansion* was dismantled in 2013. The bank is the original owner of this public artwork, as well as of a plethora of other artworks throughout the Netherlands. Initially, the bank attempted to keep the work in its place. However, owing to chiefly practical reasons and high storage charges, the bank donated *Expansion* to the municipality. This was done with the knowledge that it should stay in Eindhoven as it was created in the particular context of this city's social and cultural fabric. In a sense, due to the donation, the

FIGURE 4.1 *Expansion* (1967), Toon Slegers. Original location at Fellenoord, Eindhoven, 1967–2013.
Credit: Rabobank Kunstcollectie.

host–guest relationship between the bank and municipality was reversed. After *Expansion* was put in storage for a short period of time, the artwork was relocated in early 2014, albeit now without a pedestal on account of artistic reconsiderations. The new location is a greenbelt area adjacent to an apartment building in Lichtstraat,[5] situated in a relatively tranquil central neighbourhood in Eindhoven (Figure 4.2).

The relocation of *Expansion* to this specific neighbourhood was not entirely accidental, as the local residents' association expressed the desire to enrich this neighbourhood through a work of art. Residents generally deemed that such work should not necessarily be a new one. This was good timing for the municipality. After careful consideration with the local residents, the municipality, in cooperation with the bank, approved the relocation of the work to the neighbourhood concerned. The transportation and reinstallation costs of *Expansion* were defrayed by courtesy of the bank. As a result of this gesture, a modest acknowledgement reflecting the bank's support will soon accompany the artwork. The municipality is nevertheless still responsible for the artwork's maintenance.

FIGURE 4.2 *Expansion* (1967), Toon Slegers. New location at Lichtstraat, Eindhoven, 2014–present.
Credit: Joop van Bree.

Role-play

The World Café discussion method I implemented was based on the dialectic host–guest tenet and focused on the three central art engagers who played an active role in *Expansion*'s recent relocation: the curator of a local bank, local residents and a municipal cultural policymaker. Thirteen public art experts (seven females, six males) took part in my 90-minute role-play workshop, which occurred in what I viewed as a pleasant atmosphere in the main lecture theatre of the Van Abbe Museum (Figure 4.3). All participants in the workshop provided me with consent to use their input and exchanges as data for this research. I have processed these insights anonymously to protect the privacy of the research subjects.

It was noteworthy that the actual curator and municipal policymaker also participated in this workshop but were asked not to play-act their own professional positions. Apparently, the residents could truly be considered the missing 'significant others' during the symposium, and I tried to let their perspectives 'kiss awake' in the role-play. I acted as the panoptic host, providing a brief introduction to the workshop's objectives, setup and etiquette.

The general aim of the role-play was to gain critical understandings of the official aftercare for *Expansion* since 2013, when it was announced that the artwork had to be removed. I divided the group into three subgroups. Each subgroup represented the following roles assigned by me: the curator of a local bank, residents (one or two per subgroup) the municipal cultural policymaker, and a moderator. On the basis of the allocated roles and the knowledge provided at the symposium, the participants broadly considered the official aftercare for the artwork in the context of everyday engagements within the interrelated political, economic, social and cultural-symbolic spheres. The subgroups had to ground the debates on the following scenarios, respectively: substituting the artwork for a different one in the same place (scenario A), moving the artwork to a different location (scenario B, which happened in actual fact), placing the same artwork back in its original location (scenario C).

Three parallel discussion rounds took place. Each subgroup featured a 'fixed' moderator who also functioned as minute secretary. The other three or four 'variable' members of the subgroup collectively moved on to a different group in the second and third round. But they switched roles on both occasions so that their group conversations dynamically grew on each other throughout different perspectives. Nevertheless, seeing the rotating issue resulting from the odd number of thirteen participants, I asked two participants to retain the role of resident but to change subgroup after each round.

When the parallel discussion rounds were concluded (so after all variable members had encountered all three scenarios), it was public 'harvest time' (Brown and Isaacs 1995). That is, I asked the three moderators, in relation to scenarios A, B and C respectively, to successively provide a plenary reflection on the dynamics of the several subgroup discourses. This was attended by a critical discussion based on the three scenarios and changing roles. Afterwards, as the all-seeing host, I guided a meta-discussion with regard to the differing allocated positionalities

FIGURE 4.3 Impression of the host–guest role-play workshop pursuing the World Café discussion method.
Credit: Martin Zebracki – photograph edited for confidentiality reasons.

and ensuing viewpoints of the participants. At the end of the workshop, I invited the participants to complete an open questionnaire on paper to convey their personal view of the actually occurred scenario (i.e. scenario B) as well as desired formal aftercare for *Expansion*. In this individual paper exercise, participants were thus asked to (try to) leave the role-play and base their outlook on their everyday professional experience of public art practice. That said, I acknowledge the potential influence that the role-play might have had on the 'afterplay' where the participants (at times provocatively) steered between their real-world experiences and experiences of play-acting other perspectives. In a certain capacity, this allowed me, in the post-analysis of the workshop, to critically triangulate the role-play with the everyday professional life experiences of the participants.

Lived experiences on stage

The host–guest role-play workshop involved the positionalities of the main art engagers involved in *Expansion*'s recent official aftercare, namely the curator of a local bank, local residents and a municipal cultural policymaker. Through these different roles, the event was an enthralling agonistic 'opportunity to learn' (Stake 2000) about scenarios A, B and C for *Expansion* (i.e. respectively substituting the artwork for a different one in the same location; moving the artwork to a different location; and replacing the same artwork in the same location). The workshop's empathizing effort was seconded by one of the participants in their written evaluation:

> I was pleased with this role-play, as it gave me the chance to place and express myself in the position of the other. In the execution of my professional role I also have to transport myself mentally into the role of others in order to make a sound assessment of the various interests.
>
> *(Respondent #12, male)*

Based on my empirical experience of the workshop, I shall now critically present the three scenarios, analysed on the basis of their differing enacted positionalities and the framework of agonism. The plenary, written minutes of the moderators, as well as my discoveries regarding the respective subgroup discussions on *Expansion*, revealed commonalities and conflicts about the 'whats', 'wheres', 'whens', 'hows' and 'whys' of *Expansion*'s (alternative) public art forms and spaces, as well as its related enabling/disabling socio-spatial politics. I shall present salient observations in this regard which I have categorized under *spatialities and temporalities*, and *ownerships and accountabilities*. In so doing, notwithstanding, I need to acknowledge that the participants put their views in perspective throughout the scenario-based role-plays, as at times their perspectives were ambiguously rooted in their enacting, moderating or actual professional roles. The presentation of my findings is therefore fluid, meaning that the provided perspectives fluctuate according to the entwined roles and scenarios – as one might expect in agonistic practice.

Spatialities and temporalities

A respondent endorsed the site-specific appropriateness of *Expansion*'s relocation and the sense of public ownership among the work's new audience: "the artwork is kept for the city and has turned into an icon for the residents of the neighbourhood, and as such the work has acquired new significance for both them and the city" (Respondent #11, female; role: resident). This respondent, on the one hand, argued that the "epoch-making" artwork, made by a renowned artist, belongs to Eindhoven's cultural heritage and should therefore be kept in this city. While recognizing the art-historical relevance of the sculpture, she suggested that the initial location might not offer allure to the work any longer, as the renewal of the bank building's site has in a way disconnected *Expansion*'s meaning from its original surroundings.

As a counter-voice, another participant, from his professional role as policy intermediary on art in public space, contended that "*Expansion* has somewhat unfortunately stumbled into its new place" (Respondent #12). He emphasized the mismatch between the proportional specifics of the artwork and the new venue, and he took the view that an overly bureaucratic procedure was followed, rather than a process that puts the artwork first:

> There is now indeed a group of residents that greet the artwork with open arms, but the spatial scenery is so entirely different – concrete versus green – that the sculpture has obtained a different, out-of-place aura. So the work has lost its value.
>
> *(Respondent #12)*

This was also stressed by another participant (Respondent #7), play-acting the role of curator of the local bank. Although she appreciated that *Expansion* as a landmark piece is maintained within the city of Eindhoven, she argued that the artwork, which was tailored to the specificities of the original site, was rendered ineffective by the relocation of the work and hence it was "lost in translation". In her professional position, this respondent declared:

> It is disappointing that the previous context for which the artwork was made – think of the stone-built environment, spacious setting and the large pedestal – are less important in the artwork's new location ... That said, as might be expected, public visibility of a public artwork is always better than placing it in a depot.
>
> *(Respondent #7, female)*

According to scenario A's moderator (Respondent #4), a play-acting resident imparted that, if *Expansion* were to be replaced by a new artwork in the original location, the new work should function as a "referencing object" to *Expansion* so that it becomes "commensurable" with it and reincarnates its material pre-existence.

Respondent #9 (male), performing the role of curator of the local bank, alternatively argued that the move of *Expansion* could have been postponed till the completion of the site's architectural development: "then a worthy destination for *Expansion* could have been reconsidered on the same site, where the artwork would have full play". That said, the major practical proviso was that *Expansion* had to be displaced in any case, due to the bank's redevelopment plans. In this context, scenario C's moderator (Respondent #6) indicated that some participants in the enacting positions of cultural policymaker and curator were drastically in favour of employing *Expansion* as 'path-depending principle' for the entire local architectural redevelopment. Thus, as radically summarised by the moderator, "the location should adjust to the artwork" (ibid.).

In a personal capacity, scenario B's moderator critically imparted that the current siting of the artwork does not semantically justify the work's title: "placing a sculpture that bears the name Expansion in a little corner of a housing estate devalues its meaning". Furthermore, considering how things were experienced in reality, a participant, from her actual position as the curator of the local bank, reported that a win–win situation was achieved in view of all the imposed constraints:

> Given the limited length of time, an optimal solution was found for all parties involved. An alternative could have been devised, but then a great deal of time should have been devoted to a variety of comparative assessments
>
> *(Respondent #5, female)*

Despite this win–win situation, Respondent #12, in his professional role, condemned the lack of creativity in the actual process that occurred: "it was as if an overly official track was followed, involving officially prescribed resident participation. The bank and municipality tackled the problem in an overly pragmatic mode" (Respondent #12). Scenario A's moderator, from her professional viewpoint as local art and cultural policy adviser, affirmed the latter as well, and also for public art practice more generally: "there is little room for truly substantive debates. Procedures and practical matters are dominant" (Respondent #4).

One of those formal procedures involved a survey that the municipality conducted among the residents in *Expansion*'s new location prior to the artwork's move. This survey, as argued by Eindhoven's art and cultural policy adviser (Respondent #4), revealed that the residents were attached to *Expansion*. As indicated by a participant performing the role of resident (scenario A), this should be rendered in a purely emotional dimension of people's long-term lives:

> It is such a pity that the artwork had to move. For me, as Eindhovener as well as daughter of a father who held office at the bank, the artwork is inextricably bound up with precisely this location, even when the bank building site has been redeveloped. So, I'd be in great favour of replacing *Expansion* in the same location.
>
> *(Respondent #8, female)*

Ownerships and accountabilities

Despite the survey, the genuine public ownership of this work was critically put in perspective by several participants in the workshop. Scenario B's moderator conveyed this in regard to public surveys on outdoor art in general: "when the municipality tells us that *the residents* want an artwork, it normally concerns just a very small percentage of the local population" (Respondent #3, female). In the plenary debate, scenario B's moderator (Respondent #3), moreover, conveyed that a participant who play-acted a resident even regarded the artist as a "malefactor", judging on *Expansion*'s outward aesthetic appearance. The moderator explained that this performing resident argued that *Expansion* is "excessively abstract" and that its unintelligibility should be seen as a "morally reprehensible" case in point for a society that is meant to be transparent.

Here, the moderator reported that a participant, performing the role of cultural policymaker, provided a positive twist. He made a plea for a pedagogical intervention: an educational trip to the local museum where residents could learn more about the artist (Slegers) and gain a "proper" situated understanding and hence ownership of *Expansion*. In such a pedagogical sense, according to a participant fulfilling the role of curator in scenario C, the legibility of the artwork could be enhanced by providing information about the sculpture, the artist and the broader context of the work through various communication channels, and "as such, the value as well as public appreciation of the sculpture can be increased" (Respondent #2, male).

Scenario A's moderator (Respondent #4, female) generally noted that, throughout the subgroup discussions, the enacted curator's attitude remained authoritative about any changing conditions of the artwork. The bank's natural long-term attachment to this artwork's location, and hence its ascribed guardianship, might explain this party's monopolizing role in the debate. The moderator, moreover, indicated that two subgroup discussions overall envisaged the role of the publics in an active sense. This meant that the implementation of a new public artwork should consistently account for the voice of residents in a structured time frame. Here, the enabling parties should have the responsibility for establishing serious rapport with the various audiences throughout the whole process. In the remaining discussion group, the play-acting cultural policymaker as well as play-acting curator of the bank, on the contrary, were substantially more aligned to the idea of involving residents on an ad-hoc basis, just for the sake of formality in public art commissioning only.

Scenario C's moderator (Respondent #6, male) addressed the role of power relationships when he stated that overall the discussions walked a tightrope between preservation and displacement of *Expansion*. From his own professional position he added:

> Placing *Expansion* back in the same place would justify the historical understanding of it, whereas relocating the work would rather warrant a new aesthetic sense of the work's environmental quality … In any case, new public art locations should ideally be judged by connoisseurs and subsequently conversations should be held with residents.
>
> *(ibid.)*

This quote touches on the challenge of accountability in the everyday practice of public art as it tries to navigate between the authority, expertise and preferences (including aesthetic and utilitarian ones) of the art world, those of the local policy decision-makers, as well as the various voices and tastes of the residents. I observed that this issue was a connecting thread to both the workshop and the symposium in general. Particularly, there was tension around the issue of to what extent the opinion of (all) residents should matter or 'count', to what extent they should have the freedom to choose properties of the artwork and be empowered throughout the process, to what extent the art should be 'useful' (e.g. representative of the familiar; serving city promotion), and to what extent local art spaces should involve local or global work i.e. 'big names'.

Scenario A's moderator (Respondent #4) contended that there was overall alignment in the subgroup discussions regarding the importance of getting around the table and entering into negotiations in public art practice, no matter how tough this might be, especially given limited time frames. Yet, the moderator also noted that the play-acting policymakers were worried about the risks of inertia and not getting any artwork (or just a 'consensual' piece) off the ground, if consultation with residents were seen as an imperative while artistic experimental freedom was seen as a matter of secondary concern.

The expected division of roles between the diverse parties in the official aftercare for *Expansion* differed along various notions of ownership in the role-plays. Ownership was identified in political, social and cultural senses, but some respondents alluded to the legal context of ownership. They argued that the rightful and 'territorial' owner of the artwork, i.e. the local bank, should shoulder the responsibility for the management and maintenance of it. On this, Respondent #2, from his professional position as art restoration specialist, aired practical concerns about the artwork's durability and visibility (and hence about its site-specific 'effectiveness'):

> The sculpture in its current place now takes up a vulnerable position, as it is sited on a lawn. The maintenance of the garden could damage the sculpture as well as stonework, and growing trees could obstruct the view and potentially inflict damage. So one should enter into solid agreements about this, and annual repairs should follow.
>
> *(Respondent #2)*

Also, in the (play-acted) practical concerns about the official aftercare for *Expansion*, the bearer of the costs proved to be a recurring theme. Fascinatingly, the level of responsibility for this aftercare seemed to be repeatedly correlated with budgetary powers.

Based on the different enacted roles, I noticed that the participants by and large expressed appreciation of the charitable deed by the bank to donate the artwork to the municipality. That said, a participant, from her professional position as art and cultural policy adviser, informed that "the municipality is not properly prepared for such gifts and resulting activities, which simply don't occur that often" (Respondent #4). The present in the present, so to speak, was considered a "beautiful and apt concept" (Respondent #10, female, role: resident). I commented on this in the plenary debate by arguing that public art donations, rather than the creation of new artworks, can be gathered particularly from the current austerity context of budgetary constraints and re-established financial and political priorities. I critically referred to a headline in a Dutch op-ed circulated among the participants: "hardly any new artworks are created for public space. Both the State and firms [increasingly] dispose of their outdoor artworks" (Smets 2014, p. C2), which was argued to be a consequence of increasing social accountabilities of authorities and entrepreneurs.

Hence, the *Expansion* case might be conceived of as an epitome of the current neo-liberal climate that poses a utilitarian challenge to public art production and particularly to the destiny of existing and time-honoured public artworks. These artworks can sometimes be looked upon as 'dated' and 'needless' by some, even by the work's original patrons themselves. According to some participants, this does not necessarily mean that a new location should be found for any disposed-of public artwork: "one should more often stand the loss and give way to something different, or new, rather than pursuing the will to re-create. What provides more mental space and social progress?" (Respondent #1, male, role: resident).

In this context, the respondent noted that one should not feel diffidence about an ephemeral public artwork or even a potentially public-art-less future – such as occurred in the *Tilted Arc* case. This was also critically put into a utilitarian light by a play-acting resident, who argued that at times he prefers functional street furniture like a bike shed or bench to an artwork, for which he would rather visit a museum. Nevertheless, this respondent indicated that parties 'hosting' *Expansion*'s relocation did take on public accountability, pursued the artist's consent and yielded a sense of public ownership among the new 'guests' of the artwork:

> I'm aware that both the bank and the municipality of Eindhoven acted in the public interest. Also, the artist's heirs were informed and consulted and they fully agreed with the artwork's move and the modification to the artwork's base. The residents in the artwork's new place, moreover, saw eye to eye with the artwork, so to speak, and they also had a say in the decision-making process.
>
> *(Respondent #1, role: resident)*

Social relations and the particular balance of power and authority were core to the debates. Most of the performing residents in the role-plays regarded the municipality as a significant guardian angel in the everyday concern for the artwork, whereas a fair degree of residents' participation was still thought to be crucial.

Afterplay: the relative hospitalities of public art

The dialectic host–guest tenet, as my study's recurring theme, has conjured up queries and contentions about what artists, cultural policymakers, the diverse everyday users of public space and any individuals and civil society parties concerned with outdoor art expect from its official aftercare over space, time and in terms of ownership and accountability. The employed public art World Café model disclosed methodological potentialities as well as limitations for engaging with agonism in the public art practice of *Expansion*. Actually taking place in a lecture theatre, the public art World Café was in a sense a theatrical, staged enactment in and of itself. Following Magritte's surrealist adage '*Ceci n'est pas une pipe*', I acknowledge that the World Café did not internalize *Expansion*'s proper public art practice but was in essence a sheer performative representation thereof. The reality sense of the used method can therefore be questioned, although its role-play merits can potentially make an impact on participatory public art policy schemes.

As reinforced by the role-plays, the roles of the actors in public art practice should be seen as relative, reverberating or contradictory along diverse experiences, imaginations and aspirations. Such fluid conception ambiguously diffuses these actors' agencies in everyday life. My observations during the workshop indicated that the several role-play rounds enabled the participants to acquire a further understanding of (and empathy for) the 'other'. The plenary reflection resonated and contributed to the evolution of multifaceted perspectives crossing the various play-acted (as well as 'real') professional roles. It was obviously difficult to assess to what extent the participants could professionally 'abandon' themselves and fully embody the role of the play-acted 'other' and likewise abandon the roles they played while completing the ex-post individual paper questionnaire. Here, my intention was precisely to challenge the participants and to tease out if they were in any agony with themselves. On the next iteration of the World Café method, an ex-ante version of the paper survey – for which there was no time allowance on this occasion – would be conceptually useful. This tweaking might put the results in perspective as much as it may reassess the influence that the role-play has on ex-post responses in the plenary as well as paper exercise.

Whither public art?

For every single public art case, as I endeavoured to do for *Expansion*, one should contemplate through which political and in which economies, social lineages and cultural-symbolic contexts public art does and can potentially assemble people and instigate socio-spatial engagements. In these contexts, how can we articulate and learn about social and cultural-symbolic difference? How do the diverse modalities of agonistic engagement let public art actors trenchantly reflect on social norms, values, rights and responsibilities in regard to the living environment? How can these mirroring attitudes result in a momentum to revalue or even transgress norms, values, etc. in order to attain more socially inclusive and just spaces? That is to say, spaces wherein there is (still) trust in the positions and know-how of the various parties, transparency in knowledge production and exchange and respectful room for dissidence.

In this sense, public art can be regarded as *micropublic* (Amin 2002): an agonistic mirror countenance of society that serves simultaneously as a window thereon. Arranging this window according to individual or conventional group perspectives is akin to taking the path of least resistance. Potentially more progressive in the post-*Tilted Arc* era would be to earnestly challenge or incorporate the 'other' and any conflicting views, thus the agony of the micropublic force field, into the mental significance of public art. Consequently, this would engender a strong position to bid a farewell to the (re)production of unilateral, elitist visions and sheer top-down practices.

The *Expansion* test case provided an inspiring and provocative flight of ideas about how to deal with the multisited aspects of public art after its unveiling. This post-age of public art embodies complex co- and re-'authoring' aspects in terms of, e.g., physically renewing, replacing, dismantling, destroying or relocating the artwork in the various contexts of policy-related stipulations as well as informal social settings of everyday life. The test case also provided insights into quotidian experiences with public art. These can emotively reveal instances ranging from encouragement to revolt.

Further conceptual as well as integral experimental methodological work is needed (depending on the research specificities, one might consider in-situ [participant] observations, one-to-one interviews, participatory visual methodologies, surveys, and focus groups including audiovisual elicitation techniques, e.g. Garrett 2011; Rose 2011) to capture the art engagers' various lived experiences regarding the aftercare of public art along intersectional sociological indicators (cf. Valentine's [2007] work on examining intersectionality). The latter would further cross-analyse the human geographies of public art along identity markers of class, gender, sexuality, ethnicity, age, religion, nationality, (dis)ability, and so on. Fleshing out social engagement with public art in this intersectional manner, according to differentiated identity markers beyond the oft-assumed John Q. Public, addresses an untrodden terrain that I identify as an important research frontier in human geographical research on public art.

The complexity of public art practice is an enchanting living topic, at least to me, as it can offer unpremeditated, sagacious and (self-)critical reflections on social and cross-cultural thinkings, doings and transitions. In this vein I see public art as a 'stochastic variable' of our socially politicized everyday life. The workshop on *Expansion* provided just a glimpse of public art's still understudied *agonized* relations between authorities, the arts sector, the market and citizens.

Public art is on the edge of care as shrinking budgets have to be distributed over increasingly more policy goals. Current rigid neo-liberal thinking and actions, particularly in post-social welfare states like the Netherlands where I conducted this research, generally position the public artist as an entrepreneur. In a managerial way, the artist is consequently supposed to take heed of 'selling' art – being considered a commodified product – to citizens, i.e. consumers of the real-time experience economy who are already pampered by a profusion of both material and intangible goods.

Furthermore, in a sense, the organization of public space becomes increasingly less 'public' yet increasingly more functionalized, driven by supply and demand factors and controlled by the utilitarian thought of authorities – think especially of the growth of CCTV (Varna and Tiesdell 2010). As such, the oft-considered 'non-functional' nature of public art might come across as the strange guest in utilitarian thought. The potentially resulting sterile cultural landscape might most likely not do much to help critically disturb socio-spatial planning, not to mention *reality*. I would thus argue that such a disturbing aspect is precisely core to a sound operation of agonism.

Then, which pedagogies and heuristic methods should public art practice 'host', to stay within my metaphorical tenet, to define a meaningful social niche for public art in such a utilitarian economy? How can the legitimate and informal ownership and broader social accountability regarding public art be reconfigured through exploring alternative financial schemes? (e.g. grassroots sponsorship and crowdfunding, Bannerman 2013). How should public art, moreover, reconsider its material foci and expand its social engagement within the highly digitalized social world? (Cameron and Kenderdine 2007). These are topical issues and questions that are at the heart of daily public art practice and which may unite, reconcile or split beliefs across the actors involved.

I hope that my engagement with agonism on the basis of the public art World Café case study has provided conceptual and methodological tools for approaching the contesting interstices of everyday social public art practice. I encourage any further critical complementary work on the experimental plot that I have presented here.

Acknowledgements

I owe a debt of gratitude to the workshop participants. I am also thankful for the reviews that helped to strengthen this work. Any errors are my own.

Notes

1 All quotes in this chapter are translated from the Dutch.
2 See also Haraway's (1991) notion of situated knowledge that I have extensively engaged with in my public art studies so far.
3 Moving beyond 'public artopia' and 'the bird's-eye doctrine', I believe that enabling parties in public art practice have an innate responsibility to account for *transparent communication* with the envisaged audience, *active public participation* and *critical evaluation (and enactment thereon)* in terms of social engagement from the design phase throughout the realization and the everyday care for public art. The particular parameters of such communication, participation and evaluation are artwork-specific and hence concurrently site-specific. They are therefore to be carefully socially negotiated between the enabling and public subjects involved, resonating with collaborative planning principles applied to socially fragmented, super-diverse societies. In this regard, see particularly the seminal work by Healey (2003), who stresses the general importance of a processual understanding. Elaborating upon Giddens (1984), she also points to the essential elements of the (institutionalized) 'power over' human subjects and the 'power to' get processes going and create things in so doing. As such, we may see public art practice as a critical social interaction between subjects and matter, which is conditional upon the level of *agency* (i.e. the capacity to decide and act unreservedly) of these subjects, which in its turn is structured by broader social power dynamics over space and time. Here, in the vein of my host–guest tenet, both the enabler and audience play out, present and challenge both material and intangible resources *of* and resources *to* public art.

4 See Zebracki (2014b) for my preliminary experiment with the World Café method in the context of a participatory expert session that I led at the International Architecture Biennale Rotterdam (IABR) in 2012.

5 Noteworthily, Lichtstraat translates as Light Street in English, which refers to Eindhoven's epithet 'Light City', as it acted as an historically important host to the production of matches as well as to the Philips light bulb factory.

PART II

The education of a public artist

5

CREATING THE GLOBAL NETWORK

Developing social and community practice in higher education

Dean Merlino and Susan Stewart

Introduction

This chapter explores the pedagogy of social and community practice. It is possible to trace two pedagogic histories of community practice: these are competing but not necessarily contradictory. The first starts with the self-conscious arts-based social engagement movement that we can trace back to the 1960s. This slice of history contains both a return to community mythos (that community is the 'natural collective state' of human nature) and an emancipatory social agenda that presupposes an engagement with the arts. There is both a harking back and a looking forward that are at times in stark aesthetic contradiction. The double yearning for an older collective art and craft making, as well as for innovation and the new, at times produces interesting tensions within the practice. Over the ensuing decades, these two positions of collective mythos and aesthetic telos (constant change and development within art-making) have, however, sat side by side with an overarching desire to engage with a person's 'natural' artistic and creative expression in order to effect change in social relations and personal self-belief, not merely observe another's creative capacity under the guise of meditating upon 'great' art.

This second history, which Arlene Goldbard describes as "active participation in cultural life", and as one of the "unifying principles" of cultural development (Goldbard 2006, p. 44), is echoed throughout the literature. Such claims for the making of art have also come from schools of philosophy and psychology. For example, Erich Fromm claimed that "collective art ... is an integral part of life ... No sane society can be built upon the mixture of purely intellectual knowledge and almost complete absence of shared artistic experience" (Fromm 1963 cited in Krensky and Steffen 2009, p. 7). In this context, the underlying educative capacity of community-based arts – to learn about one's being in the world through creative action – is often traced back to the work of Brazilian educator Paolo Freire in his works *Pedagogy of the Oppressed* (1970) and *Cultural Action for Freedom* (1972), which frame the emancipatory pedagogy that runs through much of the practice.

There is a strong educative element to the framing of 'social change' in the practice of community arts that derives very much from the model of student-centred learning that rose to prominence during the twentieth century. Originally espoused by philosopher John Dewey, student-centred learning provides a learning context within which students are encouraged to ask questions, rather than be given answers, and where lived experience is recognized as knowledge. Connections made through dialogue, analysis and reflection are central to student-centred learning, and engaged participation can lead to multiple ways of knowing along with the development of critical subjectivity (Ledwith and Springett 2012).

Yet there is a deeper history of the educative/emancipatory potential of art making and creativity that is traceable back to the Socialist Realist theatre of the early twentieth century and the Makhnovist liberation plays in Ukraine during the Russian Civil War, right back to the travelling morality plays of the European middle ages. Indeed, if one were to take a more concerted anthropological position, one could say that community practice is traceable back to the fundamental aestheticized rituals of culture-making and cultural transmission.

Such pedagogic threads, apart from being significant in the genealogy of contemporary community practice, also provide the basis for our understanding of the complex amalgam of elements that make up practice: ethics and morality, politics and resistance, perfectionism and teleology, aesthetics and creativity. Many of these elements have been well covered in the literature surrounding community practice, and it is not the aim of this chapter to retread such well-worn ground. What is of interest here is the educational and pedagogic aspect of communally engaged creative practices. Though not often stated in the practice 'in general', it is heavily educational. Furthermore, there is a very strong link between community arts and the education sector, with many artists running art-based programmes in school curricula, or after school.

However, as an arts practice that consciously engages with *being in* community, indeed one reputedly built upon a social-actionist philosophy, community practice is surprisingly quiet about its own development and pedagogy. While writing exists about its ameliorative values and the educational importance of collective creativity and storytelling, next to nothing has been written about the value of education for the development of the field itself, let alone for practitioner training. The first courses in the United States to train people in community-based arts sprang up in the 1980s. There are now a number of tertiary courses dedicated to the education, training and development of community artists and community arts workers at undergraduate as well as graduate levels. Yet, despite the continued flourishing of community arts education, and indeed the impact of a growing professionalization within the community arts sector globally, there is a glaring lack of discourse dedicated to the pedagogical philosophies and methods used in training community arts workers.

There are two remarkable and rare exceptions to this: The first was *Community Cultural Development in the Tertiary Sector*, by Fotheringham and Hunter (1994). As a report written in Australia for the Australia Council for the Arts, it quite meticulously detailed every tertiary course containing one or more units teaching an aspect of community practice, and even courses that did not necessarily teach community practice as such but employed methodologies taken from the field. There are literally dozens of courses described in this report, although at that time in Australia there were no complete tertiary-level offerings in community arts. Surprisingly, when the Master of Community Cultural Development was launched at the University of Melbourne in 2005, almost all of those partial elements had disappeared across the country. Although there is a story to be told as to why, by 2005, community arts had disappeared from curricula rather than morphing into strong standalone courses, this is not the forum for that discussion. Suffice to say, community arts had formed part of a great many curricula and then disappeared from view. The second report on community practice education is an overview of the state of play in the United States produced by Arlene Goldbard, titled *Culture and Community Development in Higher Education: The Curriculum Project Report* (2008). This is equally as comprehensive as the Australian example some 14 years earlier, yet is able to show a number of standalone tertiary courses in community arts, community practice and social practice. Of further interest in this lengthy report is the discussion on the value of tertiary education for community practice (Goldbard 2008, pp. 13–15). Sadly, in the years since its publication, there has been scant engagement with Goldbard's proposals.

This chapter, therefore, begins the long overdue dialogue about the pedagogy *of the practice*. We will begin with a reflection upon the present state of pedagogic development within the field and explore the conditions for this late blooming. It will also attempt to capture some of the key questions critical to the training of practitioners such as: how does one teach *doing*? How does one teach praxis and its eventual maturation as reflexivity? Finally, what does it mean to understand practice as a field of knowledge development and, as such, what is practice as research? We will then consider the different pedagogical imperatives at the undergraduate, graduate and post-graduate research levels, and how a comprehensive teaching programme might function to link these various stages together developmentally. In doing so, we have chosen to use our own programmes as case studies. Susan Stewart will reflect on her experience of an undergraduate minor in social practice at Emily Carr University of Art + Design, and Dean Merlino will reflect on graduate coursework degrees in community practice at the University of Melbourne. Finally, we will propose the development of an international network dedicated to community and social practice pedagogy, to begin the dialogue and development of a global commitment to the future of the field.

Tertiary education and the doing of practice: why now?

Why are social practice, and community-engaged practices emerging in so many art, media and design programmes, and across such diverse global contexts? Key reasons are perhaps connected to a cultural crisis on an unprecedented scale –

climate change, economic decline, diminishing resources, large-scale inequities, and the call from younger generations for a more resilient and just society. Some have suggested that "it is a sign of the uncertainty of the moment, the unresolved play of cultural, economic, and political forces currently unfolding before us. It is this sense of possibility, and imminent threat, that animates the remarkable profusion of contemporary art practices concerned with collective action and civic engagement"(Kester 2011, p. 7). To these phenomena could be added the impact that communications technology and the networked society have had on traditional art school subjects, and the markedly different learning style of the current generations of university students. Art programmes are experiencing a radical transformation, and the best ones have undertaken to meet the needs of the twenty-first century learner. One result has been renewed interest in a field that responds with strategies that hold genuine promise for cultural transformation: social practice and community engagement.

From the perspective of practitioners/educators working in socially engaged practices for most of their creative and professional lives, this spike of interest is both surprising and affirming – surprising because community-motivated work has frequently been unrecognized and unrewarded within the status quo of the art world. Here, *community-motivated* refers to work that leads with ideals such as social justice, equality, fairness, ethics of care, along with full participation in society, and life that is grounded within a strong commitment to original and highly creative methodologies for addressing inequity. These are the bedrock values of socially engaged practice.

There is growing documentation of artists/designers, curators, artist groups, educators and administrators, whose engaged, participatory, collaborative projects and explicit social commitment are finally being recognized as a lineage leading directly to current social practices. This is an area of research that would benefit from further reflection and analysis, and which would offer a great teaching aid for educators who want to give students a sense of scope and context for both the historical and contemporary fields of social practice and community engagement. Despite the lack of a substantive history for critically engaged social practices, contemporary practitioners, scholars and educators are aware of many past projects and have been reviving and discussing creative strategies that have been in circulation for some time, as well as challenging the very idea that there can even be a narrative encompassing such a diverse set of practices. As curator and scholar Nato Thompson puts it: "socially engaged art is not an art movement. Rather, these cultural practices indicate a new social order – ways of life that emphasize participation, challenge power, and span disciplines ranging from urban planning and community work to theater and the visual arts" (Thompson 2012, p. 19). As Thompson's book *Living as Form* demonstrates, contemporary practitioners are experimenting and developing new methodologies and forms best suited to this particular historical moment. This continuation of practice and burgeoning theoretical discourse points towards a natural maturation of a field of practice and study.

Concurrently, within art and design programmes in higher education, there is a turn away from traditional silos and sharp disciplinary boundaries, towards a more poly-vocal, collaborative and transdisciplinary set of practices (Kester 2011, p. 7). This is a site of strain, debate and passionate disavowal in some programmes. It is hard to accept the pace of change, and not everyone is comfortable with the realities of these changes. Not only are the disciplines radically realigning, but the notion of the academy with its gated 'inside' and 'outside,' is also under debate. The perennial question, "but is it art?" takes on a certain poignancy in this context, as the tables turn again and traditional art modalities, from their own side, feel undermined and threatened by forms that are not dependent on individual achievement. Rather, methodologies that encourage full participation by makers and perceivers alike, training, teamwork and dialogue across multiple fields, are in the ascendancy in creative disciplines. Designers just shrug. After all, this way of working is very familiar to anyone who applies design methodologies to their practice. In a discussion about interdisciplinary research in the context of Experience Design, Ronald Jones writes: "Rarer even than flourishing interdisciplinary practices is the creation of a transdisciplinary practice. Transdisciplinarity occurs when an interdisciplinarity hybrid is no longer served by being reciprocal but transcends the limits of the original collaborating disciplines to create a third – unforeseen, and therefore entirely new – practice" (Jacobs and Bass 2010, p. 159). This definition points to the dynamic potential for socially engaged practices as well, where dialogue and collaboration across sometimes profound differences, may well lead to unexpected and vital social innovation.

The practitioner educator

Social practice educators and administrators, often artists themselves, will frame their pedagogy, as praxis. Conscious teachers have long understood the classroom as a site for radical transformation wherein all participants – teachers and students alike – can engage in a dialogic process to collectively overcome obstacles to clear thought, incisive analysis and genuine meaning making. This willingness to engage in honest assessment, and to allow transformation through conversation, connection and insight, is one of the hallmarks of the social practice classroom. It is necessary, especially at the undergraduate level, to practise these skills in the school environment before engaging with other individuals and communities. There is a substantial amount of 'unlearning' that each of us needs to take on before we use these methods in the field. In particular, students and faculty need to be self-reflexive and identify biased thinking, false assumptions and stereotypes about other people, cultures and unfamiliar situations. In the visual art classroom, reflexivity is frequently taught as the final of three competencies in critical pedagogy: production, perception and reflection (Cary 1998, p. 320). With regard to reflection, emphasis is placed on the reading of artwork and one's experience (defence) of it, in the context of the group critique that is a staple within visual art pedagogy. In the context of social practice, it is helpful to look at definitions from other disciplines such as sociology, philosophy, and politics where meaning is understood to reside at the confluence of particular social, cultural, ecological, ideological and relational contexts. Reflexivity then becomes inclusive of a broad range of concerns that are situational, empathetic and adaptive, and more in line with an ethical framework: How are we thinking about thinking, what are our influences and how do our actions impact on others?

Once teachers and students have good grounding in ethics, critical/cultural theory, and some experience in dialogue, social practice educators teach through doing. They apply theory and practice to real world situations, local and immediate, as well as sustaining long-term commitments with diverse community partners. This type of modelling is pedagogy in action, not only working with theory and self-discovery but also demonstrating methods of engagement that extend into multiple communities, and out into the world. Artist-educators are using pedagogical practice as research, leading classes of students and themselves into communities and spaces, often for the first time for all involved, with the potential to generate relationships leading to creative engagement, resilient communities and profound social change.

Case studies: overview of pedagogical and social innovation in the Faculty of Culture and Community at Emily Carr University of Art + Design

Undergraduate art and design programmes lead social practice and community engagement initiatives in very particular and vital ways. The ability to imagine new ways of conceiving what may be possible, and the application of creative process using art and design protocols is one of the things that a specialized university of art and design does best. The role of praxis and learning by doing is fundamental to art and design methodologies. When students and faculty are given a problem, and are encouraged to generate ideas and engage solutions through a creative process, they are capable of producing results that can inflame difficult issues in unexpected and sometimes astoundingly beautiful ways. Ideas of community engagement, working and dealing with local issues, pragmatic ideation and reimagining a resilient society, are finding a more willing public than ever before. This speaks to the era of crisis and change in which we find ourselves but also to the creativity, passion and resourcefulness of student artists and designers.

The Faculty of Culture and Community was constituted in 2009. Since that time, community engagement, embedded within the discourse of social practice, has played a critical and unique role in programme development and faculty research within the Faculty's undergraduate curriculum. Explicit values of the Faculty include: commitment to cultural diversity, sustainability, social justice, enhanced communication strategies and adaptive curriculum. One form these values take is an interdisciplinary Social Practice and Community Engagement minor (SPACE) that facilitates internal and external collaborations, fostering a culture of critical inquiry and reflexivity. The SPACE minor emphasizes community engagement in tandem with an increased visual and critical literacy, and prioritizes an innovative, progressive curriculum that offers students a context and ethical framework for a socially and engaged art, design or media practice.

The interdisciplinary and innovative structure of the SPACE Minor allows for engagement with the other faculties, and facilitates the potential for pedagogical innovation throughout the university. The programme is designed to allow open access for students in any of the majors and degree programmes of the university. There are two required critical studies courses in the minor (the Social Practice Seminar and the Ethics of Representation), along with a studio course requirement (Community Projects). The remainder of the credits are acquired from a range of elective courses that cross disciplines, and directly relate to social and community practices, such as Sustainable Design Strategies (Industrial Design), Social Media Projects (Dynamic Media), Audience and Communities (Photography) and Environmental Ethics (Humanities). Easy access to the minor tends to result in very mixed classes, with fine art, design and media students of any level from second to fourth year participating. This is a pedagogical asset as students learn from each other within a concrete model of student-centred learning, and discover the particular strengths and fields of knowledge that specific disciplines exemplify. For example, design students often bring communication strategies, systems thinking and presentation skills, while the visual art students may demonstrate experimental and highly original approaches to problem solving and the creative process. When focused on specific goals, these teams of students are capable of accomplishing unexpected and valuable learning outcomes. Also, the opportunity to work across their own disciplinary differences is good preparation for fieldwork and the multiple differences they will encounter in community collaborations.

Pablo Helguera characterizes the philosophical underpinning of this type of pedagogy in his exceptional handbook, *Education for Socially Engaged Art,* when he posits that

> Traditional pedagogy fails to recognize three things: First, the creative performativity of the act of education; second, the fact that the collective construction of an art milieu, with artworks and ideas, is a collective construction of knowledge; and third, the fact that knowledge of art does not end in knowing the artwork, but is a tool for understanding the world.
>
> *(Helguera 2011, p. 80)*

The three required courses in SPACE provide a strong foundation for social and critical learning in this task of understanding the world, and are presented below in more detail.

A necessary ethic

The Ethics of Representation is a required critical studies course in the SPACE minor that teaches ethics directly, relations of power when inequity is at play, and empathy for others who are marginalized and stigmatized. It is not lost on students that a large majority of people suffer acutely the world over, and this, in fact, is precisely why some students gravitate to social practice and community art courses. Students have both political and philosophical questions about the way things appear, as well as the way things *are*. Social practice students are strongly motivated by an intention to contribute to a just society, to be a voice in their communities and to find meaningful connections between art and creative practice, their education, and their lives – both within and outside school. For students, engaging in ethics embodies their first steps towards the development of a critical consciousness.

In our globalized environment, classrooms are increasingly diverse, and students and teachers come from all over the world from multiple nation states and cultures to work and study together. Some of these students and their families have experienced extreme calamities at home and oppressions of all kinds. Other students will come from sheltered, privileged and uneventful environments. This diversity of experience is a tremendous asset for an educator intent on teaching ethics as a core value. Carefully managed real stories have more potential to transform habits of thought than detached, abstract accounts. Students' own internalized biases and prejudices, especially unconscious ones, are met head-on when personal relationships are at stake. A strong grounding in ethics is essential as a fundamental learning outcome, preceding community-engaged practices. Students need the opportunity to explore ethical terrain, to identify appropriate responses to power inequities, to learn how to prioritize relationships over production and create their own ethical frameworks. Without doing this core work, they will not be able to work effectively across difference, and there is every possibility they will cause harm to themselves or others. Artist-educators should make every effort to ensure students are well prepared ethically before venturing into any public or community-engaged work.

An early assignment in the ethics class is to have small groups of students work together and present something they find in the public realm, that they feel is clearly unethical or harmful, likely found on the internet. The discussions that emerge from these group examples provide an opportunity for students to delve into questions of what constitutes ethical image making, and to form a roadmap for sound relationships in the production of documentaries and representations when working with others. Not only do students begin to constitute and strengthen their own guiding ethical framework, they also have the opportunity to explicitly articulate ethical unease among their peers. This is highly political terrain for a teacher to navigate, since in order to make sense of some of these images it is necessary to provide cultural context and analysis, explain how systems of power work, address economic and historical realities and so on. It is also an opportunity to closely examine the construction of meaning through representation, how framing and point of view work to bolster ideologies can function as propaganda. Following on from this, it is then possible to look at artists who deliberately provoke ethical questions as part of their practice, and to provide students with the critical distance necessary to understand why artists may be doing so.

Socially engaged art

> Socially engaged art, [is] a term that emerged in the mid-1970s, as it
> unambiguously acknowledges a connection to the practice of art.
>
> *(Helguera 2011, p. 5)*

A second required course for the minor is the Social Practice Seminar, offering a framework for understanding social practice both from an historical and a contemporary context, as well as providing a space for critical reflection. This is an essential requirement for students who aspire for further degrees and/or an art career that employs social practice methodologies. The Social Practice Seminar provides a space to interrogate the widely divergent practices that constitute socially engaged art, such as participatory art, various dialogic experiments within the community, public art, performance, embedded residencies and other projects that hold social relationships as the primary construct within art production (Helguera 2011, p. 5).

Since a majority of the students who currently take the SPACE minor are Bachelor of Fine Art students, it is important to focus for a time on art specifically. In the art school context, it is understood that students who attend social practice courses are already well versed in formal aesthetics through the production of discreet works and classroom critiques. It can also be assumed that they have been introduced to a variety of forms of contemporary art production, cultural theory, art history and critical thinking. Some of this thinking can seem to put them on a collision course with socially engaged art with its emergent and sometimes informal treatment of aesthetics – aesthetics, in any case, that are not prioritized over a process that is itself co-emergent, collaborative and unpredictable.

These differing approaches to aesthetics are hotly debated in the academy and can result in extreme views that sometimes act as flashpoints for reaction and disavowal of social practice artworks. This type of reception is similar to what political and pedagogical social art, such as feminist projects, queer artworks, performance art and radical theatre received in the 1980s and 1990s, when overstepping the bounds of aesthetic rigour and formalism. Fortunately for art educators, this is an excellent opportunity to unapologetically introduce these differing positions to students and interrogate conflicting ideas about aesthetics and the particular meaning and function of various artworks. The debate not only appears across disciplinary lines but also within social practice philosophy and critical theory. As well as projects that are participatory, collaborative and humanistically positive, one can also cite examples of socially engaged artworks that are deeply disturbing and provocative, which contradict and disprove any notion that there is a single set of methodologies for social interventions. Claire Bishop articulates this condition in social practice discourse:

> ... in insisting upon consensual dialogue, sensitivity to difference risks
> becoming a new kind of repressive norm – one in which artistic strategies of

disruption, intervention, or over-identification are immediately ruled out as 'unethical' because all forms of authorship are equated with authority and indicated as totalizing. Such a denigration of authorship allows simplistic oppositions to remain in place: active versus passive viewer, egotistical versus collaborative artist, privileged versus needy community, aesthetic complexity versus simple expression, cold autonomy versus convivial community.

(Bishop 2012, p. 25)

This dualistic framework that many of us seamlessly operate within provides a basis for critical inquiry in the classroom that sharpens analytical reasoning, and provides a platform for political and philosophical discussions that undergraduate students relish. Students enter into these conversations with strong positions, and simultaneously and rapidly re-form their identities relative to the art and design ideas that they are encountering in school. In the social practice seminar, part of our job as educators is to lead them into an interrogation of their views and to model a methodology for debate, disagreement and dialogue, all necessary skills in community work. Hence it is not just content that we want to provide but also to model methods of working with differing viewpoints, divergent lived experiences and an open willingness to be changed by potent ideas. As teachers, we need to embody a willingness to be changed similarly through these processes, and to let students recognize that this is happening.

In community

Educational institutions can assume a leadership role in creating partnerships with broader communities, local businesses, non-profit groups, and other institutions. Community project courses are where social practice studies and theory become applied through experience, and are the third of our required courses within the SPACE minor. In the Community Projects course, we offer a project-based curriculum that addresses the specific goals of our partners, in tandem with our own learning outcomes. Initial conversations between the prospective community partners and the social practice educator (a space where process, planning and outcomes are shaped and the nature of the collaboration explored) require sensitivity, careful attention and dialogue. The result of these meetings should be a clear understanding by both parties of what is possible, within an educational framework, for this particular community context. Parameters and aspirations can vary widely, depending on the partner organization's mandate and needs.

An important aspect of the overall strategy is to sustain long-term relationships with some collaborators, building partnerships that have depth and transformational potential for both parties and for society at large. We have found that longer-term commitment to certain community partners has actually allowed curriculum to develop and mature naturally as we learn what works and what could be improved. It also allows for a slower process overall and more time for relationship building. For the administrators, organizers and faculty who are responsible for the outcomes of these curricular partnerships, sustaining community relationships develops trust, deeper learning outcomes and shared resources. Courses that happen only once rarely get past an introduction stage. Equally, artists/educators embedded as practitioners in residence in non-art spaces is an interesting strategy that is starting to be explored in various community contexts. Unused civic spaces, parks, science labs, field houses, social service agencies, non-profit spaces, abandoned factories and empty storefronts are just a few examples of possible sites for embedded artistic activity and pedagogy. Placing teachers, students, projects and their curriculum in situ enables a new kind of praxis where the informal spaces of community-building shape the formal space of pedagogy, and vice versa.

Pedagogy/methodology

Teaching social practice and community-engaged art practice requires pedagogical methodologies that match the values and philosophical underpinnings of social practice discourse. Asking students directly what they require for their education, right here and now, makes them active partners in the learning process. It also allows for a great deal of inclusion of difference, including previous knowledge sets, learning styles and individual aspirations. All students have something to contribute. Participating in dialogue and learning to practice active listening are essential social practice methodologies. Emphasizing this fact, asking for student participation and assistance within a context of collective, conscious, co-intelligent learning has the potential to propel the entire group. When faculty and students alike are actively engaged, the classroom becomes a dynamic environment.

Classroom interconnections should encourage the same conscious investment in relationships that we encourage students to explore in social praxis. Along with dialogue, it is important to model power negotiations, reflecting what we expect students to navigate when interacting within communities. This adds a new embodied dimension to student-centred learning. With social practice, it may be useful to consider a more mutual experience within teaching and learning that is more student-focused. This might entail inclusion in the decision- making process, and a pedagogy that is willing to disassemble and reconstitute on the spot according to learning needs. In an undergraduate context, a strong classroom container is necessary. Students need this in order to feel secure exploring participatory practices, often for the first time, even with each other. A strong container does not preclude teachers modelling inter-subjective awareness, active methods of dialogue and explicit attention to power imbalances. These techniques have the potential to demonstrate appropriate and necessary skill sets for community and social work within the confines of a safe learning environment. Hence these three courses with their attendant methodology represent the core curriculum that functions to support student development and learning in SPACE at the undergraduate level.

Graduate teaching at the Centre for Cultural Partnerships, Faculty of the Victorian College of the Arts and Melbourne Conservatorium of Music, University of Melbourne

Having established the basic pillars for undergraduate or entry-level studies in social and community practice, we now turn our attention to the shape of graduate courses. Undergraduate studies are necessarily more skills-based. Students need to develop their abilities in an art form. Even if their practice is to become more hybridized in nature over time, students must still experience their own development and mastery over a practice. Furthermore, to work in collaborative and community spaces, students must be introduced to the fundamental skills and ethical demands of the work. Here, the impact of dialogue with community cannot be overstated, yet it is no easy thing to grasp. Many artists consider communities as merely the extension of the tools found in their own studio. Work in community practice is often conducted within a 'master/free labour' dichotomy, under the guise of collaboration. In this model the artist has complete control over the vision, design and construction of an artwork with little input from the community. Community practice understands this as a small aspect of what happens 'on the ground', but ideally aims for the community to be involved at all stages of the project process. Pedagogically, this participation must include more than the shift from the traditional role of audience/observer of an artist's vision to that of volunteer labour on an artist's public project. Instead, community practice argues that the making of art, the participation in the creative process itself, is what is of benefit. The non-artist as collaborator is invested in opportunities for expression on the one hand, and opportunities for responsibilities on the other, that are simply absent from the performer/audience model. Community practice goes one step further in this democratizing process, arguing for the complete democratization of the art-making process. Engaging community members (non-professionals) in the totality of the process, from vision and design to implementation and performance, presents the opportunity to enhance community capacity, self-belief and self-reliance in a number of ways beyond the simplistic meditation upon 'great art' that often masks a control of capacity and development.

The above discussion brings to light a very crucial element in the training and development of a practitioner: namely, that the engagement of communities across the totality of a project implies the welcoming of participants into both the practical *and* the conceptual/theoretical space of a project. We have seen that at the undergraduate level, students take their first steps in their theoretical and practical development and begin to grasp the notion of praxis. Graduate level begins the process of unpacking praxis, bringing theory and aesthetics into dialogue with practice and ethics. The philosophizing of practice merges here with the doing, to shape a practice where the two inform and feed on each other. Yet in this sense, praxis brings several layers of theory and practice into dialogue. The student is seeking to understand the relationship between theory and practice, not only within their own practice but also in the broader practice, and within the broader community with which they are engaged. There are complex intersections, value judgements and contradictions to be navigated in order to ensure that a project is coherent and meaningful, especially if the community is to take on key collaborative roles with the artist.

This shift from normative practice to a more sophisticated meta-level engagement with both *the* practice and *one's* practice is what distinguishes graduate from undergraduate study in community practice. As such, it is also the space for experienced practitioners to return to study and immerse themselves in this process. This learning potential for experienced practitioners is absent from the literature. Goldbard's 2008 study of the state of higher education is not explicit about the potential differences between undergraduate and graduate streams in this sense. While the study reflects the key principles of student-centred learning and the notion of student as community participant within higher education, this does not translate as a reflective frame for the retraining of practice. As such, it echoes the response to community practice education commonly voiced from within the field itself: that it is important for 'new' practitioners to learn the skills of practice and the theories and histories that underpin them but also that experienced practitioners are beyond this need.

Historically, most practitioners literally trained 'on the job'. Now there are courses for such training, yet the *development* of one's practice is still expected to occur in situ. This produces two significant problems for the practice. The first is the isolating nature of this expectation and the difficulty that individual arts workers have to conform their private developments into a global practice. The second is that in response to the staleness and 'stuck-ness' often expressed by experienced practitioners, the collective mantra is to simply keep on practising, or that *practice will find the solution to practice*. This generally fails, and many practitioners can grow increasingly frustrated and burned out, or even leave the field altogether. Graduate study, therefore, is not the space for formal training in an art form; rather it is the space for formal training in praxis. Certainly in the Master of Community Cultural Development (CCD) at the Centre for Cultural Partnerships (CCP) many experienced practitioners enter the course with a sense of their practice being *stuck*. In other words, students have refined the *doing* of their practice and are indeed experienced and accomplished, yet feel that their practice is now an automatic process that neither challenges nor stimulates. Some talk in terms of feeling stale in their work and unable to find their way out of the problem, or in terms of seeing new practice emerge and feeling unable to redevelop their own practice to keep up. Here, the need is to understand the complexity of the theories and philosophies behind community practice and to bring this into communion with the practice. We can pose a plethora of questions about *the* practice and *one's* practice to map a complex understanding of the space of community arts. These can range from the historical, aesthetic and developmental to the more abstract and contingent. The point however is to learn to apply thinking *into* practice, rather than either replicating the stultifying anti-intellectualism of practice detached from thought, or the siloing effect of critique and defence. Dialogue is therefore between four cardinal points: the doing of the practice, the thought of the practice, the doing of my practice and the thought of my practice.

To facilitate this process of praxis, the first year of the Master of Community Cultural Development contains two units focusing on theory (Theoretical Frameworks and Research Methods), and two units focusing on practice (Brokering Partnerships in a Policy Context and Practice, Process and Evaluation), though the two states are never separated. Rather, it is a question of balance – exploring theory and then reflecting on the implications for future practice, and exploring practice and then reflecting on the underlying (and often tacit) theories. The training shifts into a more reflexive space in the second year, with two units that engage student practice in the world (Community Performance and Ritual and Rethinking the Creative City), and a written 12,000-word minor thesis in which students can tackle a substantial idea. This last step is valuable for those practitioners who wish to contribute to the discourse of practice through writing and public lectures.

The collapse of certainty

Structuring the graduate exploration of practice as dialogue between the breadth of *the* practice and the depth of *one's* practice puts pressure on the student to clearly articulate their thoughts to others in a number of different ways. Since no one embodies the complete landscape of practice, the layered complexities of the landscape of practice slowly reveal themselves to students, as each grapples with and explores their own particular space while also commenting upon and enlightening each other's. As a dialogic process, indeed as a complex counterpoint, the collaborative sharing of spaces necessarily transforms each person's bounded claim to space. In other words, by recognizing that practice is performed in so many ways, students necessarily confront the limits and (self) imposed boundaries of their own practice. It provides an antidote to the constant scapegoating of a mythologized, morally bankrupt *other* (capitalism, government, etc.), and instead sees students turn a questioning gaze upon themselves and their own practice. This epistemological doubt is triggered by the undermining of the certainty of one's practice through the rich variety on display in the classroom. The doubt is challenging, as students feel the boundaries of certainty fade away. Yet it is also liberating, as practice is often unnecessarily limited.

Collective dialogue and collective articulation of practice are sufficient conditions to produce doubt. To enter a classroom certain of the parameters of *one's* practice and *the* practice, and then to experience methodological and epistemological diversity necessarily alters one's perceptions of the assumed specificities and generalities of practice. To be receptive to the perceptions, experiences, methods and language of other practitioners, different art forms, various organizational methods and needs, to name but a few, is to be receptive to the collapse of certainty. Thus begins the process at graduate level of the transformation of practice into praxis, and eventually into reflexivity; or the dawning self-awareness of both the assumptions and consequences of being in the world. The fecund uncertainty brings into doubt the unqualified certainties of normativity, and eventually demands a more sophisticated meta-level (meta-philosophical, meta-ethical) understanding and articulation. At this point, students begin to remake their practice to fit the expanded field of knowledge and to produce a deeper, more profound level of understanding. Furthermore, they can begin to reorient their practice towards the future rather than replicate the past. This is the process of becoming unstuck, which is extremely difficult to achieve outside of an educational situation.

Beyond its importance for the development of practitioners and of new understandings of practice, this is the very process that opens up the ontological possibilities of community practice. The classroom process shifts from (1) an initial certainty to (2) collective articulation and personal doubt to (3) individual and collective rearticulation and finally (4), a deeper and more complex meta-knowing awakens new modes of understanding and potential for practice. Shifting from the normative and often instrumental paradigms of community art – such as its influence upon individual and community wellbeing, mental health, urban renewal and the like – students can make the connection between their own state of being in a complex practice with the realization that community practice itself is a way of *being in the world*. This pedagogic model builds upon the student-centred learning model as collective engagement, indeed collaborative responsibility, and is aimed at evaporating the limited and self-centred horizon (what do *I* want/need to know?), eventually replacing it with a collective push into the unknown (what can *we* possibly know?). Given this collective twist, the methodological base of student-centred learning finally becomes a powerful ontological imperative.

As discussed earlier, the focus on skills training at undergraduate level implies a limit on the diversity within the classroom. Situating courses within fine art programmes, for example, focuses on the collaborative and performative potential of one art form. The field of community practice, however, is not limited to artists. There are certainly artists 'on the ground', yet community practice is an entire ecosystem requiring facilitators, creative producers, social entrepreneurs, arts and cultural managers, organizational workers and a range of other roles in order for the artist to work directly with community. Perhaps the most important differentiation at graduate level is the structuring of courses to include the development and understanding of all these possible roles. It is critical for the continuing development of the practice that all aspects of the ecosystem be represented in the graduate classroom. This changes the structure of the classroom dramatically, as the various perspectives are developed in conjunction with each other, and collectively fill out the topography of the landscape of practice. Furthermore, the Master of CCD attracts students from spaces that are interested in community practice as a methodology or a set of useful values. For example, students from community and international development, social work and urban design are attracted to the content of the graduate programme but are not interested in transferring into the field. This is significant in realizing that community practice is much more than just *a* practice. It is a space that has worked out how to weave together collaboration/participation and ethics, providing an attractive solution for other disciplines.

Graduate level studies are also the perfect place for the exploration of the hybridity of community practice. Not merely an arts practice that exists within its own bubble, many projects occur in conjunction within various federal, state and local government contexts and are part of broader cultural and community policies. Projects also occur in collaboration with health and wellbeing organizations, non-government organizations (NGOs) and within international development contexts, among others. Understanding the imperatives of these contexts becomes of the utmost importance, producing a hybrid notion of collaboration.

Finally, graduate students can make a vital contribution to undergraduate courses and projects as teaching assistants, or in some cases as co-teachers. They can also support the curriculum through assisting with public events and symposia, or assuming research assistant roles in faculty projects and courses. Strong bridges between undergraduate, graduate and research projects allow for mutually beneficial and enhanced learning outcomes for participants at all levels of learning.

Looking forward, this process leads inevitably to the establishment of research degrees. Though beyond the scope of this chapter, practice-led research can advance the field beyond praxis towards a more self-aware reflexive methodological engagement, and beyond the methods of practice towards an ontological positioning.

By way of conclusion: an international network of teaching

As the title of this chapter suggests, the ultimate aim is to encourage an international network of tertiary courses teaching community and social practice. It is a necessary step in the future development of community practice pedagogy. The detailed discussion of the three levels of tertiary education, as well as the case studies presented above, are essential in understanding the building blocks for an international pedagogic collaboration. In one sense, the classroom emulates 'good practitioner behaviour'. It is dialogic rather than unidirectional, exploratory rather than normative and future facing rather than canonical or historical. It offers a space to map out the breadth of practice, its threads and historical traces, mirroring the narrative style of working within community practice itself. The possibility of exploring new narratives requires open-mindedness and a capacity for responsive flexibility as a practitioner. It also requires a capacity to listen and unpack what is being said, in a hermeneutic sense, to unearth the deeper cultural threads of a community. Furthermore, understanding one's place within a larger landscape, and articulating the multiple relationships that this entails, reflects the work done with communities to understand and articulate themselves within local, national and international contexts.

An international network would also mirror community practice. The linking of courses into a global dialogue allows for the local, national and international frames of practice to become the frames of a broader pedagogy. By linking courses together, including the potential for staff and student exchange, we would cross-pollinate programmes and allow for more complex learning experiences. Ultimately, this is the most important step in the development of community practice pedagogy. The internationalizing of teaching will combine with the growing internationalization of practice, as well as the dialogues of practice. Furthermore, it would continue to impact upon research and the development of knowledge, both about community practice and the relationality of practice with other disciplines.

The epistemological revolution, which in one sense can only take place through teaching and research training, will hopefully spark an influx of writing and knowledge sharing. A corollary of this is the growing number of students who are willing to turn the research gaze not only upon their own practice but also upon the practice itself – to bring into question the sacred tenets of community practice, its historical contexts, as well as the changing world around practice and the influence of technologies. In doing so, the practice can now begin to freshen up, as it were, and to respond to the conditions of today and the perceived conditions of tomorrow. Here, the case is being made for the necessity for social and community practice education in art and design, at all levels of tertiary education. Yet this is just a microcosm of the argument for its inclusion in all art forms. It is imperative to provide students with the opportunity to study and train from the beginning of their undergraduate education all the way through research doctorates, if this field is to advance to its full potential.

We are keenly interested in seeing a network of pedagogy emerge, a global network of practitioners/educators with the capacity to share best practice in the field. The programmes at the University of Melbourne and Emily Carr University are just two examples of community and socially engaged art programmes, among a wide variety of both well-established and emergent programmes across a number of universities and colleges worldwide. Our hope is that this modest contribution to the discussion of pedagogy will help in moving the conversation forward and open up a space for dialogue and new research initiatives. There is also an acute need to discuss the ways in which educators and practitioners can be sustained and empowered to continue practising within this particular project of education, given the high degree of energy and commitment the pedagogy requires. Teaching in the context of social practice and public engagement requires new methodologies, new ways of thinking about faculty and administrative roles and the specific professional development that is required for educators. A good first step might be to find ways to share experiences, strategies and visions or, in other words, to work together in an act of pedagogical co-creation.

Given the complexity of the issues and conditions facing both art schools and cultures at large, an international network of social practice practitioner/educators would have the capacity to contribute to progressive educational reform where it is most needed. No one school or programme in any single nation state, can provide the depth and breadth of knowledge and experience, that will provide students with a full enough context to realize the complexity of the social, economic and environmental problems (crises) the world faces. Social practice and community-engaged educational programmes at the very least provide students with a methodology for dialogue across difference, an ethics of care and a conceptual toolbox within a field of creativity that enables understanding of mutuality and interdependence, leading to a dynamic social and cultural exchange of ideas and actions. If this were a movement, the educators would be among its leaders.

6

THROWING STONES IN THE SEA

Georg Simmel, social practice and the imagined world

Ted Purves

Introduction

In 2005, I was hired by the California College of the Arts, as a Professor of Social Practice. At the time, it was the first such appointment in the United States, and the position came with the explicit instruction to begin a graduate-level curriculum (which would evolve into the Social Practice Workshop) that specifically focused on artists' practice at the intersection between art and the public spheres.

The questions I began with are the same ones that I still consider, ten years later. How does art interact with the social world? What does it change? How does it work with specific communities, or serve to create them? How are the boundaries of a specific community even determined in a time of escalating globalization? How might the critical language of the arts apply to larger social forms? When does the practice of art bleed so far into other areas of 'participatory culture' that it becomes something else?

What has changed in the last ten years are the bodies of theories that I use to provide frameworks for the participants in the programme. Two years of graduate study is a very short time to refine one's art practice to focus on the social and public spheres – let alone to understand the complexities of sociology, political philosophy, economics and cultural studies that might be brought to bear when trying to understand even a small, local community with any level of depth. Over the past years, the theoretical framework that we work with has become increasingly considered. This chapter charts some of my own shifts in thinking about foundational texts, largely formed in response to observing and participating in the challenges that artists and other creative practitioners face when deciding 'what to do' with any given opportunity (or assignment) to work in public space.

One of the main points of this chapter that I am trying to express is that my own recent curriculum has been guided by a belief that diagnostic theoretical skills are more initially useful for artistic practices in the social/public sphere than theoretical skills in deconstruction or remediation (i.e., that the questions "where – or what or who – are we?" are more pressing to answer first than "what must be done – or what is wrong and how might it be repaired?"). Given this, it is worth stating that this text should not be taken as an inquiry into pedagogy per se. Its focus is on *what* to teach, rather than *how* to teach.

To that end, the chapter proposes that studying foundational social philosophers as well as contemporary anthropology that considers imagined communities, as well as actual ones, is perhaps a more useful theoretical beginning point than Marxist critique or Situationist aesthetics. The chapter does not recommend ignoring such critical readings; it mainly puts forward the idea that diagnostic readings provide a more solid starting point for understanding both the nature of a place, or site, or community, as well as the potential dynamics of how any action or project that they create might come to have relevance, meaning or traction, within public or social spaces.

To this end, I have found that a reading of Georg Simmel, focused specifically on his construction of the *social form*, is a solid beginning point. In general, Simmel's preoccupation with, and accounting for, the fragmentation that we experience in the course of our lives seems to predict our contemporary, information-laden, multilayered daily lives. Simmel's evocation of the ebb and flow of the self, as well as the sense that we traverse many different 'worlds' within a day of transaction, exchange and dialogue, are oddly contemporary. More specific to the context of an art programme, Simmel's writings on the existence and evolution of *social form* are equally prescient (Levine 1971, p. xxiv). His decision to base his sociology on the distinction between form and content dovetails quite functionally into foundational ideas from art education as it constructs a common language that associates more traditional ideas of form with other, more conceptual, extensions of the term. Simply put, it creates a unified field within which to understand how something as 'traditional' as a painting is connected to a relational artwork wherein daily free meals are served in a gallery.

The framework of social form has far-reaching implications for the consideration of the current landscape of social and public art practice, not simply because it extends a familiar art historical concept of form to a large group of artists' projects that seemed not to have succinct forms but, more importantly, because the consideration of social forms gives us a much more direct way to understand how such artists' projects interact with the rest of the world.

The second argument of this text is intertwined with the first, and is also concerned with the question of "what to teach?" In general, the theory curriculum of Masters'-level fine arts programmes is expected to be focused on bringing students up to date on current critical concepts of art practice, especially as these texts intersect with the goal of producing artworks that are 'in conversation' with issues and arguments within the specialized field of contemporary global art. One of the motivations for framing a curriculum in such a way is that it will help students to understand how their works will be understood in the locations within the art world (i.e. the gallery, art fair, project space or museum) that they intend to occupy.

However, for those artists who are specifically interested in making work outside of these identifiable cultural locations, such as a community or neighbourhood setting, or within a public or social space, this frame is only one of many ways that their work will be understood. To broaden this frame, I suggest it is useful to steer away from a focus on art theory and curatorial constructions, and instead to focus on contemporary thinking about the nature of the public and counter-public spheres, about how disagreement and conflict occur between individuals and groups in such spaces, and more specifically, about the experience of public space within the context of globalization. For this undertaking, authors such as Arjun Appadurai, Chantal Mouffe and Michael Warner are among those whom I have found to be particularly instructive. While highly individual in their approaches, such theorists share an underlying perspective on social and public spaces as being inherently *emergent* sites. In this way they are conceptually synergistic with the social theories of Simmel, which were similarly focused on fragmentation and change. Elizabeth Goodstein has remarked that Simmel "is a man of many renaissances, and he is discovered and rediscovered with disheartening regularity by sociologists, anthropologists, and cultural theorists of all stripes" (Goodstein 2002, p. 209). In my case, the following text is a modest, but hopeful, 'rediscovery' within the field of contemporary art.

As a final point of introduction, I would add that this 'rediscovery' of Simmel, and my subsequent incorporation of his ideas into a framework for understanding current trends in public and socially situated art, is not solely done for the sake of vindication of Simmel as a thinker. I am much more interested in using his ideas as a way to both frame and question the interplay of artists' projects and the social worlds they are attempting to act within and upon. These projects are attempting to work within the social world to alter its dynamics, based on a belief that alteration, encounter and renewal are inherently possible. This is a viewpoint that Simmel shared in his own time, and it thus makes sense to bring his ideas forward to understand how they might be used in a wholly new conversation.

The shop in two worlds

To understand Simmel's construction of the social, with its attendant forms and contents, it is useful to consider an actual event, a particular manifestation of an artwork within the fabric of the social world.

This picture (Figure 6.1) by the American artist David Hammons documents what has come to be one of his most iconic works. This particular artwork, *Blizaard Ball Sale* (1983), was a performance piece in which Hammons set up a blanket in Cooper Square (New York City) and proceeded to attempt to sell snowballs (priced according to size) amid the array of other street peddlers selling used or cast-off goods. The project took place shortly after a blizzard raged through the city that provided ample material for the production of the items for sale. This

FIGURE 6.1 *Bliz-aard Ball Sale* (1983), David Hammons. Photographer: Dawoud Bey. *Credit*: David Hammons.

work has been read as both a critique of the commodity nature of the art market, as well as a commentary on 'whiteness' and access to the art world. Steven Stern, in a 2009 article for *Frieze* magazine commented about this work as follows:

> The piece has become iconic, the single ephemeral work – a work that is essentially about ephemerality – that has come to stand for his entire practice. As it comes down to us in documentation, it is a portrait of the artist as an anonymous and disreputable pedlar, an absurdist street hustler. Hammons' notion of an artist includes a constant flirtation with notions of the illicit and the fraudulent – the ever-present suggestion that the whole business might be a scam.
>
> *(Stern 2009)*

Stern's assessment gives a good summary of how this work, which operated wholly within what could be termed 'the public sphere', has continued to accumulate meaning within the discourses of the art world. His analysis discusses the critical terms that have become leveraged in the debates of the art world – ephemerality, the image of the artist, as well as the racial and economic politics that the work elicits. In this process of estimation, we can see how *Bliz-aard Ball Sale* is understood in terms of style, how it creates *impact* within the dialogues of the art world. These impacts within the art world could be designated as its vertical effect – their movement shows us how this work, which was created in a specific place or time, rises into the art world, to take its place alongside other artworks – to argue with and among them.

Beyond the art world dialogue, and perhaps more crucially within the emerging discussions around social practice, we need to understand more about the *other* effects that this work generates, beyond simply those effects that are located within the art world. After all, one can assume that 99 per cent of the audience for this piece, at the time that it was created and in the space that it was created, would not have contextualized it as an artwork *per se*. What meanings and dialogues does this work challenge for this 99 per cent? While such a question might be almost impossible to answer with any certainty, it is nonetheless important to at least try to model such a thing. How then to understand what one might term its *lateral* or *horizontal* effects? How do we understand how this project affected the world that it actually lived in?

To accomplish this, we must imagine an alternate photograph, one where we see not only the 'performance' but also a bit more of where it took place and what was happening around it. After all, the location was Cooper Square, where, throughout the 1970s and 1980s, on any given day, one could encounter many, many street peddlers, each with a table, or rack or blanket, selling any number of reclaimed goods. It was a marketplace, albeit one of great precarity, and it was also highly specific to a particular set of racial and class constraints. So when we attempt to understand the horizontal effects of the piece, it is this horizon that must be considered. Hammon's blanket, in the eyes of the passers-by, worked its effects not on the world of art but on the immediate context of the blankets of the other merchants. To them, it might be suggested that Hammons was not creating an artwork – he was creating a *store*.

One way of understanding how this project operates for the 99 per cent[1] of its audience we considered above might, then, come from an assessment of the form that the artist chose to occupy. After all, the starting point for any traditional reading of a work of art begins with a consideration of form and content. That said, it is certainly the case that *Bliz-aard Ball Sale* did not manifest in a form that we would readily identify as an artwork. However, this does not mean that the work did not have form; rather, it means that we have to turn to other frameworks to understand the forms that it occupied.

As has been discussed earlier in this text, Georg Simmel's concept of *social form* is one place where we might turn. Simmel framed the concept of social form in this way:

> Any social phenomenon or process is composed of two elements which in reality are inseparable – on one hand, an interest, or purpose, or motive, on the other, a form or mode of interaction among individuals through which, or in the shape of which, that content attains social reality.
>
> *(Simmel 1908b, p. 24)*

Applying this framework to *Bliz-aard Ball Sale*, we could say that the artist used the social form of the peddler's shop/blanket, and filled it with specific contents, in this case the attempt to sell snowballs. Obviously, this is not a typical use of the form, but artists have rarely been required, or expected, to use forms in traditional ways; innovative occupation of forms is part and parcel of what artists do.

The useful thing about Simmel's construction of the social world in this situation is not just that his concept of social form gives us a way to understand how the shop that Hammons created functions as an artwork; he also gives us a way to understand more fully the tensions between the two different worlds that it exerts its effects upon and the differing forms that this piece seems to occupy.

It is important to begin with an understanding of 'the social' in the way that Simmel conceived it, as his construction of the social world positioned its existence entirely *between* people. Simmel writes:

> Strictly speaking, neither hunger, nor love, work nor religiosity, technology nor the functions and results of intelligence are social. They are factors in sociation only when they transform the mere aggregation of individuals into specific forms of being with and for one another.
>
> *(ibid., p. 24)*

What this means is that the social world is not something that we experience solely within ourselves. It is possible that we are incapable of truly experiencing 'the social' on our own (though we may dwell upon it); it arises only when we are in contact with others. When we are in contact with others, it is our own 'contents' that we act with and upon, the interests we seek to advance, but these contents then become negotiated or modified by others. Olli Pyyhtinen writes: "The social does not assume a lasting and substantial existence by itself . It is processual by nature and comes into existence in the brief instant of the event" (Pyyhtinen 2008, p. 189). The social, then, is inherently *between*.

Social forms, as constructed by Simmel and described above, are those structures which then can be thought to order this *between-ness*. They can be something concrete, like a shop or a trade union, or something more ephemeral, like a meeting or a lunch date, but in all instances, they function something like a grammar or a syntax for the ongoing babble of exchanges that we instigate and receive, back and forth, within the horizon of the social. A social form such as a shop, whether it is a peddler's blanket, a table at a farmers' market, or a large drugstore, will be recognizable to us in terms of its form, and through it, we will anticipate, somewhat, the range of encounters that might occur within, the ways that we are 'with and for' the proprietor, or the person at the cashier's desk. Social forms, then, help us manage our interactions with others, and organize the immensity of the social.

What is key to his thought was an essential belief in the fragmentation, or transience, that occurs between these two categories, wherein forms can take on the role of contents, and contents can accrete into forms. This structure then is based on the idea that the 'social', and thus society itself, is perpetually in formation. It is always becoming, and, as such, does not exist as a fixed entity.

Returning to the *Bliz-aard Ball Sale*, we have been able to use Simmel to account for its lateral effects, which are understood through the lens of the social world it was located in. How to account for its vertical ascent, the part of it that was never really a store at all? How do we account for the part of it that was an artwork? In his construction of contemporary life, Simmel describes not just social forms and content but also forms of culture. Culture is not social. Where the social arises between people in response to interaction, forms of culture arise in the self, how the self thinks of relations to religion, to the past, to beauty, to love, to aesthetics, etc. He theorized that as these cultural forms accrete, they become worlds, orbiting the daily, lived world (Levine 1971, p. xvii). They are separate from social forms, yet at the same time they interact fully with social forms, giving them places to belong in an individual's life.

Simmel believed that these cultural worlds grew larger and more self-referential, or autonomous, as time moved forward and the cultural thoughts and productions of humans, contributed to their evolution and ongoing articulation. *Bliz-aard Ball Sale*, the part of it that was an artwork (the performance piece) is a part of such a world – a form within it. As it grew more renowned, as it was exhibited and as it became written about, its location within that particular cultural realm, the 'art world', became more fixed, and its life as a social form in the social world slipped away to the past.

There is one more aspect of Simmel's construction of the social to consider in regard to the *Bliz-aard Ball Sale*, as well as a host of other artworks that have manifested in social forms. Simmel believed that while there were endless social forms evolving and falling into disuse across the breadth of society, these forms fell into two larger categories. The first, which we have already discussed, he saw as tied to praxis. They are the forms through which we address our needs through interaction with others. He identified the second category as "play forms" of the social. These forms, which include such things as games or coquetry, do not serve a real need, and exist because there are times in our lives when we wish to 'play' at the social. "Devoid of pragmatic content, they exist for those moments where we wish to participate in the 'world' of society as an end in itself" (Levine 1971, p. xxvi). This, then, is one further lens through which to consider the *Bliz-aard Ball Sale*. A shop, seemingly a pragmatic social form, situated amid others on Cooper Square, is doubling as another social form altogether, 'playing' at the idea of the shop, and of the sales and interactions that might arise if someone would be such a fool as to buy a white snowball. In its relationship to the stores around it, Hammon's work takes on a different creative tone, one that is wholly within the social world at the same time that it seeks to exert pressures on the boundaries of forms around it.

This, of course, was the explicit mission of a project such as the *Diggers Free Store* – an activist shop originally created in San Francisco in 1967 by members of the San Francisco Diggers, a group based in radical theatre practices, who sought to manifest actions as ongoing, social manifestations that actively performed an alternate social reality. They served free food in the Haight-Ashbury neighbourhood every afternoon, and distributed free newspapers, conducted drug awareness clinics and organized places for young vagrants to stay. Their store was like a thrift shop but one where anything within the store – even the cash register – was free. Anyone who walked in could take on the task of managing the store, or could do nothing at all. Its explicit purpose was to pose questions to the shops on either side: can they be free as well? What if there were no scarcity of things? Of food? Of clothes? What if the only thing that there was a scarcity of was money? What happens when that is removed from the equation?

We can see another aspect of this lateral pressure, (perhaps even its contrapositive manifestation) in a more recent 'shop' created by the Melbourne-based artist Anastasia Klose. Klose has worked since the mid-2000s on a body of situational, interactive work that frequently takes place in the public, or in the case of works involving her mother, the private sphere. Much of it incorporates an everyday, almost DIY, aesthetic and makes use of casual interactions with strangers and passers-by. I had an opportunity to see her recent shop project *One Stop Knock-Off Shop*, which was featured in the *Melbourne Now* exhibition at the National Gallery of Victoria. The project was set up as a shop, staffed for the entire exhibition by the artist as sole worker/shopkeeper, in the midst of the exhibition galleries, surrounded by paintings, photographs and installations.

FIGURE 6.2 *One Stop Knock-Off Shop* (2014), Anastasia Klose.
Credit: Anastasia Klose/Tolarno Galleries.

The shop sold T-shirts designed by Klose, each of which featured a slightly misspelled name of a blue-chip contemporary artist (Ai Weiwei, Tracey Emin and others) or other bits of text and team numbers. The merchandise inhabited the form and language of 'knock-off' clothing produced in peripheral markets which attempts to associate itself by look and style to name-brand fashions produced by the global brands (in other words, the real players). At the same time, the shop, as well as its contents and presentation, performed and framed a rough analogy to Klose herself – the knock-off, peripheral artist in a regional exhibition – pulling in names of the famous and the fabulous to somehow harness their marketable aura.

While it was an effective piece on its own conceptual terms, I was struck at the time how it was also subject to the lateral pressure created by tension around its form and context. In Figure 6.2 you can see the key – the artist has written a hasty sign that declares "this is a real shop". [2] It is one thing to create a shop in a storefront or a market, where the social form is readily contextualized and where we, as social participants, are ready to become shoppers (or at least browsers) without breaking stride. It is quite another to place a shop in a museum (itself an outpost of the art world) and have it push against all of the neighbouring forms (which are most likely cultural forms), and to have them push back. This pushing-back occurs every time that a person wandering into the gallery and into this 'real shop' stops being a viewer or audience member and becomes a shopper instead.

In their disruption of forms, all of the preceding shops, from the Diggers' to Klose's, align with Simmel's overall belief in the fragmented and shifting nature of social forms and contents. He believed that the trajectory of society and social form was not linear, and that its destiny was to become ever more diverse, idiosyncratic, non-unified. The forms are challenged constantly by our needs for them, by the contents we fill them with and by the interactions we wish those contents to manifest in the world. Simmel, it is likely, did not conceive of the specific possibility that artists would occupy a social form for the purpose of switching pragmatic interaction for critique and sociability, but it is also highly possible that he would understand the cultural shifts that necessitate such a manoeuvre. Moreover, it could be said that Simmel's theories actually anticipate the necessity of such a possibility.

Society does not progress towards unity and flatness – a singular future. Rather, we inhabit a landscape of change and growth, both vital and entropic. Simmel believed that "the energy inherent in life to create forms that transcend life is a force towards cultural diversity, not unity" (Levine 1971, p. *xvi*). In such a world, Simmel believed that the task of the sociologist, and the social philosopher, was to immerse oneself in that landscape and seek to discover the complexity of its forms, and understand them through discrete analysis with an eye towards revealing their structural implications (ibid.: *xxxi*). I hold forth the belief that this unfolding, shifting world of new forms and unexpected contents is brought closer by such critical, idiosyncratic occupations of social form that the preceding works utilize.

To return briefly to a thought that ended the introduction of this chapter, this is a point where we are not simply bringing Simmel forward for the sake of what Pyyhtinen calls "presentism", wherein we are simply using Simmel to account for the operations of the world. Rather, we are "mutating his 'code' to a new environment" (Pyyhtinen 2008, p. 33): in this case, a world more fragmented than the one he inhabited; one which not only has a staggering range of cultural worlds overlaid upon it but also includes layers of digital proximity and virtual *sociation*, where we are *with and for one another* in surprisingly new ways. His 'code' then, might be of some value for testing the limits and potentials of the contemporary world that despite the shift in complexity is still deeply social. The nature of this world is where we turn to next.

Artistic activity and the world-at-large

Curriculum starts with students. The students that have decided to attend our programme have arrived with a wide array of backgrounds that have led them to commit to a Master of Fine Arts course in Social Practice. In general, their interest in the programme stems from a desire to produce works such as those described in the preceding section (i.e. work within the social sphere that challenges forms and engages audiences and communities in active and innovative ways). For many years, some of the early curriculum that the students have been given is an array of contemporary art writings that give an accounting of the last two decades of work in the social and public sphere. These texts are accompanied by a series of survey lectures where a range of works and projects are shown (or screened). Taken together, these introductory readings and lectures come together to create a common language of reference through which the students come to understand the field they intend to occupy, at least insofar as it relates to the discourse of the world of contemporary art.

While these writings shed light on the art world that their projects sought to be in dialogue with, they are not always as helpful for the students as they work to understand how their projects might be understood within the various social/ public locations in which they are situated. As we have seen with the example of David Hammon's *Bliz-aard Ball Sale*, the public and social context, more often than not, makes the estimation of a work's impact or meaning more complex. When one is working in the public sphere, the meanings and dialogues of the art world run parallel to other, multiple sets of meanings and dialogues. It is difficult to account for how a work is met in public when one's critical lens is focused solely through theories crafted to secure practices within the history of art.

The important thing to note here is one of location and context. Much of the project work that is done in the context of a social/public art practice is only loosely identifiable as 'artwork' in a common sense of the word. These projects occupy places in the city that do not immediately establish them as 'official' artworks, or they manifest as media (such as a T-shirt sold in a shop, or even the shop itself) that are shared by similar, 'non-art' versions of the medium. In either case, they do not enter the public realm in places or forms that are readily associated with either artwork (or the art world). Instead they enter a much more complex place, something that I have termed the "world-at-large".

The "world-at-large" is a term that I began using in 2003 to describe a world of encounter that has the potential to take place in public and social spheres. At that time, I was not focused so deeply on a 'Simmelian' construction of the world, and saw the world-at-large simply as a space where artworks in a public space would be understood primarily in connection to the surrounding public context, to the social space they exist within, rather than being over-determined by their status as artworks. However, with a more thorough reading of Simmel in hand, the world-at-large is actually more specifically understandable as a space fully within the social that is also located *between* any particular cultural world, where no one reading of the cultural form is hegemonic. In such a space, the encounter within a social form is less bounded and more open to conscious, active and emergent exchange.

This question, the mapping out of the world-at-large, was not always the starting point for my theory courses. For many years, these courses began with a range of readings that constructed a critical view of the contemporary world with an eye towards understanding its politics, issues and inequities. These readings began, often, with Marx's writings on labour and alienation, and moved towards the present, examining power, class and privilege through feminism, decolonial theory and writings on the public and counter-public spheres. These courses would also include Situationist writings, which provided, at least, a link to art's ability to provide a powerful critique of capital, leisure and boredom. However, these readings often proved a difficult place to start for the students in our programme, as they are based on a critical analysis of the constructions of – and dynamics of power within – our contemporary world, but they provide little suggestion for how to address the various inequities and contradictions at an individual level. While these readings are extremely relevant for artists working in the public or social realms, after beginning the course in this way several times, I realized they were not axiomatic enough to allow the students to understand what the world-at-large is about, and from that, how they might come to affect it.

Making sense of this world-at-large becomes the real question for understanding how to make choices about practice, form and aesthetics when undertaking an art project in a space where it might not have any ready contextualization as such a thing. This particular challenge also underscores what might be the primary defining difference – from a pedagogical standpoint in any case – between the curricula of a wide variety of contemporary arts practices programmes and those, such as the Social Practice Workshop, that specifically focus on social and public art. On the one hand, you are mentoring students to produce works and projects that, by and large, are designed to be understood or *read* within a particular set of discourses and, on the other hand, you are teaching them the possibility that their works and projects might be read as anything but art.

How then, do we understand the world-at-large? More to the point: if one were dropped into a residency or a civic commission, or tasked by the engagement curator from a museum to work with the surrounding neighbourhood, or faced with an invitation to produce a project for a live art festival, what would one propose? From a pedagogical standpoint, what body of philosophy or range of readings would one compile to aid in navigating this transit – from the individual artist to the world-at-large – and on to the possibility of creating meaning, communication or change?

Horizons

This question of lateral effect – of making one's presence and impact felt locally, nearby, upon neighbouring sites and forms – runs against the many patterns and desires that we commonly associate with cultural production; at least as they are internalized by many, if not most, of those involved in the world of contemporary art practice. While we walk through the world, the daily lived world, where we eat, sleep, breathe and work, we feel a continued pressure to look upwards – to see how we might be reflected in those worlds that hover above us. There are many other worlds, a whole host of them: the financial world, the fashion world, the first world, the third world, and, most prominently in this discussion, the art world. Each of these worlds, however unreal they are, intrudes into the world we walk through – they demand our attention, and create the 'professional' or 'cultural' context for whatever meanings our projects or interactions might have.

This text has touched upon Simmel's conception of cultural forms and the "worlds" they create. What is important to consider is how these cultural worlds, these separate, autonomous spheres, make an impact within the world of the social. How does a social location, such as a clothing store, become tied to an orbiting cultural world, to a Prada boutique or, alternatively, to the overstocked world of a dollar store? In social terms, each of these stores is full of clothing to put on our bodies, and each is staffed with workers who will give us the clothes in exchange for money. However, the weight of cultural worlds also bears upon them, in terms of class, style and status; it makes us feel differently about them, and about ourselves in relation to them. In this way, 'autonomous' cultural forms actually become social contents that we act upon through social forms (Levine 1971, p. xxviii).

The cultural worlds of Simmel can be seen as conceptually related to an array of contemporary theories of globalization, most notably those of Arjun Appadurai, who named a the variety of 'scapes' – *technoscapes, ethnoscapes, financescapes, ideoscapes* and *mediascapes* that form a tangible, yet imaginary, set of landscapes that we move through. Each of these "scapes" is simultaneously unhinged from actual distance in time and space, yet each also overlays itself over the surface of the world (Appadurai 1990). In Appadurai's text, he remarks:

> These landscapes thus are the building blocks of what, extending Benedict Anderson, I would like to call 'imagined worlds', that is the multiple worlds which are constituted by the historically situated imaginations of persons and groups spread around the globe.
>
> *(ibid., p. 297)*

Through this invocation of an imagined world, Appadurai ties the 'scapes' directly to Benedict Anderson's idea of an "Imagined Community", whereby an idea of society is maintained not through the actual encounter with others in daily life but through an imagined idea of belonging that is contained within the self (such as being a citizen of a country).[3] This is, quite literally, a country of the mind, albeit one with very real legal and physical manifestations.

The 'scapes' also draw on the related concept of the *Social Imaginary*, which is a term that has emerged in contemporary social philosophy primarily through the writings of Charles Taylor. Taylor writes that a social imaginary is constituted through "the ways people imagine their social existence, how they fit together with others, how things go on between them and their fellows, the expectations that are normally met, and the deeper normative notions and images that underlie these expectations" (Taylor 2004, p. 24). Members of a society hold social imaginaries of many things, such as the American dream, or the idea of the rural, but they are distinguished from concepts such as cultural myths or social traditions by an inherent *plasticity*. Unlike myths, their specifics can shift over time and are highly contextual.

To help envisage the horizons that such 'scapes' produce, we can consider an artist's project created by the Polish-born, New York-based artist Elisabeth Smolarz. For this project, Smolarz travelled for a period of six years to each of the G8 +5 member countries. In each country, while in its capital, she advertised for local day labourers, or unemployed workers, to be hired for an hour of work. When the workers in each country responded to the advertisement, Smolarz negotiated with them to hire as many of them for an hour as $100.00 (in its equivalent local currency) would afford, and arranged with them what they would do for that hour. In most European countries, she was able to hire three workers. In India, she hired 36. The hired labourers would sit in a room, generally with a table, chairs and light refreshments for an hour, and do whatever they wanted. These activities included talking, playing games, singing and so on. A stationary camera recorded their activity for the hour (Purves 2014, p. 151).Through this project, then, one particular horizon of the 'finance-scape' comes into view.

Extending beyond Smolarz's work, we can look at a broad array of contemporary social-artists' projects in light of the horizons that they bring into view. Through this lens, they are not simply repurposing social form, they are contributing equally to a re-estimation of geography. In this case, however, it is not a notion of the physical world but an amalgamation of the cultural world that Simmel proposes, and our social imaginary of that world, modified by the shifting horizons of Appadurai's concept of 'scapes'.

Social practice and encounter

Shifting back to where this chapter began, to the space of teaching socially based art practices, it is worth repeating that it's difficult to 'teach' an artist how to make a public artwork. The disciplines and structures of teaching art do not favour this sort of undertaking; and, as was mentioned earlier, the constraints of a Master's programme do not often support a long-term engagement with a community, if they are even able to provide a community to work with. These conditions make the production of 'traditional' public artworks problematic within a typical art curriculum.

However, I believe that the texts we considered in the prior two sections provide a different way to think through this situation. It might not be necessary to have to teach artists a 'craft' of public art, or a medium of social practice. The manipulation of form and the exploration of the imagination, after all, are part and parcel of the very basic training that any artist undertakes. To extend this facility and training into social forms, and to explore a shared social imaginary allows for (at least on the level of analogy) a similar application of practices. Where once the primary task of an artist was to draw upon their imagination to manifest subjectivities in a given material form, we have expanded the scope of that equation to suggest that artists interested in the public and social practice work in the realm of shared imaginaries and tactically occupy social forms.

Of course, in the world-at-large, these creations in social form have just as much chance to be understood as shops, dinner parties or lotteries (for example) as they do to be understood as artworks. But I would contend that this is only a problem if your primary goal as an artist is to create artworks. In my time as educator and observer of the field, I've learned that this is not always the underlying concern for those who are interested in pursuing this type of work.

In the first place, the history of contemporary art has given decades of examples of how project-based work that unfolds through process or relation can marshal its documentation to later manifest as artworks. As *Bliz-aard Ball Sale* demonstrates, a project doesn't need to be understood as an artwork in Cooper Square for it to become an artwork in the history books. Beyond this, it has become clear that many artists who work in public and social space do not simply aspire for this art world re-estimation as the end point for their project. Instead, I would contend that many of these artists are interested in using the position of an artist and the occupation of social forms to produce moments of *encounter*.

Encounter, in this case, is that moment when we are confronted with an 'Other'. However this 'Other' is not simply a thing that is separate from ourselves; it is an encounter with someone that makes us realize our own individuality by experiencing them as an active, and largely unknown, entity – an undiscovered country. This construction of encounter and the 'Other' is clearly outlined in the spiritual philosophy of Martin Buber, who famously stated, in his book *I and Thou*, that "all life is encounter". *I and Thou* is a far-reaching work that spans between social philosophy and theology. In this work, Buber:

> Outlined a theory of existence consisting of the constant negotiation between the 'word-pairs' I-It and I-Thou. The world of the I-It is cognitive, formed by the functioning of the mind. Never gaining entry into lived experience, this world is external, uninhabited, except for a collection of objects which

one observes at a distance... The world of the I-Thou pairing is an actual world of encounter: a process of holistic subjectification in which the individual exists in relation with others and the world around her. Rooted in lived experience, to speak the I-Thou pair is to recognize the other as an active agent with whom we can speak.

(Rana 2008, p. 13)

Buber's construction of the twofold world of encounter is echoed by a host of philosophers and theorists who place the space of recognition of otherness, and the negotiation of others, at the heart of our social processes. Berlin-based writer and poet Matthew Rana, whose overview of Buber's construction of "I and Thou" is quoted above, draws connections between this work and the linguistic philosophy of Mikhail Bakhtin, who believed that the meaning of language (and thus our filter for the world) is generated primarily *between* people ("the dialogic"), rather than in the personal spaces of our minds (Rana 2008, p. 12).

The realm of the encounter finds further articulation in twentieth-century constructions of both the social world and the public sphere, and brings our attention back to the writings of Simmel, and his evocation of a social world that comes into being only between individuals. At the same time, this construction of a world where meaning arises entirely in the space of encounter can extend to such theorists as Hannah Arendt, who saw the space of the public sphere as a zone of contestation, where the *self* is measured against the *other* and, through this process, allows the individual public expression and selfhood to emerge. A third author, and one much more contemporary to our times, whose writings have bearing on this issue, is the French theorist Chantal Mouffe. Mouffe's theories of *agonism* and *dissensus* chart ways in which a contemporary society can work through the inevitable conflicts that arise when encounter creates disagreement and debate, with a particular focus on how a society, or community, can navigate disagreement without fundamental rupture – where adversaries do not necessarily become enemies.

One further layer of thought emerges from Louis Althusser's writings on the encounter that elevates the encounter from a zone of connection to one of catalytic potential. In his text, *The Underground Current of the Materialism of the Encounter*, Althusser traces a thread of aleatory materialism, beginning with Lucretius's rain of parallel atoms, in which one swerves off course to strike another. Thus begins a history of the encounter, which the author tracks through the course of western philosophy, revealing a history of materialism that ignores the overriding discourse of individual freedom and sees instead a world where encounters produce the fact of the world, not individual willpower. This construction of encounter is not simply aleatory; when an encounter 'takes hold', it becomes fixed enough to alter the world around it. The encounter is the accomplishment of the fact of the world – it produces the world in its wake (Althusser 2006, p. 6).

While much of the writing about encounter is specifically addressing the encounter between two individuals, the participatory characteristic of most public and social practices allows for a similar analysis and, in terms of Althusser, also holds out the hope of catalytic outcomes. The pressure of effect between forms and contents is an opportunity for an encounter to *take hold*. The Scottish writer Anne Douglas commented as follows on her public blog, *On The Edge Research*:

> This is an encounter between conventional social phenomena and a provocation made by the artists... that offer reversals of the convention. This is not a merging of art into the social. It appears more like an interval of distance in which the private, singular world of an individual makes a momentary appearance within the social, disrupting it gently.
>
> *(Douglas 2014)*

Conclusion

Considering *encounter* as the primary product of social and public art practices shifts its primary goal away from some of the more teleological purposes that have been required of public art throughout its history. While these earlier results-oriented goals, which include national commemoration or community representation (ranging from public sculpture to neighbourhood murals) as well as the instigation of social action (such as the tradition of posters, pamphleteering and political graphics and, by extension, graffiti and agitprop theatre) have not necessarily receded; they have become increasingly complicated within our globalized, multicultural society. While the encounter itself might be the creative goal of contemporary social and public practices, these issues of representation and social action are still potential outcomes from the accomplishment of the encounter.

Given this, the critical questions that attend public and social art are still highly relevant: What constitutes a community? Who belongs to it, and what designates its boundaries? Who has the privilege to represent it? To what effect do we commit art projects to activism, and – having aligned art with activism – how do we reconcile the art world's interests (which are meritocratic and economic) with its social interests (which may lie elsewhere)? These questions create the framework for the next layer of readings and investigations, which are chosen to examine the uses and distributions of power, the analyses of the spectacle, the politics of difference; all of these many other readings are the ones which the reader might remember were the starting point of my earlier curricula in the early years of this programme.

As I suggested at the outset, these questions are vital, as they outline the many, many things that we might want to direct our practices to affect, or to overturn. They construct a set of reasons *why* such changes have urgency. What Simmel and these other foundational readings of the world-at-large discussed in this text offer is a *where* and a *how*. They aid in the sorting of our *vertical* aspirations from our *lateral* interactions. To move the world, after-all, one must be able to see its edges. The view of the horizon is the seed of agency.

Notes

1 Such photographs are available and can be found through a diligent internet search. They rarely accompany any official documentation of the work, however.

2 In visiting the artist's website (https://anastasiaklose.wordpress.com), it is apparent that the particular handwritten sign was not part of the original set up for the shop, as it is not in the original photograph. In conversation, I was told by Klose that she had added it in after the show had been open for a bit, since the first question most people asked her was whether this was a real shop or whether it was a performance.

3 For more on this, consult Anderson (1991).

7

OPEN ENGAGEMENT

Accessible education for socially engaged art

Jen Delos Reyes

The Open Engagement (OE) conference (Figure 7.1) is the organized chaos of my life. It is perpetual trial by fire. It is also the most formative educational time of my adult life. The unruliness and emergent education I have received through these events were ones that felt akin to what Peter Marin described in his article *The Open Truth and the Fiery Vehemence of Youth: A Soliloquy of Sorts* (1970) in which he reflects on his intensive and immersive participatory research on adolescence and education. In setting up his contribution, he describes his state and the forthcoming writing as follows:

> I have chosen an eccentric method of composition, one that may seem fragmentary, jumpy, and broken. This article will be more like a letter, the letter itself an accumulation of impressions and ideas, a sampling of thoughts at once disconnected but related. There is a method to it that might appear in its mild madness, but I do not know at this juncture how else to proceed. Shuffling through my notes I feel like an archaeologist with a mass of uncatalogued shards. There is a pattern to all this, a coherence of thought, but all I can do here is assemble the bits and pieces and lay them out for you and hope that you get a sense how I got from one place to another.
>
> *(ibid., p. 134)*

Like Marin, this reflection may seem scattered. It might feel like a collection of fragments and pieces. These are what I have managed to gather over the years while in the centre of the storm, trying to organize the myriad of conversations and actions swirling around the world, reflecting on socially engaged art. I hope that this collection can serve as a kind of archive of these attempts and activities toward documenting the increased movement of artists working in this way, and that like any archive that it is imbued with the promise of agency, giving the power of

FIGURE 7.1   Open Engagement visual identity evolution, Jen Delos Reyes.
Credit: Nicole Lavelle.

making sense and meaning to its readers and users. I hope that this information, as unkempt as it is, can provide some insight and education into these gatherings. In addition, the language might feel plain, straight spoken or even veering into stream of consciousness. Like bell hooks (1994, p. 71), I have written elsewhere and shared my decisions around writing style in public talks:

> Not using conventional academic forms is not only a position motivated by the desire for accessibility, but for me it is also so that the writing about social art can be as open and public as much of the artwork. Writing about these practices needs to be as accessible as the works themselves, so they can work in tandem as allies, and together help to shape the world we want to see.
>
> *(Delos Reyes 2014, pp. 266–9)*

In socially engaged art, there is potential for an open-ended quality that allows for the viewer to become a participant and contributor to content and meaning, often in unexpected ways. These projects can be very flexible in design, allowing for the works to grow and change with immediate feedback from the audiences. Openness is at the core of this project and allows participants not only to help create the structure of Open Engagement but to also input various meanings and create numerous experiences.

Since 2007 Open Engagement has become a vital international site for the support and development of socially engaged art. It has convened presenters and attendees from around the world to share current perspectives and approaches to this work. It also brings together museum professionals and Master of Fine Art (MFA) programmes working in social and public engagement –making it a key meeting point for development in these areas. Open Engagement creates a platform that explores and supports the work of transdisciplinary artists, activists, students, scholars, community members and organizations. The conference mission is to expand the dialogue around socially engaged art, as well as the structures and networks of support for artists working within the complex social issues and struggles of our time. This accessible, low-cost/no-cost conference is an essential educational resource that delivers workshops that assist in providing attendees with skills and tools that support their work in communities and embedded contexts.

This chapter traces the evolution of the conference from its beginnings as a graduate project, its rebirth as a pedagogical framework, its role as a primary site for the emerging conversations on socially engaged art, to its ambitions to create a national consortium. What follows is a combination of writing about the conference that I have done – including reflections and previously unpublished work, case studies – and excerpts of writing that has appeared in print and online. This contribution will look at the structure of the conference, the relationship to artist-run and free culture, institutionalization, as well as year-by-year case study logistics and summaries. The overviews highlight the overarching events and contributions to the field, while the highlighted quotes from each year zoom in on specific thinking around the events and socially engaged art. The case studies outline the themes of each year, as well as the people who created the framework and made the conference happen. These year-by-year accounts make visible the networks of individual and institutional support that make the conference a reality. The case studies also chart the evolution of Open Engagement from foundation for an education, to the basis of a framework for teaching outside of the classroom, to developing a site that is in itself a free and accessible education for socially engaged art.

The origins of Open Engagement

Open Engagement: Art After Aesthetic Distance was the first iteration of the conference, and began as a hybrid project that used a conference on socially engaged art practices as its foundation, incorporating elements including workshops, exhibitions, residencies, pedagogy, curatorial practice and collaboration. I wanted to foster a different kind of conference – one that worked in the way I wanted to see it work: with a sense of togetherness, putting emerging and established voices side by side, highlighting different ways of knowing and learning and serving as a site of production as well as reflection. I wanted to contribute to the discourse on socially engaged art in a meaningful way. When Open Engagement began, it was a student project. I was a graduate student. The conversations that I wanted to engage in were not happening at my school in Saskatchewan, so I decided to create a situation that would allow me to have these discussions with people doing similar work.

Open Engagement was the basis of my education, and has been a major foundation of my work as an educator.

It is worth spending time at the beginning and seeing how the foundation of the event began, as many of these elements and approaches continue to factor into how and why the conference is organized. It remains a conference that is free, and programmed through an open call for submissions. It remains a conference that looks at the structure of organizing the event as a support for and integration of creative strategies and approaches. It continues to be a site that reflects the current climate of socially engaged art.

Open Engagement began by defining the project as my MFA thesis. After the conceptualization and research phase came the logistical organization, which consisted of assembling a conference planning committee, drafting a budget for the project and applying for funding. In an attempt to appeal to students, I promoted the planning committee as a place to develop organizational skills, work with experts and enthusiastic novices and develop friendships. I met Warren Bates during a project I did at the university gallery exploring participation and group work called *Make It Happen '06*. Bates was a regular presence in the gallery during the exhibition, participating in nearly all of the daily activities. His passion for the project was evident as each day he would explain the activities to visitors and encourage them to participate. Seeing his interest and voluntary commitment to *Make It Happen '06* motivated me to invite him to be the Lead Conference Assistant of *Open Engagement: Art After Aesthetic Distance*. Another person connected to *Make It Happen '06* and *Open Engagement: Art After Aesthetic Distance* is Kristy Fyfe. I met her during the exhibition, to which she also regularly contributed, and learned that she was a business student at the University of Regina. I encouraged her to combine her love of the fine arts with her career path and join the planning committee. Recent University of Regina MFA graduate Jeff Nye was also invited to sit on the planning committee. As a specialist in contemporary art theory, Nye offered his opinions, since his research focused on social art. The last member to join the committee was Andrea Young, who I met while a Teaching Assistant for Art 280[1] in 2006. Finally, my role on the planning committee was formally defined as the Conference Director, though my actual role was much more flexible.

In the early stages of development, the planning committee had monthly meetings to discuss progress. The first group meeting took place nearly one year prior to *Open Engagement: Art After Aesthetic Distance* in the fall of 2006. By the winter of 2006, I had written the call for submissions, designed the logo and produced a poster call for submissions. The process of disseminating the call was extensive. A mailing list of art schools and departments, galleries, museums, social practice artists and writers, artist-run centres, local high schools and local elementary schools was created. This list consisted of nearly 400 addresses worldwide, including locations in Canada, the United States, Asia and Europe. The call for submissions was also widely circulated through the internet using emails, listservs, MySpace, Facebook and the conference website. A detailed schedule of the conference was established next, along with finding local volunteers, and making connections with local art organizations and institutions to achieve the support needed for the project. *Open Engagement: Art After Aesthetic Distance* was a socially engaged art project that, like many others, had the following motivations, which Maria Lind outlines in her essay "The Collaborative Turn" (2007). Lind examines some of the possible driving forces behind some of the socially engaged art works that emerged in the 1990s:

> A common explanation is the wish to practice generosity and sharing as an alternative to contemporary individualism and the traditional role of the romantic artist as solitary genius. Self-determination in an ever more instrumentalised artworld, both commercially and publicly, and a desire to be a more powerful force in society have also been mentioned as important motivations. Not to forget the fun involved with working with others and the practical advantages of sharing tasks according to specialities and preferences. In certain cases, the need for infrastructure...self-promotion and a desire to achieve success in the artworld.
>
> *(ibid., p. 28)*

Open Engagement: Art After Aesthetic Distance enabled me to work with friends, addressed issues surrounding the notion of artist as solitary genius and allowed for the promotion of other artists. This project leveraged my organized, approachable and controlled demeanour, my strong skills as an administrator and my ability to bring together groups of individuals. Another motivation stems from the rigorous demands put on me during the course of my MFA programme. I was, and am still, in a constant state of questioning and examining socially engaged art practices. While I found this high level of critical engagement beneficial, I also saw the need for a support system of people who practice this type of art making. Through *Open Engagement: Art After Aesthetic Distance* I tested my practice, my ideas of socially engaged art and came to better understand my relationship with my work and my relationship to the pedagogy of social art. I endeavoured to include these ideas into classes, creating debates within the faculty, and exposing students to a medium – the social.

Open Engagement, artist-led culture and the value and cost of a free conference

It is important to note that the context of the first Open Engagement is in the legacy of Canadian artist-run and artist-led culture. While my personal reverence for artist-run culture was a core belief in organizing the conference in an inclusive and artist-driven way, there was criticism received about the organizational process that I had not anticipated. I reflected on this feedback for a publication by YYZ, *Decenter: Concerning Artist-Run Culture* (Delos Reyes 2008):

> As I write this I am in the aftermath of organizing a conference on socially engaged art practices titled *Open Engagement: Art After Aesthetic Distance*. This

conference would not have been possible without the support of not only my academic institution and SSHRC, but also the local community and artists who worked together to develop projects, assist artists and run the event.

For *Open Engagement* a group of artists and volunteers picked up out-of-town contributors at the airport holding a banner that read, "We are here for you". This banner made me think about some of the reasons behind the idea of an artist-run culture: a need for a system of support from your peers, encouragement and the dissemination of contemporary art.

To make this conference a reality a close-knit system of artists and volunteers has been assembled to house and feed the conference contributors and help facilitate the projects and research. One of the artists contributing to *Open Engagement* was confused by the absence of artist fees. She felt that by setting up this alternative space for the creation of new art works and research as an academic conference, which does not require paying artists fees, we were going against the work that has been done by artists to ensure fair payment for the arts in Canada. She was surprised an artist would organize this event: "If we don't stand up for each other, who will?" she proclaimed.

A system of financial support for artists is integral. I am grateful that artists worked to create some of these systems, but we must remember that all of the grassroots work done by our predecessors was not just for fair pay for the arts, it was also about creating a community of support. This is one of the greatest strengths of artist run culture. After all, if we aren't here for each other, who will be?

(Delos Reyes 2008, pp. 76–7)

Since 2007, Open Engagement has maintained its position as a free conference that does not charge presenters or attendees. How this is possible is a combination of resourcefulness, shifting what a system can do/who a system is for, institutional support and countless hours of invisible labour. What kind of space does something that is free create? What does it mean that what creates that 'free' space is an art practice? What are its unique potentials? In Irit Rogoff's (2011) essay "Free", she outlines several relevant questions:

1. First and foremost what is knowledge when it is "free"?
2. Whether there are sites, such as the spaces of art, in which knowledge might be more "free" than in others?
3. What are the institutional implications of housing knowledge that is "free"?
4. What are the economies of "free" that might prove an alternative to the market-and-outcome-based and comparison-driven economies of institutionally structured knowledge at present?

(Rogoff 2011, p. 184)

"What is the real cost of a free conference?" This question was put forward at the close of 2012 at our final panel discussion by a group of students who were involved in organizing a line of programming at Open Engagement that explored economics. The question was met with uproarious applause. We were asked to evaluate what does "free" really mean? Someone is always paying, and who pays has significance. There are underlying issues that have a reach far beyond a conference on socially engaged art: who is paid? Who is not? Who is valued? How does one pay? At what cost? From 2007–13 Open Engagement, this "free" site of knowledge was hosted primarily by universities that otherwise charge for the access to knowledge. Funds were redistributed in order to create an institutionally supported site of public knowledge sharing.

I want to reframe the original question from 2012 by asking: what is the real value of a free conference? How can this conference on all levels be a proposal for a structure that does not yet exist, and model how to be in our world in a different way? We need to address the deeper economies at play. As Open Engagement moves forward it has the potential not only to highlight, mobilize and strengthen existing networks of support through a receptive mobility but also in itself to serve as a model. There is much work to be done for this conference to reach that state; the first step forward is acknowledging where we are. The conference being free has the ability to emphasize a different kind of exchange. The exchange we seek to further is the conference as a hub for the transmission of knowledge, and as a site to further support artists working in these ways. It is important to keep the perspective that Open Engagement, while it stems from an artistic practice, is ultimately still a conference. What is typical practice is for conference presenters and attendees to pay fees to the conference in order to attend and participate as speakers. Yet, unlike the standard conference practice of charging presenters a fee to attend and present, Open Engagement has intentionally maintained the position of being a free and accessible event.

Open Engagement and Portland State University

In 2008 I joined the faculty at Portland State University (PSU) to co-direct the MFA in Art and Social Practice programme. I worked to create a pioneering and challenging programme that has brought the School of Art and Design international attention and recognition as one of the primary locations for the study of socially engaged art. One of the things that made the programme a focal point of the developing conversation around these practices in North America was that, for four years, it was the host of Open Engagement. Though never formally part of the curriculum, I worked with interested students and community collaborators outside of class time, often from my home, to discuss, shape and programme the conference. This process began in 2009, with the first Portland conference happening in 2010. The planning of the conference itself was an exercise in group work. There was voting, reviews by committee, volunteer scheduling, collective budget making, teamwork and ever-punishing group reflection and feedback sessions following each conference. As the conference grew, so did the workload, and in the final year at PSU, we began to incorporate planning sessions into our weekly group MFA workshop.

The impulse to include students in the shaping and organizing of the conference reflected my own personal experience of Open Engagement being the core of my own education in socially engaged art. It also helped to engage students in the practice of connecting and community building. Thich Nhat Hahn has written that:

> Community building is the most important action of the 21st century...We should learn to do things together, to share our ideas and deep aspirations in our hearts...We need each other in order to practice solidarity, freedom, and compassion so that we can remind each other there is always hope.
>
> *(Thich 2012, p. 104)*

Pedagogically, this was an attempt at group work within the MFA programme but also moving toward the larger goal of building a community of support for artists working in this way around the world.

During the first year at PSU it was necessary to find a new structure that worked for the context of having the conference in Portland and in collaboration with a programme focused on socially engaged art. The themes of the conference emerged from casual group conversations, on walks and in group meetings. The first group that came together around the conference was enthusiastic and hard-working. They were dedicated to creating a site for discussion and exploration. The 2010 planning committee consisted of Katy Asher, Ashley Neese, Sandy Sampson, Crystal Baxley, Laurel Kurtz, Amy Steel, Lexa Walsh, Ally Drozd, with Graphic design by Belin Liu. This core group organized all aspects of the conference: from submissions, applicant reviews and booking venues, to sewing the conference tote bags by hand. The learning curve was gruelling. The process could not have been further from streamlined. The hours were intense. But what was born of this first transitional year of the conference was the importance and significance of the core group of women who come together to make Open Engagement a reality.

In 2011 the committee structure became more defined, with set roles and committee members taking the lead on planning specific areas of the conference: housing, transportation, hospitality, welcoming committee and food. This group included Crystal Baxley, Sandy Sampson, Katy Asher, Ariana Jacob, Ally Drozd, Lexa Walsh, Jason Sturgill, Carmen Papalia, Stefan Ransom, and with faculty input from Mack McFarland, Garrick Imatani, Sara Rabinowitz and Harrell Fletcher. This group included other faculty from PSU, as well as from other local colleges to share resources and support. It was in this year that the graphic design vision for the conference was in the hands of Nicole Lavelle. Lavelle remains the primary conference graphic designer to this day.

Each year of the conference marked significant growth. Applicants and attendees were increasing in hundreds each year. In 2012 the organizational structure needed to evolve to continue to support the community emerging around the event.

Many of the core team from 2010 and 2011 remained as the primary driving force behind the conference – Sandy Sampson, Lexa Walsh, Ally Drozd, and Ariana Jacob. Crystal Baxley, an undergraduate student at PSU when she began working with me to orchestrate the first Open Engagement at PSU, stepped up to the challenge to share the increasing amount of administrative duties and communications equally, and officially became conference co-director for 2012 and 2013. In response to this growing need for conference administrative support, the MFA programme also assigned one graduate assistant to work part-time on OE. This core team made the conference run. The voluntary involvement of MFA students from the programme focused more on shaping the conference through the selection review process, and then working directly to realize some of the projects and selected events. This was in response to feedback from students the previous year that the workload and administration were too great, and that the focus of their involvement should more closely tie in to their primary interests and what they felt was of value, or to the presentation of their personal work and research at the event.

The work of organizing a large-scale international conference with no revenue and limited resources is a challenge. If that were not already enough of a feat, there was the added weight (and also benefit) of seeing the entire structure as an opportunity for learning. It was incredibly rewarding but also draining – not only for me as an educator but also for the students. Many students began to resent the conference as drudgery, especially the administrative workload that they felt should be the responsibility of someone else. There was a degree of graduate student entitlement that placed this kind of labour outside of what some students felt was what they were there for, which was solely to focus on their own artistic practice. This is the kind of thinking that shuts down learning communities and perpetuates the self-focused, scarcity-based art world that we are accustomed to. Whether or not they recognized it, administrative communication is part of the challenging work of community building. It is also the crucial work that makes these kinds of events happen.

The reality of organizing a conference in collaboration with an MFA programme is that cohorts move on, students graduate and attitudes change. While many of the main team that built up OE at PSU had graduated, a few remained involved post-graduation, like Lexa Walsh, and one who continues to be involved in organizing aspects of OE, Ariana Jacob. By 2013 the conference had reached its maximum capacity at PSU. With over 600 attendees, we physically could no longer be a comfortable host to the conference. In addition, many of the current students who did want to be involved preferred not to have meetings off-campus and outside of class time, as had been the mode of organization for years. This change in structure shut out many of the other community-based committee members who were previously involved, as well as some recent grads who could no longer attend meetings as it conflicted with their work schedules. The main involvement from the students was in the form of choosing to work on small sub-committees based on their interest in one of the guiding themes selected by the group: Institutions, Context and Publics. These teams would shape these areas of programming during the conference but took on little of the enormous amount of additional work needed to make the conference a reality. The 2013 planning process was the most overwhelming and brutal, with Baxley and I bearing too much of the weight. We emerged from Open Engagement 2013 completely emotionally, physically and intellectually exhausted, and the prospect of doing another one, even for one more year, seemed impossible. The students of the MFA programme at that time were also overwhelmed, and the end of conference feedback session for OE that year was incredibly intense, emotionally volatile and (truthfully) verging on abusive.

After four years of uncompensated and under-appreciated long hours, Baxley decided to take time to focus on other endeavours and step away from Open Engagement. I also made a decision at the end of the 2013 conference that I would no longer continue to dedicate over 20 hours a week of uncompensated labour on Open Engagement and have the university use it as "signature programme" and selling point. I presented the graduate students at the time with a proposal of the increased support that would be required for Open Engagement to continue at PSU, and the majority decided that they were uninterested in advocating for the conference by supplying the additional financial and structural support necessary for the conference to continue in collaboration with the Art and Social Practice MFA programme. My decision was met with resistance from the university, and from other faculty. After four years of this work at Portland State University, it was clearly time to find a different way to look at Open Engagement as a structure for education. Multiple factors contributed to this evolution, including internal conflict among faculty (an unfortunate toxic reality of academia), squabbles around authorship and ownership, increased budget cuts that would make it financially impossible to offer a free conference, burnout and, perhaps most importantly, the lack of joy that became evident at the end of my tenure there.

In the Frierian school of thinking, cited by bell hooks in *Teaching Community* (2003), I also contend that: "Democratic educators can only see the acts of teaching, of learning, of studying as serious acts, but also ones that generate happiness" (hooks 2013, p. 41). Now that the conference has been released from that environment, it is back to a place of discovery, expansiveness and joy.

The allies of Open Engagement

I would like to acknowledge friend and artist Paul Ramirez Jonas for his encouragement, and his belief that Open Engagement is a site that is needed. When the future of OE seemed uncertain, he was an advocate. When it was in search of a new landing point, he even generously offered his kitchen table. It was because of his belief in this event that another ally emerged in the form of past OE keynote presenter and at the time Director of the Queens Museum, Tom Finkelpearl.

The move to Queens Museum in New York City in 2014 marked another transition year for Open Engagement and an opportunity to find its footing again. Kerri-Lynn Reeves was added to the OE core team as the Program Coordinator. Reeves and I worked closely with Prerana Reddy, the Director of Public Events at the Queens Museum, to ensure the success of the overall event. To shape the conference programme, groups of selection committees were brought together that represented more holistically the diverse support ecosystem surrounding socially engaged art practices. Ariana Jacob remained involved in organizing the conversational aspect of the conference that year (and to this day) in collaboration with Sheetal Prajapati, Associate Educator in Public Programs at MoMA. Additionally, artist and scholar Gemma-Rose Turnbull was added to the OE core team to manage the conference social media and blog. Another crucial ally that emerged that year was the non-profit arts organization A Blade of Grass in New York. Continuing and refining the tradition of working within an educational framework, we also worked with the Social Practice MFA programme at Queens College, mostly through the selection process, but also closely with student Mirana Zugnr who ran the Open Platform presentations.

As you might have noticed from the overview of the labour contributions outlined in this chapter, a lot of women work on Open Engagement. What does it mean that the labour was done primarily by women year after year for free (or for less than minimum wage) for the first five years of its existence? It was not until the partnership with A Blade of Grass and the Queens Museum began in 2014 that the conference finally had partners willing, and without question ready, to ensure that the small team that make this event happen be fairly compensated.

From the direction to the graphic design, social media, committee members and volunteers, year after year the overwhelming majority of the people who push Open Engagement forward are women. In Marilyn Waring's 1999 book *Counting For Nothing: What Men Value and What Women are Worth* she examines the unacknowledged and unaccounted labour of women on a global scale and makes visible these contributions. As I take a closer look at what makes this conference run, and at what cost, acknowledging this aspect of the conference is also to ask: why is this the case? Why is it that more men are not contributing more time and energy to making this site possible for this community of practitioners?

Case studies

The budgets in each year do not reflect in-kind support, only funds raised. All quotes are from lectures, reflections or interviews given by key figures of that year's conference.

2007

> I'm feeling confident that there are brilliant people chiselling away at this, and those annoying but interesting questions of "is it art?" won't be interesting to us for long.
>
> *(Darren O'Donnell 2007)*

Summary
Over 40 national and international contributors were present during this first iteration of the conference. The contributors were selected through an open call for submissions to participate alongside three keynote presenters. This was an around-the-clock experience. It was a conference, an exhibition/performance venue, a mini-residency and a workshop. Each out-of-town presenter was billeted with a member of the local community. Participants shared meals with one another and members of the local community, commuted together and were encouraged to thank their hosts by leaving a created trace.

Location: Regina, Saskatchewan (Canada)

Dates: October 11–13

Planning timeline: September 2006–October 2007

Themes: "You are all that I see: Art and everyday experience."; "It takes two: collaborations, collectives, other team relationships"; "I'll call you: long-term relationships, communities and connectivity"

Keynotes/Featured Projects: Darren O'Donnell, Jessica James Lansdon, Harrell Fletcher

Presenters: 40

Attendees: 120

Partners: The University of Regina, The Dunlop Art Gallery

Funding: Social Sciences and Humanities Research Council of Canada, University of Regina

Venues: University of Regina, The Dunlop Art Gallery, The Mackenzie Art Gallery and homes of various local Regina residents

Talks/panels: 24

Projects/performances: 13

Events: 8

Exhibitions: 1

OE Team: Jen Delos Reyes, Warren Bates

Graphic Design: Jen Delos Reyes

Selection committee(s): Warren Bates, Jen Delos Reyes, Kristy Fyfe, Jeff Nye, Andrea Young

2010

"But what is utopia, where did it come from and if utopia is nowhere how can we get there?"

(Nils Norman 2010)

Summary
In 2010, Open Engagement resumed at Portland State University in conjunction with the Art and Social Practice students, under the banner of *Making Things, Making Things Better, Making Things Worse.* What is the role of the object in socially engaged art? Does socially engaged art have to do good? What are the ethics of this way of working? The main inquiry and interest of the students and programme became key in the framing of the conference.

Along with over 150 presenters accepted through an open call for submissions, the featured keynote presenters (Mark Dion, Nils Norman, and Amy Franceschini) framed the themes of the 2010 conference.

Location: Portland, Oregon (USA)

Dates: 14–17 May

Planning timeline: October 2009–May 2010

Themes: *Making things* – what is the role of the object in socially engaged art?. *Making things better* – does socially engaged art have to do good? *Making things worse* – what are the ethics of this way of working?

Keynotes: Mark Dion, Amy Franceschini, Nils Norman. Special guest moderator: Nato Thompson

Presenters: 150

Attendees: 400

Partners: Portland State University, Pacific Northwest College of Art

Funding: Regional Art and Culture Council Grant, Portland State University

Venues: Portland State University, Gallery Homeland, Igloo Gallery, Portland Institute for Contemporary Art, Buckman Park, Car Hole Gallery, Project Grow, Gerding Theater, Museum of Contemporary Craft, various other locations

Talks/panels: 26

Performances/projects: 21

Events: 4

Exhibitions: 2

OE Team: Katy Asher, Crystal Baxley, Jen Delos Reyes, Ally Drozd, Ariana Jacob, Laurel Kurtz, Ashley Neese, Sandy Sampson, Amy Steel, Lexa Walsh

Graphic Design: Belin Liu

Selection committee(s): Katy Asher, Crystal Baxley, Jen Delos Reyes, Ally Drozd, Garrick Imatani, Ariana Jacob, Laurel Kurtz, Mack McFarland, Ashley Neese, Sandy Sampson, Amy Steel, Lexa Walsh

2011

"Different perspectives in dialogue, various methods informing and building on one another, a repertoire of diverse forms, and different media rubbing up against one another. But compatible intentionality in the larger sense bonds the efforts and differences."

(Julie Ault 2011)

Summary
For Open Engagement 2011, we set out simply to discuss art and social practice and explore how writer and theorist Stephen Wright positioned the term as a double ontology.

Through conversations, interviews, open reflection on experiences and related projects created for, or presented at the conference, we examined five themes that encompassed ideas connected to social practice: Peoples and Publics, Social Economies, In Between Places, Tracking and Tracing and Sentiment and Strategies.

2011's keynote presenters were Julie Ault, Fritz Haeg, and Pablo Helguera, with a final dinner discussion moderated by Rick Lowe. The work by these artists touches on subjects including democracy, group work, the boundary (or lack thereof) between art and life, education and transdisciplinarity.

In 2011 Open Engagement also played host to the Bureau for Open Culture, Bad at Sports, an exhibition by the Bruce High Quality Foundation University and concurrent summits on art and education and social practice/participatory programmes and practices arising at museums. The summits featured representatives from OTIS College of Art and Design, the University of California Santa Cruz, Maryland Institute College of Art, California College of the Arts, The Walker, Portland Art Museum, The Hammer Museum and others.

Location: Portland, Oregon (USA)

Dates: 13–15 May

Planning timeline: May 2010–May 2011

Themes: Peoples + Publics: Democracy Group, Social Economies, In Between Spaces

Keynotes: Julie Ault, Fritz Haeg, Pablo Helguera; special guest moderator: Rick Lowe

Presenters: 201

Attendees: 475

Partners: Pacific Northwest College of Art, Lewis and Clark College, Portland State University, TriMet.

Funding: Portland State University, Pacific Northwest College of Art.

Venues: Portland State University, Boxxes, Candle Light Lounge, City Hall, Coalition Brewing, Field Work, Park Blocks, Portland Art Museum, Pacific Northwest College of Art, White Stag Building, Wealth Underground Farm, Xhurch.

Talks/Panels: 41

Performances/projects: 12

Events: 6

Exhibitions: 2

OE Team: Katy Asher, Crystal Baxley, Jen Delos Reyes, Ally Drozd, Garrick Imatani, Ariana Jacob, Nicole Lavelle, Mack Mc Farland, Sara Rabinowitz, Stefan Ransom, Sandy Sampson, Jason Sturgill, Lexa Walsh

Graphic Design: Nicole Lavelle

Selection committee(s): Katy Asher, Crystal Baxley, Jen Delos Reyes, Ally Drozd, Garrick Imatani, Ariana Jacob, Nicole Lavelle, Mack Mc Farland, Sara Rabinowitz, Stefan Ransom, Sandy Sampson, Jason Sturgill, Lexa Walsh

Summits: Museum Summit, Art + Education Summit

2012

"And today what we're seeing is the production of caustic, corrosive, invisible voids, where art is no longer going out into the world and in sociality in the form of objecthood, or even in the form of self-described aesthetic experience, but in the form of dark energy."

(Stephen Wright 2012)

Summary
The 2012 Open Engagement featured presentations from keynote speakers Tania Bruguera, Shannon Jackson and Paul Ramirez Jonas. The work by these artists and scholars informed the conference themes: Politics, Economies, Education and Representation. Curatorial teams made up of Portland State University Art and Social Practice MFA students developed and directed these themes by framing the programming with their own questions and concerns.

Location: Portland, Oregon (USA)

Dates: 18–20 May

Planning timeline: May 2010–May 2011

Themes: Politics, Economies, Education and Representation

Keynotes: Tania Bruguera, Shannon Jackson and Paul Ramirez Jonas

Presenters: 148

Attendees: 530

Partners: Portland State University, Portland Art Museum, OTIS College of Art and Design, Southern Methodist University, Arizona State University

Funding: Portland State University, PSU MFA Art and Social Practice, OTIS College of Art, Arizona State University, SPARC, Southern Methodist University and the Regional Arts and Culture Council.

Venues: Portland State University, Boxxes, Candle Light Lounge, City Hall, Coalition Brewing, Field Work, Park Blocks, Portland Art Museum, Pacific Northwest College of Art, Recess Gallery, White Stag Building, Wealth Underground Farm, Xhurch, Yale Union

Talks/Panels: 55

Performances/projects: 30

Exhibitions: 2

Events: 12

OE Team: Crystal Baxley, Jen Delos Reyes, Ally Drozd, Grace Hwang, Ariana Jacob, Nicole Lavelle, Travis Neel, Sandy Sampson, Lexa Walsh

Graphic Design: Nicole Lavelle

Selection committee(s): Economies committee: Jason Sturgill, Erica Thomas, Dillon De Give, Mark Menjivar, Nancy Zastudil

Politics: Sharita Towne, Alysha Shaw, Ariana Jacob, Patricia Vasquez

Education committee: Harrell Fletcher, Grace Hwang, Travis Neel, Molly Sherman, Travis Souza, Michelle Swineheart

Representation committee: Carmen Papalia, Betty Marin, Eliza Gregory, Transformazium, Julie Perini

2013

"What do we recognize as social practice? Who are the insiders? And how does such work evoke an idea of public time, as well as public space?"

(Claire Doherty 2013)

Summary
Open Engagement 2013 featured keynote presenters Claire Doherty, Tom Finkelpearl and Michael Rakowitz. It brought together these voices to reflect on the themes of publics, contexts and institutions in relation to the current state of socially engaged art, education and institutional practice. The conference included dozens of panels, workshops and lectures, as well as a continuation of the socially engaged art in an institutions summit as well as a public conversation with *Creative Time* on the roles of the Creative Time Summit and Open Engagement.

Location: Portland, Oregon (USA)

Dates: 17–19 May

Planning timeline: May 2012–May 2013

Themes: Contexts, Publics, Institutions

Keynotes: Claire Doherty, Tom Finkelpearl and Michael Rakowitz

Presenters: 178

Attendees: 640

Partners: Portland State University, Portland Art Museum

Funding: Portland State University, Regional Arts and Culture Council, Southern Methodist University, OTIS College of Art and Design, SPARC, Limerick School of Art and Design, University of Queensland, attendee donations

Venues: Portland State University, Portland Art Museum, Museum of Contemporary Craft, Field Work, Portland Institute for Contemporary Art

Talks/Panels: 67

Performances/projects: 11

Exhibitions: 2

Events: 7

OE Team: Crystal Baxley, Jen Delos Reyes, Grace Hwang, Lexa Walsh

Graphic Design: Nicole Lavelle

Selection committee(s): Publics committee: Travis Neel, Betty Marin, Erin Charpentier, Zach Gough, Patricia Vazquez

Contexts committee: Dillon De Give, Erica Thomas, Alysha Shaw, Jeff Wright, Sharita Towne

Institutions committee: Head Harrell Fletcher, Grace Hwang, Heather Donahue, Mark Menjivar

Summits: Museum Summit, Art and Education Summit

2014

"Everyone and everything that keeps life going feeds me as an artist and person. This includes people and also remediating infrastructure systems that keep the planet going; all everydayness feeds me."

(Mierle Laderman Ukeles 2014)

Summary
Open Engagement 2014 was planned in conjunction with the Queens Museum, A Blade of Grass, Social Practice Queens at Queens College and a selection of artists, educators and interested parties. This year, the selection process brought together groups of people representing the expansive and complex ecosystems that support these practices – museum perspectives, funding perspectives, education perspectives, artist perspectives and student perspectives.

Students, faculty, staff and committee members worked with one another to select the presenters and create the conference programming. That year, we brought together a diverse group of over 200 presenters from around the world, including keynote speakers Mierle Laderman Ukeles and J. Morgan Puett. We assembled these voices to reflect on subjects that are inextricable from our daily existence – life and work.

Open Engagement 2014 was sited at the newly renovated Queens Museum, with additional programming at the New York Hall of Science, Queens Theater in the Park, Immigrant Movement International and various other locations around New York including MoMA, Flux Factory, Creative Time, Aperture, Vera List Center for Art and Politics and Laundromat Projects. This year also included a number of New York-based academic programmes led by Social Practice Queens at Queens College, CUNY. We also provided an extensive suite of workshops that addressed funding, writing, curating and community organizing as it pertains to the field (see Figure 7.2 for an impression).

In an effort to better connect and support life/work, the conference partnered with the Danish art collective *Wooloo's Human Hotel* in New York City to provide free private housing for visiting cultural workers travelling with children.

Location: Queens, New York City

Dates: 16–18 May

Planning timeline: September 2013–May 2014

Themes: Life/Work

Keynotes: J. Morgan Puett, Mierle Laderman Ukeles

Presenters: 232

FIGURE 7.2 "Bodies of Knowledge: Sourcing Disability Experience", a lunchtime discussion focused on disability and access at Open Engagement: Life/Work, 2014.
Credit: Jen Delos Reyes.

Attendees: 1,100

Partners: The Queens Museum, A Blade of Grass

Funding: A Blade of Grass, The Queens Museum, Big Car Collective, attendee donations

Venues: The Queens Museum, Queens Theater in the Park, New York Hall of Science, Creative Time, Museum of Modern Art, Flux Factory, ISCP, Vera List Center for Art and Politics, Aperture Foundation, The Laundromat Project

Talks/panels: 106

Performances/projects: 18

Exhibitions: 2

Events: 20

OE Team: Jen Delos Reyes, Kerri-Lynn Reeves, Gemma-Rose Turnbull, Alex Winters, Ariana Jacob, Sheetal Prajapati

Graphic Design: Nicole Lavelle

Selection committee(s): Life/Work – Panels and Presentations: Jen Delos Reyes, Prerana Reddy, Deborah Fisher, Sheetal Prajapati, Barrie Cline and Kerri-Lynn Reeves

Life/Work – Projects: Jen Delos Reyes, Tom Finkelpearl, Maureen Connor, Deborah Fisher, Natasha Llorens and Kerri-Lynn Reeves

Immigrant Movement International: Jen Delos Reyes, Silvia Juliana Mantilla Ortiz, Elizabeth Grady, Sol Aramendi, Patrick Rowe, IMI community members and Kerri-Lynn Reeves

Panorama: Jen Delos Reyes, Prerana Reddy, Seth Aylmer, Elizabeth Grady, Gonzalo Casals and Kerri-Lynn Reeves

Watershed: Jen Delos Reyes, Prerana Reddy, Jason Yoon, Seth Aylmer, Elizabeth Grady, Gonzalo Casals and Kerri-Lynn Reeves

Open Platform: Jen Delos Reyes, Prerana Reddy, Francisco Karmelic, Deborah Fisher and Kerri-Lynn Reeves

Open Houses: Jen Delos Reyes, Tom Finkelpearl, Deborah Fisher and Prerana Reddy

Summits: Student Summit

Open Engagement: 2015 and beyond

The 2014 move of Open Engagement to the Queens Museum in New York marked the beginning of a rotation of the conference from coast to coast in order to build a national consortium for socially engaged art that will work together to shape the conference. Open Engagement is committed to expanding national and international support and awareness for socially engaged art. Part of how the conference achieves this is through the creation of partnerships and relationships with organizations that also value the social potential of art. Moving towards these goals, Open Engagement is looking to build two more host-site relationships in addition to the successful and growing partnership with the Queens Museum. We are looking for sites on the West Coast and in the Midwest so that the conference will be able to have a coast-to-coast representation of socially engaged art practices across the USA. Our ideal landing points are already centres of socially engaged art activity: the Bay Area in partnership with the California College of the Arts, and Chicago in partnership with the University of Illinois at Chicago's Art and Social Justice Cluster. Once all our sites and partners are identified, there will be a three-year annual rotation cycle beginning with the West Coast. Such national conversation is key in ensuring that OE truly represents and supports the breadth of current work and practices. My work has shifted from educator to organizer, working to build a national network to support socially engaged art practice through this conference as a site for education and development.

The year 2015 will also see the continuation of the important partnership between Open Engagement and A Blade of Grass in New York. Both organizations work together to further their mutual goals of providing resources to artists who demonstrate artistic excellence and serve as innovative conduits for social change. Both A Blade of Grass and Open Engagement, through open calls and expansive and inclusive working methods, evaluate the quality of work in this evolving field by fostering diverse and practical discourse about the aesthetics, functions, ethics and meanings of socially engaged art, resonating within and outside the contemporary art dialogue. We believe in the beauty and innovation of these works, as well as their power to enable tangible and positive social change outcomes. Together, we seek to foster a programme that pushes these practices further and promotes this way of working for artists.

Now seven years into its evolution, Open Engagement is at a critical moment of development. The conference has grown significantly each year, widening its scope and reach, as well as serving as a site of professional development and education around socially engaged art. Open Engagement is the only conference on this subject of this scale to operate on an inclusive open-call model that supports diverse publics as well as emerging and established artists. The conference has become an important site for the conversations surrounding socially engaged art practice, as well as a generative site of production. It is a space that expands to hold these conversations, support these practices and fully explore the contours of these ways of working in the world. We want to continue to be a key site for the conversations and issues that arise in socially engaged art. For as long as we can, Open Engagement will continue to promote the growth of the field and support practitioners by offering a site for continued education.

Note

1   *Art 280* is an introduction to time and lens-based media, performance, installation, site-specificity, net.art, artist's use of text and conceptual approaches to art making as defined within contemporary art practices.

8

"CONTEXT IS HALF THE WORK"

Developing doctoral research through arts practice in culture

Anne Douglas

In 2001 to 2004, a small research team of post-doctoral and doctoral artist researchers, working with five cultural partners, drew together two apparently incommensurable issues: remote rural culture and contemporary art. The thrust of their questions was speculative: what might the role of the contemporary artist be in remote rural contexts? At the time, the turn of the millennium, the dominant context of contemporary visual art was urban and metropolitan. Any ambition to develop art in alternative contexts needed to be negotiated against this dominance – its assumptions and aesthetics. "Context is half the work" was developed by the artist Barbara Steveni as a central axiom underpinning the work of Artist Placement Group (APG) (1966–89) and O+I (Organization and Imagination, 1989–present) (APG/Tate 2015). It aptly expresses the opening up of art practice to context that our research question had provoked.

In parallel, practice-led research through the arts was emerging as a new research area. Practice-led research may be defined as research that emerges out of particular questions and expertise of (in this case) arts practice. It is frequently framed by interplay between the histories and traditions of practice and current social and cultural change. This area of research is underpinned by a methodological approach that might combine qualitative and quantitative approaches, but, nonetheless, its overall purpose is discursive and critical rather than propositional or problem solving.

On the Edge[1] research responded to these parallel developments in arts practice and in research practice. On the one hand the particular context of remote rural north-east Scotland prompted a rethinking of the role of the contemporary visual artist beyond the dominant urban metropolitan conventions of gallery and museum practice. Remote rural culture significantly shaped the programme's approach, producing forms of art in which temporal, developmental and immersive qualities of engagement through the arts overshadowed the importance of the artifact as a single mode of address. Situating the challenge as a research inquiry helped to open up process over production. It enabled the team to position the artist in relation to social, cultural and economic issues, aesthetics, and communities of interest, drawing in other disciplines that could inform the unfolding research.

In aligning art with formal academic research, doctoral and post-doctoral, we not only confronted the dominance of established modes of production and reception but also established research approaches. At the time, the arts sector tended to draw on the social sciences in particular to explain the social role of art. Appropriating existing research language and concepts sought to legitimize the arts' relationship with research. These efforts restricted the kinds of questions that could originate in the arts. In foregrounding questions specific to practice, such as the role of the contemporary artist in a specific cultural context, the team needed to think through step-by-step what we believed could be known, and identify knowledge traditions that would appropriately inform practice in the world.

A remote rural context suggested some clear ground rules. Heather Delday, the doctoral researcher in this phase of work (2001–5), contributed her 30-plus years of experience of living and working in the Orkneys and Western Isles of Scotland. She investigated a 'close' relationship between artist and community as an alternative construction to the conventions of a more anonymized artist and audience relationship. This study, as part of a much larger research project, was formative in how the research developed (Delday 2006).

First, vernacular culture, in fact all human culture, is rich in creativity and meaning. The arts bring these meanings to the foreground at different times and through different media. In this sense the arts and culture are not synonymous but work in relation to each other to exploit the immense diversity of ways of being in relation to environment, culture and values. Raymond Williams defines three categories of culture. The 'ideal' is concerned with the absolute or universal, "the discovery and description, in lives and works, of those values which can be seen to compose a timeless order... a permanent reference to the universal human condition" (Williams 1973, p. 56). The second is 'the documentary'. This is a critical activity taking form through a body of intellectual and imaginative work in which human experience and thought is recorded in diverse ways. The documentary ranges close to the ideal but may also focus on a particular work and its analysis or undertake an historical criticism that, through analysis, makes connections between particular traditions. The third is the 'social' definition of culture – a description of a particular way of life that draws on expressions of culture through the arts and also in institutions and everyday practices.

This third category is possibly the closest to *On the Edge* research. Art projects emerged in response to a particular way of life, working with institutions and organizations responsible for sustaining and reflecting upon the production of culture in relation to the past, present and future of a particular region. The function of each art project or intervention was to make connections and invigorate participants, organizations and artists. The function of research was to reflect on and inform emergent arts practice from a wider context of ideas and practices, testing the significance of the approach beyond the rural, to trace change as a means to create a better understanding of social and cultural development as a whole (Williams 1973, pp. 56–7).

Second, cooperation between individuals in remote rural cultures to sustain a way of life is a greater priority than working from a particular identity or professionalized 'role'. By being open to learning, to hearing and seeing what remote rural culture could offer the research, new forms of art started to emerge that rediscovered the profound relational and interdependent nature of artistic endeavour. Artistic practice may produce a new experience, event or activity, but the work of art requires the input of others to gain traction and meaning. In this sense "the reader creates the text" (Wolff 1981). Jacques Rancière, a philosopher of culture, suggests the way that we learn is through acts of translation. By connecting signs to other signs we come to understand what another human being is trying to communicate. As a consequence "every spectator is already an actor in her story, every actor every man of action, is the spectator in the same story" (Rancière 2009, p. 17). The active spectator responds to a given narrative by creating another story true to his/her world of experience. It is this principle of iterative cycles of translation that emancipate rather than stultify community.

Third, in remote rural contexts there is minimal infrastructure that institutionalizes, and therefore secures, the roles of artist and audience. Instead, there are diverse communities of interest through which activity may stand or fall. The research team worked with individuals across arts practice, policy development and curatorial practice, exploring issues with cultural leaders, residents and academics from disciplines including anthropology and philosophy. The research process created a safe space to formally acknowledge these differences as the starting point to managing their implications through appropriate forms of action.

This chapter consists of two interrelated sections. The first half of the chapter explores the emergence and development of *On the Edge* research from 2001 onwards through two projects, *Inthrow* (Douglas et al. 2005) and *Celestial Ceiling* (Douglas 2005). Both projects developed between 2001 and 2004. It traces how the experience of living in north-east Scotland has shaped the form of the work and its underpinning values, as well as subsequent developments from 2005 onwards. As new thematics emerge, such as artistic leadership, improvisation and ecology, the research approach sustains an ethos of collaboration and participation as a mode of inquiry in and through arts practice. The programme also frequently encounters expectations of both research and arts practice that prompt critical reflection and, at times, conflict.

The second section mines a particular example of doctoral study, that of Reiko Goto Collins who in 2012 completed her doctoral dissertation entitled "Ecology and Environmental Art in a Public Place. Talking Tree: Won't you take a minute and listen to the plight of nature?". This study is situated between art and ecology. It draws on both quantitative and qualitative methodologies and confounds many of the conventional ways of thinking about an arts-led doctorate as a consequence of its interdisciplinarity.

This part draws on an analytical lens developed by Egon Guba and Yvonna Lincoln in 1994. They challenge a received view of research as predominantly propositional, by subjecting a number of research paradigms to analysis. They expose fundamental beliefs or first principles on which four different research paradigms have been built, including positivism, post-positivism, critical theory and constructivism. Their analysis is used as a critical base to position Goto's research in relation to existing paradigms, other discipline perspectives and research expectations to draw out the unique qualities of the work as practice-led research through the arts.

The chapter concludes by exploring arts-based research as knowledge-producing, i.e. not just the subject or method of research but formative of a whole approach that acts as a lens through which the world is perceived and understood. Doctoral research programmes such as *On the Edge* have the potential to prepare individuals to challenge and critique existing forms of inquiry that are tied into particular knowledge economies. In developing sound research skills, in constructing argument that is well informed and critically adept, artists interested in exploring issues of contemporary practice in a changing world become equipped to develop alternative ways of knowing and, importantly, to act through practical engagement in the world. The generative aspects of arts-based research point to a new research paradigm. If supported and developed, this paradigm should enable artists to influence forms of inquiry alongside other disciplines and expert practices. At the very least, they establish as an important principle of research that it is not possible to speak the truth in the wrong paradigm (Coessens et al. 2009).

On the edge: emergent arts-based research

Inthrow, *Lumsden, 2001–4, artist Gavin Renwick*

At the heart of the project *Inthrow* was a field at the corner of a village in Aberdeenshire. Nearer the city, many of the fields were steadily being covered with suburban housing. The village had been laid out by the estate as part of a programme of agricultural improvements nearly one and three-quarter centuries before. Now, agriculture was changing. What would happen to the field? What would happen to the village? Pat Dunn, the farmer who owned the field, would retire as the last farmer living in the village to tenant land from the estate. What happens when no-one wants to farm the land?

Chris Fremantle, then director of the Scottish Sculpture Workshop within the village of Lumsden, posed these questions in part through his experience of living in the village and in part prompted by working with Gavin Renwick, a practice-led researcher and architect. Renwick had been exploring similar themes in the Northwest Territories of Canada. The team worked with Fremantle to develop a brief – to explore the ideas, the depth and shape of the questions. They then approached Renwick to work on the project. For him it was an opportunity to deepen his understanding of the issues he had been developing in Canada.

Renwick worked with elders and young people in the village, architecture students and graduates, and other artists. He developed a number of threads in the work around the idea of home and hearth. In the local dialect, the doric, *inthrow* means hearth.

Gavin Renwick said: "My practice is about continuity – you can only go forward if you know where you come from." Ian Hunter evaluated the project as an artist and researcher of public art. He said: "This project is about revealing change." Pat Dunn, the farmer who owned the field, said: "If they dinnae (Doric for 'do not') know about things, there's nothing to be said."[2] Willie Petrie, Dunn's neighbour and also a farmer, quoted Robert Burns:

> I'm truly sorry man's dominion,
> Has broken nature's social union,
>
> *(Robert Burns, 1789, "To a Mouse, on*
> *Turning Her Up in Her Nest with the Plough")*

A discussion about the future of a field thus became a way for each contributor to position themselves. This was captured in a book of reflective texts, drawings and commissioned photography. The book tells the story of Renwick's original concept and the different forms of action that flowed from it, forming acts of translation in Rancière's sense. The artists' interventions create the conditions to open up eyes and ears to different experiences of village life undergoing change. In rural cultures these may be otherwise unmarked moments that go unnoticed but nonetheless transform lives. Art interventions allow for encounters that are more conscious and sensory, shared as a community (Douglas et al. 2006).

Celestial Ceiling, *2001–4, artists Robert Orchardson and John McGeogh*

The *Celestial Ceiling* project addressed the loss of important Scottish heritage, a sixteenth-century painted ceiling in an ancient house dating from the eleventh century, on the northern coast of Aberdeenshire. The ceiling was destroyed by fire in the 1990s. In responding to the challenge, the team gathered together art historians, painters and curators, including the custodians of the original heritage. They reflected on the loss. It became apparent that we could do one of a number of things: nothing, reproduce the lost work or commission a new work.

We asked the historian of the Scottish Renaissance, who had specialized in painted ceilings. He responded by describing how the original ceiling had come about. We asked the contemporary art curator. She contrasted the artist in the sixteenth century carrying out the desires of the patron with the expectations of autonomy and the freedom that artists look for now. She suggested names of artists of quality who make paintings. We asked a painter of heraldry who has painted many ceilings. He responded: "You might consider something like this. It is quite similar to what was there." We asked a contemporary artist and he replied: "Think about how the original was made. Think about what new materials are available to artists. Think about how we can now throw light as a medium, not trap light in pigment. There are now ways that were not possible in the sixteenth century." We asked the artist who trains other artists and he said: "It must be a genuine response – to what was there and to what we believe now." He suggested young artists whom he had taught. We asked the architect and he said: "I will keep an open mind but keep me informed. Work with me and work with my clients. They are the new patrons. They must always be informed and they must be allowed to inform what happens."[3]

The discussion generated not one but two commissions, developed with quite distinctive artists. One completed a new ceiling for the twenty-first century (Figure 8.1). The other reconstructed the original ceiling through digital media as an interactive work situated between the arts and heritage. The project drew additional resourcing to complete both works.

What is the significance of the work to remote and rural cultures and communities? A large number of Scottish Renaissance painted ceilings are found in north-east Scotland. Cullen House and Duff House are neighbours and both represent built heritage of considerable architectural interest nationally and internationally. Both had suffered disrepair and undergone restoration. Working

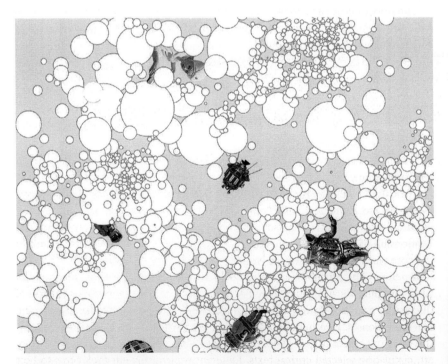

FIGURE 8.1 *New Cullen Ceiling* (2004), Robert Orchardson.
Credit: On the Edge research.

with the research team, the director of Duff House, an outstation of the National Galleries for Scotland, was keen to frame his institution as a public resource of knowledge in architectural restoration. A request from his neighbours, the private owners of the original ceiling at Cullen House, provided the opportunity for him to draw on his organization's considerable knowledge of restoration techniques and skilled networks. In fact, he supported a process of exploring, rather than resolving, the problem of heritage loss.

Many of the skilled craftsmen of the region would have worked on the restoration of both Duff House and Cullen House. The loss through disrepair or fire to either property constituted a loss to the whole community, economically as well as culturally. In some respects, the story of *Cullen Ceiling* draws attention to the relationship between the public and private in remote rural contexts. It is not the same relationship as in urban contexts. Where the National Gallery in Edinburgh functions as a visitor attraction within an urban, metropolitan setting, i.e. as a form of provision of service *to* the public, its counterpart in Duff House constructed a reciprocal relationship between the public and the private. This took the form of an exchange of shared experience and responsibility for care of the built environment, of expertise, interdependence and of mutual learning in the light of the loss of culture. Such a project and relationship might not have been possible within an urban environment or indeed outside of a research inquiry.

The story of process forms a second book, *Cullen Ceiling: Contemporary Art, Built Heritage and Patronage*, a narrative tracing the different perspectives and contributions of the participants (Douglas 2005).

Reframing research and practice

These kinds of questions and approaches drew five project partners, responsible in some way for culture in remote and rural contexts of NE Scotland, to work with the *On the Edge* research team.

Through emergent questions, we positioned the work simultaneously as research and as practice. The resulting networks were not loose connections between individuals but a clustering of interacting elements that, we envisaged, might have long-term consequences. Our different experiences of living in remote rural cultures provided an initial source of energy to explore, in new ways, the relationship of art to its cultural context. We created learning spaces that involved the core participants in two-day workshops, held every six months across a three-year period. They included artist researchers, organizational leaders, geographical rural communities and, increasingly, other artists. The workshops took the form of discussion, cross-fertilizing ideas, techniques and processes as well as challenging default responses. Heather Delday, as doctoral researcher, led a process of placing the work in a wider national and international discourse on the changing nature of art, circulating selected critical texts. Different project partners took turns to host each workshop so that we were working in the places in which a project took form. In this way the research could support a process of defining what success and failure looked like. The core concern was to uncover the value (or otherwise) of artistic intervention as it came into play within experiences of social and cultural change.

The opening question of the first phase of *On the Edge* in 2001 was: how do you articulate forms of visual arts practice of quality in remote and rural areas? The question framed some problematic assumptions of how – and by whom – quality is judged, and also produced. We asked this question as artist researchers and inhabitants of remote rural places, rather than as sociologists; as makers and dwellers within the situation, not as observers outside the situation. The question challenged our assumptions of what art might be, and where and how it might be experienced.

A conventional model within the arts involves sharing at the stage of a completed product, at a point of reception. This is frequently dependent upon an institutional frame and established protocols that position the work as art. A characteristic of *On the Edge* projects has been that artists were commissioned to realize projects. The default position in public commissions is to start with writing the commissioning brief. We adapted this procedure by foregrounding a research-based approach that focused on the visions and challenges of cultural leaders. We 'suspended disbelief' and sustained an open-ended exploration of ideas, ethics and principles of action so that projects started to emerge, to be identified through a process of recognition rather than by being pre-planned or pre-determined. The process of cross fertilization created a starting point that was deeper and more significant to the participants. By choosing not to work in conventional ways, we were free to focus on the challenges and unique character of remote and rural life. We needed to negotiate new terms of reference by exploring foundational principles – who and where were we? Who and where did we want to be?

Vandana Shiva, a quantum physicist, activist and leading opponent of genetic modification and patenting of seeds, stresses the importance of biological and cultural diversity working together. In an interview with Wallace Heim (2003), Shiva describes a ritual process, *Akti*, in central India by which different groups annually donate, mix and redistribute rice seed. This has the dual function of resisting disease and sharing through ritual exchange.

This is a vivid metaphor for the aspiration and approach of art in public life. Isolation, including that of the artist or cultural leader or participant, leads to a loss of resilience, a vulnerability to attack from conditions that threaten quality of creativity in everyday situations. A dynamic culture of inquiry through art is dependent upon infusions of new energy that might appear unexpectedly and from unpredictable sources.

Allan Kaprow, artist and theorist, is also a major point of reference in this research. He championed art's proper role as part of life – as distinct from the role that had come to be assigned to it by the institution of museum and gallery practice, as commodity. His point of entry was through an idea of play. Play is a perpetual, indeterminate state of mobility. It is an energy that avoids the traps, the fixed points, of entropy, the hardening of beliefs and ways of being. Play is the antithesis of certainty. Nonetheless, there is a paradox: mobility can be defined as going from one place to another. It relies on a negotiation between fixed points. The tension between a desire for mobility and its dependence on a contradictory force – determinacy – seems to get to the heart of an understanding of contemporary art that is situated within paradox (Kaprow 2003). In some sense mobility, as Kaprow suggests, is dependent upon a state of constantly questioning, of hovering in the intervals between points, not to "deaden the game" (Kaprow 1995). Kaprow's thinking and aesthetic approach is one of a number of artists whose work is research-led. Like John Cage, his mentor, Kaprow supported experimental practice in the world through a meta level of thinking explored through reflective writings.

It is important to say that cooperative energy did not always operate in this positive, developmental way. Four out of the five projects developed through collaboration with the research. In one case the collaborative ethos failed and a more traditionally autonomous practice resulted. Individuals consciously exercise choice and judgement in its most heightened and skilled form, in the making and experiencing of art. This is true for the artist in declaring a musical composition or drawing as a success or a failure, and also for the audience correspondingly experiencing the work as a process of completing or resisting and rejecting it. In a similar way, the exercising of choice is an important quality of the research space – to act or not to act, to participate or not despite the availability of funds to do so, to learn from the experience or to choose to learn from another source or mode of working.

Research developments from 2006 onwards: the aesthetics of leadership in social art practice

The questions have evolved beyond the remote and rural to embrace new kinds of cultural contexts. In 2005, the artist Suzanne Lacy approached *On the Edge* to support her PhD by practice. A recognized practitioner of international standing, Lacy was interested in reflecting upon a ten-year body of work in Oakland, California that involved issues of youth, race and media education. It was challenging to imagine supervising the doctorate of an individual who is so widely known and regarded internationally, an individual who had already published a number of seminal texts in the field. A clue to an approach that chimed with the artist's aesthetic lay in performativity and public space, in particular Lacy's emphasis on public dialogue. *On the Edge* took the process of critical reflection into a public setting, inviting other key practitioners interested in the issues to learn together over a 12-month period (2006-7). There would be a structured programme of invited lectures, discussions and studio sessions, ending in the most public of contexts, the Scottish Parliament (September 2007). Thus Suzanne Lacy's personal research became *Working in Public,* a seminar series across the four major cities of Scotland with the intention of reaching artists, funders, policymakers and community partners who could benefit from the specific experience of a high-level practice (Figure 8.2). In this sense, Lacy's Oakland projects acted as a case study of important experience to the whole community of public art practice. The

FIGURE 8.2 "Seminar 1: Working in Public" (2007), Suzanne Lacy, Grant Kester and participants.
Credit: On the Edge research.

research generated an analytical framework situating the different tensions at work in this kind of artistic endeavour. It drew on Lacy's specific experience and extrapolated the consequences. The framework sought to acknowledge the very real tensions between aesthetics and ethics (Seminar 1), representation and power (Seminar 2) and quality of art and quality of social process (Seminar 3) (Douglas 2007).

Lacy finalized her thesis in 2013: "Imperfect Art: Working in Public, a Case Study of the Oakland Project 1991–2001", situating her Oakland work in art historical, philosophical and cultural contexts to assess its aesthetic merits. One of the major themes underpinning the thesis is to examine how the social claims in work of its kind can be evidenced. To this end she engaged with five sites: institutions within health, education, criminal justice, civic policy and youth experience. She aligned her work with forms of pedagogy – from the expanded notion of public pedagogy to the intimate level of a mentoring relationship. Pedagogy underpins the work's claim to hold a relevant place within both the public and professional art spheres.

In parallel with Lacy's research and inspired by its complex leadership dynamic, *On the Edge* developed the *Artist as Leader* research. This was a research partnership with Cultural Enterprise Office, Scotland, a Scottish-based organization that defines itself as a specialist business support and development service for creative businesses and practitioners, and with Performing Art Labs or Pallabs, a London-based organization that specializes in a methodology of creative labs across the arts, design, science and technology. It came at a time (2006–9) in which leadership was predominantly interpreted as good management and considered to be the key to a success mainly defined in economic terms. The partners in the research wanted to distinguish leadership in the arts from arts management. The research report (Douglas et al. 2009) drew on in-depth interviews with key individuals across the arts and the cultural policy sector, predominantly in Scotland. It distinguished three forms of leadership: aesthetic, organizational and social/activist. These were not intended to act as separate categories of leadership. A single individual could manifest leadership in all three forms, but each form depended upon different skills and focus. Perhaps more importantly, the research laid down the foundations for critical discourse across the arts and policy sectors by engaging individuals in a debate on leadership and its meaning to their communities of practice. This work is currently undergoing development through new doctoral research into cultural leadership by Jonathan Price, a cultural theorist.

This history shows how *On the Edge* is formed by, and also influences, the different cultural contexts in which the research operates. The starting point in remote rural cultures established an ethos of co-created research in which questions emerge out of shared interests across institutions and organizations, disciplines and diverse interests. In other words, these questions were not driven by a single agenda, whether that of an individual doctoral researcher, or of an institution, discipline or research project. Collaboration and interdependence have involved us in raising questions through discussion, listening rather than determining, working across the academic hierarchies of doctoral and post-doctoral research experience. Methodologies have had to be constructed as part of the research process, along with relevant literature and analytical frameworks that illuminate both the aesthetic and social dimensions of the practices on the ground. The research approach has involved forms of dissemination that communicate across the diverse community partnerships involved.

What characterizes doctoral research within the *On the Edge* programme? Researchers are frequently experienced practitioners, seeking to deepen their understanding of practice in a changing world. Each research project establishes exploratory threads, and tests different analytical frameworks as a lens through which to grasp the particularity of their approach and as a contribution to a shared discourse. They include artists and also arts-related practitioners working with cultural policy or leaders of arts organizations. In the process, researchers encounter challenges of how to position their inquiries within established knowledge paradigms. They draw on mixed methods crossing different paradigms.

The following case study is a particularly complex and vivid example of doctoral research that develops in this way. Reiko Goto Collins joined the research team in 2005 at the planning stage of the *Working in Public* seminars with Suzanne Lacy and was central to the process of developing and realizing the programme. She brought her particular expertise as an ecologist artist to the team. In the following analysis, Guba and Lincoln's framework of three questions is applied retrospectively to this doctoral thesis, a process that reveals how this practice-led research does not entirely fit with the specific paradigms that Guba and Lincoln define, suggesting that this area of research may in fact offer a different paradigm in its own right.

Evidencing a paradigm shift: a case study of doctoral research

"Ecology and Environmental Art in Public Place. Talking Tree: Won't you take a minute and listen to the plight of nature?" Reiko Goto Collins.
PhD Robert Gordon University 2012. Supervisor: Anne Douglas.

"What can be known?" (Guba et al. 1994, p. 108)

Goto Collins argues that it is possible to create change in understanding and behaviour towards the natural environment if we understand that human life is interdependent and interrelated with nature in our environment. Her perspective is that of a practising artist of some 20 years, working with her partner Tim Collins on ecological issues. Prior to the doctoral study and as Carnegie Mellon Research fellows, their partnership had undertaken major projects focusing on recovering landscape and river systems in post-industrial contexts such as Pittsburgh and raising public perception and agency within riparian environments (Goto Collins, 2010). Goto Collins knew that artistic interventions in these processes worked in certain circumstances, but not necessarily *how* they worked, and when – and why – they could also fail.

"What is the nature of relationship between the knower or would-be knower and what can be known?" (ibid.)

Through the research, Goto Collins was seeking to move beyond a planning-based approach to her art practice, and reconsider earlier ideas and practice where she was focused on individual relationships with living things. From the beginning, it was important to address the popular tendency to anthropomorphize nature, the position of the activist 'tree hugger'. She aimed to contribute to moving ecology art to a respected position as a research endeavour that was well informed, clearly argued and evidence based, building on the research practices of other artists such as Helen Mayer and Newton Harrison (Harrison and Harrison 2008). It emerged early on in the research that Goto Collins' challenge was to shift the dominance of positivism within ecology discourse and open up a discursive space that increased knowledge by engaging in deeply sensory and affective experiences of nature, increasingly opening these up as shared public encounters.

"How can the inquirer (would-be knower) go about finding out? Not any methodology will do … " (ibid.)

The methodological approach was complex, comprising a literature search into existing environmental theories (Brady 2003) and analysing three carefully selected case examples of ecology art practices: Sonfist's *Time Landscape* (1978), Joseph Beuys' *7,000 Oaks* (1982) and the Harrisons' *Serpentine Lattice* (1993) as important examples of aesthetic mediation in the natural environment. In addition, Goto Collins developed her ecology art practice as a site of experimentation.

This complexity of interrelated areas of knowledge and experience demanded a pivotal concept to explore the resonances between her approach and that of other significant ecology artists in the field and to locate these artistic endeavours within a history of ideas including environmental theory, a changing field.

Each area of inquiry made a distinctive contribution to the research. Goto Collins realized that existing theories positioned the human imagination as mediating aesthetic perception and scientific constructions of nature. She went further in acknowledging that the artist could demonstrate particular skills and responsibilities towards harnessing perception if they focused on the imagination. To this end, she concentrated on the relationship between humans and other living things that share the environment, conceptualizing this in terms of 'empathy'.

Goto Collins distilled a concept of empathy drawing on the work of the phenomenologist, Edith Stein (2002). Stein approaches empathy as a sense of lived connectedness, an awareness of the relationship between body, mind and environment. Empathy is a reaching towards something that is foreign and beyond self-interest. It is different from sympathy in seeking a new level of critical understanding through a sensitive reading of the expression of others (facial, bodily or spoken). Empathy is directed towards the unknown and the strange, as opposed to sympathy in which we map onto the world our existing mood or understanding (Goto Collins 2012, p. 57).

Goto Collins chose trees as a focus of experimentation. Trees form the largest living thing that we encounter (above ground on dry land). They are at once utilitarian, aesthetic and alive. She developed a relational artwork in close collaboration with a plant physiologist and a computer programmer, in order to experience how plants 'breathe' (Figure 8.3). She translated the plant's physiological

FIGURE 8.3 *Plein Air: The Ethical Aesthetic Impulse* (2010), Reiko Goto Collins. Peacock Visual Arts, Aberdeen, Scotland.
Credit: Reiko Goto Collins and Timothy Collins.

processes of photosynthesis and transpiration into sound, using and extending an existing custom software system. At first this was played back through digital systems, but, increasingly, Goto Collins performed the data using wind instruments, imagining the data as a score or note-to-note procedure that could be explored through the performing body. Public performance imaginatively linked the human body to the breathing tree. She reinvented the *Plein Air* easel to hold the plants' physiological system so that it could become a small portable station (ibid, p. 89).

What are the implications of this methodology for what is found out?

Goto Collins' research situates and makes explicit the implicit aspects of our current utilitarian relationship to nature. She creates experiences that propose a different possibility in which human beings are conceived as part of nature. The research embodies this way of imagining through the experimental work, shared as an aesthetic experience with a public. Through the deep mining of empathy as a philosophical construct, the research provides a critical base from which to evaluate empathy as an approach that achieves dialogue between human beings and nature. The practices and specific projects of other artists that manifest empathy in these terms, develop and nuance this critical base.

Guba and Lincoln (1994), in positioning research within competing paradigms, observe that facts are only facts within some theoretical framework. These are relative, not absolute. The same facts can be used to support different theories. Critical of the dominance of positivism within academic research, they challenged the tendency to focus on methodology as the determining factor in characterizing research. Both qualitative and quantitative methods, they argued, can be used appropriately in any research (ibid, p. 105). The question of method was secondary to the question of paradigm.

Goto Collins deploys both quantitative and qualitative methods. Her starting point challenges an objectivist stance in relation to nature by establishing dialogue as a principle of empathy – knowledge is achieved through experience, through feeling in relation to what is foreign, not known or understood. Quantitative methods, adapted from plant physiology, create a point of access to the inner life of trees through their processes of photosynthesis and transpiration and beyond what can be observed directly through the human senses. However, this quantitative approach stretched conventional sampling within plant physiology to longer, deeper observation that revealed the immediate and sensitive responses that each tree makes to small changes in the CO_2 environment (Goto Collins 2012, pp. 111–14).

Guba and Lincoln claim that a paradigm is a basic set of beliefs: a world view that positions the individual within it. All paradigms are therefore human constructions that are subject to the same kinds of evaluative criteria: persuasiveness, utility, proof. In research, we need to make explicit these beliefs, understanding what falls within and outside of the limits of an inquiry.

They establish three interconnected questions that need to be taken in order. These have been used to articulate Goto Collins' research approach.

1. Ontological: what is the form and nature of reality? Therefore what can be known? If the answer is driven by a belief in a 'real' world, then only those questions that relate to 'real' existence can be addressed. The concepts of aesthetic/moral assessment and value fall outside of this area.
2. Epistemological: what is the nature of relationship between knower and what is known? This again is not just any question – a belief in a 'real' reality positions the knower in relation to the world as objective, detached and value-free.
3. Methodological: how can we go about finding out? Not any methodology will do.

This metaphysical approach has provided an important way for the *On the Edge* research programme to construct practice-led doctoral and post-doctoral research projects. It supports the individual practitioner by consciously aligning research questions with the researcher's positioning, allowing for degrees of subjectivity and deep personal engagement with a set of issues. Methodologies serve the research question, not vice versa. Language, narrative, voice follow from the intentions and position of the inquiry. The framework of questions allows the researcher to probe and critique assumptions underlying existing paradigms of research. In this way, Guba and Lincoln's framework establishes the case for interdependence between researcher, research questions, existing knowledge and methods.

In artistic research it has been crucially important to construct and render transparent the progression that a practitioner might make from research issues or questions to methodology and outcomes. This orientates the voice and experience of the practitioner as an important contributor to producing knowledge. Issues or questions emerge from the fields of practice rather than from other academic research, though this is by no means excluded.

Guba and Lincoln reference four existing paradigms: positivism, post-positivism, critical theory and constructivism. The case example of Goto Collins' PhD analysed through their framework of competing paradigms (1994), reveals a useful method for arriving at a research design. However, their framework does not account for apparently contradictory research values in a single project. Goto Collins' research aim is clearly positioned within a constructivist paradigm that foregrounds the human intellect or imagination. Constructivism operates on the assumption that there are conflicting social realities at work that may change in the light of new knowledge. From a clearly constructivist position, Goto Collins challenges an objectivist approach to nature, creating a vivid and persuasive case for reappraising human/nature relationships as interdependent. At the same time a core aspect of her methodology is apparently positivist. This is evidenced in the approach used to collect data on the transpiration and photosynthesis of trees, data that was verified by a plant physiologist.

The crossing of existing paradigms within a single project begins to tell a story of inter- or trans-disciplinary approaches in which practice may be a pivotal element. In what sense does educating the artist as researcher imply a new research paradigm?

Conclusions: positioning practice-led enquiry

At an ontological level, practice shapes what can be known, in the sense that the experience of (in this case) the making of art as an active process, adds to subsequent acts and is formative of the next experience: "Wholly independent of desire or intent, every experience lives on in further experiences" (Dewey 1997, pp. 27–8). This generative force may open up new horizons of possibility and also limit them by closing out other possibilities to create focus. The artist's relationship with what can be known is quite distinctive. It is not based on hypothesis, the truth of which is deduced by moving from the general to the particular. Nor is truth induced from a body of experience by moving from the particular to the general. The artist, and by extension the artist-researcher, holds in juxtaposition specific moments of experience with other specific moments, so that the one shows itself beside the other and produces what Agamben calls "a new ontological context" (Coessens et al. 2009, p 95). In this way, concrete experience can constitute and make sense of a whole context from a particular perspective, without losing its particularity.

To return to the case example, Goto Collins' data gathering methods are not used for the purposes of prediction and control brought about through greater levels of generalization, as fitting the aims of positivism. As readers or audiences of the thesis, exhibition or performance, we remain close to the visceral experience of the phenomenon. It is this proximity to – and experiencing of – the specific 'moment' of the breathing tree that creates an encounter and a common ground between ourselves and another organism. Through reflection, we understand our condition as interdependent with nature. By making trees present within human experience, a whole context is constructed that reframes human/environmental relationships from a different perspective.

Over a period of 14 years, *On the Edge* research has developed an epistemological base that forms common ground across individual doctoral and post-doctoral projects. The thematics within this epistemology include remote rural cultures, leadership and public pedagogies, all of which position the artist as researcher. Across time and with deepening understanding, there has been a noticeable shift from working with art research as a lens to see differently (in this case remote rural cultures), to increased levels of creative intervention within self-imposed constraints. The *Artist as Leader* research set aside the current assumptions of leadership discourse, for example, and opened up a space for artists and policymakers to generate new understanding out of their conflicted expectations and assumptions. By drawing together two apparently incommensurable positions and placing these in juxtaposition, leadership – as it relates to the arts – was configured in ways that were distinctive.

These examples lead to the realization that art can never be subsumed in generalization without losing its point as art. Challenging truth is a fundamental task of positivism, but it is oriented towards stability. In contrast, the purpose of artistic inquiry is not to end up with stable truths that accrete, but to remain mobile. Constructivism and critical theory are more mobile, constantly creating more informed and sophisticated constructions that undergo continuous revision. Like the constructivist and critical theorist, the artist moves through realms of shifting meanings and subjectivities as a permanent condition of being, acting upon experience. Unlike the constructivist or critical theorist, the artist intervenes in those subjectivities by making and experimenting rather than observing from a distance. And in making art, the world is not just observed but also reframed.

Notes

1   On the Edge (OTE) is a doctoral and postdoctoral research programme at Grays School of Art, Robert Gordon University, Scotland. Founded in 2001 through a research grant from the UK's Arts and Humanities Board, OTE has developed a number of research inquiries in which the practice of the arts forms a pivotal aspect of the research approach. Research strands include the role of the contemporary artist in remote rural culture, the artist as leader and, increasingly, art and ecology.
2   These are the author's distillation of a number of conversations that unfolded over time.
3   As above, these are the author's distillation of a number of conversations that unfolded over time.

PART III

The spatial fabric of public art and social practice

9

PUBLIC ART AS A FUNCTION OF URBANISM

John Bingham-Hall

Introduction

Art, unlike architecture, has no interior as an urban element. It works as an image, so is not interpreted as a spatial object and has therefore been largely absent from the discourse of urban morphology (the study of the shape and layout of urban form). Many writers have brought the city into valuable discussions of art in the urban public. Sara Selwood, Malcolm Miles and Lucy Lippard among others describe how cities are gendered, politicized and commodified and how art negotiates these values. The city, in this reading, is a sociological entity consisting purely of patterns of social relations. This is not at all wrong, but it *is* incomplete. What is missing is space – concrete, real, three-dimensional space. So while Dolores Hayden asserted that "no public art can succeed in enhancing the social meaning of place without a solid base of historical research and community support" (Hayden 1997, p. 75), this chapter is an attempt to argue for the addition to these criteria of an understanding of the measurable shapes and syntaxes of urban spaces designated for new public art. Drawing from space syntax, a theory of urban morphology and social form (Hillier and Hanson 1984), the chapter describes measurable attributes of urban space that can be impactful for the way art objects are encountered and experienced, and therefore the kinds of cultural effect they can have. With case studies drawn from an original study applying the methodological techniques of space syntax to public artworks in the London Borough of Lewisham, it will be argued that there are surprisingly regular ways in which the ideologies that produce different types of city layout also shape the ways art objects use space.

Before making this argument, a few terms should be clarified. We talk often of what art can do to public spaces: invoking memory, creating a site to negotiate conflicting practices, stimulating social encounters between its audiences in shared moments of spectatorship. The argument here, however, is that we know little about what public space does *back* to art. This depends, of course, upon which definition of *public* is being invoked. Public can mean being "on stage" (Goffman 1966), being visible in a crowd of strangers (Lofland 1985), negotiating their many conflicting ways of occupying that stage, and playing a supporting role in the performance of public civility (Sennett 1993). In this regard, what public does to art is constrain, asking it to serve the cause of civility as a background prop, not to disrupt the performance with demands on attention or unsanctioned incursions on space. This constraining is well explored and constantly challenged, from modes of production that aim to refine this performance by working within constraints, as part of place-making, and seeking to disrupt it by consciously breaking these constraints, to amplify political messages, for example. 'Public' is also a set of communication practices that take place through mediated, national and international media to give rise to what we perceive as public opinion. In this regard, what public does to art is to make it answerable to demands of taste and involvement in the democratic processes of city building, of which public art commissioning forms a part. But 'public' is also something else. It is a spatial and legal reality formed of the exterior spaces within settlements, to which everyone is allowed access for the purposes of mobility and social gathering (notwithstanding the current issues arising around its privatization through by-laws). In this form, publicness can be measured as an assemblage of solid and virtual boundaries between jurisdictions and varying surfaces in the urban exterior, with geometric relationships to one another in a network of routes and spaces. It is this form of public that is under question here: in what way do these measurable spatial conditions impact upon the way art is applied into the public and experienced through it?

Public space as gallery

The city cannot act as a replacement for the gallery, creating passive environments for the display of art with minimal signal interference. Art in public will always negotiate with other demands on urban space: for movement, commerce and inhabitation. If, therefore, we are to use the city to create ways to view art, we must surely learn to better describe the spatial specificities of urban places and the hierarchy of functions supported through spatial structure.

As such, the history of art objects in public space can be told not simply through style and content but also through measurable changes in their spatial conditions. These conditions in cities are not just representational of social practices but in fact form and perpetuate these practices through the structuring of patterns of movement, encounter and separation in the city. For example, a residential back street does not only become so simply because it happens to be populated mainly by homes, but inversely it is populated mainly by homes *because* its relationship to other streets in the city means it is not viable as a through-route for traffic at city-wide scales. Its limited spatial connections means that it becomes a setting for the quotidian comings and goings of residents and therefore while legally public, it is parochial, constrained in its potential as a gallery by the very immediate concerns of a clearly defined set of users.

So the spatial conditions of the residential back street mean that artworks encountered there will be so in the context of instrumental, daily activity (as opposed to occasional ceremonial events, for example) and within a social setting that is in a sense only semi-public. As a result of this position within the hierarchy of spaces, the street is also likely to be shorter and narrower, with every inch utilized to support the needs of travel and inhabitation of its residents, leaving no "value-free" ground (Miles 1997, p. 56) to act as a plinth for abstract art objects. Artwork here must instead make use of vertical surfaces such as walls, which lend themselves to forms of unfolding narrative that are encountered through movement along a street rather than in the fixed, head-on views that would be possible in larger spaces like town squares. This is just one example of the constellation of effects that could be traced between an artwork, its spatial settings and the social practices afforded by that space, showing how demands over space – formed in part by its geometric attributes – assign value across its surfaces and structure views and encounters.

A brief overview of the development of public art can be retold with these spatial concerns in mind. From the nineteenth century art began to be disseminated to a wide public through the establishment of municipal galleries and art schools but also the filling of public space with sculptures of political and colonial figures. Although the aim was mass education and enculturation, the message was fixed – on the triumph of colonialism and industrial power over the darkness of the past – and communicated one-directionally (Willett 1967). To achieve this kind of unimpeachable, rigid communication, the objects themselves were raised up on plinths, untouchable, located in state-controlled civic spaces for the largest possible audiences and positioned in the centre of large, commanding views rather than in intimate recesses or corners.

At the beginning of the twentieth century, public art was reimagined by Robinson (1904) as a civic rather than colonial expression. This came as part of the rationalization of cities at that time through transport technology and urban planning, and the freeing of the city centre from the industries of the Victorian era, leaving the possibility for open space, "trees and turf" and a project of urban beautification. Civic art was to serve a unified urban aesthetic – the "visible crown" (Robinson 1904, p. 17) of the successful modern city at the apex of its historical evolution and so it did not need to represent anything other than the ability of a society to invest in urban beautification. With the simultaneous move towards pure abstraction in art, we can see how dominance of the historical or political monument began to subside, and space be made for a public expression of increasingly autonomous and non-representational art forms. Correspondingly, public art moved from being the focus of space, positioned in the centre of a void to create monumental views, to being built into the very fabric of the city through artistic approaches to the production of built form. Artists such as Victor Pasmore were appointed as consultants to urban planning departments as part of the "town artist experiment" (Petherbridge 1979). In Glenrothes in the late 1960s, resident town artist David Harding applied abstract reliefs to the walls of road underpasses, demonstrating a new spatial ideology in which art is an embellishment of small urban spaces and a backdrop to public life rather than a monumental totem to be gazed upon in reverence. Later we will see in specific spatial terms the difference between these two ideologies. As we will also see in more detail later, modernist planning itself also created the kinds of blank urban surfaces – around road infrastructure and the raised walkways of housing estates for example – that were rare in the traditional urban layout of streets and terraces, and appeared to provide inert canvases on which to apply rarefied artistic forms.

Malcolm Miles (1997, p. 59) criticized this attempt to provide public access to a "privileged aesthetic domain" by treating these blank surfaces like the white walls of the gallery. He used feminist and Marxist readings of public space to argue for public art policy that treats space as value-loaded and personal, and for art forms that are always either applied as urban design or work with social rather than concrete forms. The archetypal example of this approach is the community mural, popular in the late twentieth century, which brings public art practice into the kind of parochial residential spaces described earlier. Public art can enter into these socially constrained spaces when artists enable a micro-population – such as that of an individual street or estate – to produce forms that represent them to themselves. This level of cultural specificity, in which an artwork depicts the unique experiences and cultures of this micro-population, is again reflected in a spatial specificity: segregated, minor streets and tight visual fields occupied by these kinds of community works naturally limit their audiences to those deeply embedded spatially and socially in this locality.

Now, though, this kind of social art practice, with its parochial modes of production and spectatorship, struggles to compete with a neo-liberal ethos that employs public art as part of an armoury of techniques in the competitive marketplace of urban real estate. Councils vie to attract business and developers by showcasing the cultural output of their borough and advertise the presence of the "creative class", to use Richard Florida's much criticized terminology (Florida 2005). As developers, in turn, compete to establish theirs as the new 'urban village' *du jour,* public art must once again angle for maximum visibility, both at the focal points of commercial plazas or luxury private courtyards and in the glossy pages of advertising brochures.

What was perhaps a final stage bringing public art to the situation we recognize today has been the amalgamation of both planning-led public sculpture and artist-led public art practice into a 'cultural economy'. In Lewisham, south-east London, the case study presented later in this chapter, the borough council runs an agency called *Creative Lewisham*, through which it promotes two distinct but now clearly interrelated agendas: public realm improvement and support for the creative industries. Art, then, is seen as a way to support desired forms of economic activity and to present a desired image of the borough to a wider public. The key distinction in the context of this study is that where previously official policy has put artists to work along specific briefs based on social betterment or civic pride, the council now supports existing forms and highlights "Creative Enterprise Zones" where culture is self-generating, such as in the dense urban north of the borough as opposed to the more suburban south.

In this section, we have seen hints of the ways that changing ideological and economic concerns within the production of public art have been intimately linked with historical paradigms in the spatial formation of cities, in terms of the ways the accessibility and visibility of artworks are structured by spatial conditions. In what follows, these terms will be elucidated further through concrete examples and reference to existing theories on the creation of monumental urban form, setting the scene for the survey of public artworks in Lewisham, which develops these notions through systematic analysis and comparison of the spatial conditions of 52 individual art objects and locations.

Monumental objects or monumental space?

Doreen Massey, in her study of public art in Milton Keynes, argued that a 'place' should be seen as a meeting point of various layers of activity which extend across urban networks, rather than as a discrete entity (Massey and Rose 2003). In other words, a place is not just a set of social conditions determined by local cultures or populations but also an intersection of movement flows at varying scales dependent on its position within the hierarchy of spatial typologies and the network of routes through the city. This is one of the central premises of space syntax theory, which models space at two scales to describe Massey's observation empirically (Hillier 1989). At the most local scale, space is enclosed into immediate sections, within which people and objects are fully co-present. These sections – distinctly bounded urban squares or stretches of street – can be measured in terms of size and shape by modelling all open space in the city as a series of 'convex' shapes (see Figure 9.1).[1] Any space with an obtuse angle within its boundary would create a corner, blocking views and meaning part of it is outside of the realm of immediate perception, and therefore within the domain of the 'elsewhere'. Every space is, though, connected to the elsewhere, and space syntax analysis measures the form of this connection mainly in terms of the degree to which it is permeable from the rest of the street network. The measurement[2] demonstrates whether a convex space, such as a street section, is integrated into or segregated from the wider network, providing a relational description that is not contained within space (in the way size and shape is) but is syntactic. Hillier illustrates the way that this syntactic aspect of space shapes its social functioning through the example of the archetypal parade ground and the market place. To paraphrase, imagine two hypothetical examples of archetypal urban forms identical in size and shape but with very different ways of being embedded into the wider urban morphology (Hillier 2004, p. 185). The parade ground, for example, is the focal point of a formal planned layout consisting of straight ceremonial routes with inactive street frontages and freestanding buildings that reproduce the fixed social hierarchies of military power through their lack of emergent, unplanned functionality. The market place, on the other hand, is embedded in a network of small streets whose form is often organic and has developed to serve the demands of unplanned, emergent commercial activity of many individuals acting independently. Space in and around the market place is instrumental and resists over-investment in the symbolic, non-functioning forms like monuments that parade grounds and other ceremonial places are structured around. So places enclosing similar amounts of space in one immediate moment can afford very different social practices according to their syntactic relations with the rest of the city. Furthermore, according to Hillier, the more space is enclosed, the greater the symbolic emphasis on the syntactic attributes. So the grander the parade ground, the more focal it is likely to be in a symbolic urban or nation-scale performance of political power, and the larger the market place, the more central it is to the instrumental workings of an urban economy.

Hillier also describes how the visibility of buildings or objects, structured by their immediate spatial environments, forms their role in what Zukin has called the "symbolic economy" of urban form (Zukin 1995, p. 5). Hillier relates religious architecture – in which the sacred focal point is almost universally placed at the end of a long line of sight through the building – to the classic morphologies of urban centres of power such as Brasilia or London's Westminster, where long, straight ceremonial routes meet symbolic buildings' façades or monuments head-on, creating fixed views or "isovists" (see Figure 9.1) (Hillier 2004, pp. 171–6).[3] In

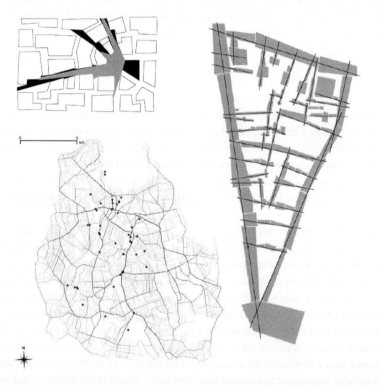

FIGURE 9.1   *Space Syntax*; clockwise from top left: isovists from a façade in a hypothetical urban layout; open space (grey) between buildings (white) split into convex spaces with axial lines showing potential movement routes; axial map of Lewisham with artwork locations starred (more integrated routes appear darker and less integrated routes appear lighter).

Credit: Hillier 2004, p. 117; Hillier 2004, p. 188; John Bingham-Hall.

contrast, places focused on trade and everyday life rather than ceremony (such as the City of London) tended to align buildings *alongside* routes through the city, so that their instrumental value as movement spaces supersedes any symbolic value. These spatial effects and the ideologies they relate to are hinted at in studies of cultural urban form but not explored in spatial terms. Doreen Massey, in her study of public art in Milton Keynes, wondered why artworks were tucked away in recesses adjacent to streets, limiting their visibility (Massey and Rose 2003), and this practice in modernist planning will be explored more later. Discussing privately managed Bryant Park in New York City, Sharon Zukin refers to how "an Alexander Calder sculpture stands in the middle of the lawn, on loan from an art gallery, both an icon and a benediction on the space" (Zukin 1995, p. 31), implicitly relating the object's spatial centrality to a quasi-religious effect symbolizing the investment of private wealth in this space.

Polly Fong undertook to quantify this by modelling the visibility of monuments in the historic layouts of the cities of London and Westminster (Fong 1999). She measured the area each monument could be seen from, finding fixed, symmetrical views along wide straight streets in Westminster as opposed to unfolding views along narrow angular routes through the city of London. A monument, it is suggested, is created as much by space as it is by content.

Spatial typologies of public art

This research is developed from a case study of 52 varied artifacts listed by the London Borough of Lewisham (at the time the study was carried out in 2011) in a guide map to public art within its jurisdiction. It was not a comprehensive survey of every artifact in every public space in the borough that could be considered 'art'. It excluded traditional monuments and instead consisted almost entirely of works made since 1970, suggesting an implicit definition of public art as a modern practice, distinct from the historical depictions of the Victorian city. However, this list was useful in defining a sample for investigation, and interesting for its framing of a collection of public art that the council wished to present as part of its civic provision and promotion of Lewisham (a somewhat unfashionable part of inner London at the time). The guide was interesting for other reasons as well. It revealed a surprising lack of knowledge on behalf of the council about what exactly the artworks were that lurked in the public spaces of its borough. The map offered only approximate locations for the artworks, and even on the corresponding council web page (since then moved and updated) most of the names given for works came without a reference image to suggest what kind of object they referred to, and where exactly they were to be found. So, even locating and identifying the objects that constituted these works was a significant first step in the investigation, requiring extensive use of non-council resources such as the Public Monuments and Sculpture Association's (PMSA) *National Sculpture Database* (http://pmsa.cch.kcl.ac.uk/). Facts such as artists' names, dates of creation and commissioning bodies were even more scant in the Council's own information, and were found instead in online chat forums about local places as well as the PMSA database. So, although public art commissioning is thought of as having reached a point of mainstream acceptability in urban planning and development, it remains marginal enough that even a council may not possess archives revealing what it holds in its very own hands.

Once every art object had been located, documented and catalogued with background information, a process of urban modelling was undertaken, based on the space syntax methods described above, in order to show the way that the visibility and accessibility of each is shaped by the urban morphology within which it is embedded, and the size of the immediate space containing it. First a map was created from Ordnance Survey geographical data showing all visual obstructions – buildings, walls, trees, raised rail lines and freestanding structures. Depthmap software (Varoudis 2012) can then generate isovists, defined by Benedikt as "the set of all points visible from a given vantage point in space and with respect to ... visible real surfaces in space" (Benedikt 1979, p. 47). As such, each artwork can be discussed in terms of the size and shape of the area from which it can be seen.

The next concern was accessibility: the way the location of each work can be encountered unexpectedly as a by-product of movement through the city. One of the 'generic functions' of urban space is to allow access from every location in the city to every other location along axes of movement, through streets and across larger open spaces (Hillier 1997). An 'axial line', in this theoretical model, is the longest possible path of continuous movement through any given space in a straight line before a change of direction must be made. So an axial map represents all our options for moving through the city and calculates, according to something like a 'path of least resistance' model the routes most statistically likely to be taken from every point in the network to every other point. For every segment of space between intersections, or changes in direction where in human terms a route decision must be taken, a value of accessibility can be calculated. This calculation takes into account how many other segments from every point on the network can be reached within a given distance, or in a limited number of changes of direction. While two streets may be only metres apart 'as the crow flies', their distance is measured along the street network itself and may be greatly increased if they are cut off from one another, as is often the case in the cul-de-sacs and dead ends of post-war residential development. This calculation gives a numerical value of 'integration' into the network, and in repeated observational studies this value has been shown to correlate positively with the volume of pedestrian traffic through that space (Hillier 1997). When analysed with a limited distance of 800 metres (around 10 minutes' walk) for example, this calculation tends to show local high streets and local shopping parades as the most integrated parts of the street network. This, according to Hillier's theory of the "movement economy", is because shopping areas have arisen organically where the network promotes pedestrian traffic, or have been planned to allow access on foot to commercial areas from the surrounding residential neighbourhood. When the whole network is analysed, showing how far every segment of street is from every other, it is the long 'spokes' – direct routes from city edge to centre with few changes in direction – that show as the most integrated, allowing quick movement at larger distances, usually vehicular, that bring people through the area on longer journeys. This 'foreground' network of integrated routes for travel and commerce tends to be superimposed on a background of much more segregated residential streets, where short segments and sharp corners segregate space and decrease the likelihood of through-traffic. So again we see how space syntax models space statistically and uses this to demonstrate how it fulfils its urban function. For each artwork then it is possible, by calculating values from an axial map of Lewisham (Figure 9.1), to say how accessible it is as a location, and what kind of space it occupies

Finally the immediate urban space containing each artwork was drawn out on a map, in relation to the physical boundaries surrounding it, once again producing shapes whose size and form can be described empirically and related to both urban functions and, as discussed above, to symbolic emphasis. Wide, regular openings in the urban fabric, such as squares that contain activities, allow us to stop and *be* in a place in static co-presence with other people. The larger that opening is, the greater the emphasis on its importance within the hierarchy of spaces: for example, distinguishing a local garden square from a grand town centre civic space. Long, narrow sections of space tend on the other hand to be streets, where our experience of sharing that space with both people and art objects is transitory and in passing.

So, for each of the 52 public artworks in the sample defined by Lewisham's Public Art Map we have a model of the size, shape, accessibility and visibility of its location. These models have measurable attributes, such as spatial integration, size, length of longest view and so on. By combining these measures statistically it begins to be possible to observe patterns in the spatial conditions of these locations that are interpreted here as morphological typologies, or categories of space. Each typology with its set of conditions, I would argue, brings spatial constraints, affordances and functions that describe in surprisingly regular ways how art is used in those spaces. Through its structuring of movement and visibility, urban form plays a large part in shaping what kind of urban functions artworks can fulfil. In what follows, some of these typologies will be illustrated through examples chosen from the survey.

The measures taken from these models can be compared in the form of data plots, comparing attributes to one another. We can compare, for example, the size of a space with the amount of spatial integration on the routes that pass through it. Using the example of the market place and the parade ground, it was shown that the larger a space, the greater the symbolic emphasis on its syntactic description. This emphasis can be shown statistically, by placing these two measures on either axis of a graph and plotting each artwork according to each attribute. Splitting the resulting plot into four quadrants gives us a systematic way to describe each location, given its distribution within the sample: small and segregated, large and integrated, and so on. A narrow high street, for example, is a highly integrated but purely functional space for movement and commercial exchange, whereas the large town square at its end is similarly integrated, but the extra investment in space lends it symbolic value as a representation of civic life and vitality.

Symbolic segregation

In these terms, large open spaces that are poorly accessible from the street system are symbolically segregated. Parks are the physical manifestation of this, where the state has given over significant amounts of valuable land to economic unproductivity, symbolizing social values centred around nature, health and well-being. In the artworks found in these large segregated spaces in Lewisham, artistic concerns are subservient to functions relating to these values. All but one of the examples with these characteristics are artist-designed mileposts for walking routes, while the last one is a windvane referencing river wildlife. None of them were commissioned by Lewisham council: the mileposts are from the green transport charity Sustrans and the windvane paid for by the Environment Agency. The park, being segregated from passing movement, is not a location valuable enough for the council to invest in promoting its creative talent or civic pride (as will be seen in other examples) and they, in fact, explicitly recognize in their cultural strategy that the abundance of open space in the south of the borough acts as a spatial barrier to home-grown cultural activity there (Creative Lewisham Agency 2002).

Non-symbolic segregation

Fourteen of the 19 artworks within the dataset representing small spaces with low integration are murals or wall-mounted reliefs applied to vertical surfaces rather than floor-standing. It is common sense that artists produce non-land-consuming work in confined spaces such as small streets, but it is also notable that murals are more likely to be found in relatively segregated locations. As was suggested previously, commercial activity is more likely to occur along routes that are spatially integrated, as statistically they are likely to attract a flow of pedestrian traffic (Hillier 1997), and shop entrances mean there are not usually the large non-permeable sections of wall required for a mural to be realized in integrated streets. Murals are found instead where street frontages are impermeable: among infrastructure like the railway underpass home to the graffiti mural *Get the Message* in Forest Hill, or quiet post-industrial areas such as Creekside in Deptford where Gary Drostle's *Love Over Gold* mural adorns the wall of a warehouse overlooked by council flats. Both works were created together with local school children with part funding from social charities and the local education authority. The mural is the classic form of community participation that art often involves, as in the case of *Pink Palace* in the Crossfields Estate, local residents. We might well expect this kind of mural to be found where lack of footfall means there is less mixing between inhabitants and strangers; residents are in greater control of this space and perhaps feel more inclined to invest in its appearance than they would in a more integrated and more publicly used space that is shared by a wider population.

Symbolic integration and consensus landmarks

In Catford, the civic centre of the borough and the location of its town hall, London's South Circular meets the A21 (see map in Figure 9.2) – two significant trunk roads that form part of the highly integrated network of long-distance movement routes described before. At this convergence they widen out, changing from linear thoroughfares to 'fat' convex spaces: from roads to move along to places to be in. This widening creates symbolic integration: large convex spaces that are highly accessible, focal points of the street network. The two public artworks here are large, abstract, three-dimensional sculptures of around 2 metres each in height, standing on lawn beds surrounded by low fences and embedded into the wide pavements. Both are by non-local artists: *Water Line,* commissioned from the prolific public artist Oliver Barratt by Lewisham Council, and *Chariot* – bequeathed to the council by the family of the Russian artist Oleg Prokofiev after his death (see images in Figure 9.2). Both these artworks were installed in Catford town centre in a project led by Creative Lewisham – the borough's arts agency,

FIGURE 9.2 Map of Catford town centre, showing isovists (hatched grey) from *Pensive Girl* (left), *Water Line* (middle) and *Chariot*. 'Consensus landmarks' have long T-shaped isovists meeting many junctions while 'backdrop' art is only visible from the building entrance.

Credits: John Bingham-Hall using Ordnance Survey data, Crown copyright and database right, 2012.

with funding from the developer Desiman Ltd, placing them firmly in the category of high-visibility cultural regeneration-led commissioning, previously outlined.

In his classic text *The Image of the City*, Kevin Lynch (1967) describes how urban elements can become landmarks. When placed for optimum visibility they reach a point of consensus, featuring repeatedly in cognitive maps of the city. "Location is crucial: if large or tall, the spatial setting must allow it to be seen … Any breaks in transportation – nodes, decision points – are places of intensified perception … Buildings at route decision points are remembered clearly, while distinctive structures along a continuous route may have slipped into obscurity. A landmark is yet stronger if visible over an extended range of time or distance" (Lynch 1967, p. 101). Reinterpreting these Lynchian criteria in the same terms used in this study, Ruth Conroy-Dalton has described a landmark location as one producing large isovists with long fingers representing views over an extended range of time or distance, overlapping with well-integrated, intersected axial lines representing decision points on well-used routes through the area (Conroy Dalton and Bafna 2003). To look for these landmark attributes in Lewisham using the spatial data collected in the survey, the size of each isovist was plotted against the number of axial lines it meets. In other words, the extent of the area from which each location can be viewed compared to the number of different routes it can be viewed from. The artworks in Catford town centre came out with the highest values in this data comparison – they can be seen from far down the wide main roads (471 metres away at the furthest) as well as the many junctions with side roads that meet them. So the locations of these two artworks provide spatial conditions that, according to Lynch's definition, can turn art objects into landmarks. But how do these objects in these particular locations respond to that potential? With their spatial conditions elevating them to landmarks, the artworks themselves are not required to have any further urban function: as depictions of local cultures, as street furniture, signage or other such elements that were common in other less conspicuous spaces like the parks or back streets described previously.

Given the spatially integrated town centre location, where land is highly valuable commercially and infrastructurally, the spatial investment made to display these works – on protected, dedicated canvases of land in almost quasi-gallery conditions – is evidence of a position of prestige. Not only are these landmarks for local people but they are also emblems intended for a wider audience of passers-through, demonstrating the ability of this borough to invest both spatially and economically in the display of 'international' art. In its cultural strategy published in 2002 (four years before the installation of these works), Lewisham identified Catford as an "emerging cluster" of the local creative economy, proposing that "Lewisham's visual environment needs a significant uplift to mark a change of attitude" and that "external recognition" was a key ambition (Creative Lewisham Agency 2002). The relationship of these artwork locations to the city-wide network of movement space means they *can* reach this "external", non-local audience, and their alignment within that location takes maximum advantage of their landmark visibility along these routes. This can also be thought of as the most public of public space. With greater volumes of local and through-movement, an intense mixing of people occurs; no-one can be thought of as a stranger and the performance of personal identities becomes subservient to civic responsibility to the generic crowd. Artworks within this kind of space seem not to respond to specific cultural identities but rather take on more abstract visual forms.

Art as backdrop

At the opposite end of the spatial spectrum to such landmarks were more hidden locations, visible from smaller areas (around 4,000 square metres) and only one or two street sections. These are works set back from linear spaces, and adjacent to the direction of movement, forming (see Figure 9.2) the effect noted by Doreen Massey in which art works are not viewed head on. Four works in the sample were positioned like this, adjacent to the street but semi-enclosed in either entrances or enclaves. *Feed the Cows*, artist-painted recycling bins in New Cross, for example, are functional objects decoratively treated. They are encountered within an enclave whose purpose is to provide a partially protected space to stop and make use of that function. The *Horniman Mosaic* adorns the entrance to a local museum in Forest Hill and *Pensive Girl* sits outside Lewisham Council's offices just off the main road in Catford (see Figure 9.2). Both are set back from the street into semi-private recesses that limit viewership to those who choose to enter that building. These are not abstract, self-sufficient objects that, like the sculptures nearby in the centre of Catford, become meaningful by being fixed in view as landmarks, but decorative interventions forming a backdrop to other moments of activity, such as taking out the recycling, or crossing a threshold into a cultural space.

Amorphous landscape

Another similarity with Milton Keynes comes when looking at the urban landscape in Lewisham with a wider lens. Lewisham centre can be thought of as one of London's 'villages', historic settlements incorporated into the metropolitan area as they grew themselves as satellites, and as London grew outwards towards them. In space syntax terms, the roads around Lewisham centre act as a 'hub' from which emanate 'spokes' towards the borough's edge and into London's large-scale movement network (Hillier 1999, p. 8). Much of the historic town centre itself, however, was destroyed by bombing in 1944 and was redeveloped from the 1950s, including the addition of an indoor shopping centre in 1977 and the pedestrianization of the adjacent section of the high street in 1994. The result is a combination of a traditional morphology of small, street-fronted shop units lining the east of the high street, and the typically post-war morphology of a large commercial building with interior permeability and inactive exterior façades facing onto busy traffic arteries. So the high street itself acts as the overlap between a landscape of streets and houses to the east surviving from before the war, and a post-war landscape of open space, roads and large residential and commercial buildings to the west.

Julienne Hanson defined this historical shift in urban morphology by calculating the ratio between built and open space. She found that in post-war developments such as housing estates, new towns and urban restructuring projects like that in Lewisham town centre, open space became more significant in proportion to built mass (Hanson et al. 2007, p. 55). Art, she suggested, would be used in this context to act as an interface between the home and this new, alienating landscape. This morphological change has also been described by Matthew Carmona as the shift from traditional to modernist space, with the latter described as an "amorphous landscape" which surrounds "freestanding pavilions" (Carmona et al. 2003) as opposed to the clearly defined streets and squares contained by solid blocks of built form.

In the 1990s the *Lewisham 2000* scheme was initiated to regenerate the commercial centre through the improvement of the public realm. Lewisham appointed renowned sculptor John Maine to the role of town artist, as had many new towns during the 1970s. In this role, Maine created *Ridgeway, Column* and *Bollards*, which a contemporaneous critique of applied arts saw as "likely to outlast many of the buildings which might more readily be taken as Lewisham's 'thereness'" as it was "to the bones of the landscape that John Maine applied his art" (Nuttgens and Heath 1992, p. 36). Though landscape is used poetically here, it describes accurately the open modernist morphology, which leaves large sections of ground unused by either building or infrastructure. The works that form part of the Lewisham 2000 project were inserted as retrospective improvements into the pre-existing open spaces and blank façades resulting from 1970s planning around the shopping centre. John Maine's work both stylistically and spatially characterizes civic art which was to be an abstract expression of the height of modernist rationality and to occupy a cleansed urban landscape of 'trees and turf', apparently removed from daily functions of space such as commerce, which are only one street away on Lewisham High Street. *Ridgeway*, if it were inched slightly south-east of its location, could fill the fixed views along the streets that approach it and become a monument. Instead, modern council-commissioned works shy away from large-scale spatial structuring of ceremonial routes in favour of localized effects. The ideology they help to project is not one of overarching order as observed by Polly Fong in Westminster but of restorative cultural intervention into pre-existing sections of unused space. The redundant surfaces created by post-war planning become blank canvasses for art and are thereby justified in their existence.

Urban scale patterns and historical shifts

Hopefully these examples have given an idea of how public art could be seen primarily as a function of urbanism, even before we start to consider the cultural and political issues raised by its content and its modes of production. As we zoom out from individual settings, however, there is also a wider pattern in the way art is produced among the urban landscapes across the area. *The Social Logic of Space* (Hillier and Hanson 1984) puts forward a model that predicts certain forms of cultural representation in certain types of urban space and does not look dissimilar to a description of the data collected in this study.

The argument, in short, is that two kinds of socio-spatial mechanisms cooperate to produce and maintain social forms. On one hand 'organic' city-building emerges from spatially dense and unritualized social negotiations, generating new socio-spatial forms that go on to become reproduced in wider society ("local-to-global" in Hillier and Hanson's terms). On the other hand planned city-building allows the state to project "a unified ideology and a unified politics over a specific territory" through representational artefacts and morphologies that reproduce existing social structures in space ("global-to-local") (Hillier and Hanson 1984, p. 21). Settlement morphology is formed by both mechanisms, in varying degrees, according to the role of that settlement. Local-to-global space appears as a "dense system, in which public space is defined by the buildings and their entrances", like the traditional street morphologies in the denser urban north of the borough. Its inverse is a "sparse system, in which space surrounds buildings with few entrances" more like the modernist landscape in Lewisham town centre (ibid.). Lewisham Council itself has noted the creative energy that seems to be produced in the north of the borough, and their main practice is to identify artists who have emerged unplanned from this social milieu and support them to produce artworks generated locally. Deptford artists Artmongers produce non space-consuming works that are applied to inactive surfaces, located in relatively small spaces along the busy, narrow Deptford High Street, which lacks symbolic emphasis but is prominent at a local scale. These works are impermanent and can easily be changed or removed with few financial implications, as social and urban forms in the area continue to emerge and change.

In the open landscape of Lewisham centre, and wide streets of Catford centre, we find a tendency towards a greater spatial and financial investment by the council and developers in permanent, freestanding sculpture through which commissioners aim to produce rather than respond to local identities, through cultural regeneration and rebranding. These works signify the cultural and economic wealth of the overarching political body, in exactly the way Hillier and Hanson suggest is indicative of the global-to-local logic in space. Again an adaptation of this logic occurs in the segregated but sparse space of the parks, which the council has recognized as a barrier to a home-grown cultural economy. Here, national environmental organizations like Sustrans and the Environment Agency have installed route markers among a sparse morphology where society's central beliefs are reproduced through representational forms; in this case the recent belief in the importance of environmental responsibility. Indeed the Cultural Strategy recognizes that "the continuing programme to naturalise the river channels...have demonstrated Lewisham's role in – and commitment to – maintaining and improving the natural environment" (Creative Lewisham Agency 2002, p. 16). These markers, as Hillier and Hanson put it, are a part of the same centrally produced system of value representation.

Hopefully this study[4] has shown that urban morphology is an important factor in structuring the way art objects in public space are produced, and the roles they can play. The city is more than an aesthetic and social 'context', on which much debate on public art has focused. This is not to suggest that these immediate contexts are irrelevant, but rather that – like architecture – public art should take these into account *alongside* spatial implications, which appear to impact greatly upon the ideologies embodied by this kind of urban object. By bringing in a social theory of space it has been proposed that well-connected streets can be more public than segregated, parochial spaces of habitation adding a spatial dimension to Massey's "meeting point" definition of public space. Whereas critical writing on public art has tended to assume that 'public' refers to a limited set of individuals living in proximity to a location and defining its socio-cultural identity, the syntactic method offers a more differentiated view of the continuum between public and private, which could be used by artists, commissioners and academics looking to add a spatial dimension to their understanding of the relation between art and the public.

Notes

1 A convex shape is contained entirely by boundaries with acute angles at its corners, so that every point within it has a direct line of sight to every other point.
2 Defined using Depthmap software (Varoudis 2012) that, in simple terms, calculates the distance and the number of turns from every segment of movement space in a street network to every other, giving a numerical value of integration for any one place. See Bafna (2003).
3 "Isovist" is a term coined in Benedikt (1979) to describe the area from which a specific point in space can be seen, or vice versa. See Figure 9.1 for example.
4 The full text of this study, including data and methodological details, can be found at http://www.bit.ly/publicartasurban.

10

LISTENING IN CERTAIN PLACES

Public art for the post-regenerate age

Elaine Speight

Almost a decade ago, in May 2005, I took up a curatorial position with *In Certain Places* – a new public art scheme in the north-west city of Preston, based at the University of Central Lancashire, UK. Freshly graduated from the art school of a larger, more culturally vibrant city, I spent the first few days reacquainting myself with what I considered to be my staid and dreary hometown. At first glance, the city appeared to have changed little in the six years of my absence. The staccato calls of street vendors still punctuated the high street; women with grey perms and shopping trolleys sipped tea in the bus station café; and the derelict buildings that I had photographed for a high school project in the late 1990s continued to crumble and flake. Yet, the more I familiarized myself with the city, the more I realized that it was no longer the place that I was once so eager to leave. Buoyed by the promise of regeneration, and imbued with optimism, Preston felt as if it was undergoing a process of metamorphosis – about to emerge from its mill town past, as a contemporary, creative city.

In this respect, Preston was not dissimilar to many other post-industrial cities in the UK during that time. Driven by the New Labour government's urban renaissance agenda – which sought to transform downtrodden city centres into economic drivers, by "creating the quality of life and vitality that makes urban living desirable" (Urban Task Force 1999, p. 3) – former manufacturing hubs set about reinventing themselves as vibrant and "attractive places to live, work and socialise" (ibid.). By the time I returned to Preston, the neighbouring city of Liverpool had cleared a 42-acre site at its core to make way for what would soon become the UK's largest outdoor shopping centre. Meanwhile, Manchester had morphed into a polished urban centre, its new glass towers shimmering above redbrick Victorian buildings, which housed loft-style apartments for aspirational city dwellers. After decades of decline, the country's inner cities were posited as economic saviours, and municipal authorities were eager to cash in.

Within this milieu, public art became regarded as an effective, yet low-cost way to add value to urban development projects. Prized for their visionary thinking, aesthetic sensibilities and cultural cachet, artists were widely employed within regeneration schemes as 'place-making' professionals. Yet, less than five years after *In Certain Places* began, this bright future would be exposed for the mirage that it was. The disintegration of the property market marked the end of large-scale regeneration, as well as the generous financial and political support for public art that it had entailed. However, while the economic crisis led to the decline of many public art schemes, it also presented opportunities to build upon the ground covered and lessons learned during the urban renaissance era, and to develop more sustainable approaches to art and regeneration.

In the following chapter, I give a brief account of such developments through the prism of my own experience of public art in Preston. Through the example of *In Certain Places*, I also outline what I describe as a 'place-listening' approach to public art. Presented as part of a wider, emerging ethos among artists and curators, place-listening denotes an attitude to public art and curatorial practice that is founded upon a situated and long-term commitment to a place. Characterized by durational, embodied interactions with the site and subject of the work, place-listening is – I suggest – a useful concept for considering new modes of public art, that respond to the opportunities and challenges presented by the post-regenerate city.

Public art and urban renaissance

In Preston, urban renaissance took the form of the Tithebarn scheme – an ambitious retail and leisure development, which proposed to reconfigure around one-third of the existing city centre. Ten years in the planning, the project was a partnership between the city council and Grosvenor Ltd. – one of the largest landowners in Britain. Although widely supported by the people of Preston, like all forms of change, the plan was not without its detractors. While some people worried that the council would be pressured to sell land to the developers, others believed that the scheme, which included a proposal to remodel the city's covered markets as a glassed-in deli-style food court, catered to a wealthier demographic than the general population. Most notably, the redevelopment also involved the planned demolition of the city's brutalist bus station, whose immense stature and iconic curves became a cause célèbre for modernist architecture enthusiasts.[1]

For people involved in the arts, however, the Tithebarn scheme's main limitation was that it contained no reference to culture. Given the size of the project and the mood of the time, this omission was somewhat unusual. Heralded by advocates as a key factor in the revitalization of cities such as Bilbao, Barcelona and Chicago, culture was widely promoted as a panacea for urban decline and, despite limited evidence of its efficacy, local authorities eagerly embraced it as a regenerative tool. Between the late 1990s and mid-2000s, *cultural* and *culture-led* regeneration schemes flourished across the UK.[2] The derelict waterfronts of cities such as Newcastle, Salford and Glasgow were revived as highbrow entertainment complexes, and contemporary art galleries, designed by prominent architects, were commissioned for such working-class towns as West Bromwich and Middlesbrough.

Traditionally sympathetic to the notion of 'art for the masses', the New Labour Government was quick to extol the contribution of art to the nation's economic and social wellbeing. However, the cross-pollination of arts and urban policy, which occurred during their time in office, was also informed by wider cultural debates. Notable among these were François Matarasso's 1997 study, 'Use or Ornament?' – which argued that it was necessary for the arts sector to "start talking about what the arts can do for society, rather than what society can do for the arts" (Matarasso 1997, p. v) - and US urban theorist Richard Florida's *The Rise of the Creative Class* (2002). While the former outlined a series of social benefits derived through participation in the arts, such as reduced crime, increased health and more 'cohesive' communities, the latter identified the arts as an essential factor within the financial fortunes of a place. Specifically, Florida claimed that the economic viability of post-industrial cities lay in their capacity to attract 'creative professionals', through access to culture and a high quality of place, which could largely be achieved through the arts.

Yet despite its rising currency it was not culture but retail that lay at the heart of the Tithebarn scheme; and attracting a 'flagship' store, rather than constructing a new art gallery, developing a festival or commissioning public art, was the council's primary concern. In response, Preston's creative professionals took it upon themselves to assimilate art within the city. In addition to local artists, who explored the implications of regeneration through site-specific projects and events, creative responses to the Tithebarn scheme were driven by a handful of individuals with links to Preston's foremost institutions – the city council and the University of Central Lancashire. Among these were James Green – programme manager at the council-run Harris Museum & Art Gallery, and artist and lecturer Charles Quick, who together devised what would eventually become *In Certain Places.*

For Quick and Green, the Tithebarn scheme represented a valuable opportunity to engender the type of public art culture that they believed the city lacked. Having instigated a number of art initiatives in Preston, the pair sought to develop a more integrated role for artists in the city. To this end, they devised a programme of activities designed to inform the entire Tithebarn planning process. This consisted of three mutually supportive projects: a series of public talks about art and regeneration; a three-year programme of temporary public artworks in Preston city centre; and, after much negotiation, the appointments of Quick and New York-based artist Alfredo Jaar as lead artists within the Tithebarn master-planning team.

Initiated in 2003, this three-pronged approach was designed to lay the groundwork for a long-term commitment to public art in Preston. The programme of talks and debates disseminated new ideas about the role of artists within urban development, while the series of temporary artworks aimed to demonstrate the range of possibilities for permanent or large-scale commissions. The plan was for Jaar and Quick to build upon these activities by creating opportunities for themselves, as well as other artists, to influence specific aspects of the scheme, and developing the necessary infrastructure for subsequent artworks and events. By the time I joined *In Certain Places,* the project had gathered momentum. A critical mass of people – predominantly artists but also architects, urban planners and other civic-minded people – had coalesced around the project, and Green and Quick had successfully lobbied the council to employ a public art development manager within their urban planning department. In this way, the duo sought to engender a holistic model of public art commissioning that would not only create opportunities for artists within the Tithebarn scheme but also ensure their involvement in the city's future as a whole.

The burgeoning public art culture in Preston during the early 2000s reflected a wider national trend. Across the country, there was an increasing sense that artists were moving outside of the gallery and that public art was, very slowly, losing some of its former stigma. Rather than the oft-cited and much caricatured model of 'roundabout sculpture' or earnest community art, perceptions of the genre were beginning to expand to include more avant-garde forms of practice. This shift was partly informed by the groundwork laid by artists, curators and commissioners during the late 1980s and 1990s. Commissioning agencies such as Artangel in London and Newcastle's Locus + had demonstrated that art in urban spaces could be as, if not more, challenging and critically engaged than works in a white cube context. Moreover, artists began developing intellectual frameworks for their practice by convening conferences and events that articulated the type of critical, participatory and place-specific art with which so many were engaged. Notable among these was the 1994 conference 'Littoral: New Zones for Critical Art Practice' in Salford – organized by Projects Environment, now called 'Littoral' – which attempted "to locate the theoretical and aesthetic coordinates" of collaborative and "socially engaged" practices (Littoral 2014); and, across the Atlantic, Suzanne Lacy's influential 1991 conference, 'Mapping the Terrain', which yielded a book of the same name and the still current neologism "new genre public art'" (Lacy 1995).

Collectively, these activities generated a renewed interest in public art as a dynamic and critical practice. This was embodied by the emergence, during the late 1990s and early 2000s, of a series of commissioning agencies for art in the public realm – including Modus Operandi, London (established in 1999), Ginkgo Projects, Somerset (2001), Situations, Bristol (2002) and General Public Agency, London (2003–10) – many of which operated within urban development contexts. Likewise, more established cultural and civic institutions began developing their own artistic interventions within the urban public realm. In 1999, for example, the Royal Society of Arts launched a series of temporary commissions for the Fourth Plinth in Trafalgar Square; while a year later London Underground began its 'Platform for Art' project. Further north, Arttranspennine98 – a three-month exhibition of public art organized by Tate Liverpool and the Henry Moore Foundation, Leeds – and the Liverpool Biennial created new encounters between art and everyday life.

Alongside the work of arts institutions and agencies, this attitudinal shift was also driven by the advocacy of research and media organizations, which collectively endorsed public art as an agent of urban change. Significant among these were *Art & Architecture Journal*, Public Art Forum – a 'think tank', later rebranded as 'ixia' – and Comedia, whose 'Creative City' paradigm helped to position public art within wider discussions about the role of art within urban planning.[3] Such debates helped to shift perceptions away from the pervasive 'sculpture in the plaza' model, which had characterized the commissioning of public art since the mid-1900s, towards an understanding of the art form as a multifaceted and versatile practice. Rather than a mere decorative addition to otherwise faceless developments, public art was championed as an active and engaging process, capable of producing tangible effects within a city's environment, community and economy.

As a result, central and local government embraced public art as a vehicle for urban change and a way for cities to compete for tourism and business. As local authorities attempted to emulate the perceived regenerative effects of Gateshead's *Angel of the North* through their own commissioning projects, New Labour also enshrined public art within their urban policy. Promoted as a way to generate a sense of place and local distinctiveness within regeneration projects, the commissioning of public art was posited as an antidote to the threat of homogenization posed by standard approaches to urban design and the dominance of chain stores. Additionally, participatory forms of the genre were posited as a "flexible, responsive and cost-effective" (Matarasso 1997, p. vi) means of stemming local opposition to redevelopment schemes and engendering social cohesion.

Rather than the detached producer of stand-alone artworks, these discourses positioned the artist as an urban "problem solver", "*creative lateral thinker*" (Farrell cited in Minton 2007) and valuable urban strategist, who could provide a new development with "something unique and engaging" within an otherwise crowded market (Landry 2008). No longer romantic outsiders, artists became regarded as key players within the construction and coordination of the neo-liberal city. As Jonathan Vickery suggests in his Creative City critique, as the creative industries began to replace manufacturing as the driver of urban economies, it became a tacit belief among cultural advocates that "the artist would displace the engineer as the model of professional labour in the hard physical contexts of the urban realm" (Vickery 2011, p. 2). Lauded for their entrepreneurialism, intuition and perceived ability to act as a conduit between local communities and urban professionals, artists were endorsed as a cost-efficient means of securing the competitive advantage necessary to ensure urban success.

Specifically, artists became valued for their contribution to 'place-making'. Derived from progressive responses to the tabula rasa approach of mid-twentieth-century urban renewal, place-making has become shorthand for the practice of creating, maintaining or enhancing a location's identity and sense of place as part of the regeneration process. More an ethos than a method, it constitutes "a multi-faceted approach to the planning, design and management of public spaces" (Project for Public Spaces 2010) that draws on existing cultural and physical resources to create places that "promote people's health, happiness and wellbeing" (ibid.). Not simply an aesthetic embellishment, place-making has been promoted as "a key driver for economic prosperity" (CABE, English Heritage and Sustainable Development Commission 2008, p. 4) that can transform struggling cities into places in which people choose to "live, work, play and invest" (CABE 2004, p. 1).

As producers of collective meaning and experience, artists were recruited as place-making professionals within public realm developments. In many cities, such schemes followed the traditional model of place-making as "urban design allied with public art" (Miles 1997, p. 117). In these instances, artists contribute to place-making initiatives by producing decorative additions to landscape and urban design features, or creating sculptural works that fit within an overarching design aesthetic. In other cases, art was regarded as part of a 'soft' place-making approach, with artists employed to engage local communities within the redevelopment process through forms of 'creative consultation'. In more ambitious scenarios, however, such as the *In Certain Places* scheme, artists had the opportunity to actively inform the early stages of public realm developments as lead artists and consultants.

The early 2000s therefore marked a renaissance for public art in the UK and increased opportunities for artists. Sustained by the engorged property market, fine art graduates, who had anticipated the customary struggle for survival, found themselves in demand as place-making professionals. As itinerant workers, many were able to make a living – albeit frugally – by undertaking short-term commissions within a continual stream of regeneration contexts. This was facilitated by the emergence of a new class of creative worker, who variously described themselves as 'public art commissioners', 'administrators' and 'project managers', and acted as intermediaries between local authorities, regeneration agencies, developers, artists and communities. Previously viewed by some sectors of the art community as a mediocre occupation, the practice and management of public art was reframed within the creative industries as a smart career choice.

Yet, within a few short years, the landscape would shift again. As the economic recession took hold, following the property crash in 2007, and the Liberal Democrat/Conservative coalition government replaced New Labour in 2010, funding streams and the public art roles they supported began to dissipate. In turn, what had appeared to be a budding cultural sector was suddenly recast as an unaffordable luxury. Although unapparent at the time, the formation of *In Certain Places* coincided with the decline of the country's urban renaissance and associated public art culture. For Preston, this meant the failure of the Tithebarn scheme, which was finally abandoned in 2011, and the untimely termination of the Lead Artist initiative. Nevertheless, despite this setback, *In Certain Places* endured and, as part of a wider cultural trend, began to explore new ways to operate within the post-regenerate city.

Post-regenerate public art

The collapse of the property market in 2007 had a perceptible and devastating effect upon the UK's urban centres. As the economy slowed, so too did the incentive of businesses to expand, making it difficult for developers to secure tenants for retail projects. Many regeneration schemes were consequently put on hold or abandoned altogether, creating modern ruins from half-completed construction sites. The disintegration of New Labour's Housing Market Renewal Initiative had a similar effect on the country's urban fringes, reducing rows of Victorian housing to wasteland and scattering communities. Fortunately, a series of complications delayed the construction of the Tithebarn scheme and spared Preston the fate of cities such as Bradford, which was left with an abyss at its core.

Despite leaving its centre intact, the recession produced a sense of lethargy and despondency in Preston. After more than a decade of working towards a new urban identity, the art community felt deflated. Injured by governmental budget decisions, the council attempted to save money by reducing cultural provision and cutting resources, such as its recently established art and design gallery, and the public art development manager. For *In Certain Places*, the Tithebarn's decline also marked the official end of the Lead Artist project, which in reality had never begun. Although outwardly supportive, the council and developers had been reluctant to involve Quick and Jaar at the master-planning stage and sidestepped the artists' persistent attempts to be included in the process. By the time the development was cancelled, the Lead Artist project was already defunct.

This frustrating experience was echoed by the accounts of other artists and curators, who had become disillusioned with the relationship between public art and regeneration. Like Quick and Jaar, many had discovered that their elevated status within regeneration discourses failed to translate into practice. Held at arm's length from strategic decision-making processes, and prevented from developing meaningful forms of engagement due to limited timescales and funds, artists had come to view their involvement within the development of places as shallow and tokenistic. Furthermore, a common emphasis upon predetermined outcomes, rigid commission briefs and a dominant 'tick box' culture had blunted their ability to provoke questions or to critique a situation. Instead, it appeared that art practice had become reduced to a low-cost social ameliorant or creative place-marketing tool.

Even as the revived public art industry unfurled in the early 2000s, artists began to question the social and ethical implications of their various place-making roles. Described by critics as gentrification disguised as urban renewal,[4] urban renaissance was, after all, predicated upon a belief that the economic viability of urban centres could be achieved by catering to middle-class tastes and concerns. Within this context, artists not only provided the creative cachet deemed necessary to attract this demographic, but also, through their engagement with existing, less wealthy inhabitants, helped to produce – or at least construct the illusion of – strong and harmonious communities. The model of the artist as social worker was a particular concern for artists, who worried that their involvement within challenging social contexts was simply an alternative to more expensive, yet effective, forms of community development. Cultural commentators similarly criticized artists as helping to generate the impression of wholesale physical and social regeneration, while masking "the unaltered or worsening conditions that affect the urban majority as welfare is dismantled, public assets sold off and free spaces enclosed" (Slater and Iles 2010, p. 7).

The ensuing backlash against place-making models of public art led to the dissemination and cultivation of more critical approaches. Initiatives, including the long-running Project Row Houses in the US city of Texas (established in 1993) and Jeanne van Heeswijk's *The Blue House* in Amsterdam (2005–9), were widely cited as exemplary artist-led responses to urban renewal. Closer to home, organizations such as the Barrow-in-Furness-based Art Gene (established in 2002) vocalized their commitment to moving beyond economic models of urban development towards "projects which stimulate sustainable, self-sufficient, locally distinctive economies and cultures" (Art Gene 2014). Allied by their negative experiences of public art commissions, new groups of artists also instigated 'regeneration' projects. Initiatives such as Insitu – set up in 2012 in the east Lancashire town of Brierfield, Primary's community engagement programme in the Lenton area of Nottingham and AIR, which operates in the Archway and Kings Cross areas of London – are emblematic of a wider movement to influence urban processes through sustained and situated forms of practice.

As the dust settled amid the remnants of the bright new urban era, what at first looked like a crisis began to resemble a series of opportunities. While undoubtedly restrictive on a number of levels, the diminished financial resources for public art incurred by the recession were also a welcome source of respite. Freed from excessive policy objectives and the pressured timescales of developers, public artists, curators and commissioners had space to evaluate their experiences over the last decade and to test new ways of working. In the case of *In Certain Places*, the economic slowdown allowed a more measured and long-term approach within our curatorial practice. Rather than rushing to secure place-making roles for artists within a pre-existing plan, we were able to engage them within wider discussions about the city's form and functions. This, in turn, enabled us to have a much more profound involvement with Preston than would have been possible had the Tithebarn scheme transpired. Despite the initial setback to the city's budding cultural scene, the abrupt end to its regenerative ambitions marked the beginning of a more creative and sustainable approach to its future.

Place-listening

Mainstream urban regeneration is a fundamentally visual process. Designed to enhance the economic prospects of a place by making it more appealing, the activity relies heavily on the production of simulacra. Years before the first digger breaks ground, or the wrecking ball commences, a development site will already exist as a series of architect's drawings, populated with smiling citizens, swinging shopping bags or sipping lattes beneath a Mediterranean sky. Once completed, buildings, public art works and urban design features are transformed into sleek promotional images, designed to sell the place as a desirable residence or tourist destination. Yet, while place-making models of public art are generally part of this process, rather than appealing to the gaze, artist-led projects, including *In Certain Places*, more commonly possess what geographer Paul Rodaway describes as an "auditory sensitivity" (Rodaway 1994). Concerned with "flows and continually changing relationships, rather than objects or parts and compositions or views" (ibid., pp. 110–11), such approaches strive to articulate and shape the experience of a place through practices that are akin to the act of listening.

As a corporate and political buzzword, listening has, in recent years, become a somewhat meaningless concept. Mobilized to create a semblance of democracy to disguise undemocratic processes – for example as a form of community consultation for a predestined development scheme – it has gained a reputation as a shallow, one-dimensional practice. In its true form, however, listening is an engaged and vigorous process that involves a concerted effort to make sense of a complex mass of information. Jean-Luc Nancy, for example, points out that the French expression to denote listening – *tendre l'oreille* – means literally "to stretch the ear", denoting a conscious effort to know or understand something which is not immediately to hand (Nancy 2007, p. 5). Unlike the passive act of hearing, listening involves a "straining toward a possible meaning" (ibid., p. 6), and constitutes the embodied enactment of "an intensification and a concern, a curiosity or an anxiety" (ibid., p. 5). As such, public art practices which possess an auditory, rather than visual, sensibility are informed by a desire to experience, comprehend and attend to a place through a conscious communion with it.

What I describe as a 'place-listening' form of public art can be identified by two main features that are interrelated aspects of listening. The first is a durational and open-ended approach to the development of the practice, and the second is an embodied and sensory engagement with a place. Characteristic of most artist-led public art projects, this durational and corporal approach could be seen as a reaction to the top-down, time-restricted nature of many place-making commissioning models. By grounding themselves socially, physically and culturally in a place, artists and curators are able to develop an intimate connection with the context of their practice, and contribute to the future of their locale as part of a wider community. At the same time, their surroundings also provide a testing ground, collaborators and audiences for new artworks and ideas, and a context in which to examine the significance and impact of wider social themes.

For *In Certain Places*, the city of Preston as a lived and practised place is the focus of our work. Although our long-term engagement with the city stems partly from our involvement within the Tithebarn scheme's drawn-out decline, the project's durational nature is also a curatorial strategy. Our guiding principle has always been that artists produce the most interesting work when given the freedom to do so. When we invite an artist to participate in the programme, we ensure, as far as possible, that they are neither restricted by a fixed brief nor pressured to meet a deadline. Instead, we provide them with the necessary time and support to develop a physical understanding of the city, and to form their responses to it through social interactions. Despite the project management challenges that such fluidity incurs, this policy has proved fruitful. By enabling artists to connect to Preston over a sustained period of time, the programme has generated a series of projects that have transcended their status as one-off public artworks to become part of an ongoing dialogue with and within the city.

Originally designed as 'warm-up' activities for the impending Lead Artist initiative, the temporary public artworks, along with the talks and debates, have gradually become the main focus of *In Certain Places*. In addition, without the need to comply with developer-imposed timeframes, the project has morphed into an ongoing and open-ended scheme. In this way, our work shares similarities with a small number of organizations across the UK that offer artists the opportunity to engage with a place as part of an evolving curatorial project. Organizations such as Grizedale and Deveron Arts, for example –which operate in the rural communities of Coniston and Huntly respectively – provide alternative models of public art commissioning that are predicated upon a long-term commitment to one particular place. Like *In Certain Places*, both initiatives have, over a number of years, developed robust social and professional networks within their immediate locale that provide a framework in which to commission art and to engage with neighbourhood issues.

Such situated and durational practices constitute what Paul O'Neill describes as "an always-emergent praxis", through which a "constellation of activities" develops over time (O'Neill 2014, p. 195). In the case of *In Certain Places*, the project resembles a meandering, yet critical conversation with various stakeholders in Preston, to which a procession of 'outside' interlocutors – including economists, urbanists, cultural sociologists, architects, city planners, product designers, curators, historians and artists – are invited to listen and respond. Their contributions – which take the form of public artworks, performances, workshops, talks, tours, exhibitions and films – provoke insights into the nature of the place, and suggest possible solutions to current urban problems. In turn, visitors are likely to gain new perspectives on their work, and have the opportunity to intervene within the city's infrastructure as part of a collective and iterative process.

As opposed to the biennial model of commissioning, where artworks are presented concurrently as part of an orchestrated event, *In Certain Places* comprises a "series of cumulative and dispersed encounters over time" (O'Neill and Doherty 2011, p. 14) that generate a forum for experimentation, imagination and discussion. Originally conceived as distinct, yet interrelated activities, the temporary public art commissions and the series of talks and debates have gradually morphed into a singular, yet multifaceted, line of enquiry. The 'Open City' symposium, for example, demonstrates how a durational approach can engender a symbiotic relationship between art practice and debate. This two-day event was the development of an earlier artwork by Dutch and German artists Wouter Osterholt and Katja van Driel, entitled *Open to the Public* (2013), which mapped over 300 disused city centre properties (Figure 10.1). Building on debates around the politics of space initiated by the work, 'Open City' involved 80 artists, urban planners, architects, city council directors, local councillors, students and residents in explorations of the changing role of the city centre, and the potential to reframe empty properties as an important community resource.

FIGURE 10.1   *Open to the Public* (2013), Wouter Osterholt and Katja van Driel.
Credit: Wouter Osterholt.

Prolonged through our involvement with the city council and local groups, these conversations sparked an attitudinal change. Rather than viewing the city in purely commercial terms, decision-makers began to see the value in other approaches. Almost a year after the 'Open City' event, the first artist studios in the city centre were set up in a local authority-owned building, supported by a business rates subsidy. In addition, the council is striving to enhance access to empty properties by tackling 'absentee landlords' and developing 'tool kits' to help communities negotiate the bureaucratic barriers to such use. Whether these developments are sustainable or simply represent an interim solution to a hollowed-out urban centre presently remains to be seen. However, for a city that, for the last two decades, had pinned its hopes upon the agendas of property developers, the shift towards a more grounded and inclusive approach to its future surely represents progress.

It is important to note that duration does not, in itself, guarantee artistic integrity or engender social benefits. As David Beech warns, "the ideology of duration is … deeply embedded in contemporary practices of *business management and social control*" (Beech 2011, p. 320), and can thus hinder, rather than enable, critical approaches to art practice and place. However, curatorial projects which adopt a longitudinal outlook provide a framework in which artists can disrupt the normative configurations of a place through activities which deal with "delay, interruption, stages, flows…temporary objects…repetition, echo and seriality" (ibid., p. 315). The enduring presence of initiatives, such as *In Certain Places*, within the fabric of a place also provides a foundation from which the personal relationships and bonds of trust that make the commissioning of public art possible can lay down roots and mature. For instance, whereas the first large-scale *In Certain Places* commission was almost thwarted by red tape, more recent artworks, such as the *Harris Flights* (Figure 10.2) – which involved the construction of a temporary staircase on the front of the Harris Museum & Art Gallery – have been realized through the active support of the city council and local groups. As Nigel Roberts, principal urban designer at Preston City Council explains:

> You go through a process of change and testing and I think it energises people. They don't feel like it is being imposed upon them, it's something they can use and interact with. There's been a journey that's got us to where we are now, where something like the *Harris Flights* doesn't frighten people as much as it would have done five or six years ago... I think that's part of the advantage of these *In Certain Places* events. It's about allowing some of that debate to happen... People are interested in where we could go next and want to do something creative, not just sit back and wait for Grosvenor. There's an understanding that there are some smaller-scale actions that we can take... But you do need that creative and collaborative approach to move a city forward.
>
> *(Roberts 2014, p. 31)*

FIGURE 10.2 *Harris Flights* (2013), *In Certain Places* and Research Design.
Credit: Craig Atkinson, Café Royal Books.

As "processual rather than procedural or instrumental" (O'Neill 2011, p. 228) activities, public art commissions that are informed by a place-listening ethos facilitate the dissemination of ideas beyond the confines of the artworld and contribute towards wider cultural projects. While the time-restrictive nature of traditional commissioning models can curtail the creative process, more auditory outlooks promote iteration and reflection, and embrace detours and distractions as potential routes of knowledge. In encouraging projects to unfold slowly "like a tune" (Rodaway 1994, p. 82), durational commissioning practices leave room for the unexpected, and generate other additional collaborative acts and interventions through creative forms of listening.

A durational approach to public art also goes hand in hand with a corporeal and sensory engagement with a place. As opposed to the bird's eye view of the master-plan, which converts the backdrops of everyday life into models or representations, place-listening modes of public art attend to a site through physical on-the-ground encounters. The situated nature of *In Certain Places*, for example, is both the product and producer of embodied forms of knowledge that we continually acquire through our interactions with the city. As the provenance as well as the subject of the project, the way that Preston functions and *feels*, rather than how it appears to the outside world, is central to our practice. Moreover, as people who eat, shop, sleep and socialize in the city, we have a vested interest in the place, and our work is shaped by our personal, as much as our professional, relationships with it.

Michel de Certeau (1984) likens the difference between viewing and interacting with the urban environment to that of reading and writing. While the "totalizing eye" of the developer transforms the world into a "text that lies before one's eyes" (ibid., p. 92), the practitioners of a place exist "below the thresholds at which visibility begins" (ibid., p. 93). As walkers or "*Wandersmänner*, whose bodies follow the thicks and thins of an urban 'text'", these inhabitants collectively "compose a manifold story that has neither author nor spectator, shaped out of fragments of trajectories and alterations of spaces" (ibid.). In this way, the inherent characteristics of a city can be understood as the amalgamation of countless movements, textures, rhythms and flows that coalesce to generate a distinctive sense of place. It follows then, that in order to gain an insight into the true nature of a city, one must immerse oneself fully and physically within it, and become part of its cadence and pulse.

City planners have long acknowledged the value of walking as a way to acquire intimate urban knowledge. In the same way, *In Certain Places* is underpinned by an ambulant engagement with Preston. When an artist from outside the city arrives to undertake a commission, our first priority is to lead them on a walking tour. As their project develops, subsequent and frequent explorations reveal other more subtle or obscured aspects of the place. As a result, their artworks engage with Preston in multisensory ways, and generate new perspectives of the city through bodily encounters. Such responses have included: Susan Walsh's short film, *To Scatter* (2010), which examines the significance of music and song for the city's Irish migrant communities; David Henckel's collaboration with a local craft brewer that produced a new taste for Preston in the form of the *Transit of Venus* ale (2012);

and Chantal Oakes's animation *Thoughts that Make Actions in the World* (2008), which depicts the bus station as a site of embodied experience, rather than simply a fetishized object for the architectural gaze.

The development of place-responsive artworks such as these resembles the process of listening as an embodied and situated practice. Unlike the detached act of looking, which concerns "surfaces and stability" (Rodaway 1994, p. 92), listening involves an immersive, shifting and multidirectional engagement with a subject. In the same way, within a place-listening approach to public art, the compound meanings of a site are established and reinforced through the senses of the body. Rodaway describes how the dual readings of 'sense' – in terms of "*making sense*" through "order and understanding", and a "sensation or feeling" produced through the body's faculties of smell, sight, taste, hearing and balance – "are closely related and often implied by each other" (ibid., p. 5). As such, public artworks that are predicated upon sensuous interactions with a place entail "a reaching out to the world as a source of information and an understanding of that world so gathered" (ibid.).

Suzi Gablik describes artworks that are "rooted in a 'listening' self" as part of a wider paradigm of "connective aesthetics" that is founded upon reciprocal, open modes of conversation and debate (Gablik 1995, p. 82). Within this dialogical model, "social context becomes a continuum for interaction, for a process of relating and weaving together" and "creating a flow", in which the barriers between "artist and audience, creative and uncreative, professional and unprofessional" dissolve (ibid., p. 86). For initiatives such as *In Certain Places*, which explore ways to understand and inhabit a place outside of mainstream development contexts, a connective approach to curatorial practice is especially conducive. In particular, the inclusion of other voices within the curatorial process has enabled the project to expand beyond its urban renaissance remit and to have an influence upon the post-regenerate future of the city. More than participants, the people of Preston have become collaborators and advisers, who increasingly inform all aspects of our work, and help to steer its direction.

We first presented the programme for scrutiny in 2007 with the development of *The Family*. Devised by artist Chris Davis, the project involved members of the Moores family who live in the Ribbleton area of Preston – two miles north of the centre and the site of Davis's practice for over 20 years. Characterized by high levels of unemployment and social housing provision, the area presents a much different urban perspective than our city centre view. Moreover, families such as the Moores, who do not own a car, can find travelling to the centre time-consuming and costly. With this in mind, Davis orchestrated a series of online video chats about art and regeneration between the family and *In Certain Places*. As a 'neutral' space, the conversations allowed us to experience the city from a different point of view, and generated ideas about how we could involve residents like the Moores in our activities and in our discussions. In turn, the family gained insights into the methods of public artists and curators, and an understanding of urban processes as something they could inform, rather than the inevitable outcome of detached, disembodied agendas.

One of the values often claimed for listening as an expressive or artistic medium is that subjects gain a sense of empowerment through the experience of being heard. While this may be true, such assertions create a distinction between the 'listening' and 'listened to' subjects, which implies a particular power dynamic. As *In Certain Places* has evolved, we have attempted – where time and resources allow – to create spaces in which listening as a two-way, equitable process can occur. Most prominent among these is the recently established Critical Friends group, which was formed under the guidance of creative practitioner and researcher Sophie Hope. Made up of around 15 core members – including artists, architects, local authority planners, university lecturers, students and other local residents – the group meets regularly to hear updates, offer advice and critically appraise our practice.

As enablers and ambassadors, these critical friends have proved instrumental in helping to raise the visibility and profile of *In Certain Places*. Yet, it is through their more demanding roles as interlocutors that they have begun to inform our work at a more systemic level. By posing questions – such as, *What is the importance of being placed within the university (does the university engage with the city through* In Certain Places*)? Is* In Certain Places *for the people of Preston? How can* In Certain Places *better facilitate a 'passing on' of responsibility for developing projects in the city?* – the group has encouraged us to reflect upon our methods and motivations, to consider alternative approaches and to better articulate the aims and objectives of the project.

Being held to account in this way is not always comfortable and involves a level of exposure and lack of control that can, at times, prove daunting. However, as Grant Kester describes in his account of 'dialogical' models of practice, active forms of listening necessitate a "willingness to accept a position of dependence and intersubjective vulnerability relative to the viewer or collaborator" (Kester 2004, p. 110). By failing to open up and be transparent in this way, public art schemes run the risk of generating projects which are unable to connect to a place in meaningful ways, and function merely as window dressing or urban spectacles. While decorations and distractions contribute towards the complexion of a place, they also tend to obscure its inner workings. In contrast, projects that are founded upon durational, embodied, critical and collective forms of listening are more likely to disrupt and redirect a city's flows in surprising and generative ways.

Currently entering its second decade, *In Certain Places* is a project that continues to evolve. Originating from curatorial responses to the regeneration of a place, the scheme has, in the words of John Newling, morphed into a type of "ecosystem" which, "alongside the already existing histories", has become "part of a city's soil" (Newling 2014, p. 6). The space for reflection and discussion, which emerged as the urban renaissance age receded, has enabled us, with our interlocutors in Preston and colleagues in other parts, to test new configurations of urbanism and art that are specific to a location. Non-linear and undefined, this has been an intuitive and iterative process that has been shaped as much by chance and error as by well-considered plans. Dialogical and sensory, embedded and prolonged, the project has produced – albeit often indiscernible – shifts within the foundations of the city.

Collectively and over time, these have engendered wider constellations of activities and debate about how Preston might become a more equitable, open place.

We took the name 'In Certain Places' from a passage in the novel *Invisible Cities* by Italo Calvino. In the book, the merchant traveller Marco Polo regales the Chinese ruler Kublai Khan with tales of ostensibly disparate cities that are all, in fact, versions of Venice. In his account of a city named Fedora, the narrator describes "a metal building with a crystal globe in every room" (1997, p. 28). Contained within each globe is an imagined version of Fedora as an individual's ideal city. Engrossed in the construction of their visions, however, the creators of each globe had failed to realize that the city had already changed around them, thus rendering their efforts nothing more than "a toy in a glass globe" (ibid.). As an allegory for recent approaches to urban development, the narrative is pertinent. Driven by a conception of the city as its own post-industrial product, and a perceived need to conform to elitist urban ideals, regeneration schemes have, in many cases, achieved little more than superficial slogans and the destruction of homes and communities.

The challenge for today's towns and cities, therefore, is to find new ways to evolve and survive. As forms of employment and local services are cut, and public freedoms curtailed, the need to engender new resistant, resilient and critical urban practices is increasingly urgent. For public artists, curators and commissioners, rather than advancing predetermined futures, this implies an engagement with cities as they exist in the here and now. One, among a number of situated initiatives across the country and beyond, *In Certain Places* presents an approach to public art as an integral part of urban life. By no means a solution or definitive model of practice, the project nonetheless demonstrates how artists can contribute to the lived realities of a place. As we progress further into the post-regenerate age, it will be interesting to observe how new artistic methods emerge in order to critique, provoke, interpret and disrupt urban situations, as part of wider conversations and, always, with a close ear to the ground.

Notes

1   The bus station was awarded Grade II Heritage Listed status in October 2013.
2   See Evans (2005) for a full account of the differences between cultural and culture-led regeneration.
3   See Landry (2009) and Landry et. al. (1996).
4   See, for example, Smith (1996).

11

ANTAGONISTIC SPACES

On small, interventionist and socially engaged public art

Justin Langlois and Danielle Sabelli

We're in this together

Broken City Lab started as a conversation while doing the dishes. It was March 2008. We were living in a west-end apartment: a brick building that formerly housed the mayor's office of then-Sandwich in Ontario, Canada, which amalgamated with the neighbouring towns of Windsor and Walkerville in 1935. The surrounding neighbourhood was diverse – a mix of students, low-income residents, recent immigrants and a few middle-class holdouts from a better time. Directly beside our apartment was a small courtyard next to a community centre, which was also attached to a small jail. Further west were increasingly abandoned commercial buildings and apartments, followed by the sewage treatment plant and a park built on top of a decommissioned garbage dump. A ten-minute walk to the east stood the privately owned Ambassador Bridge, one of the two border crossings to Detroit, which was surrounded by hundreds of boarded up homes awaiting the bridge's long-stalled and yet to be realized 'twin-span'. A five-minute walk to the north was the Detroit River, where you could see the outlines of south-west Detroit and the emissions from Zug Island. To the south was a local high school slated for closure, and south of there was a converted factory and showroom, which now housed the University of Windsor's Visual Arts building. This was the neighbourhood that we moved through on a daily basis, and it continually presented us with explicit examples of the economic and social shifts brought by decades of industrial prosperity meeting the earliest moments of the financial crisis. It was a place that articulated a very specific sense of locality, the kind of place that Lucy Lippard (1997, p. 7) has described as being simultaneously understood through "temporal and spatial, personal and political" lenses.

Our conversation shifted from a reflection on the neighbourhood to what it meant for us to be living there. We wondered about how things could change and then wondered if we might be able to help change them. We argued around models of action: protest versus guerrilla tactics; large gatherings versus small groups; planning versus acting. The latter models won out. Drawing from a number of public and socially engaged practices best encapsulated by Rosalyn Deutsche's (1991, p. 53) assertion that art's greatest potential is in its capacity "to participate in the creation of social life", which ranged from the long-term place-based work of Bonnie Sherk to the interventionist letter-writing and postering of the Guerilla Art Action Group and from the incendiary *détournement* of the Situationists to the interdisciplinary conceptual art of Stephen Willats, we imagined ways of working that could be urgently applied to the city around us. This imagination would guide our work towards something not wholly new but rather a distinct merging of a lineage of socially engaged public practices and a set of concerns around the locality of the urban environment. In her seminal text, *Mapping the Terrain: New Genre Public Art*, Suzanne Lacy (1995, p. 19) described these kinds of practices as being driven by an "internal necessity perceived by the artist in collaboration with his or her audience". We understood that these practices were, as Tom Finkelpearl (2013, p. 343) suggests, indeed most meaningful when they opened up a creative process that could activate local knowledge and imagination, and we aimed to create projects that might stir a localized political imagination. Building from these practices, our activities were most potent at the overlap between public art and creative activism, a space perhaps best described by Brian Holmes (2007: 290) as the intersection of social movements and artist collectives' efforts towards social and political transformation.

As the dishes were drying, we moved to the kitchen table and wrote a manifesto, essentially a to-do list, trying to spell out the forms of activity we would tackle, and titled it Broken City Lab.[1] In the following weeks, we started gathering allies, drawing mostly from our peers in the student body at the School of Visual Arts. We met regularly with Joshua Babcock and Michelle Soullière, and then Cristina Naccarato and Rosina Riccardo; for a while, Steven Leyden Cochrane, Immony Men and Karlyn Koeser; later on, Hiba Abdallah, Kevin Echlin and Sara Howie. We collectivized, intent on acting (out) in the city, trying to explore the ways in which we could shape and enact a sense of agency, and modelling that process of discovery in the space of the city. We continued to build on a trajectory of practices that took trouble-making seriously and aimed to foster new relationships with audiences and participants, finding affinities in Fluxus tactics and Augusto Boal's *Theatre of the Oppressed*, while also seeing compelling models for organizing larger and longer-term projects in the earlier infrastructural efforts of the Artist Placement Group and the work of Rick Lowe's *Project Row Houses*. We set up an institution of our own to host the kind of 'embedded' practice that artist and activist Marisa Jahn (2010, p. 15) suggests has the capacity to "re-sensitize us to affective relations", allowing us to consider our work not only in the interventions we mounted but the collectivity we fostered as we did them. Operating our institution as a collective allowed us to further extend our creative practice into our everyday lives, bending the formal structures of a 'lab' to the informality of an open studio workshop. The starting point of all of our projects, however, was a distinctively antagonistic intensity for the city we encountered and a commitment to what Blake Stimson and Gregory Sholette (2007, p. 12) describe as "engaging with social life itself as the medium of expression", framing ourselves as the authors, participants and audience for our projects. We were also acutely aware of the necessity to maintain an internal focus with our projects, whether or not they unfolded in a public setting. As Finkelpearl (2013, p. 357) has suggested, just as an Impressionist painting is not necessarily made better by virtue of it having more impressions, nor is the success of a socially engaged practice necessarily measurable by virtue of the number of socially engaged participants.

We were also inspired by the work of the N.E. Thing Co. and their work exploring corporate systems as sites for artistic intervention, and some of our first projects were sparked by an early exercise in organizational role-playing. We took our self-designation as a lab seriously, and set out to engage in our DIY version of a strategic planning process, eventually capturing a particular sentiment over and over again. The text, "send a message to Detroit", seemed to be at the intersection of a number of our inclinations. It captured a distinctive gap that existed for us in our sense of locality – a relationship between Windsor and Detroit, two post-industrial cities so deeply connected through labour, geography and infrastructures, and yet so symbolic of the things that made these cities so broken. Our interest was in sending a message from Windsor to Detroit in order to commiserate with unknown and imagined colleagues and peers across the border. We wanted to declare a loss of connection, a sense of empathy and a course of impossible action. We looked to the interventionist tactics of Jenny Holzer's text-based projections and the poetics of Rafael Lozano-Hemmer's large-scale public installations as reference points, interested not in suggesting an ameliorative stance per se but rather displaying a set of text-based sentiments that would be legible through a variety of political, social or economic lenses. *Cross-Border Communication* (2009) presented a series of symbolic, poetic and declarative statements projected onto a large building on Windsor's waterfront: such as, "We're in this together", "We need to talk" and "We're lost with(out) you", which were legible from downtown Detroit. The texts were not based on any large consultation or engaged community input, but they captured our own antagonistic sensibility in response to the situations we were encountering in our city. This work, like so many of our projects, was based on the interests and desires of our collective unfolding in public spaces and based on the social engagement we had with one another, and it is this model of socially engaged practice that we wish to advocate for in this chapter. Despite what our name may have suggested, the aim of our work was never to fix the city on behalf of anyone but to imprint our agency into the places we encountered. We maintained that if we acted towards any particular outside mandate, we would be compromising what we did best – essentially acting in ways and spaces that formal organisations, other artists or the city itself would not.

In this chapter, we will aim to discuss some of the challenges of practices associated with socially engaged public art, based on our experiences as co-founders of Broken City Lab. While we recognize the earnestness of framing critical issues in our own work and that of our peers, we will also explore the limits and liabilities of the critical rhetoric that so often surrounds these kinds of projects, to offer a grounding for emphasizing antagonistic practices as a useful foundation for socially engaged public art. We will also work to unpack the neo-liberal tendencies that we often encounter in readings and expectations of socially engaged public art, and then make an argument for new groundings of practice that could help to reorient it towards a set of ideals better aligned to the experiences of its practitioners and participants. We will work towards unpacking some large and challenging questions, including: what if socially engaged public art worked without any focus on audience, and instead solely concentrated on the political development of its authors and participants? And, how might we be able to articulate a constant sense of antagonistic affectivity as a foundational part of our political imagination, informed by frontline creative experiences? Throughout, we will not necessarily work to develop deep readings of works outside of our own, and so we acknowledge that there is further thinking to be done around the applicability of our ideas to the field of socially engaged public art in general. Finally, and most pertinently, it is important to note that we write as artists, interested in more deeply understanding the work we have done and the forces that have shaped it, with an eye towards anticipating where our practices will lead us next.

Translation and exchange: the foreclosure of our political imagination

Socially engaged public art is often challenged with having to operate in two rhetorical registers simultaneously: first, for a general public; and second, for a group of artists, peers or critics. For a general public, socially engaged public art is often presented as ameliorative, generously collaborative and widely accessible. For a group of artist peers or critics, socially engaged public art is often circulated with expectations for it to constructively engage in critical discourses around power, access and art history. Take, for example, the presentation and circulation of Paul Ramirez-Jonas's *Key to the City* (2010), where individuals were invited to exchange a ceremonial key that also opened a series of private and common spaces across New York City, or Thomas Hirschhorn's *Gramsci Monument* (2013) where residents of the Morrisania neighbourhood in the Bronx could engage with a series of 'pavilions' providing art workshops, guest lectures and community concerts. These works each presented a particular generosity and an example of socially compelling ways of gathering but simultaneously hinted at something more deeply political, whether an exploration of ownership and access in a city, or modelling experimental forms of grassroots community services at the block level. That hinting is not just an underlying aspect of the work but is very much an incredibly valuable component of the work that makes it possible to circulate as a successful, socially engaged public art project. There is a need, then, to think about the presentation of a project as critically relevant, and the rhetoric that brings that relevance to the fore as not just one rhetorical register but really *the* rhetorical register. The rhetoric that supports this kind of work is not only a frame through which we can see certain aspects of the project but also the precarious scaffolding for it. In tracing a lineage of North American socially engaged art practice stemming from the Happenings in the 1960s, feminist educational efforts and performance, to post-minimalism, installation art and relational aesthetics – all of which were framed by the political leanings of the avant-garde (Helguera 2011, p. ix) – we can see the expectation for the work to be politically informed or responsive, anti-capitalist and blurred with everyday life (Bishop 2012, p. 11) Yet we can also begin to see that this same expectation can feel increasingly like a platform for a *performance* of these criteria, rather than a realized aspect of the works themselves (Davis 2013, p. 46). Rhetorical criticality is the performance of those criteria. It is the scaffolding for the work. It is the currency with which these projects are circulated.

This criticality turned rhetoric can be seen everywhere, and our works in Broken City Lab were no exception. Art professionals at all scales and pay grades enact the duplicity of rhetorical criticality through project descriptions, press releases and commissioned essays, and the linguistic inflation that this produces is arguably most damaging for socially engaged works. When potentially transformative language, such as words like 'critical' or 'community' or 'participation' or 'democratic' or 'resistance', is invoked irresponsibly, the collective understanding of these terms becomes further limited, used primarily as a tool of order rather than transformation. The instrumentalizing potential of the language that might surround a socially engaged public art project, framing it as critical or democratic or participatory, is therefore especially challenging in the way it sets new limits and boundaries on our sense and understanding of those words. The damage from the limitation of this language, which fluctuates and evolves depending on how it will be manipulated for a particular end at any point in time, is most pronounced when considering the capacity and power embedded within it – once the language is limited, it can no longer serve as an instrument of transgression. It changes and weakens the work it describes. Whether in the art world, or as a community project, socially engaged art as a site of exchange implicates audiences and participants as actors in the real world; and there is an exchange implied in much of socially engaged public art, based on the contingency of the work to require some form of participation[2] from other people. While the form of that participatory exchange might best be captured by an understanding of the service economy, as investigated by Nicolas Bourriaud (2002) in his *Relational Aesthetics* thesis - that is, cultivating an experience in place of manufacturing a product, as even social relationships can be packaged and commodified – there is also a utility in understanding the ways in which we are primed to think about exchange based on more fundamental economic cues and frameworks. Marx suggests that by placing something into a system of exchange where it becomes objectified and abstracted, we also develop a commodity relation or relationship. This relationship will also include the creation of a subject who performs the exchange. The movement of labour towards service occupations where that exchange *is* the delivery of human relations insists that all human relations can become wrapped in instrumental logic and be prepared for commodification. Such a framework is essential to the understanding of the ways in which we receive and produce cultural products or, rather, experiences. 'Experience' no longer seems to be subjective, active and embodied; instead, it tends to be passive, objective and virtual. It is the product, and in its production we further devalue the critical capacity of that experience. In socially engaged public art, the translation of critical rhetoric from scaffolding for performance to script for a market logic means that the work not only limits the capacity of the criticality embedded in it but also turns it into an identifiable boundary. While critical language may aim to destabilize order, it may ultimately stabilize it instead. We must be aware of how language, especially resistive language, becomes instrumentalized for the purposes of containment logic, towards the preservation of societal order and dominant market logic.

Beyond language, the political imagination and vernacular from which we draw, as radically assumed as it may be, is already limited and bound as soon as we begin to exercise it. Socially engaged public art projects continually draw from Dada aesthetics, avant-gardist tendencies to use art for the political imagination, Fluxus leanings to dissolve artist and audience, the Situationists' desire to decouple lived experience from the spectacle and the pedagogical impulses of Joseph Beuys' social sculpture. The application of these critical framings to contemporary practices is commendable, but their capacity to continue to do the work they set out to do in their original framings, as mentioned, is severely limited. We can see that there is an endless expansion of Dada-veneer into everyday consumer culture (from the rise of DIY capitalism to hipster depots like Urban Outfitters). The dissolution of divisions between art and audience has built participatory cultures and social media (perhaps best exemplified by YouTube). Decoupling everyday life from the spectacle remains an arms race towards the blurring of the two (witness the spread of sponsored content). Any radical pedagogical impulses are all-too-quickly tethered back to the neo-liberal educational complex. The tactics of these practices have been taken up by capitalism, and any effort to redeploy them only more clearly articulates their limits. Of course, the implication of these limits is not only troubling for the political or critical capacity of socially engaged practices but rather the larger sense of political imagination across our communities. Take, for example, the momentarily exciting expression of a nascent (or perhaps reawakened) political imagination in the Occupy movement. Even in this political project, we can find tracings of the logic of late-capitalism. The legibility of Occupy was both a call-to-arms and an all-too-familiar marketing tactic. When we consider the ways political imaginations and tactics can function as a marketable brand, we can better understand the ways in which their flexibility actually makes them completely compatible with – and containable within – late-capitalism (Dean 2012, p. 222). The compatibility and containability of a socially engaged project is used as leverage both for and against it, ultimately smoothing its edges until it can no longer cause any friction. Even artists that have intentionally aimed for friction or antagonism have enjoyed an (arguably slow) eclosion into contemporary art, and in turn, late-capitalism. In thinking about the political aims of early works by Gran Fury, REPOhistory or Group Material, even with their arguable aesthetic overlap with what we now might think of as civic initiatives or guerrilla marketing, the real danger of the increasing legibility of these kinds of works is in their ability to be scaled and translated by much more instrumentalizing forces – including at the very least, outreach activities by municipal governments, strategic directives of countless organizations and the business plans of social entrepreneurs. Those expressions of creativity that met the built environment – and the forces controlling it – head on were all-too-easily brought under umbrellas of practice and policy designed to make the entry points and exits clear for participation. This clarity then limits what else we might be able to do together. It encloses and contains any radical possibility of participation, and any assumption that it remains valuable must be questioned (Miessen 2010, p. 14). From social media memes, to tourism campaigns, to utopian urban design consultancies, we see the ways in which antagonistic practices can be eventually compromised and rearticulated. This is the essence of the instrumentalization of socially engaged public art – the transformation from antagonistically founded creative gestures to highly controlled engagement strategies. Socially engaged public art that can be supported or framed without the tethers noted above may not necessarily be as legible in the ways that we have come to expect but by virtue of that illegibility may in fact more readily cultivate the forms of change and expressions of agency we actually want to enact.

In trying to circumvent such a seemingly unavoidable outcome, the political imagination we wanted to encourage for ourselves in Broken City Lab runs counter to a common expectation of political engagement and the way we experience it. Rather than limiting the scope and practice of politics to things like elections, demonstrations or city council chambers, a new political imagination opens opportunities for expression far outside of these limitations. It finds political expression and action embedded deeply into everyday life and creative practice. A new political imagination may entirely ignore the potential for change in the ways that we so often otherwise experience politics. It might move away from expectations that anything politically worthwhile is translatable to the pre-articulated political spectrum of issues, parties and policies. This is not to suggest that these areas are not worth exploring but rather to try to offer a counterpoint to the tendency to allow those areas and issues to take up all of the space and time and energy we have for political imagination. In doing so, we must consider the embedded barriers to reimagining and developing the capacity for a new political space. The political capacity of large-scale socially engaged public art is inherently limited in its scope by virtue of the support required to make much of it possible. Works that require particular permissions or assurances are limited by the need to adhere to the edges of those permissions and assurances. Works that require particular financial resources are limited by the scope of eligibility built into the funding applications that make those financial resources accessible. For example, we ran into challenges in securing the resources to support our two-year-long *CIVIC Space* (2012–14) storefront, a project that originally aimed to build on the work we did in the *Storefront Residencies for Social Innovation* (2010), as the grants that could best support it had priorities far outside the artistic concerns we had for the project. The work ended up shifting considerably to accommodate the requirements of the grant, and in some ways compromised the kinds of activities we had envisaged for it. Because of the scale and duration of this kind of work and the resources required to realize them, it is therefore rather difficult to articulate projects that might be able to act outside or beyond those limitations (and in turn, all the more interesting to imagine when and how they can). However, the limitations of infrastructures that support these works are not the only hurdles to clear.

The assumptions, and as we have tried to argue, the predispositions of the ideas that go into constructing notions of criticality and social change ultimately foreclose the larger potential for socially engaged public art to do what it can do best. If socially engaged public art sets out to make social change tangible, it is measured against non-profits, government services and wider civic engagement efforts, all of which necessarily have very specific goals and outcomes in mind. In turn, an artwork that aims to do that same work is likely to be viewed as inadequate or an outright failure of response. Perhaps for this very reason, Nato Thompson (2012, p. 28), chief curator of Creative Time, has argued for the opposite, wherein we might set a wider set of boundaries around socially engaged practices to include all forms of cultural production, including non-profit organizations and even spontaneous political events such as the celebration of Barack Obama's 2008 presidential victory in Harlem. The inclusion of these arguably non-art entities flexes our imagination of what socially engaged public art is and perhaps, by virtue of that, raises our imagination around political creativity. However, the value in harnessing a political imagination through doing, by showing ways to enact forms of agency in the built environment, becomes the foundation for demonstrating and enacting different ways to be in the world, together. Untethered from the needs of partnering institutions, funding objectives and any otherwise identifiable goal, socially engaged public art provides us with the opportunity to explore how we can act towards the interests we have, as antagonistically informed they might be, and ultimately cultivate a sense of possibility that cannot otherwise exist.

Within Broken City Lab, it was never the emails from student groups or other artists asking for details on our process or works that were unsettling. We were happy to share, and ensured our website was open for those purposes under the Creative Commons licensing scheme. It was the requests from business accelerators, design consultancies and government-initiated task forces that were so difficult for us to deal with. These requests made clear that the legibility of our project was such that it no longer provided the antagonistic framings that we ourselves had found so useful. It was ready to be packaged and transformed into a playbook for engagement strategies for youth, or consumers or voters, which, to be sure, are important kinds of efforts in their own right. What was absent from that translation was the actual work, and the experiences gained from that work that we took on to enact our own spaces of practice, as well as the tensions that arose from those actions. It did not matter if it was a large-scale projection, a small guerrilla gardening project or a temporary text installation, the work was rooted in the act of having an impulse to do something one day and then acting on that impulse the next day. This is the political imagination that we work towards.

Antagonism as form

Antagonism is the starting point for the type of socially engaged public work we have attempted to describe throughout. Claire Bishop (2012, p. 16) has argued that the capacity of artistic practices to maintain a sense of antagonism is vitally important, as it allows a distance from the neutralizing and instrumentalizing forces of capitalism and government policy. This distance provides for works that can act on their own, rather than in service of something or someone. Antagonistic work, as compared to ameliorative work, locates its foundation in a mode of deep frustration and anger with the world it encounters. It assumes that there is important energy and value in harnessing that frustration towards a series of experiences that allow such frustration to be explored and realized. It tries to find the possibility for social actors to react to, rather than act within, a frame of an event or action. Ameliorative practice, meanwhile, assumes from the perspective of a specific group of individuals that there is work to be done and that art has a role to play in that work. It slides all too easily into the mandates and strategic directives of larger organizations. It also halts the creative capacity of conflict and tension, preferring to channel that energy and creating a release valve into something 'productive', something that can defuse the tension and offer a sense of relief in action, no matter how trivial, or vacant of actual change. Ameliorative work masks political leverage points under expressions of sympathetic or altruistic effort. As we have argued above, it makes it impossible for socially engaged public art to articulate a political capacity or the imagination to act outside or beyond what is known, understood and sanctioned. In the event that ameliorative art can offer a novel sense of hope or potential, it is immediately enclosed by neo-liberal forms of encapsulation and subjection towards efficient and measurable outcomes. Where antagonistic work fails in achieving legible social transformation, it succeeds in reintroducing a distance from permissible and therefore pre-configured actions deemed to be ineffective within the articulated boundaries of practice. It acts against the intentionality of ameliorative practice with urgency. It resists exploitation. It counteracts through illegibility. It provides a basis for pedagogical shifts as well as shifts in consciousness. It reintroduces us to solidarity in the absence of the kinds of contested spaces that were once experienced as factories. It cloaks itself in its unmeasurability. These capabilities are precisely what make antagonism so important to locate at the base of the political imagination: they can't stop us if they can't see us coming.

   In our work, an imprint of agency was driven by an antagonism, a constant and dialogic frustration targeted at the range of political and social structures we encounter. This antagonism is infinite and its work is never done because its affectivity is constant in everyday experiences. The exercises of power expressed through policies, and the built environment and the resulting ennui of small-city urban life, were catalysts for bringing a set of common concerns and practices together. The efforts of these common practices were perhaps legible as ameliorative, but their starting point was always rooted in antagonistic lack and frustration. For instance, in our project *City Counselling* (2011), we acted in response to a series of failed community consultation sessions that the city had organized around an upcoming infrastructure project by hosting an open discussion about the future of Windsor's infrastructure in the plaza in front of City Hall and projecting our hand-written notes onto its exterior in real time. In situations where tension or anger bring people together, the larger rehearsed narrative arc may eventually lead us to a point at which those tensions *appear* resolved. We encounter a wrong and this narrative of resolution, this instrumentalized rhetorical criticality, assumes we should make it right. This kind of equation removes the political capacity of that tension and eases the discomfort of any unresolved aspects of the experience by insisting on an outcome, a finishing point and a resolution. Further, it is a resolution made from diluted compromise, wherein power is surrendered for a small and often insignificant gain. This resolution may even appear reasonable, but the conditions catalysing the conflict and the subsequent resolution actually remain unreasonable and oppressive. To maintain a focus on (or tether to) the antagonistic intensities that so often spark action is to resist the tidiness of vernacular expressions of activism and unrest.

Our work continually circled back to antagonistic intensities to remind ourselves of the infinite capacity of neo-liberal and bureaucratic violence to drive creative political action. There was no destination or end point; there was only ongoing struggle, and this is when a sense of antagonism can shift to a radical agonism – what Chantal Mouffe describes as a continual and infinite hegemonic battle within democratic spaces. The challenge in reading this infinite form of exchange, however, is in understanding that there is no resolution to be had, nor any ultimate result to achieve. The least violent situations we can cultivate, Mouffe (2013, p. 7) would suggest, are the ones that are most ready to receive and host antagonism. Making space for two sides in hegemonic struggle to meet again and again on the infinite horizons of everyday life forms the basis for the ideals of democratic forms of public practice: everyday life as political struggle in which the act of encountering hegemonic forces is the method for overcoming, or undoing, institutional forms of power expressed as throttling bureaucratic policies, bylaws and strategic planning. The spaces for encountering power are no longer in the traditional battlefields of protests, factory floors or city squares but in the meeting and disruption of the expectations and highly curated actions within urban public space – curated acts as a practice of loitering and as exercising embodied agency in the built environment; loitering as a general mode of operating; loitering as the ideal framing for activity by virtue of its disinterest in any larger aim or goal. Simply taking up space, staking claim to a fleeting moment in urban negotiations, becomes highly useful in its uselessness and its disinterest in larger aims. It actively counteracts any co-opting forces that might otherwise want to embark on partnerships or total encapsulation of creative activity unfolding in public. The act of loitering compromises and short circuits instrumentalizing forces through its aimlessness, as it actively pursues a refusal of reason or rationale other than the desire to make a temporary place that is organized around non-dominant interests or use-values. Socially engaged public art as loitering provides a shorthand for the intensity required to enact the true political capacity of these practices. In refusing from the outset to frame or corral the activity, it becomes untethered from the inescapable requirements of institutional forces. In its antagonistic stance, it captures the basis of affective intensity that so often drives our interests in taking on the work in the first place, and allows us to more honestly address the concern at hand at the most basic of levels.

The ways in which this translates to art and, more specifically, socially engaged public art, is in the legibility we can provide to its starting point. Art projects that can be positioned and communicated as being built on the complexities and awkwardness of antagonism as form are more readily aligned to their political capacities. They can resist instrumentalizing framings better because they are not aligned to the goals and outcomes of transformative or even exploratory processes. Rather, they exist, ideally in limbo, in an antagonistic space, understanding the role of agonism in cultivating an infinite exchange. They are not easily resolved or surrendered. They are primarily hosting a sense or potential of antagonism over a period of time and in a particular place. They are responsive but not necessarily responsible. By allowing artworks the space to exist without what we will term as 'resolutionary' inclinations of funding bodies, strategic plans or institutional mandates, they can better take up the task of creatively addressing and inciting social and political change as a constant effort and hegemonic struggle rather than a task list waiting to be cleared. At the core of this is valuing the ability of everyday actors to enact social and political transformations as a constant part of everyday life. Goals not only get in the way of these efforts, muddying the clarity of their antagonistic foundations, but also pave the way for enclosure by political and institutional forces. Leaving spaces for official partnerships and acceptable-use policies undoes the affective and political intensities of the work, which in turn makes those intensities so muted as to render them illegible even to those artists and participants engaged in the frontlines of the work. The danger in all of this is by framing so many activities around goals and outcomes, we become unable to read the political potential of actions that do not meet these same endpoints. We cease being capable of understanding that acting on an antagonistic intensity moves us towards an experience and realisation of agency. We no longer allow ourselves to act outside of predefined plans or mandates and so we cede control over our actions to the boundaries that someone else established. This form of control is so dangerous because we cannot even see or realize that it is happening. We simply stop engaging in activities that are unable to meet an outcome that someone else set out for us because we assume that any energy and time spent with our political imaginations must be accountable to some measurable change. This is the neo-liberal condition and the socially engaged practices that we so often encounter are already compromised by its presence before we can even see that it has entered the room. Of course, the challenges in aiming for goal-less activity within the realm of public and socially engaged practice are significant. As projects enter these terrains, especially when they are not legible within a common lineage of socially engaged art or activism, they are frequently enclosed within a set of assumed strategic aims. On its face, this may not be altogether different than the ways in which we receive any artwork in any space – short of didactic panels, are we not continually hardpressed to sort out all the precise intentions or references embedded in artworks (and isn't this imprecision one of the most important things that art can provide?) – and yet, what is at stake in public and socially engaged practice is the potential for these assumed strategic aims to compromise and foreclose their actual radical potential.

Over and out: between radicality and pragmatism

As artists in Broken City Lab, we were able to take ownership of the capacity to imagine our way into public space in new forms and through new practices. These new forms and practices we experienced together enabled us to act on our antagonistic inclinations in ways that simultaneously flexed the boundaries of action (that is, we had not limited ourselves to particular goals or outcomes or metrics of success) and provided a platform for demonstrating engagement. While we never set out to take on a mandate to necessarily demonstrate creative political activity, it became clear that the ways in which we organized and acted coincided with the existing efforts of other people and organizations in our community. The balancing point between keeping our actions, which had helped to articulate our agency, untethered from these coinciding efforts and remaining open to the potential for cross-pollination was precisely where we found the greatest impact for socially engaged public art to be located. Being able to draw from, and maintain a focus on, the antagonistic affectivity that drove our projects, provided the very means through which other organizations, institutions and efforts became interested in working with us. New projects that led us to more formal collaborations were only possible because of the way we had worked against these considerations in the first place. This sense of *working against* had always been productive, if not always necessarily broadcasted, and it was the very reason that the limits of what was possible through Broken City Lab became clear. The more we tried to embed antagonistic leanings into larger projects, the more we had to make them distanced from the surface in order to find the partnerships and resources to realize the work. That distance also unfolded across time and, ultimately, the work was so legible, it was no longer interesting to us. If city departments and business accelerators and design consultancies could make sense of our work (and for that matter, wanted to borrow the tactics embedded in our work), it seemed that our work was done.

Undoubtedly, the work we did in Broken City Lab provided a set of experiences in which we had to continually struggle over the legibility of our activity in the wider community. We worked hard to document our projects for archiving and distribution, and we were always flattered to see where the images of our work ended up. However, the question of value in relation to something's scarcity or availability, or more usefully its legibility or illegibility, is tied to the framing one provides vis-à-vis the constructs of neo-liberal productivity logic. Is a project widely circulated through a range of media sources? Is a project repeatable? Is a project's outcome measurable? Is there evidence of change that can be attributed to the resources utilized to create the project in the first place? It would seem clear that once this logic and language is introduced to the planning of a project, it could drastically change not only what is accomplished but also what is discussed in the first place. We also have to wonder how much this kind of thinking and framing not only limits a potential project but also encloses the political imagination. When a socially engaged public art project is asked to address an issue, or indeed be useful – this is not to suggest an absolute critique of Tania Bruguera's (2011) *Manifesto on Useful Art*, "where art's function is no longer to be a space for 'signaling' [sic] problems, but the place from which to create the proposal and implementation of possible solutions" – as something other than art, its capacity to (re)charge the political imagination is severely limited. Of course, an argument could be made around the potential good that could come from utilizing artistic tactics and gestures in service of a larger and more legible issue. One might even suggest that this is necessary, as late-capitalism continues to harness the fervent inclination of the general public to produce and distribute media through social media channels. However, it is the orientation of the imposition that is most worrying. If a socially engaged public art can retain its capacity to act beyond and outside of the limits of organizational mandates, bureaucratic policies and funding infrastructures, it remains possible for it to act towards the ignition of the political imagination of at least its authors, if not its immediate participants, let alone a wider public. If, instead, the project immediately seeks to position itself in relation to the larger moving parts of the needs of a pre-articulated issue, it compromises its potentiality to act unencumbered towards the realizing and exercising of a political imagination autonomous from the pressures and forces of neo-liberal organizing logic and semio-capitalistic[3] production models.

In closing, there are of course even more pressing questions that we have arguably failed to address. What about work that wants to engage in an accessible and legible form of ameliorative practice? What about funding agencies, and galleries, and universities, and BIAs and non-profit organizations that want to partner on socially engaged public art projects? And, what about the ones that want to do it as responsibly as possible? Have we written ourselves into a corner, insisting that only through ostensibly anarchic creative gestures completely untethered from real world expectations and any goals that might help others, can artists actually make good or truly socially engaged public art practice? Though these may be valid questions, this would be a misunderstanding of our argument. We wanted to argue that the additional weight and drag affixed to socially engaged art – when we read it as though it is trying to, or indeed required to, fit more or less neatly into the mandates and goals of any of the aforementioned parties – is harmful to the practice and, perhaps more usefully, misses the point of some of it altogether. Socially engaged practices that are incubated in such a way as to allow them to do what they do best – create emancipatory political moments for those most deeply and directly involved – not only have the capacity to 'act' more responsibly by virtue of their proximity to a very real and present cause and effect but also create more sustainable paths for scaling the work. Rather than essentially proofreading a large work for errors around ethics, colonial tendencies and political economies by positioning the 'art' on one side and the 'issue' and 'community' on the other, we could spend more time understanding the ways in which a small work not only addresses those issues in organic and constant ways but also in ways that more legibly outline new tactics and methodologies for existing and enacting a post-capitalist world. The things we want most from this work, anyway, are examples of other ways to bend the political imagination and live together. However unrealistic and unmeasurable this might be, it serves as an incredibly helpful lens through which we can see these kinds of practices for what they truly are – either a platform for actors in numerous and complex relations formed around autonomous actions, or a platform for large-scale and comprehensive efforts to control, hone and shape those actors and their relations and actions. Should we want to engage and support the very real political efforts that the former platform represents, then we have to find ways to cultivate the infrastructures needed to make those practices feasible and sustainable. These infrastructures may take on forms that are familiar yet productively destabilizing. Perhaps the introduction of financial support (tethered to phases of exploration that move from non-goal-oriented research, to audits for the potential of goals, to a final phase of additional funding should the artist wish to exploit those goals), could make this work more sustainable while maintaining the potential for radical unproductivity. If institutions could more readily support multiyear and durational projects, artists would have the opportunity to consider taking on riskier projects that may have illegible outcomes, and simultaneously create opportunities to further explore the display and dissemination of this kind of work that could unfold beyond documentation or archives. Academic programmes trying to model or teach socially engaged practices might remove the insistence of finding partnering organizations for students to be placed within, and instead focus on fostering the student's own development of agency and capacity to act in the world beyond predefined programmatic requirements. The urgency with which we might imagine these kinds of infrastructural changes being deployed is necessarily going to be scaled to the language we have to describe them, and infrastructures are rarely responsive enough to show us the way. We may have to invent our own. Undoubtedly, this invention will include infrastructures that are disinterested in trying to articulate grand narratives and much more sincerely interested in making way for the small and agile, and all of the complications they bring.

Notes

1   At the time, we had been looking at projects like Graffiti Research Lab, an initiative launched by Eyebeam residents Evan Roth and James Powderly in 2007. We thought

that the term 'lab' captured a certain way of working and could immediately allow us to role-play in ways that went beyond our current practices (at the time, Danielle was an MA Candidate in the Department of Communications and Justin was an MFA candidate at the School of Visual Arts at the University of Windsor).

2 Participation may mean a number of different things, or gradients of action. One way to explore them is through the Ladder of Participation diagram, accessible at http://lithgow-schmidt.dk/sherry-arnstein/ladder-of-citizen-participation.html, and originally published by Arnstein (1969).

3 For a full exploration of the term 'semio-capitalism', see Berardi (2012).

12

WHY PUBLIC ART? URBAN PARKS AND PUBLIC ART IN THE TWENTY-FIRST CENTURY

Joni Palmer

Introduction

Talking about public art in urban parks today is a complicated venture because we must address what is an interesting paradox involving public art, urban public parks and neo-liberalism, and thus ask the following questions: What are the motivations behind, the rationale and support for art in urban parks, particularly in a neo-liberal environment in which parks are a curious mix of 'privately public' spaces? The aim of this chapter is to explore the *why* and *how* of public art in urban parks today. This is an important question now because parks and public art are at an interesting juncture given the fragile state of city budgets, which inevitably tend to cut both public arts and open space budgets. Public art programmes and parks departments are struggling in many cities in the United States, and have been for over a decade. Public–private ventures have helped fill the gap in terms of the production of both public art and urban parks, suggesting a new era for this particular spatial, political and economic conversation in cities today. It is not just each on its own that makes this conversation compelling but the intersection of interests and agendas, and the physical manifestation of these interests and agendas.

The main point of departure for this essay was an article in the *New York Times*, "Eye candy or eye sore" (Johnson 2012). The author provocatively states: "does the High Line need art on top of all that? [The person quoted in the article is referring to the popularity of the park as a promenade, its vendors, design etc.] I'm not convinced that it does." This is a daunting and difficult question, particularly at a time when arts budgets are being slashed, and municipal public art programmes in the United States have been erased or severely diminished.

There are three things the *New York Times* piece prompted me to think about: first, what kind of model is the High Line, given its popularity, inciting replication in cities all over the United States, and what are the implications of the production and operation of the park and its public art programme? Many cities see the High Line as both a model and as a solution to a lack of green space and for reuse of derelict landscapes – yet without a sense of what these kinds of spaces mean to the socio-cultural and political landscape of the city. Second, public art has become something of a requisite element in urban spaces – in the United States – today. Public art has become part and parcel of urban spaces, whether it is 1 per cent for art or art that is funded in some other manner. Though at first it seems a boon for public art, this kind of ill-conceived or purely administrative insertion does not instil confidence, or a sense that public art truly is a meaningful component of urban space today. Third, park designers – landscape architects and architects – often do not critically assess the role of public art; that is, they are only responding to requirements or making artistic insertions without asking, why public art here and for what purpose (Senie 2003; Cartiere 2008). As such, the High Line serves as a kind of foil to explore urban parks and the role of public art in urban parks today, because it is such a prominent fixture in contemporary urban park conversations, particularly given the recent (August 2014) successful completion of the third and final section of the park. I end this chapter with some 'conclusions', intended as a means of moving this conversation forward, since, I imagine, this conversation is far from over.

What does public art 'do' for the urban park and its publics?

A key question that must be asked by those of us who are involved in the making of cities today is: "What does public art *do* for urban parks, and for its publics?" Public art, more often than not, has been relegated to being merely a beautifying or enlivening element (Deutsche 1988; Phillips 1989a; Sharpe et al. 2005). Beautification of and enlivening public spaces is far from inconsequential as both can 'do' a great deal in terms of increasing people's awareness of, and enjoyment and appreciation for, their environment. Yet public art has far greater reach than this. It has been depoliticized to such a degree that public art has become, in many instances, individual aesthetic insertions that are not considered a substantial component of the social, cultural, political and economic fabric of the urban environment.

For its time, Patricia Phillips' piece *Out of Order*, was a provocation to think critically about for whom, and for what reason, public art is created and placed in public spaces. And it is apropos to what has become an increasingly curatorial approach to public art in the public realm today (Phillips 1989a). Creative Time has enabled a great number of provocative, edgy, critical installations and performances in New York City. It has been able to do so through a seasoned curatorial, expertise-based, professional artist- in-action approach. The works this organization has produced have expanded notions of the possibilities and potentialities of art in the public realm, without relying on the municipal percentage for art. This does not mean it is better or worse than publicly subsidized public art but that it is makes possible art that might otherwise be found only in galleries, museums, private or isolated venues.

The most common and all-encompassing definition of public art is: "work created by artists for places accessible to and used by the public" (Becker 2004, p. 4). Local government/municipal public art programmes, according to Becker, "are charged with administering the development and management of public art in their communities", and they – by ordinance – demand a public process that takes into account the site and other contextual issues (ibid., p. 1). The problem is that such programmes thus maintain the pervasiveness of mediocre public art: the intentions for public art are either modest (mere amenities) or obviously ornamental (Phillips 1989a). Public art, though, has the potential to be imagined in multiple ways. One way to imagine public art is as a visually accessible object that is located within spaces of open public access (Eaton 1990; Miles 1997). Yet, just what is 'public space' is under extreme debate, given the privatization of the public realm. What one can see (thereby privileging the visual aspects of public art) is not necessarily what one can physically encounter *in* a/the space. Another way to imagine public art focuses on the social aspects, which Deutsche encourages as a way to question the artist's approach to the public dimensions of public art. She argues that art *becomes* public when the art is intended to engage or address the public. A third way to imagine public art is to consider the selection process, which takes into account the level of public engagement, involvement and participation (Doss 1995; Lacy 1995; Hall 2007). Yet another way one might imagine public art is to emphasize its *becoming public*; that is, art *becomes* public through the public's engagement with it, which manifests itself through, for example, ownership, by attaching 'pet names' to the project (Massey and Rose 2003; Palmer 2012). There are, of course, "degrees of publicness" of public art, by which I mean the extent to which public art is made a part of peoples' everyday lives (Hall 2007; Palmer 2012). The notion that public art is for places accessible to and used by the public is a simplistic way of thinking about public art, because it does not interrogate the accessibility of public art nor does it consider what is a rather clinical phrasing – *how* it is used by the public. Visuality is just one dimension of the potential of public art. Rather, as Deutsche (1988), Massey and Rose (2003), and Hall (2007) all note, public art becomes public through various processes, actions and everyday activities. As such, what public art 'does' for people is related to how people and the built environment are engaged.

The benefits of public art can be divided into three broad categories: quality of life, community image and identity, and economic stimulus. In terms of quality of life, public art offers a benefit because it enhances peoples' experience of the built environment by stimulating their attention to the world around them. Public art also serves as a means by which to promote a community image and identity. In this way, public art expresses a pride of place, bolstering the community's image of itself. The economic stimulus component of the benefits of public is much harder to prove, though Americans for the Arts' research has shown that arts and culture are an important revenue generator (AFTA 2011). Public art has the potential to stimulate the (creative) economy because it makes places more attractive to productive individuals and business.

A clear and universal definition of public art is difficult to pin down, but this can be a productive point of departure in that this 'muddiness' suggests the potential of public art. But this potential is only possible if we acknowledge and critically engage this further-expanded field (Cartiere 2008, p. 9). Public art is, in its many manifestations, a reflection of society/ies. In some instances public art reflects a civic-minded society, one that values arts, culture, a liveable environment and the contentment of its citizens. In its physical and material form (whether, for example, that be permanent or temporary, object or performance), public art enhances public spaces and provokes dialogue. As a community art/engagement tool, public art provides people with the opportunity to participate in the making of a city, and generates conversation amongst its publics.

Given a further-expanding field, and even more so since Cartiere published her piece in 2004, there is a real need for disseminating information, tracking use and response, and what Seine calls "responsible criticism" (Senie 2003). For Senie, all of these are responsibilities that those involved in public art are not only burdened with but to which they should feel obligated. It seems quite possible that informing, tracking and responsibly critiquing will enable a deeper and more resonant understanding of this expanding field. Responsible criticism is at the core of advancing the field if it includes "a discussion of the requirements of the commission and the curatorial role of the public art administrator, an analysis of the site, and a consideration of audience response. ... and the artist's intention" (ibid., p. 3).

This further-and ever-expanding field of public art includes a wide variety of sites and venues, financing and funding scenarios, media and mediums, as well as individuals and collectives. Unfortunately, public art continues to be considered a luxury or a burden, a requirement or an add-on, a constraint or an opportunity. It is by addressing and unpacking the specific geo-political, economic and socio-cultural contexts of public art that we might better be able to responsibly critique it in its many forms – and thus answer the question: why public art (in this particular place)? In other words: what does public art do for *this* space and for *its* publics?

Hybridity and the future of urban parks

The twenty-first-century large urban park

The High Line has become an influential model for large urban parks in the United States, and suggests what one might think of as a hybrid reality for large urban parks in the twenty-first century. In Czerniak and Hargreaves's (2007) volume *Large Parks*, Julia Czerniak ruminates on the notion of "large" in relation to parks. She notes that the editors (and contributing authors) "provisionally take Downing's advice and define 'large' as 500 acres" (p. 23). Later she adds: "In addition to size, the term 'large' implies ambition" (p. 26). In the case of the High Line, although it is just less than 400 acres, I would argue that it should be considered a large park because of the extent of its urban linear coverage (1.45 miles), as well as its presence and ambition.

Large urban parks have the potential to "afford a rich array of social activities and interactions that help forge community, citizenship and belonging in dense, busy cities" (Corner 2007, p. 11). Yet 'privately public' parks don't always allow for this array of interactions. James Corner, principal of Field Operations (the landscape architecture firm that co-designed the High Line) asserts: "large parks will always exceed singular narratives. They are larger than the designer's will for authorship, they exceed over-regulation and contrivance, and they always evolve into more multifarious (and unpredictable) formations than anyone could have envisaged at the outset" (ibid., p. 13). Corner is correct in that parks are much more than plans on paper, but his claim that they exceed over-regulation and contrivance is typical of an apolitical naivety employed by design firms to strengthen support for redevelopment projects. John Beardsley notes, in the same volume of *Large Parks*, that "it is increasingly difficult to find a large park anywhere in the world that is fully public – that is, entirely free and accessible in all places at all times, and fully supported by public funds" (Beardsley 2007, p. 199). It is difficult, as Beardsley observes, to finance and maintain parks in today's economic climate, thus an increasing number of urban parks are the result of public–private partnerships (ibid.). These public–private partnership parks represent what Beardsley calls an "erosion of commitment" among public institutions, which have "troubling public policy implications" (ibid., p. 200). Beardsley provides the Central Park Conservancy as an example while – in 1988 – Deutsche provided Battery Park.

In the past decade we have seen an explosion of the "physical and fiscal erosion of parks" (Ibid.: 211); clearly, city parks departments are ill-suited to stem this tide. Thus, "we can no longer speak simply of public as opposed to private space; we are increasingly dealing with a hybrid that is not entirely one or the other" (ibid., p. 202). These partnerships blur the lines between public and private that are often difficult to ascertain in some or even many instances. In New York and in San Francisco, it is necessary to first read nameplates before one can determine the status of a park, because some of these seemingly public spaces are, in fact, fully private. The negative aspects of these partnerships are manifest in the formalization and privatization of activities and spaces, as parks have become gentrified, along with their neighbourhoods. The positive aspects of these partnerships are the funds, clout and additional resources that add value to these parks. In terms of public art, staff, programmes and installations (permanent and, particularly, temporary) can be developed and sustained because of private investment. In this manner, city parks/recreation and public art departments can supplement their minimal funds to accelerate opportunities and promote arts and culture to their publics.

This new hybrid park reality highlights what Don Mitchell and Richard Van Deusen contend: namely, that public space is "largely depoliticized and highly controlled" (Mitchell and Van Deusen 2001, p. 103). Their argument is that urban parks are "decidedly not public" because their "purpose is to control and direct interaction, to police it, rather than to provide a stage on which various publics can come together in all their often contentious differences, and spark a conflagration of public, political, and social interaction" (ibid., p. 103). Thus, we have parks like the

High Line, sanitized landscapes that re-present the type of public art the city wishes to produce. However, Beardsley does not agree, believing instead that large urban parks, though they are "representative of uneven development" (Beardsley 2007, p. 201), "are still one of the principal places where people are least subject to social control". He contends that "parks are among the few places where people are most free to pursue the ordinary and extraordinary expressions of everyday life" (ibid., p. 209).

Interestingly, Beardsley cites the claims that parks provide "unaccounted economic benefits to cities: increased property values and enhanced revenues in surrounding neighbourhoods, and advantages for their towns over less green cities in the competition for tax-paying businesses and residents, to cite just two". This is similar to what Hall and Robertson list as the difficult and unwieldy claims of advocates for public art (Hall and Robertson 2001): "Parks," Beardsley astutely notes, "were once believed to be of value for their own sakes", which could be said as well of public art. Now both are "caught up in demographic, political, and economic transformations that they can neither hope to contain, nor fully represent" (Beardsley 2007, p. 212).

Interrelated taxonomies: Urban parks and public art

Public art has long been a part of urban parks. Yet, there has not been an explicit conversation about how public art has come to be a component of parks and what role, if any, it is intended to play. Additionally, it is useful to consider what Mitchell and Van Deusen call the "new hybrid park reality," in relation to parks of other eras.

Galen Cranz, in her 1982 book *The Politics of Park Design*, identified four eras of (urban) park design and development: 1850–1900, the pleasure ground; 1900–1930, the reform park; 1930–1965, the recreation facility; and 1965–1980, the open space system. At the time, this taxonomy was revelatory since it provided a means by which to think about how parks responded to changing political, economic and social forces and conditions. In 2004, she (along with Michael Boland) proposed a fifth model or era of park design, the sustainable park, which they believe emerged in the mid to late 1990s. It is their assertion "that park models tend to dominate for 30 to 50 years, and they conclude that these models are generational" (Cranz and Boland 2004, p. 104). As generationally created, parks represent each generation's "ideas about how parks can help cities, its own experience in putting these ideas into practice, and its own frustrations and successes with those models" (ibid., p. 104). The sustainable park model emerged at a time when city administrators, designers and planners were beginning to actually grapple with issues of social justice as well as concerns about restoration, ecology, and – importantly – the attempt to operationalize the notion of sustainability in urban parks.

It is not the intent of this chapter to advance the taxonomy of park design, but rather to extend Cranz's argument in order to include one particular element of parks: *public art*. Public art has long been part and parcel of parks and park design. The oft-referenced Lacy quote about the white guy on a horse is relevant here, given that public art (aka statuary or memorial) was often inserted after the fact or given a prominent place in parks in order to celebrate a particular historical figure (typically a white male, and frequently riding high up on a horse).[1] According to Cranz, "if the pleasure ground had been a pious patriarch, the reform park a social worker, and the recreational facility a waitress or car mechanic, the new park [the open space system] was something of a performance artist" (Cranz 1982, p. 138). Along this line of thinking, the sustainable park might be a naturalist or an ecologist. And, relative to public art, the art that is representative of each of these various types of park would be as follows: monuments to war heroes and the like would populate the pleasure ground, celebrating the growing might of the nation; statues of civic persons and state leaders would announce (and educate the populace about) the civic values of a new century in the United States; functional and abstract sculpture would inhabit the recreational facilities of mid-century; while large, monumental sculpture would land in the open spaces of the park systems of the mid-1960s through the 1980s; and public art signage and wayfinding educational works would colonize the sustainable park.

Urban parks in the USA have always reflected power dynamics, though who wields the power, and what/who they wish to monitor or control, has changed over the decades (ibid., p. 157). Based on Cranz's park model life cycle, we are not yet ready for a new model of urban parks. Yet, I believe a new era of park planning and design overlapped with the emergence of the sustainable park. I will call this new park era the neo-liberal park. The poster child for this kind of park, particularly in terms of public art, is the High Line. Such a park would not be represented by a pious patriarch (because this kind of park is more flamboyant than his piousness would be able to tolerate), nor would it be represented by the social worker, waitress or mechanic (because they probably would not be welcome or comfortable there). The performance artist would be welcomed there, but for different reasons than in an earlier era – because performance and aesthetics are crucial to the way this new kind of park operates and attracts people, and the naturalist/ecologist would be seen as a curious interloper exploring the park's claims of being sustainable. Instead, the representative of this kind of park is the corporation or the entrepreneur, and its public art is highbrow work, curated for an urbane and sophisticated public.

The new hybrid park reality: the neo-liberal park

From a political standpoint, this new park era is not all that different from the era of the pleasure ground or the reform park, because those parks served, and in serving produced particular kinds of publics. However, what I am referring to as the neo-liberal park is a distinctly new typology, not only because it is a gated, surveilled and policed urban park, but also because they are the result of a "reduction of corporate taxes, the shrinking and/or privatization of public services... the enhancement of international capital mobility, the intensification of interlocality competition, and the criminalization of the poor" (Brenner and Theodore 2002, p. 3). The public art that is installed as part of these park projects is only possible because of this corporate business model and because of the extensive management of these parks. That said, such parks are not to be disparaged for what they can offer – well-manicured, surveilled and seemingly safe environments, comfortable and rich in amenities. Yet, they must be considered as very particular types of parks that are not possible in all cities or urban conditions.

Neo-liberal parks are parks that are instrumentalized for economic development, and the public art therein is a value-added component, one that is visual and marketing-ready. The arts and cultural components of these parks are critical because they "attract the 'creative class' that makes regions economic winners" (Flanagan 2008, p. 149). The creative class are not only desirable populations to visit the park, but they are wooed as financers (of the park) as well.

The neo-liberal park is a hybrid financially, politically and socially. As Mitchell and Van Duesen note, these parks are depoliticized in order to redirect attention – away from the concerns about lack of public funding (e.g., dwindling city budgets for city parks departments) and away from the corporate entities (and other private actors) that control access to (and behaviour in) these parks. These parks, which play critical roles in urban regeneration initiatives, are complicated due to the challenges of "coordinating diverse and multiple agencies" (Haughton and Allmendinger 2007, p. 306). Because of the multiplicity of interests and actors, these parks operate in a fuzzy area of planning where, as Haughton et al. suggest, progressive or regressive actions can be enacted. These parks can thus be "deliberate tactic[s] to create uncertainty or mask clarity" (Haughton et al. 2013, p. 217). In this way they might make possible parks that could not be produced within formal, visible, democratic processes. As such, they can be considered physical manifestations of soft spaces because these parks operate "outside, alongside or in-between the formal statutory scales of government, from area master plans to multiregional growth strategies" (ibid., p. 217).

Deutsche's influential and prescient 1988 article ("Uneven Development: Public Art in New York City") was a reaction to New York City Mayor Koch's (Mayor of New York City from 1978 to 1989) instrumentalization of the power of his office and urban development to rid the city of what were deemed undesirable populations and activities. Koch supported urban redevelopments that were "attempts to restore to the city a surface calm that belies underlying contradictions" (Deutsche 1988, p. 5); as such, these urban "improvements" were, as Deutsche says, "imposed from above by state institutions or private interests, one that is dictated by the necessities of control and profit but legitimized by concepts of efficiency or beauty" (ibid., p. 6). Urban revitalization projects during Koch's term were, admittedly, an attempt to rescue the city from bankruptcy and deterioration. And, in many ways this rescuing mentality buttressed public support of these efforts. In the first decade of the twenty-first century, another New York City mayor supported similar structural practices that further exacerbated the uneven development of the city in an attempt to elevate its global stature. These practices are examples of a city that is "produced by a group in order to be bought or even used by others" (Deutsche cited Ledrut, ibid., p. 6).[2] Deutsche's 1988 article is indeed still significant, because it foreshadowed what is now rampant uneven development throughout the city. That she linked public art to uneven development is equally important. Recent scholarship in public art is directly confronting exclusionary practices, attending to the lack of attention to multiple publics' voices and thus attempting to engage communities that have been ignored (Pratt 2009; Pollack and Sharp 2012; Zebracki 2014a). Deutsche's work is useful here because her work, though it focused on the development process, foreshadowed the rampant, ambiguous instrumentalization of public art in urban parks. Stated in a different way, public art has become part and parcel of the symbolic economy of park design without express attention to the why, what and how of public art. That is, how might public art – as a public/community process and as an integral element of community planning and park design – be a productive force, not a stand-alone thing/object in the landscape?

Uneven development today is exemplified, in New York City and other global cities, by development of urban parks that serve particular segments of the populations, and exclude counter and subaltern publics through a range of means, ranging from explicit to more subtle approaches. Public art became a priority for the Koch administration because it was a means by which to re-present the city as hospitable to real estate interests, private development and tourism. This redevelopment of the city as beautiful and safe was intended for specific publics, publics that would spend, invest and reproduce themselves as 'the public' of the new New York. Public art, as such, was aestheticized to the point that it was meant to signal safety and comfort. Equally, the High Line's public art signals safety, comfort and status, particularly given that it is a curated collection that touts big names and big money. Deutsche's concern that public art was fetishized is relevant here as well, because public art at the High Line is in – and of – the development of this site. Cheeky and often times apolitically political, it announced its elevated status in ways that symbolize a cultural economy that is mainly concerned with an aesthetic urge – along with the reproduction of wealth and further development – rather than strengthening the local economy in order to create a liveable urban environment for the existing community (Zukin 1998).

Consider this: news about the opening of the final phase of The High Line – a much anticipated and celebrated event – ran alongside weeks of articles about the poor funding for parks throughout New York City's boroughs. On 6 October 2014, a *New York Times* article relayed that the new mayor of New York (Bill de Blasio) would be announcing "an ambitious initiative that would channel some $130 million into tattered parks and playgrounds in low-income neighbourhoods across New York City". This was big news, particularly in a city where the High Line and other parks (Brooklyn Bridge Park and Governors Island, for example) had been garnering a great deal of attention and private money while: "There are the hardscrabble neighbourhood parks that, advocates say, were overlooked during the Bloomberg administration, even as billions of dollars flowed to big-ticket legacy projects in wealthier parts of the city." De Blasio's initiative will be funded by public dollars, and will serve thousands of people in underserved communities across the city.

The ruin(ed) and rescued child: the High Line as neo-liberal poster child

What does a park such as the High Line offer, in terms of urban parks and public art? I believe that it offers much in the way of lessons, cautionary tales as well as lessons by which other cities and park systems might develop public art works/ programmes in relation to urban parks. As such, it provides a means by which to observe and critique the *why* and the *how* of public art in urban parks.

The High Line has gained a great deal of notoriety, particularly given that the final phase of the park has been completed and has been widely celebrated as a success in many circles. The High Line is an elevated, linear park on Manhattan's lower West Side. The park occupies a former 1930s freight train (infra)structure; the last train ran in 1980. The park is owned by the City of New York (Department of Parks and Recreation) but maintained, programmed and operated by Friends of the High Line, which raises private funding to support more than 90 per cent of the park's annual operations.

The High Line resurrects an urban space that was in disuse and had become an urban ruin of large proportions. The founders of the Friends of the High Line addressed this space at a consequential time, when cities were developing urban revitalization strategies that operated at the intersection of culture, economy and politics (Harvey 1989; Scott 2006; Champion 2008). Thus, the High Line became one of the leading players in the competition between cities, with both the park and its art playing an important cultural symbolic role in the revitalization of an entire district. It has become emblematic of cities' efforts to rescue urban spaces and infrastructures that have fallen into ruin(s), and recreate them as recognizable and economically viable public spaces that will attract people and development.

Pseudo-public space/art

The High Line is a 'privately public' space because of the process through which it was created, and by which it is maintained, policed and occupied. Such spaces are not uncommon today and, I might add, they are not necessarily in and of themselves negative aspects of the urban experience today. Increasingly, these spaces are part of what one might call a 'cultural public space network', which would include a wide variety of arts and cultural objects, installations and institutions.

What is at issue here is the fact that the public being served by these parks is not a *citizen* public; rather, the approach is to focus on narrow market or niche segments. Their public is a customer, audience or target market, rather than a broad spectrum or inherently diverse public (Palmer 2012). Therefore, such spaces do not attend to varied interests, needs and abilities; rather, they provide for (and thus reproduce) a public that can then be instrumentalized in the name of promoting an elite arts and cultural public.

This public, in urban parks such as the High Line, identifies as consumers and spectators rather than as a civic public. This is the public that is mass reproduced by an increasingly privately held public realm, which I argue is a pseudo-public space by virtue of the "Exclusions enacted to homogenize public space by expelling specific differences" (Deutsche 1988, p. 11). Admittedly, all public space involves exclusions, which are enacted in both small and large ways. For example, many public spaces today prohibit certain activities, from skateboarding to drinking alcohol. Such requirements and prohibitions exclude certain individuals and populations. Yet, the concern here are the larger – and more insidious – exclusionary practices that surveillance and policing enforce (enforcement by both security personnel and by park users).

What is important to the current and future state of public art at the High Line is the fact that the art is "presented by Friends of the High Line and the New York City Department of Parks and Recreation. Major support for High Line Art comes from Donald R. Mullen, Jr. and the Brown Foundation, Inc. of Houston, with additional funding provided by David Zwirner Gallery and Vital Projects Fund, Inc." (High Line Art 2015). This is important because the art at the High Line is continually being (re)presented in order to uphold its innovative and cutting edge status, thus maintaining and growing its body of supporters and donors. Private funding for art is not problematic (donated works and privately funded art in public spaces is nothing new); nor are the public–private partnerships because these partnerships are a growing force behind the production of public art in cities across the country. The hybrid and soft space park takes advantage of the fuzzy zone within which it operates, particularly with regard to public art. Calling art 'public art,' suggests a publicity that it may not be the result of. And, importantly, as curated art it is appealing to a cultured, creative class audience.

Seductive and selective

An obvious observation to be sure (and this is what makes the High Line unique, though not unprecedented) is that the High Line creates an unmistakable and profound relationship between the vertical and the horizontal, instigating relationships and possibilities between the spaces and people above, below and beside it. Opportunities created by this condition include what can happen on the vertical and horizontal surfaces situated beside, above and below the park. The building walls become possible sites for projection, addition and subtraction. The space above, both the sky and anything that overhangs, are potential sites for art, as are the spaces below, beside and on the High Line rail structure itself. Thus the High Line provides for a wide array of public art – public in the sense that it is accessible, particularly visually – to whomever can see it, whether or not it is in – or of – the public realm or public space. In this way, the High Line provides a regular dose of public art in ways, places and times that other public parks are not able to – or have not had the opportunity to – pursue.

Curated space, art and public(s)

Furthermore, this sectional condition makes possible a threefold curation of space, art and public(s). The art programme at the High Line is curated by Cecilia Alemani. Public art at the High Line is, according to its website, "presented by Friends of the High Line. High Line Art commissions and produces public art projects on and around the High Line…to foster a productive dialogue with the surrounding neighbourhood and urban landscape" (High Line Art 2015).

Several years ago I gave a talk to a group of public art administrators in Colorado. An interesting debate ensued when I asked people what their role was as a public art programme administrator. Everyone agreed, and several adamantly so, that they were not curators because they did not choose the 'best' art or decide which art they wanted/preferred on a site. That is, they believed that what museums do is very different from what they do: often catering to current trends or creating exhibits that are of particular interest to the curator or the institution at a particular moment in time. Municipal public art programmes, as managers made clear, are intended to be democratic, following a public process that allows for community input, particularly because the art is from public funds. Not all municipal public art is the result of a public process. Increasingly, municipalities are working with private developers, forming public–private partnerships in order to ensure the creation, execution and maintenance of both permanent and temporary works.

The High Line, however, is definitely a mix of public and private funding. The sectional nature of this park provides for a museum or gallery-like curation. The park is set apart from the profane space below (outside it), similar to a museum. This park does cater to a particular public, namely the gallery and museum-going public that sponsors and supports the High Line. As such, taking a curatorial approach makes sense: appealing to and appeasing the public that has made the park possible, and the public the park continues to cultivate. Ultimately, the High Line continues what, in the late 1980s through the early 2000s, was considered the serious potential of public art to attract tourists and investors.

Art at the High Line incorporates performance art, something that is increasingly a part of public art programmes' dossiers. As a performative space, it is producing publics through the curatorial aspect of the park's art, and in a way this is how it curates its inhabitants. People enter the park at particular intervals along the street (there are nine entry or exit points along the 1.45 mile length of the park), and are constantly under surveillance as soon as they ascend the stairs or elevator: by cameras, security staff and other park inhabitants. This orchestration of entries and exits suggests both possibility and restriction, or containment.

The High Line is a stage in and of itself, where people perform for one another but also perform for people in the adjacent spaces. The street, as well, is a stage; the amphitheatre at 10th Avenue is set-up for just this purpose, appealing to peoples' desire to people-watch. An example of this is *SEEWATCHLOOK,* the public play created by the multimedia Brazilian artist Michel Melamed. The artist created situations where his performers enacted seemingly everyday acts that are just slightly out of place. Through his work he poses questions about how the city can be a stage, where there is a blurring of the boundary between everyday life and theatre, performance and reality.

The High Line presents a unique situation as hybrid urban park and public art. Wesselman discusses the High Line as an otherworldly space, which he says, "invites an understanding of Foucault's concept of heterotopia" (Wesselman 2013, p. 20). He believes that heterotopic spaces demand greater critical reflection with regard to understanding them, not just theoretically but also as fictional spaces as well as actual spaces. Wesselman's otherworldly space is germane to the High Line with regard to the neo-liberal park, because the park is a space that operates at a seductive remove, above and beyond the street and just out of reach for many. And, it is relevant considering the recent theoretical work being conducted with regard to neo-liberalism, the fictional realm within which it simultaneously exists, along with its reality as a material space.

Conclusions

The High Line is, admittedly, not the only example of the neo-liberal park; rather, it is one of the most recently celebrated and completed urban park and public art projects. It is the next version of what has been called 'the Bilbao effect' that drove much development and debate in the 1990s, and the 'Millennium effect', which suggests the need for a more sophisticated and fine-grain understanding of the means by which public art and urban parks are accomplished in the new millennium (Flanagan 2004). Both of these flagship projects highlighted "innovative and unusual architecture [and art] to lure the tourist dollar" (Flanagan 2008, p. 147). The High Line was not initially or overtly created as a tourist draw (though this is what it has become), but as with the conceptualization and development of Millennium Park, the visual quality of the park and its art were crucial to enticing donors and supporters so that the park would be built. Critical to this conversation about the why and the how of public art in urban parks today are the geographically specific political, economic and social actors, forces and factors. These are important questions because art in urban parks is clearly not just public altruism. Instead, in this twenty-first century the motivations behind, and rationale and support for art in urban parks is a complex mix of local–global agendas with very particular results on the ground and in the everyday lives of people who live in cities.

Inevitability of the neo-liberal park/public art?

I began this research thinking about the following precept: it is the responsibility of designers, planners and parks and public arts supporters to consider the potential role(s) of public art. Without doing so, they are merely following a normative conception of public art and urban parks, which – as we see at the High Line – is a changing condition given the social, political, cultural and economic conditions in cities today. As a landscape architect, public art scholar, and urban planner, I think it is imperative that comparative critical studies be conducted so that designers, planners and public art administrators become more cognizant of the realities of the socio-political and economic implications of the work they conduct, even though it involves the difficult position of resolving the innovative nature of the park with the neo-liberal implications of the urban park development.

The High Line is a novel park in the United States, where one is suspended above the city with views of the city that one does not typically have access to. As such, it is an 'other' space, a heterotopic public space, where one is in "a relational disruption in time and space" (Wesselman cited Johnson 2006, p, 17). Foucault's definition of such places is applicable here: "outside" places, even though they are actually localizable (e.g. honeymoons, theatres, etc.) are material spaces that are "out of the order of things" (ibid., pp. 17, 21). The High Line might have been out of the order of things several decades ago, but now it suggests the future of urban parks and public art. It lends itself to the potential of public art to shift one's way of thinking about, and *being* in the city: Public art that is specific to – and contingent on – this condition, creates a unique discourse between park, street and sky.

Does the High Line represent the philosophical, cultural, political, aesthetic future of urban parks and public art? Is this not just the inevitable product of both a hard and a soft neo-liberalism, and an example of Peck's neo-liberalism as a lived phenomenon? Did the founders of the High Line succumb, whether naively or not, to the wholesale marketization of the park and its public art through a public privatization?

Degrees of public art: a continuum

A hybrid reality just might be the new normal in urban parks and public art in the twenty-fist century, which is not necessarily a problem. Instead, the High Line should alert us to the complicated geopolitical processes at work in the making of public spaces and public arts in cities today. Parks and public art are an important part of urban life; the reality in these fragile economic times is to consider how cities will continue to provide these essential amenities. Concern arises when the interests of publics are ignored or dismissed, and when there is no transparency in the production of parks and public art. Do these public–private partnerships that enable the production of both urban parks and the public art that populates them signal what Beardsley calls an "erosion of commitment" of cities or is it a call to new means of engagement? The High Line provides an example of a particular scenario of motivations behind, and ways of accomplishing the development of, an urban park and public art. It also begs for conversations about the role of tactical public arts in the city.

Read in light of all that I have written here, Patricia Phillips' "public art machine" has been, in some instances, dismantled, and curatorial practices have instantiated themselves into the production of publics and public art. Phillips made a call for moving beyond a "minimum basic standard" for public art, no matter the flavour. For instance, Phillips notes the contributions of the Public Art Fund and

Creative Time to a more dynamic ecology of art in public spaces. These organizations were able to side-step the mind numbing bureaucracy of per cent for art programmes, and actually produce provocative, often temporary, pieces that engaged publics in meaningful ways.

Without the funding that came through the Friends of the High Line, this park would not have been possible. In some ways this represents a "grassroots neo-liberalism", which might just be considered a necessary means of survival of urban parks and for providing green space and public art to the public. And, as such, must we learn to negotiate this uneasy yet necessary twenty-first-century relationship? Municipal public art programmes in the United States are exploring a wide range of ways to provide arts in the public realm. As such, public art is truly further expanding its field, not just in terms of physical manifestations but also in terms of its politics, finances and social responsibilities. The High Line, then, operates at one end of the continuum, enacting the possibilities of the neo-liberal urban park/public art scenario. Tactical public arts operate at the other end. What else lies along this continuum? An exploration of the breadth and depth of this continuum is, I believe, the future of public art. We cannot ignore or dismiss any of these possibilities, but rather, as Seine points out, we must responsibly critique all of them in order to better understand the costs and benefits, and the challenges and consequences.

In this chapter I suggest that the new era of the neo-liberal park cannot be responsibly critiqued without taking into account geographically specific spatial politics. Public art in the neo-liberal park is, too, a result of these spatially based contingencies. Together they play important symbolic roles in the city. It is not just the park but the amenities therein, art being one of these, that draws people in great numbers. The amenities include the security and surveillance that makes these places appealing (and available) to particular publics. Further research needs to be conducted in order to better understand this new type of urban park/public art that operates in terms of degrees of publicness. The publicity of parks and art are, in this neo-liberal condition, highly contingent processes that are manifest differently across spaces, cultures and time. It is to this I recommend research be focused – comparative studies that help us deepen the conversation about the future of arts, culture, and urban public space in particular places and times.

Notes

1 "Our tradition of representational statues is dedicated to reinforcing authority, interpreting significant events in culturally specific ways, and eulogizing idealised and heroic traits that support particular views of history. Often these ideals are vested in a single person, often a white man, often a military or political figure astride a horse" (Lacy 2010, p. 197)

2 "The group" being real estate interests and private development, and the "others" being those who were not the permanent residents and businesses that had inhabited certain parts of the city for generations.

PART IV

Visual timeline

13

A COLLECTIVE TIMELINE OF SOCIALLY ENGAGED PUBLIC ART PRACTICE 1950–2015

Cameron Cartiere, Sophie Hope, Anthony Schrag,
Elisa Yon and Martin Zebracki

All histories are subjective. We cannot hope to fully capture the timeline of socially engaged artworks over the past half-millennium, but we can present a highly subjective one that acts as a starting point for inquiry. In the spirit of the collaborative underpinnings of 'new genre public art' we present selected, intertwined histories chosen by five individuals. These individuals operate from diverse locations within the field, and their selections reflect varied interests—from activist to aesthetic, from historical to happenings. While the legacies of socially engaged art stretch back much further, the boundaries for this timeline are 1950–2015 to allow for a relatively focused chronology of an already complex and expansive topography.

(CC) Cameron Cartiere's choices are grounded in her personal experience with the influential public project Mapping the Terrain. From this key point, she reaches both forwards and backwards to explore how public art is connected to performance, political action, pedagogy, cultural mapping, and theories of the everyday. Her selection focuses on what she identifies as moments that caused dramatic shifts in the genre, opening up new possibilities for producing public work.

(SH) The broad scope of the practice resonates with Sophie Hope, whose starting point to the selection explored her "own approaches to living in a socially engaged way." She takes as her pivotal moment Grant Kester's paper "Dialogical

Aesthetics" delivered at the 1998 Littoral conference in Dublin, and spins around to capture other references that link geographically disparate practices to their social and political contexts.

(EY) Elisa Yon chose artist-initiated works that catalysed cultural, social, political dialogues on issues around urban regeneration, gentrification, city planning, and policy-making, reflecting the place of social practice in a globalised, post-industrial world. The projects she selected invite multiple publics to participate, creating temporary communities within the place, town, or city through the activation of abandoned urban sites, buildings, or systems of infrastructure.

(AS) Anthony Schrag, in turn, chose to select works that explore the position of practice in regards to the institutions that fund it, and its self-reflexivity in the face of its professionalisation. His selection of artworks leans towards those projects that resulted in a questioning of the relationship between artists and institutions, such as the collective work of the Artist Placement Group in the 1960s and 1970s and hopes to trace a lineage that explores contemporary instrumentalised uses of these practices.

(MZ) Lastly, Martin Zebracki's selected key works and moments are situated in his cultural geographical engagement with public art. His compilation stresses public art as being part and parcel with everyday multiscalar social relationships, that is to say the interplay between agency, art/medium and space in the spheres of politics, economy, society, and culture; ranging from the bodily level and the home to the city, region, state, (art) world and, more recently, virtual-augmented contexts.

The contributors recognise the North American/Northern European bent of their selections; this has been for practical rather than conceptual concerns, and note that the practices of Southern, Eastern and 'non-centralised' geographies are brimming with significant and critical histories of this sort of work, which the Global North can – and should – value and learn from.

In the same vein, this limited timeline does not try to present a holistic definition of the practice but aims to incorporate events that surround, shape and guide this way of working, including changes to political landscapes, policy shifts and social movements. The drawback of the timeline format is that it extracts only a title, author and date from processes that are not easily summarised, and tells very little of the complex politics, social, economic factors of the time and place they occurred.

The act of selecting 'cultural objects' (such as art projects, policies and theoretical texts) invites epistemological questions about how and why these particular reference points are on our radars, what has dropped off, and what remains out of sight? How have we been influenced by these moments over time? Do these seemingly disparate selections have things in common (and do they need to)? Are there threads to be drawn geographically and temporally? It is perhaps what is left out of this timeline that leads to further discoveries and inspirations of this area of practice?

Finally, it is hoped that these conversations with the extensive history of public practice can offer up challenges and helpful guidance that provoke us to re-interpret, to re-think, and continue to problematize our current and future narratives.

1950 ●————————

CC (1948–1951) CoBrA: International artist collective whose working methods were based on spontaneity and experimentation. Emphasis was placed on versatility and diversity rather than any kind of formalism.

1951 **MZ** (1951) The Netherlands sees the birth of a state percent-for-art regulation The Netherlands and Sweden were the first European countries to set out that 1–2% of public building costs should be spent on art.

1952 **CC** (1952–1957) Lettrist International appropriated type as the core of a visual language, which formed the basis of their new culture.

CC

Figure 13.1 (1952) *Theater Piece No. 1* John Cage. Black Mountain College, North Carolina. Composer John Cage organized *Theater Piece No. 1*, an unscripted performance considered by many to be the first Happening. The event took place in the Black Mountain College dining hall and also included choreographer Merce Cunningham, pianist David Tudor and painter Robert Rauschenberg. Photo: Cage and Cunningham (1953), Black Mountain College Research Project, courtesy Western Regional Archives, State Archives of North Carolina.

1953 **CC** (1953–1957) International Movement for an Imaginist Bauhaus (IMIB). A precursor to the Situationists, IMIB focused on the value of irrational and poetic architecture. IMIB was also foundational for Fluxus and the Interventionists.

1954 **EY** (1954–1972) Gutai Artist Association (Gutai Bijutsu Kyokai). Founded by artist Yoshihara Jirō, Gutai's early outdoor staged events sought to break new ground between art and everyday life. Members explored the boundaries of collective creativity and participation between artist and audience.

○**1959**

SH (1958) Launch of the Campaign for Nuclear Disarmament in the United Kingdom with the first march to Aldermaston organised by the Direct Action Committee galvanised support amongst artists.

CC (1958) Theory of the Dérive, Guy Debord. A manual for psychogeographic procedures, executed through the act of dérive ("drift").

1958 **SH** (1958) In his essay "Culture is Ordinary", Raymond Williams explores the idea of culture as both a whole way of life as well as a process of creative discovery.

Figure 13.2 (1957) Founders of the **CC** Situationist International at Cosio d'Arrosica, Italy. From left to right: Guiseppe Pinot Gallizio, Piero Simondo, Elena Verrone, Michèle Bernstein, Guy Debord, Asger Jorn, and Walter Olmo. Active from 1957–1972, the Situationists have often been cited as the genesis of social practice. The group began at the Situationists' first international congress in Cosio d'Arrosica, Italy. Founding members included: Guy Debord, Michèle Bernstein and Asger Jorn. Photo: Courtesy Fonds Guy Debord, BNF.

1957 **AS** (1957) Allan Kaprow first coined the term "happening" in the spring of 1957.

1956

1955

1960 o⸺

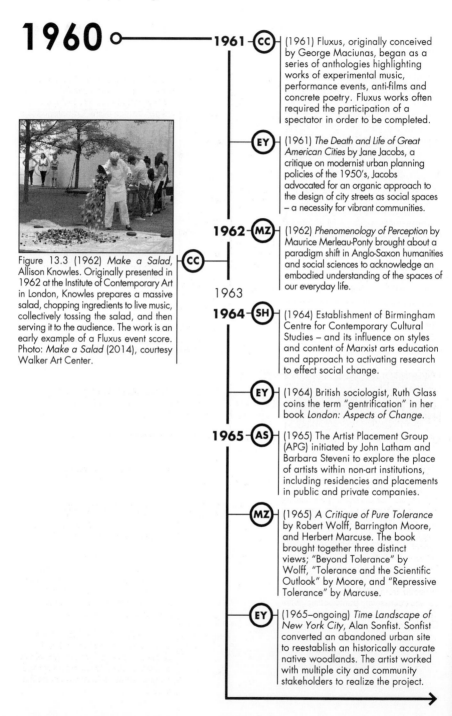

Figure 13.3 (1962) *Make a Salad*, Allison Knowles. Originally presented in 1962 at the Institute of Contemporary Art in London, Knowles prepares a massive salad, chopping ingredients to live music, collectively tossing the salad, and then serving it to the audience. The work is an early example of a Fluxus event score. Photo: *Make a Salad* (2014), courtesy Walker Art Center.

1961 – (CC) (1961) Fluxus, originally conceived by George Maciunas, began as a series of anthologies highlighting works of experimental music, performance events, anti-films and concrete poetry. Fluxus works often required the participation of a spectator in order to be completed.

(EY) (1961) *The Death and Life of Great American Cities* by Jane Jacobs, a critique on modernist urban planning policies of the 1950's, Jacobs advocated for an organic approach to the design of city streets as social spaces – a necessity for vibrant communities.

1962 (MZ) (1962) *Phenomenology of Perception* by Maurice Merleau-Ponty brought about a paradigm shift in Anglo-Saxon humanities and social sciences to acknowledge an embodied understanding of the spaces of our everyday life.

(CC)

1963

1964 (SH) (1964) Establishment of Birmingham Centre for Contemporary Cultural Studies – and its influence on styles and content of Marxist arts education and approach to activating research to effect social change.

(EY) (1964) British sociologist, Ruth Glass coins the term "gentrification" in her book *London: Aspects of Change*.

1965 (AS) (1965) The Artist Placement Group (APG) initiated by John Latham and Barbara Steveni to explore the place of artists within non-art institutions, including residencies and placements in public and private companies.

(MZ) (1965) *A Critique of Pure Tolerance* by Robert Wolff, Barrington Moore, and Herbert Marcuse. The book brought together three distinct views; "Beyond Tolerance" by Wolff, "Tolerance and the Scientific Outlook" by Moore, and "Repressive Tolerance" by Marcuse.

(EY) (1965–ongoing) *Time Landscape of New York City*, Alan Sonfist. Sonfist converted an abandoned urban site to reestablish an historically accurate native woodlands. The artist worked with multiple city and community stakeholders to realize the project.

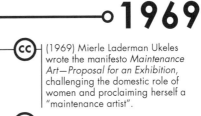

Figure 13.4 (1968–1978) As Town Artist, David Harding was officially embedded into the civic and social construction of the New Town of Glenrothes. The Town Artist project influenced the Community Arts Movement that developed in the 70s and 80s in the UK. Photo: Courtesy David Harding.

(CC) (1969) Mierle Laderman Ukeles wrote the manifesto *Maintenance Art—Proposal for an Exhibition*, challenging the domestic role of women and proclaiming herself a "maintenance artist".

(EY) (1968–1978) Ant Farm, a radical architecture collective founded by Chip Lord and Doug Michels in Texas. As the group expanded, they developed projects such as *Inflatables* (1970).

(AS) **(MZ)** (1968) First published in Portuguese, *Pedagogy of the Oppressed* was translated and published in English in 1970. The methodology of Paulo Freire has empowered impoverished and illiterate people throughout the world.

(MZ) (1968) France – May Protests, student occupations and protests against capitalist systems inspired and supported by Situationist International visual propaganda to catalyze collective action.

(AS)-**1968**

(CC) (1967) Experiments in Art and Technology (E.A.T.), founded by artitsts Robert Rauschenberg and Robert Whitman with engineers Billy Klüver and Fred Waldhauer to create collaboratative performance opportunities. Their works were some of the first to use video projection, optical effects, and wireless sound transmission.

1967-**(SH)** (1967) Philippine Educational Theatre Association (PETA) was established to train critical, cultural workers in social transformation.

1966-**(SH)** (1966) The Destruction in Art Symposium (DIAS) organised by Gustav Metzger at the Africa Centre, London connected destruction in art to destruction in society with happenings across the city.

(EY) (1965–1968) Civil rights activists used nonviolent protest and civil disobedience to effect change. News media was used to raise and spread a collective consciousness across the world.

Figure 13.5 (1968) *La Familia Obrera*, (Blue Collar Family). Oscar Bony draws attention to the lived experience of a non-art 'public' and highlights a rift between the 'internal' art world and an 'external' art world. As a 'participatory' artwork, it considered lives that were excluded from artistic inquiry, as well as the ethics of participating with #non-art' audiences. Photo: Courtesy Carola Bony.

1970 o————

(CC) (1970) Joseph Beuys begins a public lecture tour introducing the concept of "Social Sculpture".

1971 (AS) (1971) The Theater of the Oppressed, established by Brazilian director and political activist Augusto Boal, as a form of popular theater, of, by, and for people struggling for liberation.

1972 (SH) (1972) "The Tyranny of Structurelessness" by Jo Freeman – this essay is a useful reminder of the traps of collective, co-operative working and the elitism within seemingly inclusive forms of practice.

(EY) (1972–1976) *Running Fence* Christo and Jeanne-Claude, Sonoma and Marin Counties, California. USA. The work encompassed 42 months of collaborative efforts, was 24.5 miles long and 18 feet high, with one end dropping down to the Pacific Ocean. Funded entirely by the artists, the project engaged multiple jurisdictions, landowners and volunteers. The completed work was installed for two weeks in September, 1976.

1973 (EY) (1973) Daniel Bell coins the term "postindustrial" in *The Coming of Post-Industrial Society: A Venture in Social Forecasting*. It describes characteristics of a postindustrial society, identifying a fundamental shift from production of goods to production of services.

(SH) (1973–1975) *Women and Work* was a study of women who worked in a metal box factory in Bermondsey, London by artists Margaret Harrison, Kay Hunt and Mary Kelly. They used interviews, archival research, observation, film, and photography to make art works.

1974 (AS) (1974) Creative Time is founded in New York by Anita Contini, Karin Bacon, and Susan Henshaw Jones as a platform for experimental public art interventions in the city.

(EY)

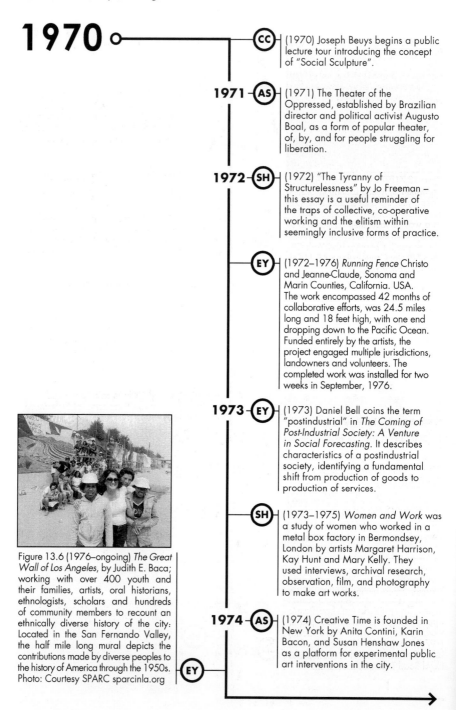

Figure 13.6 (1976–ongoing) *The Great Wall of Los Angeles*, by Judith E. Baca; working with over 400 youth and their families, artists, oral historians, ethnologists, scholars and hundreds of community members to recount an ethnically diverse history of the city: Located in the San Fernando Valley, the half mile long mural depicts the contributions made by diverse peoples to the history of America through the 1950s. Photo: Courtesy SPARC sparcinla.org

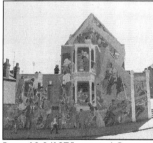

Figure 13.7 (1979–1980) *Touch Sanitation Performance*, Mierle Laderman Ukeles. Over a year the artist shook hands with every New York Sanitation worker (8,500) as a way to value their contribution to society. With each handshake she said, "Thank you for keeping New York City alive." Photo: Courtesy Ronald Feldman Fine Arts, New York.

Figure 13.8 (1975–ongoing) Greenwich Mural Workshop founded by 'art workers' Carol Kenna, Stephen Lobb, and Rick Walker as a service to council estates. They painted murals from 9am to 5pm to highlight their labour as a "proper working day." Photo: Floyd Road, (1974), courtesy Carol Kenna & Stephen Lobb, Greenwich Mural Workshop and Floyd Road Tenant's Association.

(AS) ○**1979**

1978-(SH) (1978) Su Braden's Artists and People published by Gulbenkian Foundation. A pivotal study of self-organised community arts projects and a critique of parachuting in artists to solve social problems.

(CC) (1977) Skulptur Projekte Münster. Held every 10 years (1977, 1987, 1997, 2007) in the German city of Münster examining the ambivalent relationship between art and public space through site-specific works that respond to the urban context and encourage active public participation.

(SH) (1977) Dip HE course, Art and Design in Social Contexts was established at Dartington College of Art, England by Paul Oliver. Chris Crickmay and David Harding joined the college in 1978 turning the course into a BA in 'Art and Social Context', formalised as a degree in 1986.

(MZ) (1977) Yi-Fu Tuan's *Space and Place: The Perspective of Experience* elaborates on how sensorial connections (everyday thoughts, feelings and attachments) to spaces and places are linked to the micro-scale of the human body, location, and time: past, present, and future.

1977-(AS) (1977–1985) Stephan Willats creates participatory artworks for tower blocks in the UK, Finland, Germany, and Holland; developed as 'modes of resistance and critical conciseness' with residents to critique bureaucratic and civil engineering plans.

1976-(SH) (1976–1988) *Structuring the Self*, Lygia Clark used everyday materials (plastic bags, stones, air, shells, water) which she called 'relational objects, to interact with participants in a therapeutic context aimed at emotional healing and tapping a body's memory'.

(SH)- **1975**

1980 o

(AS) (1980) The Artist Placement Group becomes I + O.

(EY) (1980) *The Social Life of Small Urban Spaces* by William H. Whyte. The book presents Whyte's seminal research on the Street Life Project and work with the New York City Planning Commission. Whyte critically reflects on his pioneering studies of pedestrian behavior and city dynamics.

1981 (CC) (1981) Tim Rollins and KOS (South Bronx, New York) began as a project initiated by Rollins to integrate art practice into an afterschool literacy program. Rollins shares authorship of the resulting artworks with the Kids of Survival. The original students coined the name KOS.

1982 (SH) (1982) The Culture and Resistance Festival, in Garobone Botswana. This festival was organised by Medu Arts Ensemble, a group of South African exiled artists, writers, musicians, designers, and theatre practitioners.

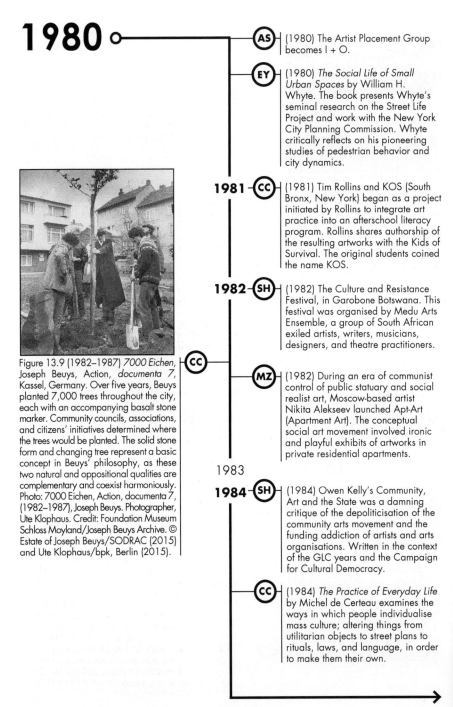

(CC)

(MZ) (1982) During an era of communist control of public statuary and social realist art, Moscow-based artist Nikita Alekseev launched Apt-Art (Apartment Art). The conceptual social art movement involved ironic and playful exhibits of artworks in private residential apartments.

1983

1984 (SH) (1984) Owen Kelly's Community, Art and the State was a damning critique of the depoliticisation of the community arts movement and the funding addiction of artists and arts organisations. Written in the context of the GLC years and the Campaign for Cultural Democracy.

(CC) (1984) *The Practice of Everyday Life* by Michel de Certeau examines the ways in which people individualise mass culture; altering things from utilitarian objects to street plans to rituals, laws, and language, in order to make them their own.

Figure 13.9 (1982–1987) *7000 Eichen*, Joseph Beuys, Action, *documenta 7*, Kassel, Germany. Over five years, Beuys planted 7,000 trees throughout the city, each with an accompanying basalt stone marker. Community councils, associations, and citizens' initiatives determined where the trees would be planted. The solid stone form and changing tree represent a basic concept in Beuys' philosophy, as these two natural and oppositional qualities are complementary and coexist harmoniously. Photo: 7000 Eichen, Action, documenta 7, (1982–1987), Joseph Beuys. Photographer, Ute Klophaus. Credit: Foundation Museum Schloss Moyland/Joseph Beuys Archive. © Estate of Joseph Beuys/SODRAC (2015) and Ute Klophaus/bpk, Berlin (2015).

○**1989**

Figure 13.10 (1986) *Chambres d'Amis* by Jan Hoet ("the Belgian art pope", 1936–2014), Ghent. Breaking out of Ghent Museum for Contemporary Art's limited gallery space, this ground-breaking exhibition featured public artworks displayed by 50 national and international artists in 58 ordinary homes across the city. The installations radically shifted conventional notions of the museum and its social audiences. Photo: Courtesy Dirk Pauwels/Herbert Foundation.

1988 (EY) (1988–1989) *Homeless Vehicles,* Krzysztof Wodiczko. The artist collaborated with a local population of people who were experiencing homelessness in New York City to create a tool for living and surviving on the streets.

(MZ) (1987) *Science in Action: How to Follow Scientists and Engineers Through Society* by Bruno Latour lays the foundation of the poststructuralist Actor-Network-Theory. This theory involves a material-semiotic approach to life where knowledge production is analysed in interplay with networks and actors, including both human and non-human agencies.

(AS) (1987) The formation of Critical Art Ensemble, an artist collective whose work explores and models the possibilities for resistant activity within capitalist democracies in various public contexts.

1987 (MZ) (1987–ongoing) Public Art Forum is established in the UK (renamed ixia in 2004). Positioned as a public art think tank to conduct research, provide training and support networking events in the public art realm. The agency published *Public Art* Journal from 1999–2002.

Figure 13.11 (1986–ongoing) *Heidelberg Project,* Tyree Guyton, Detroit, USA. Artist Tyree Guyton initiated a project to transform his neighbourhood into a living indoor/ outdoor art gallery. Guyton used found debris in the neighbourhood to compose site installations on facades of houses and assemblages on abandoned lots. The *Heidelberg Project* has raised awareness of the plight of Detroit's forgotten neighbourhoods and has become a platform to induce discussion and action. Photo: Courtesy The Heidelberg Project.

(EY) **1986**

1985 (AS) (1985) Environmental Art Programme at the Glasgow School of Art. The course was set up and developed by artist David Harding in response to the awareness of more and more artists working from context-led situations, especially within the public domain. This included a large emphasis on art in the public realm as well as participatory arts, and produced a strong generation of participatory working artists.

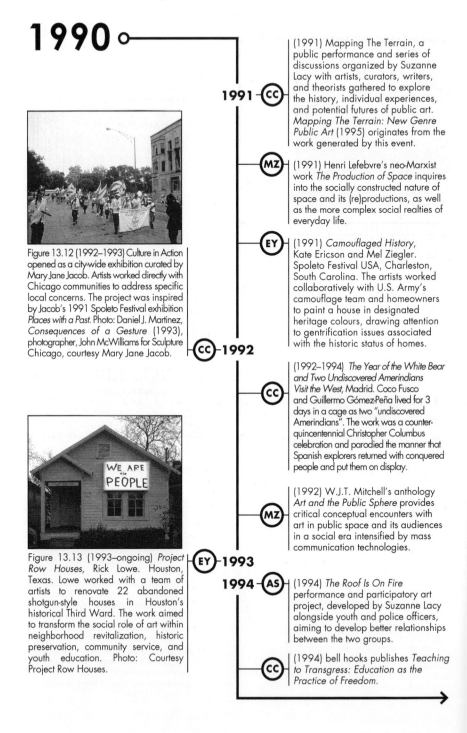

1990 o⎯⎯⎯⎯⎯⎯⎯⎯⎯⎯⎯⎯

1991–(CC) (1991) Mapping The Terrain, a public performance and series of discussions organized by Suzanne Lacy with artists, curators, writers, and theorists gathered to explore the history, individual experiences, and potential futures of public art. *Mapping The Terrain: New Genre Public Art* (1995) originates from the work generated by this event.

(MZ) (1991) Henri Lefebvre's neo-Marxist work *The Production of Space* inquires into the socially constructed nature of space and its (re)productions, as well as the more complex social realties of everyday life.

(EY) (1991) *Camouflaged History*, Kate Ericson and Mel Ziegler. Spoleto Festival USA, Charleston, South Carolina. The artists worked collaboratively with U.S. Army's camouflage team and homeowners to paint a house in designated heritage colours, drawing attention to gentrification issues associated with the historic status of homes.

Figure 13.12 (1992–1993) Culture in Action opened as a city-wide exhibition curated by Mary Jane Jacob. Artists worked directly with Chicago communities to address specific local concerns. The project was inspired by Jacob's 1991 Spoleto Festival exhibition *Places with a Past*. Photo: Daniel J. Martinez, *Consequences of a Gesture* (1993), photographer, John McWilliams for Sculpture Chicago, courtesy Mary Jane Jacob.

(CC)–**1992**

(CC) (1992–1994) *The Year of the White Bear and Two Undiscovered Amerindians Visit the West*, Madrid. Coco Fusco and Guillermo Gómez-Peña lived for 3 days in a cage as two "undiscovered Amerindians". The work was a counter-quincentennial Christopher Columbus celebration and parodied the manner that Spanish explorers returned with conquered people and put them on display.

(MZ) (1992) W.J.T. Mitchell's anthology *Art and the Public Sphere* provides critical conceptual encounters with art in public space and its audiences in a social era intensified by mass communication technologies.

Figure 13.13 (1993–ongoing) *Project Row Houses*, Rick Lowe. Houston, Texas. Lowe worked with a team of artists to renovate 22 abandoned shotgun-style houses in Houston's historical Third Ward. The work aimed to transform the social role of art within neighborhood revitalization, historic preservation, community service, and youth education. Photo: Courtesy Project Row Houses.

(EY)–**1993**

1994–(AS) (1994) *The Roof Is On Fire* performance and participatory art project, developed by Suzanne Lacy alongside youth and police officers, aiming to develop better relationships between the two groups.

(CC) (1994) bell hooks publishes *Teaching to Transgress: Education as the Practice of Freedom*.

Figure 13.14 (1999–2000) North London Link, Camden Arts Centre – a series of public art projects in communities and businesses around Finchley Road, including Anna Best's project in a Mecca bingo hall and Maurice O'Connell's 'make-over' of Midland Crescent. Photo: Courtesy Anna Best.

(SH) ──────○**1999**

(SH) (1999) "Dialogical Aesthetics" was a Littoral Conference paper by Grant Kester, creating the foundation of his pivotal work, *Conversation Pieces: Community and Communication in Modern Art* (2004).

(CC) (1998) Shelly Sacks establishes the Social Sculpture Research Unit at Oxford Brooks University.

1998 **(AS)** (1998) *Relational Aesthetics* by Nicolas Bourriaud, exploring the development of social artworks within gallery/museum contexts. While problematic, the text is useful in considering how museum/gallery institutions understand participatory work.

(EY) (1997) *paraSITE*, Michael Rakowitz, Boston. The artist designed inflatable and transportable street shelters with a group of homeless people, whom he befriended during his daily commutes to college.

(CC) (1997) Visual and Public Art Program launched at California State University at Monterey Bay. One of the first degree programs focusing on public art with a social practice influence in the USA. Founding faculty included Suzanne Lacy and Amalia Mesa-Bains.

1997 **(AS)** (1997) Election of New Labour to power within the UK is a key moment within the emerging field of participatory art practices, seeing a policy shift to include the establishment of the Social Exclusion Unit to combat (economic) social ills via a variety of methodologies including participatory projects.

1996

1995 **(CC)** (1995) Futurefarmers – founded by Amy Franceschini in San Francisco as an international collective of artists, activists, researchers, farmers and architects who work together to propose alternatives to the social, political and environmental organization of space.

2000

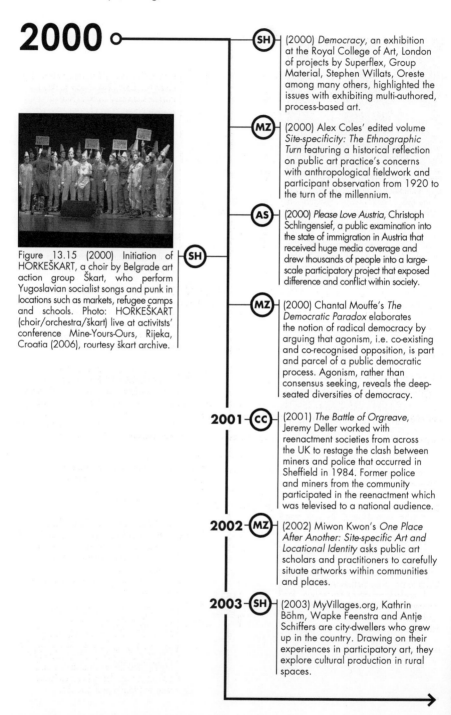

(SH) (2000) *Democracy*, an exhibition at the Royal College of Art, London of projects by Superflex, Group Material, Stephen Willats, Oreste among many others, highlighted the issues with exhibiting multi-authored, process-based art.

(MZ) (2000) Alex Coles' edited volume *Site-specificity: The Ethnographic Turn* featuring a historical reflection on public art practice's concerns with anthropological fieldwork and participant observation from 1920 to the turn of the millennium.

(AS) (2000) *Please Love Austria*, Christoph Schlingensief, a public examination into the state of immigration in Austria that received huge media coverage and drew thousands of people into a large-scale participatory project that exposed difference and conflict within society.

(MZ) (2000) Chantal Mouffe's *The Democratic Paradox* elaborates the notion of radical democracy by arguing that agonism, i.e. co-existing and co-recognised opposition, is part and parcel of a public democratic process. Agonism, rather than consensus seeking, reveals the deep-seated diversities of democracy.

2001 (CC) (2001) *The Battle of Orgreave*, Jeremy Deller worked with reenactment societies from across the UK to restage the clash between miners and police that occurred in Sheffield in 1984. Former police and miners from the community participated in the reenactment which was televised to a national audience.

2002 (MZ) (2002) Miwon Kwon's *One Place After Another: Site-specific Art and Locational Identity* asks public art scholars and practitioners to carefully situate artworks within communities and places.

2003 (SH) (2003) MyVillages.org, Kathrin Böhm, Wapke Feenstra and Antje Schiffers are city-dwellers who grew up in the country. Drawing on their experiences in participatory art, they explore cultural production in rural spaces.

Figure 13.15 (2000) Initiation of **(SH)** HORKEŠKART, a choir by Belgrade art action group Škart, who perform Yugoslavian socialist songs and punk in locations such as markets, refugee camps and schools. Photo: HORKEŠKART (choir/orchestra/škart) live at activitsts' conference Mine-Yours-Ours, Rijeka, Croatia (2006), rourtesy škart archive.

○2009

Figure 13.16 (2009) C-Words, a 100 day exhibition/event (counting down to the G8 summit in Copenhagen) on carbon, climate, capital and culture at the Arnolfini in Bristol organised by Platform, involving artists, activists and campaigners engaged in the global justice movement. Photo: *Become the Bike Bloc Laboratory for Insurrectionary Imagination*, courtesy Platform.

Figure 13.17 (2005–2009) Het Blauwe Huis (The Blue House). Jeanne van Heeswijk in collaboration with Hervé Paraponaris and Dennis Kaspori. Amsterdam, Netherlands. A durational project initiated by van Heeswijk who negotiated for a large villa in a housing block to be taken off the private market and re-designated as a space for community research, artistic production, and cultural activities. Photo: Courtesy Het Blauwe Huis.

(SH)

(CC) (2009) *One and Other*, Antony Gormley. Over 100 days, 2,400 people stood in succession on the Fourth Plinth in Trafalgar Square, London for one hour each. All participants had full authorship of their time in the public spotlight.

2008 (AS) (2008–ongoing) Paul Hamyln Foundation develops the initiative "ArtWorks: Developing Practice in Participatory Settings."

(SH) (2007–2013) *The Hidden Curriculum*, Annette Krauss involved high school students exploring the informal, unrecognised forms of (un)learning that happen within the gaps of formal education.

2007 (MZ) (2007) *The Affective Turn: Theorising the Social* by Patricia Clough and Jean Halley places mundane feelings and emotions at the forefront of biosocial research across the humanities and social sciences.

2006 (EY) (2006–ongoing) *Operation Paydirt/ Fundred Dollar Bill Project* originally developed by Mel Chin in New Orleans to engage grassroots communities with creative actions drawing awareness and solutions for the crisis of lead-contamination in cities across the United States.

(MZ) (2005) *For Space* by Doreen Massey examines politicised 'spatial times' – how time involves change and space involves the social in understanding our sense of place.

(MZ)-2005

(SH) (2004) *Beyond Social Inclusion: Towards Cultural Democracy* published by Cultural Policy Collective was a pamphlet that provided a critical analysis of New Labour's social inclusion policy, asking "inclusion into what, and to what end?"

2004 (CC) (2004) *The Interventionists: Art in the Social Sphere* opens at MASS MoCA. The exhibition and accompanying "Users' Manual for the Creative Disruption of Everyday Life" highlighted the work of artists and collectives applying interventionist methods in the public realm.

2010

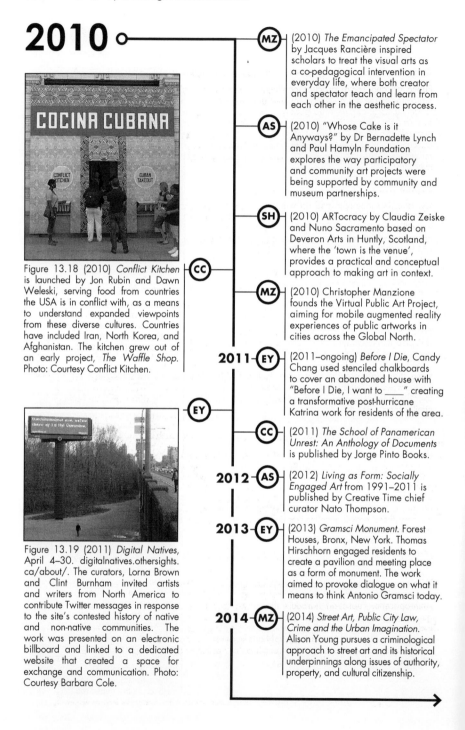

Figure 13.18 (2010) *Conflict Kitchen* is launched by Jon Rubin and Dawn Weleski, serving food from countries the USA is in conflict with, as a means to understand expanded viewpoints from these diverse cultures. Countries have included Iran, North Korea, and Afghanistan. The kitchen grew out of an early project, *The Waffle Shop*. Photo: Courtesy Conflict Kitchen.

Figure 13.19 (2011) *Digital Natives*, April 4–30. digitalnatives.othersights. ca/about/. The curators, Lorna Brown and Clint Burnham invited artists and writers from North America to contribute Twitter messages in response to the site's contested history of native and non-native communities. The work was presented on an electronic billboard and linked to a dedicated website that created a space for exchange and communication. Photo: Courtesy Barbara Cole.

(MZ) (2010) *The Emancipated Spectator* by Jacques Rancière inspired scholars to treat the visual arts as a co-pedagogical intervention in everyday life, where both creator and spectator teach and learn from each other in the aesthetic process.

(AS) (2010) "Whose Cake is it Anyways?" by Dr Bernadette Lynch and Paul Hamyln Foundation explores the way participatory and community art projects were being supported by community and museum partnerships.

(SH) (2010) ARTocracy by Claudia Zeiske and Nuno Sacramento based on Deveron Arts in Huntly, Scotland, where the 'town is the venue', provides a practical and conceptual approach to making art in context.

(CC) **(MZ)** (2010) Christopher Manzione founds the Virtual Public Art Project, aiming for mobile augmented reality experiences of public artworks in cities across the Global North.

2011 (EY) (2011–ongoing) *Before I Die*, Candy Chang used stenciled chalkboards to cover an abandoned house with "Before I Die, I want to ____" creating a transformative post-hurricane Katrina work for residents of the area.

(EY) **(CC)** (2011) *The School of Panamerican Unrest: An Anthology of Documents* is published by Jorge Pinto Books.

2012 (AS) (2012) *Living as Form: Socially Engaged Art* from 1991–2011 is published by Creative Time chief curator Nato Thompson.

2013 (EY) (2013) *Gramsci Monument*. Forest Houses, Bronx, New York. Thomas Hirschhorn engaged residents to create a pavilion and meeting place as a form of monument. The work aimed to provoke dialogue on what it means to think Antonio Gramsci today.

2014 (MZ) (2014) *Street Art, Public City Law, Crime and the Urban Imagination*. Alison Young pursues a criminological approach to street art and its historical underpinnings along issues of authority, property, and cultural citizenship.

2015

Cameron Cartiere *[Pedagogy, Public Practice, Social Engagement, Conflict Resolution]*

Public art and social practice continues to evolve through pedagogy. The role of education is deeply embedded within the field and each of us working in this vein is connected through shared pedagogical histories. My lineage runs from John Cage to Allan Kaprow to Suzanne Lacy. Using similar lines, countless students can trace themselves back to Cage, or taking a different turn, follow the threads through other educational influences to equally significant practitioners. Understanding our historical influences allows the field to embrace new means of engagement and influences on everyday life.

Sophie Hope *[Anger, Hope, Action, Change]*

Cynically, socially engaged art will become increasingly orthodox, professional, de-politicised and the reserve of the privileged with spare labour power to invest. Hopefully, we will recognise our complicity in power and inherent neo-liberalism. We will question commissioners, challenge injustices, and fight to control our labour and leisure. We will keep things complex, inventive, disobedient, messy, and at times inappropriate, uninvited, and uncomfortable. We will give up proving our efficiency, popularity, and value for money. We will collectively, poetically, unexpectedly, and consistently talk back until our voices become louder and harder to ignore.

Anthony Schrag *[Professionalisation, Institutionalisation, Resistance, Reinvention]*

Policy and institutions continue to exert influence on the practice while slowly being co-opted into the pantheon of traditional artistic works. Professionalisation will provide support and control the way artists choose to work with people. Limitations will provide rules for some people to enforce, but also structures for other people to challenge in ways that might provide new subjectivities. Artists work best when pushing against boundaries. Institutionalisation will create new opportunities to work with people only to fall out of favour and then be re-animated by another generation in a different but similar form.

Elisa Yon *[Artist-initiated, Post-industrial, hyper-multidisciplinary, Collectives]*

Durational artist-initiated projects situated in communities will continue to evolve from grassroots initiatives into sophisticated organized artist-run communities, but what is their future? How will they continue to respond to the artist's original intentions and the growing needs of the community? We see the expansion of Hyper-Multidisciplinary artist groups working across fields of public art, social practice, architecture, urban design, cultural policy, engineering, and environmental sciences. The challenge will be how these growing collectives inform and evolve social practice art forms and methodologies.

Martin   Zebracki *[Super-diversity,   Social   Justice,   Financial-cultural   Revaluation, Anthropocene Sustainability]*

Western societies are progressively challenged by social issues of super-diversity and pressing concerns about sustainable environmental conditions in the era of the Anthropocene. Public art harbours the power to set the agenda for the future by questioning the accountability of public policies, delineating methods for more socially inclusive and environmentally just spaces while navigating through grand economic-financial priorities and increasingly tight arts budgets. The social practices of public art will continue to urge us to critically reflect on our cultural values and build grounded futures of everyday 'glocal' citizenship.

Moving forward into the future . . .

REFERENCES

Althusser, L., 2006. The underground current of the materialism of the encounter. In: F. Matheron and O. Corpet, eds. *Louis Althusser, philosophy of the encounter: later writings, 1978–1987*. Trans. G. Goshgarian. London: Verso, 163–207.

Americans for the Arts, 2011. *Arts & economic prosperity iii: the economic impact of nonprofit arts and culture organizations and their audiences*. Washington, DC: Americans for the Arts.

Amin, A., 2002. Ethnicity and the multicultural city: living with diversity. *Environment and Planning A*, 34 (6), 959–80.

Anderson, B., 1991. *Imagined communities: reflections on the origin and spread of nationalism*. New York: Verso.

Anholt, S., 2011. *Step outside somewherelands for nowhereisland* [online]. Available from: http://nowhereisland.org/resident-thinkers/#!/resident-thinkers/1/ [Accessed 12 Nov 2014].

APG/Tate, 2015. *Artists' placement group – Chronology* [online]. Available from www2.tate. org.uk/artistplacementgroup/chronology.htm [Accessed 20 Feb 2015].

Appadurai, A., 1990. Disjuncture and difference in the global cultural economy. *Theory, Culture & Society*, 7 (2), 295–310.

Arnstein, S., 1969. A ladder of citizen participation. *Journal of the American Institute of Planners*, 35 (4), 216–24.

Art Gene, 2014. *Mission statement* [online]. Available from: www.artgene.co.uk/nb/index. php?option=com_content&view=article&id=147&Itemid=246 [Accessed 11 Sep 2014].

Bafna, S., 2003. Space syntax: a brief introduction to its logic and analytical techniques. *Environment and Behaviour*, 35 (1), 17–29.

Bannerman, S., 2013. Crowdfunding culture. *Journal of Mobile Culture*, 7 (1). [online] Available from: http://wi.mobilities.ca/crowdfunding-culture [Accessed 15 Oct 2014].

Barthes, R., 1999. Rhetoric of the image. In: J. Evans and S. Hall, eds. *Visual culture: the reader*. London: Sage, 33–40.

Beardsley, J., 2007. Conflict and erosion: the contemporary public life of large parks. In: J. Czerniak and G. Hargreaves, eds. *Large parks*. New York, NY: Princeton Architectural Press, 199–213.

Becker, J., 2004. Americans for the arts. *Public art: an essential component of creating communities*. [online]. Available from www.americansforthearts.org/sites/default/files/pdf/2013/by_program/networks_and_councils/public_art_network/PublicArtMonograph_JBecker.pdf [Accessed 26 Mar 2015].

Beech, D., 2011. The ideology of duration in the dematerialised monument: art, sites, publics and time. In: P. O'Neill and C. Doherty, eds. *Locating the producers: durational approaches to public art*. Amsterdam: Valiz, 313–25.

Beech, D., Hewitt, A. and Jordan, M., 2007. *Functions, functionalism and functionlessness: on the social function of public art after modernism*. In: M. Jordan and M. Miles, eds. *Art and theory after socialism*. Bristol: Intellect Books, 114–25.

Bell, K., Jarman, N. and Lefebvre, T., 2004. *Migrant workers in Northern Ireland*. Belfast: Institute for Conflict Research (ICR).

Benedikt, M., 1979. To take hold of space: isovists and isovist fields. *Environment and Planning B*, 6 (1), 47–67.

Benhabib, S., 1992. *Models of public sphere: Hannah Arendt, the liberal tradition, and Jurgen Habermas*. In: C. Calhoun, ed. *Habermas and the public sphere*. Cambridge, MA: MIT Press, 73–98.

Berardi, F., 2012. *The uprising: on poetry and finance*. Los Angeles: Semiotext(e).

Bishop, C., 2004. Antagonism and relational aesthetics, *October*, 110, 51–79.

Bishop, C., 2006. The social turn: collaboration and its discontents. *Artforum*, 44 (6), 178–83.

Bishop, C., 2012. *Artificial hells: participatory art and the politics of spectatorship*. London: Verso.

Bluedorn, A., 2002. *The human organization of time: temporal realities and experience*. Stanford, CA: Stanford University Press.

Bourriaud, N., 2002. *Relational aesthetics*. Paris: Les presses du réel.

Brady, E., 2003. *Aesthetics of the natural environment*. Tuscaloosa: University of Alabama Press.

Brenner, N. and Theodore, N., eds, 2002. *Spaces of neoliberalism: urban restructuring in North America and Western Europe*. Malden, MA: Blackwell Publishing.

Brenson, M., 1991. Review/art; visual arts join Spoleto festival U.S.A. *New York Times* [online], 27 May. Available from: www.nytimes.com/1991/05/27/arts/review-art-visual-arts-join-spoleto-festival-usa.html [Accessed 31 Dec 2014].

Brenson, M., ed., 1995. *Culture in action: a public art program of Sculpture Chicago*. Seattle: Bay Press.

Brenson, M., 2013. PLACES WITH A PAST: new site-specific art in Charleston belongs to its place and time. *The Brooklyn Rail* [online], Jul 15. Available from: www.brooklynrail.org/2013/07/criticspage/places-with-a-pastnew-site-specific-art-in-charleston-belongs-to-its-place-and-time [Accessed 31 Dec 2014].

Brown, J. and Isaacs, D., 1995. *The World Café book: shaping our futures through conversations that matter*. San Francisco, CA: Berrett-Koehle.

Bruguera, T., 2011. *Introduction on useful art* [online]. Available from: www.taniabruguera.com/cms/528-0-Introduction+on+Useful+Art.htm [Accessed 25 Sep 2014].

Büchler, P. and Harding, D., 1997. *Decadent: public art: contentious term and contested practice*. Glasgow: Foulis Press.

Büscher, M., Urry, J. and Witchger, K. eds, 2010. Mobile methods. London: Routledge.

Calvino, I., 1997. *Invisible cities*. London: Random House.

Cameron, F. and Kenderdine, S., eds, 2007. *Theorizing digital cultural heritage: a critical discourse*. Cambridge, MA: MIT Press.

Carmona, M., Heath, T., Oc. T. and Tiesdell, S. 2003. *Public places, urban spaces: the dimensions of urban design*. Oxford: Architectural Press.

Cartiere, C., 2008. Coming in from the cold: a public art history. In: C. Cartiere and S. Willis, eds. *The practice of public art*. New York, NY: Routledge, 7-17.

Cartiere, C. and Willis, S., eds, 2008. *The practice of public art*. New York, NY: Routledge.

Cary, R., 1998. *Critical art pedagogy: foundations for postmodern art education*. New York, NY: Garland Publishing.

Champion, K., 2008. The business of creative cities. *Journal of Urban Regeneration and Renewal*, 2 (2), 111–23.

City of Philadelphia Mural Arts Program, 2015a. *Our mission statement* [online]. Available from: http://muralarts.org/about/our-mission-statement [Accessed 10 Mar 2015].

City of Philadelphia Mural Arts Program, 2015b. *What we sow* [online]. Available from: http://muralarts.org/whatwesow [Accessed 10 Mar 2015].

Clough, P., ed., 2007. *The affective turn: theorizing the social*. Durham, NC: Duke University Press.

Cockcroft, E. and Barnet-Sanchez, H., eds, 1993. *Signs from the heart: California Chicano murals*. Albuquerque: University of New Mexico Press.

Coessens, K., Crispin, D. and Douglas, A., 2009. *The artistic turn*. Leuven: University of Leuven Press.

Commission for Architecture and the Built Environment (CABE), 2004. *Manifesto for better public spaces*. London: CABE.

Commission for Architecture and the Built Environment (CABE), English Heritage and Sustainable Development Commission, 2008. *Housing market renewal: action plan for delivering successful places*. London: CABE.

Conroy Dalton, R. and Bafna, S., 2003. The syntactical image of the city: a reciprocal definition of spatial elements and spatial syntaxes. In: *Proceedings of the 4th International Space Syntax Symposium*, 17–19 Jun 2003 London. London: Space Syntax, 29.1–29.20.

Corner, J., 2007. Foreword. In: J. Czerniak and G. Hargreaves, eds. *Large parks*. New York, NY: Princeton Architectural Press, 11–14.

Cranz, G., 1982. *The politics of park design: a history of urban parks in America*. Cambridge, MA: MIT press.

Cranz, G. and M. Boland, 2004. Defining the sustainable park: a fifth model for urban parks. *Landscape Journal*, 23 (2), 102–20.

Creative Lewisham Agency, 2002. *Lewisham local cultural strategy*. London: London Borough of Lewisham.

Cresswell, T., 2006. *On the move: mobility in the modern western world*. London: Routledge.

Czerniak, J. and Hargreaves, G., eds, 2007. *Large parks*. New York, NY: Princeton Architectural Press.

Davis, B., 2013. *9.5 theses on art and class*. Chicago: Haymarket Books.

Dean, J., 2012. *The communist horizon*. London: Verso.

De Certeau, M., 1984. *The practice of everyday life*. Trans. S. Rendall. London: University of California Press.

Delday, H., 2006. *Close as a construct to critically investigate the relationship between the visual artist and the everyday*, Thesis (PhD). Aberdeen: Robert Gordon University.

Delos Reyes, J., 2008. We are here for you. In: E. Chang, A. Lalonde, C. Lloyd, S. Loft, J. Middleton, D. Roy and H. Sivanesan, eds. *Decentre: concerning artist-run culture*. Toronto: YYZ, 76–7.

Delos Reyes, J., 2014. Creative rebellion for the twenty-first century: the importance of public and interactive art to political life in America. *Public Art Dialogue*, 4 (2), 266–7.

Derrida, J., 2001. *On cosmopolitanism and forgiveness*. London: Routledge.

Derrida, J. and Dufourmantelle, A., 2000. *Of hospitality: Anne Dufourmantelle invites Jacques Derrida to respond*. Trans. R. Bowlby. Stanford, CA: Stanford University Press.

Deutsche, R. 1988. Uneven development: public art in New York City. *October*, 47, 3–52.

Deutsche, R., 1991. Alternative space. In: B. Wallis, ed. *If you lived here: the city in art, theory, and social activism*. New York, NY: The New Press, 45–67.

Deutsche, R., 1992. Art and public space: questions of democracy. *Social Text*, 34–53.

Deutsche, R., 1996. *Evictions: art and spatial politics*. Cambridge, MA: MIT Press.

Deutsche, R., 1998. Public art and its uses. In: H. Senie and S. Webster, eds. *Critical issues in public art: content, context, and controversy*. Washington, DC: Smithsonian Institution Press, 158–70.

Dewey, J., 1997. *Experience and education*. New York, NY: Touchstone.

Dia Art Foundation, 2013. *Gramsci Monument* [online]. Available from: www.diaart.org/gramsci-monument/index.php [Accessed 10 Oct 2014].

Doss, E. L., 1995. *Spirit poles and flying pigs: public art and cultural democracy in American communities*. Washington, DC: Smithsonian Institution Press.

Douglas, A., 2005. *Celestial ceiling: contemporary art, built heritage and patronage*. Aberdeen: Robert Gordon University in collaboration with the National Galleries of Scotland and Historic Scotland.

Douglas, A., 2007. *Working in public seminars* [online]. Aberdeen, Robert Gordon University. Available from: www2.rgu.ac.uk/subj/ats/ontheedge2/workinginpublicseminars/seminar_menu.html [Accessed 20 Feb 2015].

Douglas, A., 2014. Notes from spectres of evaluation conference, rethinking art, community, value. *On the Edge Research* [online]. Available from: www.ontheedgeresearch.org [Accessed 14 Feb 2015].

Douglas, A. and Fremantle, C., 2009. *The artist as leader*. AHRC Research Report. Aberdeen: Robert Gordon University

Douglas A., Fremantle, C. and Delday, H., 2006. Inthrow. Aberdeen: Robert Gordon University in collaboration with Duncan of Jordanstone College of Art, University of Dundee.

Eaton, T., 1990. Art in the environment. *The Planner*, 23, 71–4.

El Puente Lab, 2014. [online] Available from: www.elpuentelab.org [Accessed 12 Oct 2014].

Evans, G., 2005. Measure for measure: evaluating the evidence of culture's contribution to regeneration. *Urban Studies*, 42 (5/6), 959–83.

Evans, J. and Hall, S., 1999. *Visual culture: the reader*. London: Sage.

Fincham B., McGuinness M. and Murray L., eds, 2010. *Mobile methodologies*. Basingstoke: Palgrave Macmillan.

Finkelpearl, T., 2013. *What we made: conversations on art and social cooperation*. Durham, NC: Duke University Press.

Flanagan, R., 2008. The millennium park effect: a tale of two cities. In: C. Cartiere and S. Willis, eds. *The practice of public art*. New York, NY: Routledge, 133–51.

Florida, R., 2002. *The rise of the creative class: and how it's transforming work, leisure, community and everyday life*. New York, NY: Basic.

Florida, R., 2005. *Cities and the creative class*. London: Routledge.

Foderaro, L., 2014. 35 overlooked parks in poor city neighbourhoods to get makeovers. *New York Times* [online], 6 Oct. Available from: www.nytimes.com/2014/10/07/nyregion/35-overlooked-parks-in-poor-new-york-city-neighborhoods-to-get-makeovers.html?_r=1 [Accessed 26 Mar 2015].

Fong, P., 1999. The role of the monument. In: *Proceedings. 2nd international space syntax symposium*, 29 Mar–2 Apr 1999. Brasilia. London: Space Syntax.

Fotheringham, R. and Hunter, M., 1994. *Community cultural development in the tertiary sector*. Redfern: Australia Council for the Arts.

Fraser, N., 1990. Rethinking the public sphere: a contribution to the critique of actually existing democracy. In: C. Calhoun, ed. *Habermas and the public sphere*. Cambridge, MA: MIT Press, 109–42.

Freire, P., 1970. *Pedagogy of the oppressed*. Harmondsworth: Penguin.

Freire, P., 1972. *Cultural action for freedom*. Harmondsworth: Penguin.

Gablik, S., 1995. Connective aesthetics: art after individualism. In: S. Lacy, ed. *Mapping the terrain: new genre public art*. Seattle, WA: Bay Press, 74–87.

Garrett, B., 2011. Videographic geographies: using digital video for geographic research. *Progress in Human Geography*, 35 (4), 521–41.

Giddens, A., 1984. *The constitution of society: outline of the theory of structuration*. Cambridge: Polity Press.

Goffman, E., 1966. *Behavior in public places*. New York, NY: Simon and Schuster.

Goldbard, A., 2006. *New creative community: the art of cultural development*. Oakland: New Village Press.

Goldbard, A., 2008. *Culture and community development in higher education: the curriculum project report*. Syracuse, NY: Imagining America.

Goodstein, E., 2002. Style as substance: Georg Simmel's phenomenology of culture. *Cultural Critique*, 52, 209–34.

Goto Collins, R., 2012. Ecology and environmental art in public place. Talking tree: won't you take a minute and listen to the plight of nature? Thesis (PhD). Aberdeen: Robert Gordon University. [online] Available from: https://openair.rgu.ac.uk/bitstream/10059/788/1/Reiko%2520Goto%2520Collins%2520PhD%2520thesis.pdf+&cd=1&hl=en&ct=clnk&gl=us [Accessed 1 Aug 2015].

Goto Collins, R. and Collins, T., 2010. *3 Rivers 2nd nature (2000–2005)* [online]. Available from: http://3r2n.collinsandgoto.com. [Accessed 20 Feb 2015].

Guba, E. and Lincoln, Y., 1994. Competing paradigms in qualitative research. In: N. Denzin and Y. Lincoln, eds. *Handbook of qualitative research*. Thousand Oaks, CA: Sage, 105–17.

Habermas, J., 1989 [1962]. *The structural transformation of the public sphere: an inquiry into a category of bourgeois society*. Cambridge, MA: MIT Press.

Hackworth, J. 2007. *The neoliberal city: governance, ideology, and development in American urbanism*. Ithaca, NY: Cornell University Press.

Hall, T. 2007. Artful cities. *Geography Compass*, 1 (6), 1376–92.

Hall, T. and I. Robertson. 2001. Public art and urban regeneration: advocacy, claims, and critical debates. *Landscape Research*, 26 (1), 5–26.

Handelman, D., 2011. Folding and enfolding walls: statist imperatives and bureaucratic aesthetics in divided Jerusalem. *Social Analysis*, 52 (2), 60–79.

Hanson, J., Zako, R., Bendon, H. and Thom, J., 2007. Opening up the open spaces through space syntax. In: E. Huijbens and O. Jonsson, eds. *Sensi/able spaces: space, art and the environment – Proceedings of the SPARTEN conference*, 1–2 Jun 2006, Reykjavik. Cambridge: Cambridge Scholars, 39–68.

Haraway, D., 1991. *Simians, cyborgs, and women: the reinvention of women*. New York, NY: Routledge.

Harrison, N. and Harrison, H., 2008. Public culture and sustainable practices: peninsular Europe from an ecodiversity perspective, posing questions to complexity scientists. In: *Structure and Dynamics: eJournal of Anthropological and Related Sciences* 2 (3). [online], Available from http://escholarship.org/uc/item/9hj3s753 [Accessed 20 Feb 2015].

Hartnett, A., 2011. Aestheticised geographies of conflict: the politicisation of culture and the politics in Belfast's mural tradition. In: H. Silverman, ed., *Contested cultural heritage: religion, nationalism, erasure and exclusion in a global world*. New York, NY: Springer, 69–108.

Harvey, D., 1989. *The urban experience*. Baltimore: Johns Hopkins University Press.

Haughton, G and Allmendinger, P., 2007. 'Soft spaces' in planning. *Town & Country Planning*, 76 (9), 306–8.

Haughton, G., Allmendinger, P. and Oosterlynck, S., 2013. Spaces of neoliberal experimentation: soft spaces, postpolitics, and neoliberal governmentality. *Environment and Planning A*, 45 (1), 217–34.

Hayden, D., 1997. *The power of place: urban landscapes as public history*. Cambridge MA: MIT Press.

Healey, P., 2003. Collaborative planning in perspective. *Planning Theory*, 2 (2), 101–12.

Heim, W., 2003. *The Ashden directory – Begin with the small* [online]. Available from www.ashdendirectory.org.uk/featuresView.asp?pageIdentifier=2013724_25858706&view [Accessed 15 Nov 2014].

Hein, H., 1996. What is public art? Time, place and meaning. *Journal of Aesthetics and Art Criticism*, 54 (1), 1–7.

Helguera, P., 2011. *Education for socially engaged art: a materials and techniques handbook*. New York, NY: Jorge Pinto.

Hercbergs, D., 2012. Narrating instability: political detouring in Jerusalem. *Mobilities*, 7 (3), 415–38.

High Line Art, 2015. *High Line Art* [online]. Available from: http://art.thehighline.org/about [Accessed 26 Feb 2015].

Hill, A. and White, A., 2011. Painting peace? Murals and the Northern Ireland peace process. *Irish Political Studies*, 27 (1), 71–88.

Hillier, B., 1989. The architecture of the urban object. *Ekistics*, 56 (334–5), 5–21.

Hillier, B., 1997. Cities as movement economies. In: P. Droege, ed. *Intelligent environments: spatial aspects of the information revolution*. Amsterdam: Elsevier, 295–344.

Hillier, B., 1999. Centrality as a process. In: *Proceedings. 2nd international space syntax symposium*, 29 Mar–2 Apr 1999. Brasilia. London: Space Syntax.

Hillier, B., 2004. *Space is the machine*. London: Space Syntax.

Hillier, B. and Hanson, J., 1984. *The social logic of space*. Cambridge: Cambridge University Press.

Hirschhorn, T., 2014. Personal communication with authors by email, 4 Sept 2014, from Hirschhorn's unpublished document *Timeline texts*, 2003.

Holmes, B., 2007. Do-it-yourself geopolitics: cartographies of art in the world. In: B. Stimson and G. Sholette, eds. *Collectivism after modernism: the art of social imagination after 1945*. Minneapolis: University of Minnesota Press, 273–95.

hooks, b., 1994. *Teaching to transgress*. New York, NY: Routledge.

hooks, b., 2003. *Teaching community*. New York, NY: Routledge.

Independent Research Solutions, 2009. Cited in Hill, A. and White, A., 2011. Painting peace? Murals and the Northern Ireland peace process. *Irish Political Studies*, 27 (1), 71–88.

Interface Project, 2011. [online] www.belfastinterfaceproject.org/interfaces-map-and-database-overview [Accessed 1 Aug 2015].

Jacob, M. and Boltanski, C., 1991. *Places with a past: new site-specific art at Charleston's Spoleto Festival*. New York: Rizzoli International Publications.

Jacobs, M. and Bass, J., eds, 2010. *Learning mind: experience into art*. Berkeley: University of California Press.

Jahn, M., ed., 2010. *Byproduct: on the excess of embedded art practices*. Toronto: YYZ.

Johnson, K. 2012. Eye candy or eyesore? Work by Niki de Saint Phalle and Bruce High Quality Foundation. *New York Times* [online], 23 Aug. Available from: www.nytimes.com/2012/08/24/arts/design/work-by-niki-de-saint-phalle-and-bruce-high-quality-foundation.html [Accessed 26 Mar 2015].

Johnson, P. 2006. Unravelling Foucault's "different spaces". *History of the Human Sciences*, 19(4), 75–90.

Jordan, M., 2011. We are all everyday superheros. *Art & the Public Sphere*, 1 (3), 239–41.

Kaprow, A. 1995. Success and failure when art changes. In: S. Lacy, ed. *Mapping the terrain: new genre public art*. Seattle, WA: Bay Press, 152–58.

Kaprow, A. 2003. The education of the unartist, part II. In: J. Berkeley ed. *Essays on the blurring of art and life*. Berkeley, CA: University of California Press, 110–26.

Kelly, M., 1996. Public art controversy: the Serra and Lin cases. *Journal of Aesthetics and Art Criticism*, 54 (1), 15–22.

Kester, G., 2004. *Conversation pieces: community and communication in modern art*. Oakland, CA: University of California Press.

Kester, G., 2006. Letter in response to Bishop. *Artforum*, 44 (9), 22.

Kester, G., 2011. *The one and the many: contemporary collaborative art in a global context*. Durham, NC: Duke University Press.

Kimmelman, M. 2014. The climax in a tale of green and gritty: the high line opens its third and final phase. *New York Times* [online], 19 Sep. Available from: www.nytimes.com/2014/09/20/arts/design/the-high-line-opens-its-third-and-final-phase.html [Accessed 26 Mar 2015].

Krauss, R., 1979. Sculpture in the expanded field. *October*, 8, 31–44.

Krensky, B. and Steffen S., 2009. *Engaging classrooms and communities through art: a guide to designing and implementing community-based art education*. Lanham: AltaMira.

Kwon, M., 2004. *One place after another: site-specific art and locational identity*. Cambridge: MIT Press.

Lacy, S., ed., 1995. *Mapping the terrain: new genre public art*. Seattle, WA: Bay Press.

Lacy, S., 2010. *Leaving art: writings on performance, politics, and publics, 1974–2007*. Durham, NC: Duke University Press.

Lacy, S., 2012. *Imperfect art: working in public, a case study of the Oakland Projects 1991–2001*. Thesis (PhD). Aberdeen: Robert Gordon University.

Landry, C., 2008. Can artists create great places? In: E. Holding, ed. *Artists and places: engaging creative minds in regeneration*. London: CABE/Arts and Business, 1–11.

Landry, C., 2009. *The creative city: a toolkit for urban innovators*. London: Comedia/Earthscan.

Landry, C., Greene, L., Matarasso, F. and Bianchini, F., eds, 1996. *The art of regeneration: urban renewal through cultural activity*. Stroud: Comedia.

Latour, B., 2007. *Reassembling the social: an introduction to actor-network-theory*. Oxford: Oxford University Press.

Ledwith, M. and Springett, J., 2012. *Participatory practice: community-based action for transformative change*. Bristol: Policy Press.

Lefebvre, H., 1991. *The production of space*. Oxford: Blackwell.

Lefebvre, H., 1996. *Writings on cities*. Trans. E. Kofman and E. Lebas. London: Wiley-Blackwell.

Levine, D., 1971. Introduction. In: D. Levine, ed. *Georg Simmel on individuality and social form*. Chicago: University of Chicago Press, ix–xv.

Lind, M., 2007. The collaborative turn. In: J. Billing, M. Lind and L. Nilsson, eds. *Taking the matter into common hands*. London: Black Dog, 15–31.

Lippard, L., 1997. *The lure of the local: senses of place in a multicentered society*. New York: The New Press.

Littoral, 2014. *Littoral: new zones for critical art practice* [online]. Available from: www.littoral.org.uk/programme_littoral.htm [Accessed 1 Jul 2014].

Lofland, L., 1985. *A world of strangers: order and action in urban public space*. Long Grove, IL: Waveland Press.

Lossau, J. and Stevens, Q., eds, 2015. *The uses of art in public space*. London: Routledge.

Lynch, K., 1967. *The image of the city*. Cambridge, MA: MIT Press.

Marin, P., 1970. The open truth and the fiery vehemence of youth: a soliloquy of sorts. In: S. Repu, ed.. *This book is about schools*. New York: Random House, 133–166.

Massey, D., 1994. A global sense of place. In: *Space, place and gender*. Cambridge: Polity Press, 146–56.

Massey, D., 2005. *For space*. London: Sage.

Massey, D. and Rose, G., 2003. *Personal views: public art research project*. Milton Keynes: Art Point Trust and Milton Keynes Council.

Massey, D. and Warburton, N., 2013. *Interview with Massey. Social science bites in association with SAGE* [online]. Available from: www.socialsciencebites.com [Accessed 12 Oct 2014].

Matarasso, F., 1997. *Use or ornament? The social impact of participation in the arts*. Stroud: Comedia.

McCormack, D., 2008. Thinking-spaces for research creation. *Inflexions*, 1 (1) [online]. Available from: www.senselab.ca/inflexions/Inflexions%20Issue%20One%20McCormack%20final%20word%20version.doc.pdf [Accessed 30 Sep 2014].

McCormick, J. and Jarman, N., 2005. Death of a mural. *Journal of Material Culture*, 10 (1), 49–71.

McDowell, S., 2008. Commemorating dead 'men': gendering the past and present in post-conflict Northern Ireland. *Gender, Place & Culture,* 15 (4), 335–54.

Miessen, M., 2010. *The nightmare of participation: crossbench praxis as a mode of criticality*. New York: Sternberg Press.

Miles, M., 1997. *Art, space and the city: public art and urban futures*. London: Routledge.

Minton, A., 2007. Project: a review. *Art & Architecture Journal*, 64, 27–30.

Mitchell, D. and Van Deusen, R., 2001. Downsview park: open space or public space? In: J. Czerniak, ed. *CASE: Downsview Park Toronto*. Cambridge, MA: Harvard University Graduate School of Design, 102–13.

Mitchell, W., 1992. *Art and the public sphere*. Chicago: University of Chicago Press.

Mouffe, C., 2000. *The democratic paradox*. London: Verso.

Mouffe, C., 2007. Artistic activism and agonistic spaces. *Art & Research*, 1 (2) [online]. Available from: www.artandresearch.org.uk/v1n2/mouffe.html [Accessed 23 Oct 2014].

Mouffe, C., 2008. Public spaces and democratic politics. In: J. Boomgaard, ed. *Highrise – common ground. Art and the Amsterdam Zuidas Area*. Amsterdam: Valiz, 135–56.

Mouffe, C., 2013. *Agonistics: thinking the world politically*. London: Verso.

Murray, L., 2009. Looking at and looking back: visualisation in mobile research. *Qualitative Research*, 9 (4), 469–88.

Murray, L., 2010. Contextualizing and mobilizing research. In: B. Fincham, M. McGuinness and L. Murray, eds. *Mobile methodologies*. Basingstoke: Palgrave Macmillan, 13–24.

Murray, L. and Sara Upstone. S., eds, 2014. *Researching and representing mobilities: transdisciplinary encounters*. Palgrave Macmillan.

Nagle, J., 2009. Sites of social centrality and segregation: Lefebvre in Belfast, a 'divided city'. *Antipode,* 41 (2), 326–47.

Nancy, J., 2007. *Listening*. Trans. C. Mandell. New York: Fordham University Press.

Newling, J., 2014. Foreword. In: C. Quick, E. Speight and G. van Noord, eds. *Subplots to a city: ten years of In Certain Places*. Preston: In Certain Places, 5–7.

Nowhereisland, 2014. *Welcome to the embassy* [online]. Available from: http://nowhereisland. org/#!/embassy [Accessed 10 Sept 2014].

Nuttgens, P. and Heath, J., eds, 1992. *The furnished landscape: applied art in public places*. London: Bellew.

O'Neill, P., 2011. Edgware Road Project. In: P. O'Neill and C. Doherty, eds. *Locating the producers: durational approaches to public art*. Amsterdam: Valiz, 187–235.

O'Neill, P., 2014. The curatorial constellation – durational public art, cohabitational time and attentiveness. In: C. Quick, E. Speight and G. van Noord, eds. *Subplots to a city: ten years of In Certain Places*. Preston: In Certain Places, 195–202.

O'Neill, P. and Doherty, C., eds., 2011. *Locating the producers: durational approaches to public art*. Amsterdam: Valiz.

Palmer, J., 2012. *The politics of 'the public': public art, urban regeneration and the postindustrial city – the case of downtown Denver*. Thesis (PhD). Boulder, CO: University of Colorado at Boulder.

Parkinson, J., 2012. *Democracy and public space: the physical sites of democratic performance*. Oxford: Oxford University Press.

Parry, W., 2010. *Against the wall: the art of resistance in Palestine*. London: Pluto Press.

Petherbridge, D., 1979. The town artist experiment. *Architectural Review*, 166 (990), 125–9.

Phillips, P. 1989a. Out of order: the public art machine. *Artforum*, 27 (4), 92–6.

Phillips, P. 1989b. Temporality and public art. *Art Journal*, 48 (4), 331–5.

Phillips, P., 1999. Dynamic exchange: public art at this time. *Public Art Review,* 11 (1), 4–9.

Pollock, V. and Sharp, J., 2012. Real participation or the tyranny of participatory practice? Public art and community involvement in the regeneration of the Raploch, Scotland. *Urban Studies*, 49 (14), 3063–79.

Pratt, A., 2009. Urban regeneration: from the arts 'feel good' factor to the cultural economy: a case study of Hoxton, London. *Urban Studies*, 46 (5–6), 1041–61.

Prins, A., 2002. Kunst van de openbare ruimte. Een pluriculturele oriëntatie [Art of public space. A pluricultural orientation]. In: H. Oosterling and S. Thissen, eds, InterAkta5: Grootstedelijke Reflecties over Kunst & Openbare Ruimte [InterAkta5: Metropolitan reflections on art & public space]. Rotterdam: CFK, 94–9.

Project for Public Spaces, 2010. *About: place-making for communities* [online]. Available from: www.pps.org/reference/what_is_placemaking/ [Accessed 1 Jun 2013].

Purves, T., 2014. Artisis' projects. In: T. Purves and S. Selzer, eds. *What we want is free: critical exchanges in recent art*. Albany: State University of New York Press, 107–84.

Pyyhtinen, O., 2008. *Bringing the social alive: essays on Georg Simmel's social theory*. Thesis (PhD). Turku: University of Turku.

Rana, M., 2008. Names for what we do: thoughts on encounter and art. In: F. Lewinger, A. Marcellini and J. Rhoades, eds. *There is no two without three*. San Francisco: Social Practice Workshop Publications, 11–15.

Rancière, J., 2009. *The emancipated spectator*. Trans. G. Elliot. London: Verso.

Roberts, N., 2014. Reflections. In: C. Quick, E. Speight and G. van Noord, eds. *Subplots to a city: ten years of In Certain Places*. Preston: In Certain Places, 31.

Robinson, C., 1904. *Modern civic art, early urban planning*. London: Routledge.

Rodaway, P., 1994. *Sensuous geographies: body, sense and place*. Abingdon: Routledge.

Rogoff, I., 2011. Free. In: J. Aranda, B. Kuan Wood and A. Vidokle, eds. *E-flux journal: are you working too much? Post-fordism, precarity, and the labor of art*. New York: Sternberg Press, 182–203.

Rolston, B., 1987. Politics, painting and popular culture: the political wall murals of Northern Ireland. *Media, Culture & Society*, 9 (1), 5–28.

Rolston, B., 2004. The war of the walls: political murals in Northern Ireland. *Museum International,* 56 (3), 38–45.

Rolston, B., 2009. 'The brothers on the walls': international solidarity and Irish political murals. *Journal of Black Studies,* 39 (3), 446–70.

Rolston, B., 2012. Re-imaging: mural painting and the state in Northern Ireland. *International Journal of Cultural Studies*, 15 (5), 447–66.

Rose, G., 2007. *Visual methodologies: an introduction to the interpretation of visual materials*. London: Sage.

Scott, A., 2000. *The cultural economy of cities: essays on the geography of image-producing industries*. London, UK: Sage Publications.

Scott, A., 2006. Creative cities: conceptual issues and policy questions. *Journal of Urban Affairs*, 28 (1), 1–17.

Senie, H., 2001. *The Tilted Arc controversy: dangerous precedent?* Minneapolis, MN: University of Minnesota Press.

Senie, H., 1998. Baboons, pet rocks, and bomb threats: public art and public perception. In: H. Senie and S. Webster, eds. *Critical issues in public art: content, context, and controversy*. Washington, DC: Smithsonian Institution Press, 237–46.

Senie, H., 2003. Responsible criticism: evaluating public art. *Sculpture* 22 (10) [online]. Available from: www.sculpture.org/documents/scmag03/dec03/senie/senie.shtml [Accessed 1 Jan 2014].

Senie, H. and S. Webster, eds, 1998. *Critical issues in public art: content, context, and controversy*. Washington, DC: Smithsonian Institution Press.

Sennett, R., 1993. *The conscience of the eye: the design and social life of cities*. London: W.W. Norton & Company.

Sennett, R., 2006. The open city, housing and urban neighbourhoods. *Urban Age* [online]. Available from: http://v0.urban-age.net/0_downloads/Berlin_Richard_Sennett_2006-The_Open_City.pdf [Accessed 21 Jul 2014].

Sharp, J., Pollock, V. and Paddison, R., 2005. Just art for a just city: public art and social inclusion in urban regeneration. *Urban Studies,* 42 (5), 1001–23.

Shirlow, P., 2003. 'Who fears to speak': fear, mobility, and ethno-sectarianism in the two 'Ardoynes'. *Global Review of Ethnopolitics,* 3 (1), 76–91.

Shirlow, P. and Murtagh, B., 2006. *Belfast: segregation, violence and the city.* London: Pluto Press.

Simmel, G.,1908a. How is society possible? In: D. Levine, ed. *Georg Simmel on individuality and social form.* Chicago: University of Chicago Press, 6–22.

Simmel, G.,1908b. The problem of sociology. In: D. Levine, ed. *Georg Simmel on individuality and social form.* Chicago: University of Chicago Press, 23–35.

Simmel, G., 2002 [1903]. The metropolis and mental life. In: G. Bridge and S. Watson, eds. *The Blackwell city reader.* Malden, MA: Wiley-Blackwell, 103–10.

Slater, J. and Iles, A., 2010. *No room to move: radical art and the regenerate city.* London: Mute.

Smets, S., 2014. Opvang voor overtollige beelden: kunst in de openbare ruimte [Looking after surplus sculptures: art in public space]. *NRC Handelsblad,* pp. C2–C4, 14 Aug 2014.

Smith, N., 1996. *The new urban frontier: gentrification and the revanchist city.* London: Routledge.

Smith, S., 2011. Mapping the terrain, again. *Afterall* [online], 27 (1), 67–76. Available from: www.afterall.org/journal/issue.27/mapping-the-terrain-again [Accessed 30 Dec 2014].

Stake, R., 2000. Case studies. In: N. Denzin and Y. Lincoln, eds. *The handbook of qualitative research.* Thousand Oaks, CA: Sage, 435–54.

STEALTH.unlimited, (2015). [online] Available from: www.stealth.ultd.net [Accessed 12 Oct 2014].

Steele, T. and Taylor, R., 2004. Marxism and adult education in Britain. Policy Futures in Education, 2 (3–4), 578–92.

Stein, E., 2002. *On the problem of empathy.* Trans W. Stein. Washington, DC: ICS Publications.

Stern, S., 2009. A Fraction of the whole. *Frieze Magazine* [online], 121. Available from: www.frieze.com/issue/article/a_fraction_of_the_whole [Accessed 14 Feb 2015].

Susen, S., 2011. Critical notes on Habermas's theory of the public sphere. *Sociological Analysis,* 5 (1), 37–62.

Svašek, M., 2008. Shared history? Polish migrant experiences and the politics of display in Northern Ireland. In: K. Burrell, ed. *Polish migration to the UK in the new European Union after 2004.* Farnham: Ashgate, 129–48.

Taylor, C., 2004. *Modern social imaginaries.* Chapel Hill, NC: Duke University Press.

Thich, N., 2012. *Fear : essential wisdom for getting through the storm.* New York, NY: HarperOne, 104.

Thompson, N., ed., 2012. *Living as form: socially engaged art from 1991–2011.* Cambridge, MA: MIT Press.

Thrift, N., 2008. *Non-representational theory: space, politics, affect.* New York, NY: Routledge.

Timson. B and Sholette, G. (eds), 2007. *Collectivism after modernism: the art of social imagination after 1945,* Minneapolis, MN: University of Minnesota Press.

Ukeles, M., 1969, Maintenance art manifesto. In: L. Lippard, ed., 1973. *Six years: the dematerialization of the art object from 1966 to 1972.* Berkeley, CA: University of California Press, 220–1.

UN 2014. *Article 20 of the universal declaration of human rights* [online]. Available from: www. un.org/en/documents/udhr/index.shtml#a20 [Accessed 20 Oct 2014].

Urban Task Force, 1999. *Towards an urban renaissance: report of the Urban Task Force – Executive summary*. London: HMSO.

Valentine, G., 2007. Theorizing and researching intersectionality: a challenge for feminist geography. *The Professional Geographer*, 59 (1), 10–21.

Varna, G. and Tiesdell, S., 2010. Assessing the publicness of public space: the star model of publicness. *Journal of Urban Design*, 15 (4), 575–98.

Varoudis, T., 2012. *DepthmapX multi-platform spatial network analysis software*. London: Space Syntax Laboratory.

Vickery, J., 2011. *Beyond the creative city – cultural policy in an age of scarcity*. Birmingham: MADE.

Wesselman, D. 2013. The High Line, 'the balloon', and heterotopia. *Space and Culture,* 16 (1), 16–27.

Whybrow, N., 2011. *Art and the city*. London: I.B. Tauris.

Wiedenhoft Murphy, W., 2010. Touring the troubles in west Belfast: building peace or reproducing conflict. *Peace and Change*, 35 (4), 537–59.

Willet, J., 1967. *Art in a city*. London: Methuen.

Williams, R., 1973. *The long revolution*. Harmondsworth: Pelican.

Wolff, J., 1981. *The social production of art*. London: Macmillan.

Young, I., 1990. *Justice and the politics of difference*. Princeton, NJ: Princeton University Press.

Zebracki. M., 2014a. Just art, politics and publics: researching geographies of public art and accountability. *Art & the Public Sphere*, 2 (1–3), 117–27.

Zebracki, M., 2014b. Public art as conversation piece: scaling art, public space and audience. *Belgeo: Belgian Journal of Geography*, 14 (3).

Zebracki, M., 2015. Art engagers: what does public art do to its publics? The case of the 'Butt Plug Gnome'. In: J. Lossau and Q. Stevens, eds. *The uses of art in public space*. London: Routledge, 167–82.

Zebracki. M, Van Der Vaart, R. and Van Aalst, I., 2010. Deconstructing *public artopia*: situating public-art claims within practice. *Geoforum*, 41 (5), 786–95.

Žižek, S., 2011. *Living in the end times*. London: Verso.

Zukin, S., 1995. *The cultures of cities*. Oxford: Blackwell.

Zukin. S., 1998. Urban lifestyles: diversity and standardization in spaces of consumption. *Urban Studies,* 35 (5-6), 825–39.

INDEX

accountability: in everyday practice of public art 76–7; in relocation *of Expansion* 75–8; toward permanent public art 68

ACT UP 13

Actor-Network-Theory 235

aesthetics: dialogic 32; differing approaches to 93; relational 31–2; in SPACE minor 93; tension with ethics 150; utilitarian uses vs, of public space 64

The Affective Turn (Clough; Halley) 239

After the Unveiling symposium, Van Abbe Museum (Eindhoven) 64

aftercare: and agonism 67; for *Expansion* 65, 71–2, 77; fluidity of approach and 68; lived experience(s) in 80; of permanent public art 64, 67, 68; social engagement in 68

Agamben, Giorgio 156

agonism: about 63; aftercare and 65, 67; change to public artwork's status quo and 67; confrontation and 64, 65; encounter and 117; and *Expansion* 65, 72, 78, 80; hospitality and 65, 66–7; limitations for engaging with 78; and non-functional vs utilitarian public art 80–1; and power 67; and public art as micropublic 79–80; and social relations around public art 80; in World Café method 65, 72, 78, 81

AIDS 4–5

AIR (Archway/Kings Cross, London) 184

Akti 148

Alavi, Seyed, *Where is Fairfield?* 22

Alekseev, Nikita 234

Alemani, Cecilia 219

Alison Lapper Pregnant (Quinn) 22–3, **23**

Allmendinger, P. 215

Althusser, Louis, *The Underground Current of the Materialism of the Encounter* 117–18

ameliorative art 32, 201

Americans for the Arts 210

Amsterdam, Heeswijk's *Blue House* in 184

Anderson, Benedict 114–15

Anholt, Simon 34

Ant Farm 231

antagonistic art/antagonism: and agency 201–2; ameliorative art vs 201; Broken City Lab and 195, 200–1, 202, 204; built environment and 199; capabilities of 201; cross-pollination from social engagement and 204; eclosion into contemporary art 198–9; as form 203; legibility of 199, 200, 204–5; loitering and 203; new practices/forms and 204; participation and 32; and political imagination 201; and radical agonism 202; resolution of 202; and social

change 201; and socially engaged art 196, 201; translation of 199
Appadurai, Arjun 105, 114–15
Appropriations Bill (1990) 18–19
Apt-Art (Apartment Art) 234
Arendt, Hannah 117
Art and the Public Sphere (Mitchell) 236
Art & Architecture Journal 181
art education: current critical concepts of art practice in theory curriculum 104–5; Dartington College, Art and Social Context degree programme 233; difficulties in teaching public art in 115–16; Open Engagement conference in 122–3, 124; reflexivity in 89; Simmel's form vs content and 104; in SPACE minor 93; turn toward collaborative/transdisciplinary practices 88–9; *see also* social/community practice pedagogy; socially engaged practice pedagogy
Art Gene (Barrow-in-Furness) 184
Artist as Leader research 150–1, 156
Artist Placement Group (APG) 141, 230, 234
Artists and People (Braden) 233
'Artists Taking the Lead' 33
Artmongers 175
ARTocracy (Zeiske; Sacramento) 239
art(s): changes to traditional modalities of 89; contributions to public spaces and vice versa 161–2; culture and 142–3; drawing on social sciences for social role of art 142; and ecology 143; economic/social benefits of 179; emergence of projects in response to particular way of life 142–3; and formal academic research 142; and social life 194, 195; as urban element 161; *see also* murals; public art; sculpture
Arts Council of Northern Ireland 46
Arttranspennine98 180
"ArtWorks" (Paul Hamlyn Foundation) 239
audience(s): artist's relationship with 142; encounters with public art 65–6; impact on 19, 23; for murals 48, 49, 51, 60; for

Nowhereisland 34, 35; for social practice public art 19–21; translation and 143
Australia Council for the Arts 87

Baca, Judith, *The Great Wall of Los Angeles* 57–8, **232**
Bacon, Karin 232
Bad at Sports (Bureau for Open Culture) 133
Bakhtin, Mikhail 117
Banksy, *Santa's Ghetto* 45, 57–8
Barratt, Oliver, *Water Line* **171**, 171–2
Barrie, Dennis 18–19
Bates, Warren 123
Battery Park (New York City) 212
The Battle of Orgreave (Deller) 238
Bauman, Zygmunt 68
Baxley, Crystal 127, 128, 129
Beardsley, John 212, 213, 221
Beatles 62n3
Becker, J. 210
Beech, David 187
Before I Die (Chang) 239
Belfast: alleyway murals 51–3; east 45–6; ethnic diversity in 50; international peace wall 58, 62; Massey's spatial characteristics in 47; murals in 4–5, 45, 47, 50–7, 61–2; nationalism vs unionism in 45–6; over-determination of space in 48; peace walls in 45, 48; re-imaging of 54–5; regeneration of 45; west 46
Bell, Daniel, *The Coming of the Post-Industrial Society* 232
Benedikt, M. 168, 176n3
Best, Anna 237
Beuys, Joseph: *7,000 Eichen (7,000 Oaks)* 152, **234**; social sculpture 198, 232
Beyond Social Inclusion (Cultural Policy Collective) 239
Birmingham Centre for Contemporary Cultural Studies 230
Bishop, Claire 32, 42, 93–4, 201
Black Mountain College 228
A Blade of Grass 130, 139
Het Blauwe Huis (The Blue House) (Heeswijk) 184, **239**

Bliz-aard Ball Sale (Hammons) 105–9, **106**, 112, 116

Bloomberg, Michael 216

Bluedorn, A. 68

Boal, Augusto 232; *Theatre of the Oppressed* 194

Böhm, Kathrin 238

Boland, Michael 213

Bollards (Maine) 174

Bony, Oscar, *La Familia Obrera* **231**

bourgeois public sphere 27, 28, 29–30

Bourriaud, Nicolas, *Relational Aesthetics* 31–2, 197, 237

Boyne, Battle of the 50

Braden, Su, *Artists and People* 233

Brenner, N. 214

Brenson, Michael 18

Broken City Lab: about 8, 194–5; and antagonism 195, 200–1, 202, 204; *City Counselling* 202; *CIVIC Space* 199–200; as collectivity 194–5; *Cross-Border Communication* 195; and Detroit-Windsor relationship 195; legibility of 200–1; limits to possible 204; manifesto 194–5; models of action 194; naming of 194; origins of 193–5; political imagination in 199, 200–1; rhetorical criticality and 197; *Storefront Residencies for Social Innovation* 200; strategic planning process 195; translation of 200–1

Brown, Lorna 240

Bruguera, Tania 24; *Manifesto on Useful Art* 205

Bryant Park (New York City) 167

Buber, Martin, *I and Thou* 116–17

built environment *see* urban space(s)

Bureau for Open Culture, Bad at Sports 133

Burnham, Clint 240

Burns, Robert 145

C-Words **239**

Cage, John 149; *Theater Piece No. 1* **228**

Calder, Alexander 167

California College of the Arts: Master of Fine Arts in Social Practice 112; Open Engagement (OE) conference and 139; Social Practice Workshop 6, 103

California Scenario (Noguchi) 22

California State University, Visual and Public Art Program 237

Calvino, Italo, *Invisible Cities* 192

Camden Arts Centre, North London Link **237**

Camouflaged History (Ericson; Ziegler) 25n6, 236

Campaign for Nuclear Disarmament 229

CARE (exhibition) 24

Carmona, Matthew 174

Cartiere, Cameron 225, 241; *The Practice of Public Art* 2–3, 14

Catford (Lewisham) 171–3, 175

Celestial Ceiling project 143, 145–7

Central Park Conservancy (New York City) 212

Certeau, Michel de 189; *The Practice of Everyday Life* 234

Chambres d'Amis (Hoet) **235**

Chang, Candy, *Before I Die* 239

change *see* social change/transformation

Chariot (Prokofiev) **171**, 171–2

charity, neo-liberalism and 41, 43

Chin, Mel: *Operation Paydirt/Fundred Dollar Bill Project* 239; *Revival Field* 22

Christo: *Gates* 22; *Running Fence* 232

Cincinnati Contemporary Arts Center (CAC) 18–19

cities: art in 161; back streets in 162–3; creative professionals in 179; engagement with, in here and now 192; new ways to evolve/survive 192; as patterns of social relations 161; territorial edges, and diversity in 48; town artists in 163, 174; *see also headings beginning* urban; *and names of individual cities*

City Counselling (Broken City Lab) 202

"City Sites: Artists and Urban Strategies" 25n3

CIVIC Space (Broken City Lab) 199–200

Clark, Lygia, *Structuring the Self* 233

Clough, Patricia, *The Affective Turn* 239

CoBrA 228

Coles, Alex, *Site-specificity* 238

collaboration: in community practice 96; hybridity of 100; international teaching network and 100–2; in murals 49; in new genre public art 9; in research 7, 150, 151; in sharing of spaces 98

"The Collaborative Turn" (Lind) 124

Collins, Reiko Goto *see* Goto Collins, Reiko

Collins, Tim 152

Column (Maine) 174

The Coming of the Post-Industrial Society (Bell) 232

commissions/commissioning: agencies for 180; and attitudinal shift in public art practice 181; holistic model of 180; place-listening and 186, 188–9; projects for remote rural life 148; in rural communities 186; urban regeneration and 7–8

community/-ies: artist's relationship with 142; and denial/politics of difference 47; dialogues between 50, 60; diversity of notion of 57; exclusion and 50; graduate education and understanding of 6; maintenance art and 24; monuments/ statues as commitments by 36; murals/ muralists and 5, 50–1, 53, 56, 57, 60, 61; porosity of 48–9; public art and 45, 57; re-imaging of 53–5; social/public art practice and nature of 118

Community, Art and the State (Kelly) 234

Community Arts Movement 231

community arts/practice: democratization of art-making process in 96; diversity of roles in 99; education sector link with 86; educative capacity of 85–6; Freire and 85–6; hybridity of 100; international teaching network as mirroring 100–1; master/free labour model 96; normative paradigms in 96; ontological possibilities of practice in 99; performer/audience model in 96; research into 101; social change in 86; training in US 86; *see also* socially engaged art/practice

Community Cultural Development in the Tertiary Sector (Fotheringham; Hunter) 86–7

community diversity: and art in public life 148; in Belfast 50; and murals 5, 54, 61; territorial edges of cities and 48

community engagement/participation: community-motivated work and 88; emergence of 87–8; in murals 170; in practical and conceptual/theoretical space of project 96; SPACE minor and 90–1, 94–5; in totality of project 96; undergraduate art/design programmes and 90; *see also* participation; social engagement

community practice pedagogy *see* social/ community practice pedagogy

Conflict Kitchen (Rubin; Weleski) **240**

Conroy-Dalton, Ruth 172

Consequences of a Gesture (Martinez) 20, **20**, **236**

constructivism 144, 155, 157

contents: cultural forms and 114; and encounter 118; in social contacts 108; social forms and 108–9, 111, 118

Contini, Anita 232

Conversation Pieces (Kester) 237

Corner, James 212

Counting For Nothing (Waring) 130

Cranz, Galen, *The Politics of Park Design* 213–14

'Creative City' paradigm (Comedia) 181

creative class/professionals 164, 179, 215

creative labs 150

Creative Lewisham 164, 171–2

Creative Time 15, 200, 209, 222, 232

Crickmay, Chris 233

Critical Art Ensemble 235

critical theory 144, 155, 157

A Critique of Pure Tolerance (Wolff; Moore; Marcuse) 230

Cross-Border Communication (Broken City Lab) 195

Cúchulainn 51

Cullen Ceiling (Douglas) 147

Cullen House 146, 147

Cultural Action for Freedom (Freire) 86

Cultural Enterprise Office (Scotland) 150

cultural form(s) 111; globalization and 114; Simmel on 109; and social contents 114; social forms vs 109, 114; world-at-large and 113

Cultural Policy Collective, *Beyond Social Inclusion* 239

culture: and arts 142–3; and context of projects/interactions 114; documentary 142; ideal 142; and public arts practice 7; research developments and contexts of 149, 151; and social change 40; social definition of 142; and urban renaissance 178–9

Culture and Community Development in Higher Education (Goldbard) 87

Culture and Resistance Festival (Garobone, Botswana) 234

Culture in Action 13, 19, 20, 21, 22, **236**

"Culture is Ordinary" (Williams) 229

curating: connective approach to 190; and encountering power 202; in High Line 214, 216, 218, 219; as increasing approach to public art 209; place-listening and 178, 185; *for* a public 17; *in* public 17, 19–20; *with* a public 17; in public art 221–2; and relocation of *Expansion* 74, 76; responsible criticism and 211; and role of public arts administrators vs curators 219

Czerniak, Julia, *Large Parks* 211, 212

Davis, Chris, *The Family* 190

de Blasio, Bill 216

The Death and Life of Great American Cities (Jacobs) 230

Debord, Guy, Theory of the Dérive 229

Decenter: Concerning Artist-Run Culture (Delos Reyes) 124–5

Delday, Heather 142, 147

Deller, Jeremy 31; *The Battle of Orgreave* 238

Delos Reyes, Jen, *Decenter: Concerning Artist-Run Culture* 124–5

The Democratic Paradox (Mouffe) 238

Deptford 175

Depthmap software 168, 176n2

Derrida, J. 65, 66

Desiman Ltd 172

Destruction in Art Symposium (DIAS) 231

Detroit-Windsor relationship, in *Cross-Border Communication* 193–4, 195

Deutsche, Rosalyn: on art's participation in creation of social life 194; and Battery Park 212; and bourgeois public space 27; on colonization of public space 48; on

desirable vs undesirable publics 28; on exclusions from public space 218; and social aspects of public art 210; on *Tilted Arc* 64; "Uneven Development" 215–16

Deveron Arts 186, 239

Dewey, John 86, 156

Dia Art Foundtion 36

dialogic aesthetics 32

"Dialogical Aesthetics" (Kester) 225–6, 237

dialogue(s): agonism and 63; empathy and 154; international, in higher-education programmes 5–6; and Lacy in *On the Edge* 149; murals and 50–1, 60, 61–2; place-listening and 186–7, 190–1; in social/community practice education 95, 96–8

Diggers Free Store (San Francisco) 109–10

Digital Natives **240**

Donal (community worker) 54–5, 57

Douglas, Anne: *Cullen Ceiling* 147; *On the Edge Research* 118

Driel, Katja van, *Open to the Public* 186, **187**

Drostle, Gary, *Love Over Gold* 170

Drozd, Ally 127, 128

Duff House 146–7

Dufourmantelle, A. 65, 66

Dunn, Pat 144, 145

durational approach/practices: as always-emergent praxis 186; and art practice-debate relationship 186–7; and *Het Blauwe Huis* **239**; in *In Certain Places* 186, 188; and corporeal/sensory engagement with place 189; curating and 185, 187; and management/social control vs critical approaches to 187; 'Open City' symposium and 186–7; and place-listening 178, 185, 189, 191; public art 186–9; and riskier projects 206; in socially engaged art/practice 206; and *Touch Sanitation* 24

ecology 143, 152–4; *see also* environment

"Ecology and Environmental Art in a Public Place" (Goto Collins) 143–4, 151–4

education: adult 37–8; international networking and progressive reform of 101–2; of public artists 5–7; *see also* art

education; practice-led research; social/
community practice pedagogy; socially
engaged practice pedagogy
Education for Socially Engaged Art (Helguera)
91, 93
Eindhoven: *Expansion* in 69–78; Van Abbe
Museum 64–5, 69, 71, **72**
The Emancipated Spectator (Rancière) 239
Emily Carr University of Art + Design 87,
101; Faculty of Culture and
Community, Social Practice and
Community Engagement (SPACE)
minor (*see* SPACE minor)
encounter(s) 116–18; with environment
156; public art and situated 66; social
forms and 108; social geographies of 63;
and world-at-large 113; *see also* social
engagement
environment: change towards 152;
empathy toward 153–4, 155, 156;
murals and 51, 52; *Nowhereisland* and
33–5, 42
Ericson, Kate, *Camouflaged History* 25n6, 236
essentialism 66
ethics: aesthetics tension with 150; in
social/community practice education
96; in SPACE minor 91–2
*The Everyday Agonistic Life after the
Unveiling* 8
exclusion(s): community and 50; public art
and 216; from public spaces 218; from
space 57; from urban parks 216
Expansion (Slegers) **69**, **70**; aftercare for 65,
71–2, 77; and agonism 65, 72, 78, 80;
dismantling of 69; donation to
municipality 69–70, 77; history of
69–70; host–guest role-play 72–8;
ownerships/accountabilities in
relocation of 75–8; pedagogical
intervention for 76; relocation of 5, 65,
68, 69, 70, 71, 72–9; replacement of 73,
76; social engagement with 65; spatial/
temporal aspects of relocation 73–5;
World Café method and 68 (*see also*
World Café method)
Experiments in Art and Technology
(E.A.T.) 231
"Eye candy or eyesore?" (Johnson) 208–9

La Familia Obrera (Bony) **231**
The Family (Davis) 190
Feed the Cows 173
Feenstra, Wapke 238
Field Operations 212
Finkelpearl, Tom 129, 194, 195
Finn (tour guide) 55
Florida, Richard 164; *The Rise of the
Creative Class* 179
Flow City (Ukeles) 24
Fluxus 198, 228, 230
Fong, Polly 167, 174
For Space (Massey) 239
Forest Houses (Morrisania) 36–7
Fotheringham, R., *Community Cultural
Development in the Tertiary Sector* 86–7
Foucault, Michel 220, 221
fragmentation 104, 105, 108–9, 111–12
Franceschini, Amy 237
Fred (tour guide) 58
"Free" (Rogoff) 125
Freeman, Jo, "The Tyranny of
Structurelessness" 232
Freire, Paolo 85–6, 129; *Pedagogy of the
Oppressed* 86, 231
Fremantle, Chris 144
Freshkills Park (Ukeles) 24
Fromm, Erich 85
Fusco, Coco, *The Year of the White Bear and
Two Undiscovered Amerindians Visit the
West* 24–5, 236
Futurefarmers 237
Fyfe, Kristy 123

Gablik, Suzi 16, 190
Garobone (Botswana), Culture and
Resistance Festival in 234
Gates (Christo; Jeanne-Claude) 22
Gateshead, *Angel of the North* in 181
A Gathering (Martin; Muñoz) 19, 20
The German Ideology (Marx) 37
Get the Message 170
Ghent Museum for Contemporary Art **235**
Giddens, A. 81n3
Gillick, Liam 31
Ginkgo Projects 180
Glasgow School of Art, Environmental Art
Programme 235

Glass, Ruth, *London: Aspects of Change* 230

Glenrothes New Town, Harding as town artist in 163, **231**

globalization: and community practice 6; and cultural forms/worlds 114; and international dialogue in higher-education programmes 5–6

Gog & Magog (Platform) 22

The Gold Rush (McCarthy) 55–7, 60

Goldbard, Arlene 85, 97; *Culture and Community Development in Higher Education* 87

Gómez-Peña, Guillermo, *The Year of the White Bear and Two Undiscovered Amerindians Visit the West* 24–5, 236

Goodstein, Elizabeth 105

Gormley, Antony, *One and Other* 239

Goto Collins, Reiko 143–4, 151, 155, 156; "Ecology and Environmental Art in a Public Place" 143–4, 151–4; *Plein Air* **153**, 154

Graffiti Research Lab 206n1

Gramsci, Antonio 38, 43, 239; *Prison Notebooks* 37

Gramsci Monument (Hirschhorn) 29, 35–8, **38**, 40, 43, 196, 239

Gran Fury 199

The Great Wall of Los Angeles (Baca) 57–8, **232**

Green, James 179, 180

Greenwich Mural Workshop **233**

Grizedale 186

Group Material 13, 199

Guba, Egon 144, 151, 152, 154–5

Guernica (Belfast mural) 58–60, **59**

Guernica (Picasso) 58–60

Guerrilla Art Action Group 194

Gutai Artist Association (Gutai Bijutsu Kyokai) 228

Guyton, Tyree, *Heidelberg Project* **235**

Habermas, Jürgen 27, 28, 29–30, 42, 43

Hall, T. 210, 213

Halley, Jean, *The Affective Turn* 239

Hammons, David: *Bliz-aard Ball Sale* 105–9, **106**, 112, 116; *House of the Future* 25n6

Handelman, D. 54

Hanson, Juliette 174; *The Social Logic of Space* 174–5

happenings 15, 197, 229

Haraway, D. 81n2

Harding, David 163, **231**, 233, 235

Hargreaves, G., *Large Parks* 211, 212

Harris Flights 188, **188**

Harris Museum & Art Gallery (Preston) 188

Harrison, Helen Mayer 152; *Serpentine Lattice* 152

Harrison, Margaret, *Women and Work* 232

Harrison, Newton 152; *Serpentine Lattice* 152

Hartley, Alex, *Nowhereisland* 29, 33–5, **35**, 40, 42–3

Haughton, G. 215

Hayden, Dolores 161

Healey, P. 81n3

Heeswijk, Jeanne van, *Het Blauwe Huis (The Blue House)* 184, **239**

Heidelberg Project (Guyton) **235**

Heim, Wallace 148

Hein, Hilde 29; "What is Public Art?" 27

Helguera, Pablo, *Education for Socially Engaged Art* 91, 93

Helms, Jesse 18

Henckel, David, and *Transit of Venus* ale 189

Hercbergs, D. 49

heterotopia 220

The Hidden Curriculum (Krauss) 239

High Line (New York City): about 8–9, 217; art in 202, 208, 216, 218, 219, 220, 221; art programme at 219; competition between cities and 217; completion of third/final section of 209, 216; curatorial approach to 219; Field Operations and 212; Friends of the High Line 217, 218, 219, 222; funding of 217, 222; and future of urban parks/public art 221; hybrid urban parks and 213, 220; implications of 208–9; as model 208–9, 211; museums compared to 219; as neo-liberal park 214, 217–20, 222; novelty of 221; as otherworldly space 220, 221; performance art at 219–20; as privately public space 217–18; prominence of 209; public–private funding of 219; signification of public art in 216; size of

211; surveillance in 214, 219; urban
revitalization and 217; vertical–
horizontal relationship in 218–19
Hill, A. 53–4
Hillier, B. 168, 170, 173; *The Social Logic of
Space* 174–5; *Space Syntax* 165–6
Hirschhorn, Thomas 40; *Gramsci Monument*
29, 35–8, **38**, 40, 43, 196, 239
Hoet, Jan, *Chambres d'Amis* **235**
Holleman, Arnoud 64–5, 67
Holmes, Brian 194
Holzer, Jenny 195
Homeless Vehicles (Wodiczko) 235
Honoré de Balzac (Rodin) 64–5
Hood, Walter Jr 16
hooks, bell 121; *Teaching Community* 129;
Teaching to Transgress 236
Hope, Sophie 191, 225–6, 241
HORKEŠKART **238**
Horniman Mosaic 173
hospitality/host–guest tenet 5, 65, 66–7,
71–8, 79
House (Whiteread) 22
House of the Future (Hammons) 25n6
Hunt, Kay, *Women and Work* 232
Hunter, Ian 145
Hunter, M., *Community Cultural
Development in the Tertiary Sector* 86–7
hybridity: of collaboration 100; of
community arts/practice 100; of
neo-liberal park 215; of public vs
private space 212; of urban parks 8,
211–14, 221

I and Thou (Buber) 116–17
The Image of the City (Lynch) 172
"Imperfect Art" (Lacy) 150
In Certain Places 8; about 177; and
conversations/encounters 186; Critical
Friends group and 191; durational
nature of 185–6, 187–8; evolution of
191–2; Lead Artist project and 179,
182, 183; momentum/coalescence
around project 180; 'Open City'
symposium 186–7; as open-ended 186;
origins of 179; and place-listening
approach to public art 178, 184–92; and
place-making 182

Insitu 184
interdisciplinarity: "Ecology and
Environmental Art in a Public Place"
and 143; paradigm crossing in research
and 156; in SPACE minor 91;
transdisciplinarity vs 89
International Movement for an Imaginist
Bauhaus (IMIB) 228
Interventionism 8, 32, 228, 239
The Interventionists (MASS MoCA) 239
intervention(s): and charity 41; and
corporate systems 195; creative listening
and 189; and *Cross-Border Communication*
195; and environment 152; fixed notion
of public space and 48; and mobilization
of community through public art 46;
Node and 43; *Nowhereisland* and 42–3; in
public space by authoritative
organizations 48; in rural culture 142,
145, 156; and social critique 27; and
social/cultural change 148; STEALTH
and 40, 41, 43; in urban public realm
173, 174, 180; variety of methodologies
for 94–5
Inthrow 143, 144–7
Invisible Cities (Calvino) 192
isovists 166, 168, 172, 176n3
Israel-Palestine separation wall 48, 54, 58

Jaar, Alfredo 179–80, 183
Jacob, Ariana 128, 130
Jacob, Mary Jane 236; and *Culture in Action*
19; and *Places with a Past* 17–18
Jacobs, Jane, *The Death and Life of Great
American Cities* 230
Jahn, Marisa 194
Jarman, N. 52, 60, 61
Jeanne-Claude: *Gates* 22; *Running Fence* 232
Jerusalem, separation wall in 48, 54, 58
Johnson, K., "Eye candy or eyesore?" 208–9
Jones, Ronald 89
Jones, Susan Henshaw 232

Kaprow, Allan 15, 148–9, 229
Kaspori, Dennis 239
Keenan, Claudia 18
Kelly, Gerard *see* Mo Chara (Gerard Kelly)
Kelly, Mary, *Women and Work* 232

Kelly, Owen, *Community, Art and the State* 234

Kenna, Carol 233

Kester, Grant 32, 88, 89, 191; *Conversation Pieces* 237; "Dialogical Aesthetics" 225–6, 237

Key to the City (Ramirez Jonas) 196

Klose, Anastasia, *One Stop Knock-Off Shop* **110**, 110–11

Klüver, Billy 231

Knowles, Allison, *Make a Salad* **230**

Koch, Ed 215, 216

KOS (Kids of Survival) 234

Kozinn, Allan 18

Krauss, Annette, *The Hidden Curriculum* 239

Krauss, Rosalind, "Sculpture in the expanded field" 15

Kwon, Miwon, *One Place After Another* 238

Lacy, Suzanne: audience model 20; and California State University Visual and Public Art Program 237; and *On the Edge* 149–50; and expansion of public art from sculptural forms to public practices 15–16; Hein on installations of 27; "Imperfect Art" 150; *Mapping the Terrain* 3–4, 13, 16–17, 21–2, 180, 194, 236; on public art as statuary/memorial 213–14; *The Roof Is On Fire* 236; and *Working in Public* 149–50, 151

Large Parks (Czerniak; Hargreaves) 211, 212

lateral effect 114

Latham, John 230

Latour, Bruno 66, 68; *Science in Action* 235

Lavelle, Nicole 127

leadership, in social art practice 149–51

Lefebvre, Henri 62, 65, 66; *The Production of Space* 236

Lettrist International 228

Lewisham: about 7; amorphous landscape in 174; artworks in 161, 167–9, 170, 174, 175; centre 173; consensus landmarks in 172–3; Creative Enterprise Zones 167; *Creative Lewisham* 164; Cultural Strategy 175; *Lewisham 2000* scheme 174; murals in 170; open vs built space in 174; Public Art Map 169; sculpture in 170–1, 175; space syntax

and artworks in 161, 167 (*see also* space: syntax); survey of artifacts in 167–8; symbolically segregated/integrated spaces in 170–3; traditional vs post-war morphology in 7, 173–4

Lincoln, Yvonna 144, 151, 154–5

Lind, Maria, "The Collaborative Turn" 124

Lippard, Lucy 161, 193

listening 185, 190

'Littoral: New Zones for Critical Art Practice' conference 180

lived experience(s): in aftercare of public art 80; as knowledge 86; of public art 22, 63, 66; and social practice 4, 15–16, 22; World Café discussion method and 72–8

Liverpool 177; Biennial 180

Liverpool Mural Project 62n3

Living as Form (Thompson) 15, 88, 239

Lobb, Stephen 233

London: Aspects of Change (Glass) 230

Lord, Chip 231

Love Over Gold (Drostle) 170

Lowe, Rick, *Project Row Houses* 194, **236**

Lozano-Hemmer, Rafael 195

Lucy + Jorge Orta, *70 x 7 The Meal, act XXXIV* 1–2

Lumsden (Scotland) 144–5

Lynch, Bernadette, "Whose Cake is it Anyways?" 239

Lynch, Kevin, *The Image of the City* 172

McCarthy, Tim, *The Gold Rush* 55–7, 60

McCormick, J. 52, 60, 61

McDowell, S. 61

McGeogh, John 145–7

Maciunas, George 230

Magritte, René 78

Maine, John: *Bollards* 174; *Column* 174; *Ridgeway* 174

maintenance art 24

Maintenance Art (Ukeles) 24, 231

Make a Salad (Knowles) **230**

Make It Happen '06 123

Making Things, Making Things Better, Making Things Worse 132

Manchester 177

Manifesto on Useful Art (Bruguera) 205

Manzione, Christopher 239

Mapping the Terrain (Lacy) 3–4, 13, 16–17, 21–2, 180, 194, 236

Mapplethorpe, Robert, *The Perfect Moment* 18

Marcuse, Herbert, *A Critique of Pure Tolerance* 230

Marin, Peter, *The Open Truth and the Fiery Vehemence of Youth* 120

Martin, Walter, *A Gathering* 19, 20

Martinez, Daniel J., *Consequences of a Gesture* 20, **20**, **236**

Marx, Karl 104, 113, 197; *The German Ideology* 37

MASS MoCA, *The Interventionists* 239

Massey, Doreen: on geographical fragmentation and segregation 47; on hidden artworks 167, 173; and limits to social engagement with artwork 68; and mobilization of place/space 46, 47–8; on multiplicity of space, and turning space into time 30; and *Nowhereisland* 44n2; on Occupy movement 30–1; on place as activity meeting point 165; on place as relational 47; on play of social relations in democratic public spaces 42–3; and public art becoming public 210; on public space as meeting point 176; and social relations as political 30; *For Space* 239; on space as formal/physical/static and public sphere theory 28; on space as product of relations 31; on space as social construction 27; theory of space, and political public 43; on "throwntogetherness" of space 33

Matarasso, François 181; 'Use or Ornament?' 179

May Protests (1968) 231

MDM Props 33

Medu Arts Ensemble 234

Melamed, Michel, *SEEWATCHLOOK* 219–20

Melbourne, University of, Centre for Cultural Partnerships, Master of Community Cultural Development degree 87, 96–8, 99, 101

Menotti, Gian Carlo 18

Merleau-Ponty, Maurice, *Phenomenology of Perception* 230

Mesa-Bains, Amalia 237

Metzger, Gustav 231

Michels, Doug 231

Miles, Malcolm 161, 164

Millennium Park (Chicago) 220

Mitchell, Don 212, 213, 215

Mitchell, W. J. T. 27; *Art and the Public Sphere* 236

Mo Chara (Gerard Kelly) 51–2

Modus Operandi 180

monuments 7, 36, 167; *see also* sculpture

Moore, Barrington, *A Critique of Pure Tolerance* 230

Moravia (Colombia) 39–41

Morrisania 36–7, 43, 196

Mouffe, Chantal 63, 105, 117, 202; *The Democratic Paradox* 238

movement economy 168–9

Muf 31

Muñoz, Paloma, *A Gathering* 19, 20

muralists: and community 61; community support and 53; and *Guernica* mural 58–9; interviews with 49; on origins of murals 51; and re-imaging of murals 55, 57

murals: audiences 48, 49, 51, 60; in Belfast 47, 50–7, 61–2; and community 5, 50–1, 53, 60, 61, 164; community diversity and 54, 61; and community-state dialogue 50–1; and cultural divergence 5; and cultural identity 51–2; and dialogue 60; disappearing of 60; environmental 51, 52; international aspects 57–8; in Lewisham 170; location of 170; mobility of 5, 60–1; nationalism vs unionism in 46; negotiation of 46, 52; politicization in tours of 49; practical collaboration in 49; range of issues in 58–60; re-imaging of 46, 55–7; research methodology 49; in segregated spaces 170; and social justice 45, 60; and social practice 1–2; state policies and 53–4; street 5, 45; territory marking by 50; tour guides regarding 49; and urban space 5, 46

MyVillages.org 238

Nagle, J. 50

Nancy, Jean-Luc 185

National Endowment for the Arts (NEA) 18; public art programmes 2

National Gallery (Edinburgh) 147

National Sculpture Database (Public Monuments and Sculture Association (PMSA)) 167–8

N.E. Thing Co. 195

negotiation(s): Belfast murals and 50; and change 46; and collaborative planning principles 81n3; community–state and public art 57; of complexity and diversity 49; and definition of 'public' 162; and development of art in alternative contexts 141, 148; and future of artwork 67, 77; and mobility 149; modelling of power in social practice pedagogy 95; of murals 5, 46, 52; of place 48; public art and 47–8; of public art in Belfast 5; of social difference 60; of state policies on visual landscape in Belfast 53; of urban public space 46

neo-liberalism: and ameliorative art 201; and charity 41, 43; and donations of vs creation of new public art 78; 'grassroots' 222; and High Line 214, 217–20; and hybridity of urban parks 215; and legibility 205; and political imagination 205; and public art 8, 164, 215, 222; and public artists 80, 181; and public spaces 31; and social media 205; and socially engaged public art 196, 198; and urban parks 8, 208, 214–16, 222

New Cullen Ceiling (Orchardson) **146**

new genre public art 3, 4, 9, 16, 180

New Labour: on contribution of art to economic/social wellbeing 179; and culture-led regeneration 40; election of 237; Housing Market Renewal Initiative 183; and public art 181; replacement of 182; urban renaissance agenda 177

New York City: Battery Park 212; A Blade of Grass 130, 139; Bryant Park 167; Central Park Conservancy 212; MTA 19; Queens Museum 6–7, 130, 139; urban redevelopment/revitalization in 215–16; *see also* High Line (New York City)

Newling, John 191

Nodos de Desarrollo Cultural No. 1 (Cultural Development Node No. 1) (STEALTH) 29, 39–41, 43

Noguchi, Isami, *California Scenario* 22

Nowhereisland (Hartley) 29, 33–5, **35**, 40, 42–3

Nye, Jeff 123

Oakes, Chantal, *Thoughts that Make Actions in the World* 190

objectivism 154, 155

Occupy movement 30–1, 198

O'Connell, Maurice 237

O+I (Organization and Imagination) 141, 234; *see also* Artist Placement Group (APG)

Oliver, Paul 233

On the Edge research: about 141–2, 157n1; and *Artist as Leader* research 150–1; and *Celestial Ceiling* 143; characteristics of doctoral research 151; commissioning of artists 148; and cultural contexts of research 151; epistemology of 156; and *Inthrow* 143, 144–7; Kaprow and 148–9; Lacy and 149–50; metaphysical approach 155; in national/international discourse on changing nature of art 147; and participation 143; potential of 144; project partners 147; project success rate 149; projects 144–7; remote rural culture and 141–2; as research and practice 147; and social definition of culture 142; workshops 147–8

On the Edge Research (Douglas) 118

One and Other (Gormley) 239

One Place After Another (Kwon) 238

One Stop Knock-Off Shop (Klose) **110**, 110–11

O'Neill, Paul 186, 189

'Open City' symposium 186–7

Open Engagement: Art After Aesthetic Distance 122–5

Open Engagement (OE) conference: about 6–7, 120, 121–2, 123; as accessible 126; allies of 129–30; and A Blade of Grass 130, 139; and California College of the Arts 139; call for submissions 123; case studies 130–8; core team 128; evolution of 122; feedback 129; first 126–7; as free conference 125–6; future development of 139–40; growth of 127–8, 139; logistical organization 123; mission 122; and national consortium 139; numbers of attendees 128, 131, 132, 133, 134, 136, 138; openness and 121; origins 122–4; planning tasks/workload 126–7, 129; platform 122; at Portland State University (PSU) 6, 126–9, 132–6; potential of 126; in Queens Museum 6–7, 130, 137–8, 139; in Regina 123, 131; rotation from coast to coast 139; and socially engaged art 6, 121–2, 124, 127, 139–40; structure 121–2, 127–8; as student project 122–3, 124; students in 127, 128–9; and University of Illinois at Chicago, Art and Social Justice Cluster 139; and visual identity evolution **121**; women vs men workers in 130

Open to the Public (Osterholt; Driel) 186, **187**

The Open Truth and the Fiery Vehemence of Youth (Marin) 120

Operation Paydirt/Fundred Dollar Bill Project (Chin) 239

Orchardson, Robert 145–7, 146

Orta, Lucy + Jorge, *70 x 7 The Meal, act XXXIV* 1–2

Osterholt, Wouter, *Open to the Public* 186, **187**

otherness 116–17

Out of Order (Phillips) 209

Oxford Brooks University, Social Sculpture Research Unit 237

Paddy (muralist) 51, 53, 55, 57, 58, 59, 60, 61

painted ceilings 145–7

Paraphonaris, Hervé 239

paraSITE (Rakowitz) 237

participation: in creative process in community practice 96; *On the Edge* and 143; encounter and 117–18; as interventionist 32; meanings of 207n2; and public art 23–4; in relational aesthetics 32; *see also* community engagement/participation

participatory art: and critical analysis 42; public art as 31–2; space/public concepts in 29

Pasmore, Victor 163

Paul Hamlyn Foundation: "ArtWorks" 239; "Whose Cake is it Anyways?" 239

pedagogy *see* education; social/community practice pedagogy; socially engaged practice pedagogy

Pedagogy of the Oppressed (Freire) 86, 231

Pensive Girl **171**, 173

The Perfect Moment (Mapplethorpe) 18

Performing Art Labs (Pallabs) 150

permanent public art: aftercare for 5, 64, 68; changes to status quo of 67; negotiation of future of 67; site specificity 67; spatial fixity of 67; *see also* *Expansion* (Slegers)

Petrie, Willie 145

Phenomenology of Perception (Merleau-Ponty) 230

Philadelphia Mural Arts Program 1–2; *What We Sow* 2

Philippine Educational Theatre Association (PETA) 231

Phillips, Patricia 16, 29, 43, 221–2; *Out of Order* 209

philosophers, Hirschhorn's monuments to 35–7, 43

Picasso, Pablo, *Guernica* 58–60

Pink Palace 170

place: as meeting point of activity layers 165; mobilization of 46; myth of 48; as relational 47; *see also* space

place-listening 8, 178, 185–91

place-making 7–8, 181–2, 183–5

Places with a Past 13, 17–18, **236**

'Platform for Art' project 180

Platform, *Gog & Magog* 22

play, art as 148–9

Please Love Austria (Schlingensiet) 238

Plein Air (Goto Collins) **153**, 153–4

political imagination: and agency 200; antagonism and 201; in Broken City Lab 199, 200–1; marketability of 198; neo-liberalism and 205; socially engaged art and 198, 199–200, 205

The Politics of Park Design (Cranz) 213–14

Portland State University (PSU): Art and Social Practice programme 126, 129; Open Engagement (OE) and 6, 126–9

positivism 144, 152, 154, 155, 156, 157
post-positivism 144, 155
Powderly, James 206n1
power: in agonism 67; ameliorative vs
    antagonistic effects of 201–2; and
    colonization of public space by public
    art 48; loitering and 202–3; negotiations
    in social practice pedagogy 95;
    place-listening and 191; and
    preservation/displacement of *Expansion*
    76; rhetorical criticality and 197; spaces
    for encountering 202–3; and urban
    parks 214
practice-led research: about/defined 141;
    Artist as Leader and 150–1; in art(s)
    practice 141; and changing public arts
    practice 7; choice in 149; collaboration
    in 7, 150, 151; construction of
    methodologies 151; as discursive/critical
    vs propositional/problem solving 141;
    "Ecology and Environmental Art in
    Public Place" 151–4; and emergent
    practice 149–50; as knowledge-
    producing 144; metaphysical questions in
    155; methodology vs paradigm in 154–5;
    paradigms 144, 151–6; positioning
    156–7; and practice as shaping what can
    be known 156; quantitative vs qualitative
    methods 141, 143, 154; questions
    regarding art(s) practice 142; reflection
    on/informing art(s) practice 142–3; in
    remote rural culture 7, 151; *see also On
    the Edge* research
The Practice of Everyday Life (Certeau) 234
The Practice of Public Art (Cartiere; Willis)
    2–3, 14
Prajapati, Sheetal 130
praxis: in social/community practice
    pedagogy 90, 96–8; social practice
    pedagogy as 89; and social practice
    pedagogy in non-art spaces 95; socially
    grounded nature of 66; theory vs 96–8
presentism 111–12
Preston: attitudinal change by city council/
    local groups in 187; Lead Artist project
    in 179–80, 183, 186; 'Open City'
    symposium 186–7; public art in 179–80;
    regeneration of 8, 177, 178; Tithebarn

scheme 178, 179–80, 182, 183, 184,
    185; walking tours in 189; *see also In
    Certain Places*
Price, Jonathan 151
Primary (Lenton area of Nottingham) 184
Prins, A. 67
Prison Notebooks (Gramsci) 37
private space(s): and privately public spaces
    217–18; public art and 14; public space
    vs 212
private–public partnerships *see* public–
    private partnerships
The Production of Space (Lefebvre) 236
Project Row Houses (Lowe) 194, **236**
Projects Environment, and 'Littoral'
    conference 180
Prokofiev, Oleg, *Chariot* **171**, 171–2
public art: accessibility of 168–9, 170; art
    criticism and 42; artist attributes for
    23–4; attitudinal shift over time in
    180–1; auditory vs visual sensibility in
    185; as backdrop 173; benefits of 210;
    as colonial vs civic expression 163;
    colonization of public space 48; and
    community 45, 57; contextualization of
    113; and controversy 3; critical
    recognition of 14; definition 2–3, 210,
    211; donations, vs creation of new
    77–8; durational practices in 186–9;
    early 2000s renaissance for 182;
    economic crises and 178, 182, 184;
    entrepreneurship in 80; essentialism in
    66; everyday vs structural issues in
    practical care of 64–5; exclusionary
    practices in 216; as focus of space vs
    built into fabric of city 163–4; future of
    241; governments' advocacy of 181;
    history of 22, 162–5, 180–1;
    homogenization vs 181; human
    geographies of 80; impact of 19, 23, 48;
    influential works 24–5; isolation vs
    diversity and new energy in 148; as
    landmarks 172; locations 3; "machine"
    of 221–2; as micropublic 79–80;
    mobility of 64–5; movement outside
    gallery to 180; multisiting of 80; naming
    of art as 218; non-functional vs
    utilitarian nature 80; opposition to/

destruction of 63–4; placement of 167; potential of 209, 210, 211; 'public'/ publicness in 29, 31, 42, 43, 210, 222; public sculpture vs 2; and 'public' space 31; as reflection of society 211; research/media organizations' advocacy of 180–1; roles of 220–1; scope of 3, 14, 148, 211; selection process 210; social aspects of 210; social groundedness of praxis 66–7; social responsibility in 24; spatial conditions changes and 162–3; tactical 221, 222; temporary vs permanent works 14; time for settling/reactionary emotions 21; uneven development and 216

Public Art Forum 181, 235

Public Art Fund 221–2

public assembly 4, 30–1

.Public Monuments and Sculture Association (PMSA), *National Sculpture Database* 167–8

'public'/publicness: charity and 41; as communication practices 162; constraints upon art 162; definitions of 162, 176; degrees of, in public art 210, 222; limited vs expanded understanding/engagements with 29; meaning of, in public artworks 31, 42; measurement of 162; *Nowhereisland* as folly to 43; as picturing/educating/ benefiting publics 29; political in term 42; in public art 29, 31; within public art 29, 31, 42, 43, 210; public sphere vs space and internal contradictions of 27; as spatial/legal reality 162; traditional uses of word 27–8; wide range of use of 42; *see also* public(s)

public realm: culture-led regeneration projects in 31; defining, within public art context 14; privatization of 210, 218; public space/sphere vs 4

public space(s): aesthetic vs utilitarian uses of 64; changes in conditions of 162–3; colonization by public art 48; contributions of art to 161–2; contributions to art 162; defined 30; disputes over 30; as emergent sites 105; exclusions from 218; as gallery 162–5;

hybridity of 212; negotiation of public art in 48; neo-liberalism and 31; neutrality vs commercial uses of 4; place-making and 181–2; privatization of public realm and 210; pseudo- 218; public assembly vs 30; public realm/ sphere vs 4; public sphere vs 27; state interventions and 31; state policies and 53–4; STEALTH and lack of 39; utilitarianism and functionalization of 80

public sphere: art's autonomy from 34–5; bourgeois 27, 28, 29–30; Habermas and 27, 28, 29–30, 42; misuse of publicity and 42; *Nowhereisland* and 35; opinion formation in forms of 29–30; opinion in, and artwork's 'publicness' 31; as performative arrangement 28; public realm/space vs 4; public space vs 27; publication of opinions in 28; and social/political interactions 28

Public Works 31

public–private partnerships: and funding of High Line 219; and public art 219, 221; in public art 218; in remote rural contexts 147; and urban parks 8, 208, 212, 221; and urban public art 208

public(s): benefiting of 29, 39–41, 43; curating for/in/with 17, 19–20; educating 29, 35–8, 43; picturing of 29, 33–5, 42–3; as political public 43; within public art 43; in public assembly 30–1; *see also* 'public'/publicness

El Puente Lab 39–40

Pyyhtinen, Olli 108, 111–12

Queens Museum (New York City) 6–7, 130, 139

Quick, Charles 179–80, 183

Quinn, Marc, *Alison Lapper Pregnant* 22–3, **23**

Radio Balzac 64–5

Rakowitz, Michael, *paraSITE* 237

Ramirez Jonas, Paul 129; *Key to the City* 196

Rana, Matthew 117

Rancière, Jacques 143, 145; *The Emancipated Spectator* 239

Rauschenberg, Robert 231

Re-Imaging Communities Programme 46, 48, 49, 53–4, 55, 56, 59
Reddy, Prerana 130
Reeves, Kerri-Lynn 130
reflexivity 89, 90, 98–9
relational aesthetics 31–2
Relational Aesthetics (Bourriaud) 31–2, 197, 237
remote rural culture(s)/communities: and art-cultural context relationship 147; articulation of forms of quality visual arts practice in 148; co-created research in 151; commissioning of projects for 148; and contemporary art 141; cooperation between individuals in 143; doctoral research in 7; and *On the Edge* research 141–2; lack of institutionalizing infrastructure 143; painted ceilings and 146–7; public-private relationship in 147
Renwick, Gavin 144–5
REPOhistory 199
research *see* practice-led research
responsible criticism 211
"Responsible Criticism" (Senie) 42
Revival Field (Chin) 22
Ridgeway (Maine) 174
The Rise of the Creative Class (Florida) 179
Rivera, Diego 58
Robert Gordon University, Grays School of Art 157n1
Roberts, Nigel 188
Robertson, I. 213
Robinson, C. 163
Rodaway, Paul 185, 190
Rodin, Auguste, *Honoré de Balzac* 64–5
Rogoff, Irit, "Free" 125
Rollins, Tim 234
Rolston, B. 46, 53, 55
The Roof Is On Fire (Lacy) 236
Rose, G. 46, 47–8, 49, 68, 165, 167, 210
Roth, Evan 206n1
Rubin, Jon, *Conflict Kitchen* **240**
Running Fence (Christo; Jeanne-Claude) 232

Sacks, Shelly 237
Sacramento, Nuno, ARTocracy 239
Sampson, Sandy 127, 128
San Francisco Diggers 109–10

San Francisco Museum of Modern Art (SFMOMA) 16
Santa's Ghetto (Banksy) 45, 57–8
'scapes,' as imagined worlds 114–15
Schitters, Antje 238
Schlingensiet, Christoph, *Please Love Austria* 238
The School of Panamerican Protest 239
Schrag, Anthony 226, 241
Schreurs, Mary-Ann 64
Science in Action (Latour) 235
sculpture: dense vs sparse systems of settlement in 175; expansion from plinth to public practices 15–16; in Lewisham 170–1, 175; of political/colonial figures in mass education 163; public, as public art 2; roundabout 180; *see also* monuments
"Sculpture in the expanded field" (Krauss) 15
Seamus (tour guide) 51–3, 58
SEEWATCHLOOK (Melamed) 219–20
Selwood, Sara 161
Senie, Harriet 64, 211, 222; "Responsible Criticism" 42; *The Tilted Arc Controversy* 3
Sennett, R. 48
Serpentine Lattice (Harrison; Harrison) 152
Serra, Richard, *Tilted Arc* 3, 13, 63–4, 65, 67, 78, 79
7,000 Eichen (7,000 Oaks) (Beuys) 152, **234**
Sherk, Bonnie 194
Shirlow, P. 54
Shiva, Vandana 148
Sholette, Gregory 195
shops, as social forms 109–11
Simmel, Georg 6; and cultural forms/worlds 109, 114; and diversity/complexity of forms 111; and form vs content 104; and fragmentation 104, 105, 108–9, 111–12; on the 'social' 108; and social form(s) 104, 107–8, 109; and social world as being between individuals 117; and world-at-large 113, 118
Site-specificity (Coles) 238
Situationism 15, 104, 113, 194, 198, 228, 229, 231
Škart 238
Skulptur Projekte Münster 233

Slegers, Toon, *Expansion* 65, 68, **69**, 69–79, **70**, 80
Smith, Stephanie 21
Smolarz, Elisabeth 115
'social': as perpetually in formation 109; Simmel on 108
social change/transformation: aftercare of public art and 68; antagonistic work and 201; artistic intervention within 148; of Belfast public space 47; in community arts practice 86; community politics of difference and 47; culture and 40; mural mobility and 61; negotiation of Belfast murals and 46; social practice classroom and 89; socially engaged public art and 8, 200; STEALTH and bottom-up practices for 40
social/community practice pedagogy: and artist/educator practitioners resident in non-art spaces 95; in Australia 87; certainty vs uncertainty in 98–9; dialogue in 96–8; diversity in 98; educators 89–90; and engagement 90; ethics in 96; globalization and 6; graduate courses in 96–100; graduate students as teaching assistants/co-teachers 100; history of 85–6; and hybridity of community practice 100; international dialogue/ networking in 5–6, 100–2; literature/ discourses on 86–7; methodologies 95; on-the-job training 97; ontological possibilies of community practice and 99; power negotiations in 95; praxis in 96–8; and public space within globalization 105; public vs counter-public spheres in 105; reflexivity in 89–90, 98–9; social engagement movement and 85; student-centred learning in 86, 91, 95, 97; teaching through action in 90; undergraduate studies in 90–5, 96, 97; in United States 87; *see also* socially engaged practice pedagogy; SPACE minor
social engagement: in aftercare 68; agonism and 63; and antagonism 204; community-motivated work and 88; and community practice pedagogy 85; contents in 108; enabling public art parties' responsibility for 81n3; fluid

approach 68; with *Nowhereisland* 35; public art and 63, 65, 67; social practice pedagogy and 90; *see also* community engagement/participation; encounter(s); socially engaged art/practice
Social Exclusion Unit 237
social form(s): and between-ness 108; *Bliz-aard Ball Sale* and 107–8, 109; and contents 108–9, 111, 118; contextualization of 111; cultural forms vs 109, 114; diversity of 111; and encounter(s) 108, 113, 118; fragmentation of 111; organic vs planned city-building 175; play forms of 109; shops and 109–11; Simmel and 104, 107–8, 109; and socially engaged practice 104; and socially engaged practice pedagogy 116; and urban space 161
social imaginary 115, 116
The Social Life of Small Urban Spaces (Whyte) 234
The Social Logic of Space (Hillier; Hanson) 174–5
social/public practice *see* socially engaged art/practice
social transformation *see* social change/ transformation
socially engaged art/practice: and aesthetics 93; antagonism and 196, 198–9, 201; as art movement vs new social order 88; audience for 19–21; and authorship 94; avant-garde and 197; controversial 93–4; cultural economy and 164; democratic forms of 202; diagnostic vs deconstruction/remediation theoretical skills in 103–4; discursive boundaries of 15–16; documentation on 88; durational projects in 206; emergence of 87–8; encounter in 118; horizons of 115; infrastructural limitations to 199–200; infrastructures for 206; instrumentalization of 199; language/ translation in 8, 200–1; leadership in 149–51; legibility vs illegibility of 199; lineage of 197; and lived experience 4, 15–16, 22; as loitering 203; and nature of community 118; neo-liberalism and 196, 198; non-art entities in 200;

numbers of participants and success of
195; open-ended quality in 121; Open
Engagement and 6, 121–2, 124, 127,
139–40; outstanding role of 9; political
imagination and 198, 199–200, 205;
within public art 3–5, 14, 15; radicality
vs pragmatism in 204–6; and research 7,
149–51; results-oriented goals 118;
rhetorical criticality in 196–8; service
economy and 197–8; and shared
imaginaries 116; and social change/
transformation 8, 118, 200; social
form(s) and 104, 116; in SPACE minor
93–4; and urban environment 194; and
world-at-large 112–14, 116; *see also*
community arts/practice
socially engaged practice pedagogy: changes
in body of theories 6, 103–5; diagnostic
vs deconstruction/remediation
theoretical skills in 103–4; difficulties in
teaching 115–16; ethics and 91–2; and
foundational philosophers vs Marxist
critique/Situationist aesthetics 104; and
foundational texts 103; and
infrastructures for socially engaged art/
practice 206; methodologies 95; Open
Engagement and 6–7, 124 (*see also* Open
Engagement (OE) conference); social
forms and 116; and transformation 89;
world-at-large in 113; *see also* social/
community practice education/pedagogy
Sonfist, Alan, *Time Landscape of New York
City* 152, 230
space: assignment of value in 163; charity
and 41; collaborative sharing of 98;
exclusion from 47; *Expansion* and 73–5;
fluidity of parameters 68; free 125–6;
geography and production of 46–7; and
globalization 30; limited vs expanded
understanding/engagements with 29;
mural mobility and changing of 60;
Nowhereisland and 34, 35; as physical vs
social/contingent 27; privatization of
48; public art and mobilization of 47–8;
shared 4, 39, 40, 50, 170; as social
construction 27; STEALTH and 40;
syntax 7, 161, 165–6, 168, 173, 176;
territorialization of 47, 50; turning into

time 30; *see also* private space(s); public
space(s); urban space(s)
Space and Place (Tuan) 233
SPACE minor: about 90–1; artist/educator
practitioners resident in non-art spaces
95; community engagement in 90–1;
community partners and relationship
building in 94–5; Community Projects
courses 91, 94–5; Ethics of
Representation course 91–2;
interdisciplinarity in 91; pedagogy/
methodology 95; required courses in
91; Social Practice Seminar 91, 93–4;
student-centred learning in 91; *see also*
social/community practice education/
pedagogy
Space Syntax (Hillier) 165–6, *166*
Spoleto Festival U.S.A. 17, 18, 236
state: and destruction of *Tilted Arc* 64;
interventions into public spaces 31; and
murals 51, 53–4; and public space 53–4
statues 36; *see also* sculpture
STEALTH, *Nodos de Desarrollo Cultural No.
1 (Cultural Development Node No. 1)* 29,
39–41, 43
Steele, Tom 37
Stein, Edith 153
Stern, Steven 106
Steveni, Barbara 141, 230
Stimson, Blake 195
Street Art, Public City Law (Young) 239
Structuring the Self (Clark) 233
Susen, S. 28
Sustrans 175

Taylor, Charles 115
Taylor, Richard 37
Teaching Community (hooks) 129
Teaching to Transgress (hooks) 236
Tele-Vecindario 20
territorialization: murals and 50; northern
Ireland state and 53–4; of space 47, 50
Texas (city), Project Row Houses in 184
Theater of the Oppressed 232
Theater Piece No. 1 (Cage) **228**
Theatre of the Oppressed (Boal) 194
Theodore, N. 214
Theory of the Dérive (Debord) 229

Thich Nhat Hahn 127

Thompson, Nato 22, 23, 88, 200; *Living as Form* 15, 88, 239

Thoughts that Make Actions in the World (Oakes) 190

Tilted Arc (Serra) 3, 13, 63–4, 65, 67, 78, 79

The Tilted Arc Controversy (Senie) 3

time: charity and 41; *Expansion* and 73–5; fluidity of parameters 68; and globalization 30; *Nowhereisland* and 34; turning space into 30

Time Landscape of New York City (Sonfist) 152, 230

Tithebarn scheme (Preston) 178, 179–80, 182, 183, 184, 185

To Scatter (Walsh) 189

Tom (muralist) 59, 61

Touch Sanitation (Ukeles) 24, **233**

town artists 163, 174, **231**

Trafalgar Square, Fourth Plinth 180, 239

transdisciplinarity *see* interdisciplinarity

transformation *see* social change/ transformation

Transit of Venus ale 189

translation: of antagonistic art/antagonism 199; of Broken City Lab 200–1; learning through acts of 143; *Lumsden 2001–4* and 145; in socially engaged art/practice 8, 200–1

Tuan Yi-Fu, *Space and Place* 233

Turnbull, Gemma-Rose 130

"The Tyranny of Structurelessness" (Freeman) 232

Ukeles, Mierle Laderman 24; *Flow City* 24; *Freshkills Park* 24; *Maintenance Art* 24, 231; *Touch Sanitation* 24, **233**

Ulster Defence Association (UDA) 55

The Underground Current of the Materialism of the Encounter (Althusser) 117–18

"Uneven Development" (Deutsche) 215–16

Universal Declaration of Human Rights (UN) 34; and right to public assembly 30

University of Illinois at Chicago, Art and Social Justice Cluster 139

University of Melbourne *see* Melbourne, University of, Centre for Cultural Partnerships, Master of Community Cultural Development degree

urban parks: city budgets and 208; consumer/spectator vs civic public in 217–18; and creative class 215; depoliticization of 215; designers, and role of public art 209; economic benefits of 213; eras of design/ development 213–14; exclusions from 216; functions of public art in 209–11; funding for 216; future of 221; "grassroots" neo-liberalism and 222; High Line and future of 221; hybridity of 8, 211–14, 221; neo-liberalism and 8, 208, 214–16, 222; physical/fiscal erosion of 212; power dynamics and 214; 'privately public' 212; public art in 208, 213–14, 215, 216, 220, 222; public–private partnerships and 8, 208, 212, 221; security/surveillance in 214, 215, 218, 222; size of 211–12; social control and 212–13; as soft spaces 215; sustainable 213, 214; symbolic segregation of 170; uneven development and 216; and urban regeneration 215; *see also* High Line (New York City)

urban public art(s): budgeting/funding for 209; city budgets and 208; councils and creative class in 164; geopolitics in making of 221; museums compared to 219; public–private partnerships in 208; urbanism and 174; *see also* murals

urban regeneration: culture and 178; gentrification disguised as 183; and High Line 217; and instrumentalization of public art in urban parks 216; New Labour agenda 177; of New York City 215–16; post-, and public art 182–4; in Preston 8, 178; property market collapse and 178, 182–3; public art and 7–8, 178, 180–1, 183–4, 216; results of 192; urban parks and 215; as visual process 184

urban space(s): amorphous landscape in 174; and antagonistic art 199; blank surfaces in 164; consensus landmarks in 172–3; geopolitics in making of 221; market place in 165–6; modelling of

168–9; morphology of 7, 161, 173–4, 176; movement in 168–9; murals and 5, 46; negotiation of 46; non-symbolic segregation in 170; open spaces in 169, 170; open vs built space in 174; over-determination of 48; parade ground in 165–6; parks 170; place-making and 182; public art as part and parcel of 209; settlement morphology in 175; social theory of 176; socially engaged public practices and 194; STEALTH and 40; symbolic segregation/integration in 171–3; viewing vs interacting with 189; visibility of buildings/objects in 166–7; walking in 189
'Use or Ornament?' (Matarasso) 179

Van Abbe Museum (Eindhoven) 64–5, 69, 71, **72**
Van Deusen, Richard 212, 213, 215
Vickery, Jonathan 181
Virtual Public Art Project 239

Waldhauer, Fred 231
Walker, Rick 233
Wallinger, Mark 31
Walsh, Lexa 127, 128
Walsh, Susan, *To Scatter* 189
Waring, Marilyn, *Counting For Nothing* 130
Warner, Michael 105
Washington Project for the Arts 18
Water Line (Barratt) **171**, 171–2
Weleski, Dawn, *Conflict Kitchen* **240**
Wesselman, D. 220, 221
"What is Public Art?" (Hein) 27
What We Sow 2
Where is Fairfield? (Alavi) 22
White, A. 53–4
Whiteread, Rachel, *House* 22
Whitman, Robert 231

"Whose Cake is it Anyways?" (Lynch; Paul Hamlyn Foundation) 239
Whyte, William H., *The Social Life of Small Urban Spaces* 234
Wiedenhoft Murphy, W. 49
Willats, Stephen 194, 233
William of Orange, Prince 50
Williams, Raymond 142; "Culture is Ordinary" 229
Willis, Shelly, *The Practice of Public Art* 2–3, 14
Wodiczko, Krzysztof, *Homeless Vehicles* 235
Wolff, Robert, *A Critique of Pure Tolerance* 230
Women and Work (Harrison; Hunt; Kelly) 232
Working in Public 149–50, 151
world-at-large 116; social/public art practice and 112–14
World Café method **72**; about 65, 68; agonism in 65, 72, 78, 81; host–guest role-play 5, 71–2, 78, 79; lived experiences 72–8; ownerships/accountabilities in 75–8; spatialities/temporalities in 73–5; *see also* Expansion (Slegers)
Wright, Stephen 133

The Year of the White Bear and Two Undiscovered Amerindians Visit the West (Fusco; Gómez-Peña) 24–5, 236
Yon, Elisa 226, 241
Yoshihara Jirō 228
Young, Alison, *Street Art, Public City Law* 239
Young, Andrea 123
Young, I. 47

Zebracki, Martin 226, 241
Zeiske, Claudia, ARTocracy 239
Ziegler, Mel, *Camouflaged History* 25n6, 236
Žižek, S. 68
Zugnr, Mirana 130
Zukin, Sharon 166, 167